Drugs and Drug Policy in America

ADVISORY BOARD

DRUGS AND DRUG POLICY IN AMERICA

A Documentary History

Edited by STEVEN R. BELENKO

Primary Documents in American History and Contemporary Issues

GREENWOOD PRESS
Westport, Connecticut • London

Library of Congress Cataloging-in-Publication Data

Drugs and drug policy in America : a documentary history / edited by
Steven R. Belenko.
p. cm.—(Primary documents in American history and
contemporary issues, ISSN 1069–5605)
Includes bibliographical references and index.
ISBN 0–313–29902–1 (alk. paper)
1. Drug abuse—United States—History. 2. Drug abuse—Government
policy—United States. 3. Narcotics, Control of—United States.
I. Belenko, Steven R. II. Series.
HV5825.D7884 2000
362.29'0973—dc21 99–32530

British Library Cataloguing in Publication Data is available.

Library of Congress Catalog Card Number: 99–32530
ISBN: 0–313–29902–1
ISSN: 1069–5605

First published in 2000

Greenwood Press, 88 Post Road West, Westport, CT 06881
An imprint of Greenwood Publishing Group, Inc.
www.greenwood.com

Printed in the United States of America

The paper used in this book complies with the
Permanent Paper Standard issued by the National
Information Standards Organization (Z39.48–1984).

10 9 8 7 6 5 4 3 2 1

Copyright Acknowledgments

The editor and publisher are grateful to the following for granting permission to reprint from their materials:

Excerpts from Documents 1, 4, 7, 28, 92, 93, 96, 101, 194, 211, 212, 213, 217, 227, and 245 are taken from *Licit and Illicit Drugs* by Edward M. Brecher, et al. Copyright © 1972 by Consumers Union of United States, Inc. By permission of Little, Brown and Company.

Excerpts from Documents 6 and 59 are taken from *Dark Paradise: Opiate Addiction in America Before 1940* by David T. Courtwright. Copyright © 1982 by the President and Fellows of Harvard College. Reprinted by permission of Harvard University Press.

Excerpts from Documents 8, 10, 11, 15, 18, 25, 26, 32, 53, 83, 163, 164, 165, 166, 167, 168, 169, 174, 175, 179, and 180 are taken from Charles E. Terry and Mildred Pellens, *The Opium Problem* (1928; reprint, Montclair, NJ: Patterson Smith, 1970), and are reprinted courtesy of Patterson Smith Publishing Company.

Excerpts from Documents 20, 21, 22, 23, 30, and 41 are taken from Joseph Spillane, *Modern Drug, Modern Menace* (Santa Monica, CA: RAND Corporation, 1994), and are reprinted courtesy of Joseph Spillane.

Excerpts from Documents 31, 33, 35, 38 and 49 are taken from Arnold Taylor, *American Diplomacy and the Narcotics Traffic, 1900–1939*. Copyright 1969, Duke University Press. All rights reserved. Reprinted with permission.

Excerpts from Documents 39, 54, 128, 136, 154, 162, 196, and 246 are taken from New York Academy of Medicine, "Report on Drug Addiction," *Bulletin of the New York Academy of Medicine* 31, no. 8 (1955), pp. 592–607 and are reprinted courtesy of the New York Academy of Medicine.

Excerpts from Documents 43, 44, 56, 127, 132, 135, 170, 183, 191, 195, 198, 218, 222, and 254 are taken from *The American Disease: Origins of Narcotic Control, 3/E* by David F. Musto. Copyright © 1999 by David F. Musto. Used by permission of Oxford University Press, Inc.

Excerpts from Documents 63, 66, 68, and 210 are taken from Alfred R. Lindesmith, *The Addict and the Law* (Bloomington: Indiana University Press, 1965), and are reprinted by permission of Indiana University Press.

Excerpts from Documents 64 and 87 are taken from Rufus King, *The Drug Hang-up* (New York: W. W. Norton, 1972), and are reprinted courtesy of Rufus King.

Excerpts from Documents 84, 113, and 119 are taken from *The Strange Career of Marihuana*, Jerome Himmelstein. Copyright © 1983 by Jerome Himmelstein. Reproduced with permission of Greenwood Publishing Group, Inc., Westport, CT.

Excerpts from Documents 97, 102, 106, 107, 110, and 111 are taken from Richard J. Bonnie and Charles H. Whitebread, *The Marihuana Conviction: A History of Marihuana Prohibition in the United States* (Charlottesville: University Press of Virginia, 1974), and are reprinted courtesy of Richard J. Bonnie.

Excerpt from Document 149 is taken from John Gerrity, "The Truth About the 'Drug Menace.' " Copyright © 1952 by *Harper's Magazine*. All rights reserved. Reproduced from the February issue by special permission.

Excerpts from Documents 150, 161, and 250 are taken from Lawrence Kolb, "Let's Stop This Narcotics Hysteria!" *Saturday Evening Post*, July 28, 1956, and are reprinted courtesy of the Benjamin Franklin Literary and Medical Society.

Excerpts from Documents 185 and 186 are taken from Dan Waldorf, Martin Orlick, and Craig Reinarman, *Morphine Maintenance: The Shreveport Clinic, 1919–1923* (Washington, D.C.: Drug Abuse Council, 1974), and are reprinted courtesy of Craig Reinarman.

Contents

Series Foreword

This series is designed to meet the research needs of high school and college students by making available in one volume the key primary documents on a given historical event or contemporary issue. Documents include speeches and letters, congressional testimony, Supreme Court and lower court decisions, government reports, biographical accounts, position papers, statutes, and news stories.

The purpose of the series is twofold: (1) to provide substantive and background material on an event or issue through the texts of pivotal primary documents that shaped policy or law, raised controversy, or influenced the course of events, and (2) to trace the controversial aspects of the event or issue through documents that represent a variety of viewpoints. Documents for each volume have been selected by a recognized specialist in that subject with the advice of a board of other subject specialists, school librarians, and teachers.

To place the subject in historical perspective, the volume editor has prepared an introductory overview and a chronology of events. Documents are organized either chronologically or topically. The documents are full text or, if unusually long, have been excerpted by the volume editor. To facilitate understanding, each document is accompanied by an explanatory introduction. Suggestions for further reading follow the volume.

It is the hope of Greenwood Press that this series will enable students and other readers to use primary documents more easily in their research, to exercise critical thinking skills by examining the key documents in American history and public policy, and to critique the variety of viewpoints represented by this selection of documents.

Acknowledgments

The conceptualization and preparation of this book have benefited greatly from the earlier work of several drug policy historians. Dr. Charles Terry and Mildred Pellens, in their 1928 book *The Opium Problem*, chronicled in rich detail the often problematic early history of opium in the United States. Two general reviews of the history of American drug policy stand out for their thoroughness and keen analyses, and I gained much insight into the development of American drug policy from them: Dr. David Musto's *The American Disease: Origins of Narcotic Control* (1987) and Edward Brecher's *Licit and Illicit Drugs* (1972). The reader is urged to consult these sources and the other important works in the list of Suggested Readings.

I give special thanks to Ellen Benoit, a doctoral candidate in the New York University Department of Sociology, who was my primary research assistant for this book. Her advice and comments, insights into American drug policy, and ability to track down many of the documents were so important in the preparation of this book. For her excellent work, I am extremely grateful. Duren Cowan and Nicole Smith also assisted ably in preparing some of the documents.

To the Advisory Board for this book, my sincere thanks for their guidance and suggestions: Dr. Richard Dembo, Dr. Jeffrey Fagan, Anita Pfluger, and Judy Williams.

Finally, my editor at Greenwood Press, Emily Birch, helped to guide me throughout the writing of this book. Her patience and encouragement, as well as her substantive comments on the manuscript, are most appreciated.

Introduction

This book reviews the origins and development of America's official policies toward illegal drugs, beginning in the mid-19th century, using original documents from enacted laws, other government documents, court decisions, scholarly writings, and articles in the popular print media. For the past 100 years, drug abuse and addiction have remained among the most difficult and intractable social issues. Although the level of public attention has waxed and waned, drugs and drug policy have never really been far from the forefront of public concerns. The emphasis of this book is on the control of illegal drugs, rather than alcohol or prescription drugs. It is understood that in anti-drug policies the line between legal and illegal drugs has often been blurred, not always reflecting their relative health or social consequences.

The evolution of American drug policy is viewed in this book primarily through the lens of federal and state laws, funding priorities, and policies. In addition, cities and counties often have had local health or sanitary ordinances that have had important effects on the sale and use of drugs—some of these are highlighted in this book. However, the official response to drugs has largely been shaped by the federal and state laws against various aspects of drug trafficking, sale, and use, and by budgetary priorities that have largely flowed from these laws. Drug policies have also been influenced by government-supported studies that have tried to illuminate the dangers of drug use, the patterns and consequences of use, the factors shaping the development and maintenance of drug abuse and addiction, and the methods for most effectively reducing the impact of drugs on individuals and on society.

There have been several important eras in drug policy beginning in the late 1800s and early 1900s, when the bulk of problem drug use (mostly opium and its derivatives) could be traced to prescriptions by physicians and the use of patent medicines.

Several key themes characterize the history of American drug policy. One is the periodic concentration on particular drugs: the cocaine drug scares of the early 1900s, the concern over the spread of marijuana and heroin use in the 1920s, the reemergence of heroin and the emergence of LSD in the 1960s, cocaine once again in the early 1980s, and crack beginning in the mid-1980s.

A second recurring theme has been the tension between the "medical" approach to controlling drugs and the punitive enforcement approach. This debate has yet to be resolved, although the rise of drug treatment beginning in the 1950s is an important part of the story of American drug policy. Although the punitive approach has generally dominated, the medical and public health fields have sometimes played an influential role in setting anti-drug policy. The latter have in part reflected changing attitudes toward the nature of addiction, which has been viewed at different times as a moral shortcoming, a psychological problem, or a physical disease.

A third theme can be seen in shifts in drug policies that often seem to have been impelled more by political and media events than by scientific advances or actual trends in drug use or drug problems. Examples are the influx of Chinese laborers in the 1870s who smoked opium, the spread of opiate addiction in the late 19th century to the middle class through patent medicines and doctors' prescriptions, the rise of the Mexican farm laborer population in the West in the 1920s with their cultural acceptance of marijuana smoking, the high rates of heroin and marijuana use among returning Vietnam veterans in the early 1970s, and the spread of marijuana and other drug use to the middle class during the social upheavals of the 1960s.

Finally, it has been the case throughout the history of American drug policy that the goals of most laws and policies have rarely been achieved. Most major policies were developed and enacted in the hope that drug use and drug trafficking would be eliminated or at least greatly diminished. Yet drug use has remained a difficult problem for more than 100 years. This suggests either that some policies have been ill-advised or that policy makers often misunderstand the dynamics of drug addiction and the economic and social forces that shape and support illegal drug markets. At other times, social or economic forces have intervened to alter the situation: the emergence of new popular drugs or new groups of users, and the adaptability of drug traffickers to changing drug markets and changing law enforcement strategies are examples. The main parts of this book delineate these key drug policy eras, as well as basic issues such as the treatment of addiction and the debate over drug legalization.

Because of the complexity and breadth of drug problems and drug policy, it was not possible to discuss every aspect of American drug policy and its influences in this book. For example, the international control of drug production, drug trafficking, and drug smuggling has had a number of important effects on American policies, but is only addressed relatively briefly. Policies toward alcohol and tobacco, the two most commonly abused drugs in society, were likewise outside the scope of this book, as was any detailed discussion of the nature of drug addiction and the behavioral, physiological, and social determinants of drug abuse. The reader is urged to explore these topics in other excellent sources, some of which are listed in the Suggested Readings.

Recent advances in neuroscience have identified many of the effects of opiates and other drugs on brain chemistry. Such scientific discoveries have greatly illuminated the physiological determinants of drug addiction, abstinence, and relapse, and thus may have profound effects in the future on how society views drug addiction. Consequently, the next cycles of laws and policies toward illegal drugs could very well change significantly. Yet the lessons learned from the first 100 years of American drug policy must be well understood so that future responses to drug problems can be improved. In the end, the overarching goal of drug policy must not simply be to selectively punish users and sellers of certain drugs, but to reduce the health, social, and economic impacts of drugs in the most humane and cost-effective way possible.

Significant Dates in the History of American Drug Policy

1860 First anti-morphine law enacted, Pennsylvania

1875 First law against opium smoking enacted, San Francisco

1885 First state law against opium smoking, Ohio

1887 Federal law against opium importing and exporting

1897 First state law against cocaine, Illinois

1898 Discovery of heroin in Germany

1906 Pure Food and Drug Act

1908 Towns-Lambert opium addiction "cure" announced

1909 International Opium Commission meeting, Shanghai

1909 Federal law against importing or using opium for nonmedicinal purposes

1912 International Opium Convention, The Hague

1914 Harrison Act

1915–1925 Passage of local and state anti-marijuana laws

1919 *Webb et al. v. United States* and *United States v. Doremus* Supreme Court decisions

1921 American Medical Association denounces ambulatory narcotic treatment

1922 *United States v. Behrman* Supreme Court decision

1922 Narcotic Drugs Import and Export Act

1923 Shreveport (LA) narcotic clinic closes

1925 *Linder v. United States* Supreme Court decision

1929 Act to Create Federal Narcotic Farms

1930 Creation of Federal Bureau of Narcotics, Harry J. Anslinger, Commissioner

1932	Uniform State Narcotic Act approved by National Conference of Commissioners on Uniform State Laws
1937	Marihuana Tax Act
1941–1945	Discovery of methadone
1942	Opium Poppy Control Act
1943	Discovery of LSD
1951	Boggs Act
1952	Eisenhower Committee Report
1955	New York Academy of Medicine Report on Addiction
1956	Narcotic Control Act
1960s	Development and expansion of methadone maintenance treatment for heroin addiction
1961	Joint ABA-AMA Committee on Narcotic Drugs report, recommending experimental narcotic clinics
1962	*Robinson v. California* Supreme Court decision
1963	Kennedy Commission on Narcotic and Drug Abuse
1966	Narcotic Addict Rehabilitation Act
1969	Operation Intercept
1970	Comprehensive Drug Abuse Prevention and Control Act
1970	Revised Uniform State Drug Law adopted by National Conference of Commissioners on Uniform State Laws
1972	Drug Abuse Office and Treatment Act
1972	National Commission on Marihuana and Drug Abuse report
1973	"Rockefeller Drug Laws" enacted in New York State
1973	First states enact marijuana decriminalization laws
1985	Crack cocaine appears
1986	Anti-Drug Abuse Act of 1986
1988	Anti-Drug Abuse Act of 1988
1989	First National Drug Control Strategy
1993	Presidential Commission on Model State Drug Laws
1996	California and Arizona adopt "medical marijuana" laws

Part I

American Drug Policy in the 19th Century

The roots of American policies to control and regulate drugs date back to the mid-19th century. From the Civil War of 1861–1865 through the end of the century, the use and sale of opium, morphine, cocaine, and other psychoactive drugs were legal and quite common in the United States. In addition to being prescribed by physicians for numerous health conditions, patent medicines containing opiates and other drugs were readily available without prescription. As this use spread, and concerns began to emerge about the dangers and negative effects of drug use, public sentiment and official policies began to shift. New laws were passed by the states and the federal government to place controls on the sale and use of drugs.

In his important 1972 study of American drug policy, Edward Brecher described the wide availability of opium in the 19th century.

DOCUMENT 1: Easy Availability of Opium (Edward M. Brecher, 1972)

[In the 19th century] opium was on legal sale conveniently and at low prices . . . ; morphine came into common use during and after the Civil War. . . . These opiates and countless pharmaceutical preparations containing them "were as freely accessible as aspirin is today." They flowed mostly through five broad channels of distribution, all of them quite legal:

(1) Physicians dispensed opiates directly to patients, or wrote prescriptions for them.

(2) Drugstores sold opiates over the counter to customers without a prescription.

(3) Grocery and general stores as well as pharmacies stocked and sold opiates. An 1883–1885 survey of the state of Iowa, which then had a population of less than 2,000,000, found 3,000 stores in the state where opiates were on sale—and this did not include the physicians who dispensed opiates directly.

(4) For users unable or unwilling to patronize a nearby store, opiates could be ordered by mail.

(5) Finally, there were countless patent medicines on the market containing opium or morphine. They were sold under such names as Ayer's Cherry Pectoral, Mrs. Winslow's Soothing Syrup, Darbys Carminative, Godfrey's Cordial, McMunn's Elixir of Opium, Dover's Powder, and so on. Some were teething syrups for young children, some were "soothing syrups," some were recommended for diarrhea and dysentery or for "women's trouble." They were widely advertised in newspapers and magazines and on billboards as "pain-killers," "cough mixtures," "women's friends," "consumption cures," and so on. One wholesale drug house, it is said, distributed more than 600 proprietary medicines and other products containing opiates.

Most of the opium consumed in the United States during the nineteenth century was legally imported. Morphine was legally manufactured here from the imported opium. But opium poppies were also legally grown within the United States.

Source: Edward M. Brecher and the Editors of Consumer Reports, *Licit and Illicit Drugs* (Boston: Little, Brown, 1972), 3.

* * *

H. Wayne Morgan, in his history of 19th-century addiction, described a nation increasingly awash in addicting drugs.

DOCUMENT 2: Spread of Opium Use (H. Wayne Morgan, 1974)

Drug abuse seemed to increase rapidly after the 1850's, and by the 1870's authorities estimated that only one-fifth of the opium imported annually went into legitimate medical channels. People also used more medication in general. Between 1880 and 1910, the national population increased about 83 per cent, while the sale of patent medicines rose sevenfold. . . . "America is a nation of drug-takers," an eminent authority on nervous disorders warned. "Nowhere else shall we find such extensive, gorgeous, and richly supplied chemical establishments as here; nowhere else is there such a general patronage of such establishments."

Source: H. Wayne Morgan, *Yesterday's Addicts: American Society and Drug Abuse, 1865–1920* (Norman: University of Oklahoma Press, 1974), 8.

* * *

An 1872 report by Dr. F. E. Oliver, prepared for the Massachusetts State Board of Health, describes the variety of drugs used in the 19th century. In addition, this document shows how even infants were commonly given patent medicines containing opiates.

DOCUMENT 3: Opium Use in Massachusetts (F. E. Oliver, 1872)

The preparations of opium reported as more commonly used are, besides the drug itself, laudanum, paregoric, sulphate of morphia and, occasionally, McMunn's Elixir. When a more prompt and stimulating effect is desired, as is often the case with those who have been addicted to alcohol, laudanum may be preferred. The sulphate of morphia seems to be growing in favor, its color and less bulk facilitating concealment, and being free from the more objectionable properties of opium. This salt is not only taken internally, but is sometimes used hypodermically. In one case reported in Boston, the whole body was covered with the scars left by the punctures of the injecting instrument. Paregoric is also largely used as a stimulant, although, as a sedative in nursery practice, it has been to a great extent superseded by the so-called "soothing sirups," in which opium is the active ingredient, as it is also in the various other abominable compounds which pass under the name of cough sirups, pectorals, cholera medicines, pain killers, etc.

Our Scituate correspondent reports that infants in that town are unmercifully drugged with soothing sirups.

In Winchester, also, these nostrums are mentioned as quite common, having quite displaced paregoric in the nursery. The basis of what is known as Winslow's Soothing Sirup is morphia. A recent analysis of a sample of this medicine gave one grain of the alkaloid to an ounce of the sirup; the dose for an infant, as directed, being four or five times that usually regarded as safe. Godfrey's Cordial is also used for a similar purpose, containing more than a grain of opium to the ounce.

Source: F. E. Oliver, M.D., Massachusetts State Board of Health, *Third Annual Report* (Boston: Wright and Potter, 1872). In H. Wayne Morgan, *Yesterday's Addicts: American Society and Drug Abuse, 1865–1920* (Norman: University of Oklahoma Press, 1974), 50–51.

* * *

Opium poppies were widely grown in the United States through the 1870s. Dr. Oliver's report for the Massachusetts Board of Health, extracted above, suggested that hundreds of pounds of opium poppies were produced annually in New England alone. Opium was an important crop in the West as well, with an acre of poppies producing an estimated 120 pounds of opium.

The use of opiates such as morphine became more common during the Civil War to relieve the pain of battlefield wounds. But opiates were viewed by many physicians as a panacea for numerous maladies, and so were prescribed for a variety of medical and psychological conditions.

DOCUMENT 4: Prescription of Opiates (Edward M. Brecher, 1972)

Physicians in the nineteenth century as now prescribed opiates for pain. They were also widely prescribed, however, for cough, diarrhea, dysentery, and a host of other illnesses. Physicians often referred to opium or morphine as "G.O.M."—"God's own medicine." Dr. H. H. Kane's 1880 textbook, entitled *The Hypodermic Injection of Morphia. Its History, Advantages, and Dangers. Based on Experience of 360 Physicians*, listed 54 diseases which benefited from morphine injections. They ranged from anemia and angina pectoris through diabetes, insanity, nymphomania, and ovarian neuralgia, to tetanus, vaginismus, and vomiting of pregnancy.

To modern readers, this list may appear to be evidence of the incompetence of nineteenth-century physicians. Yet, for the great majority of these conditions, morphine really was of help—especially in the absence of more specific modern remedies (such as insulin for diabetes). . . . The nineteenth-century physician used morphine for a wide range of disorders much as the physician today uses . . . tranquilizers and sedatives. . . .

Yet another nineteenth-century use of opiates was as a substitute for alcohol. As Dr. J. R. Black explained in a paper entitled "Advantages of Substituting the Morphia Habit for the Incurably Alcoholic," published in the *Cincinnati Lancet-Clinic* in 1889, morphine "is less inimical to healthy life than alcohol." It "calms in place of exciting the baser passions, and hence is less productive of acts of violence and crime; in short the use of morphine in place of alcohol is but a choice of evils, and by far the lesser."

Source: Edward M. Brecher and the Editors of Consumer Reports, *Licit and Illicit Drugs* (Boston: Little, Brown, 1972), 8.

* * *

The profile of the typical drug abuser of the 19th century differed from that of the present day. Abuse of opiates was primarily a problem of the middle class, and was much more prevalent among women. In part this reflected the frequent prescribing of these drugs to women, reflecting the prevailing male-centered view that women were more prone to "nervous" conditions and "female troubles" that required medical intervention.

DOCUMENT 5: Why People Used Opium (F. E. Oliver, 1872)

The fact generally remarked that women constitute so large a proportion of opium takers, is due, perhaps, more to moral than to physical causes. Doomed, often, to a life of disappointment, and, it may be, of physical and mental inaction, and in the smaller and more remote towns, not unfrequently, to utter seclusion, deprived of all wholesome social diversion, it is not strange that nervous depression, with all its concomitant evils, should sometimes follow, opium being discreetly selected as the safest and most agreeable remedy.

We must not omit, however, one other most important cause of this habit referred to by our correspondents, and the most general one of all that predispose to it. We allude to the simple desire for stimulation,—in the words of another, "that innate propensity of mankind to supply some grateful means of promoting the flow of agreeable thoughts, of emboldening the spirit to perform deeds of daring, or of steeping in forgetfulness the sense of daily sorrows." . . . In an age, too, like our own, of unprecedented mental and physical activity, the constant over-exercise of all the faculties, together with the cares and perplexities incident to a condition of incessant unrest, create a keener appetite for some sort of stimulus. No clearer confirmation of the truth of this statement is needed than the present enormous consumption of alcohol and tobacco, as well as of those milder stimulants, tea and coffee, for which there is an ever-increasing demand.

Source: F. E. Oliver, M.D., Massachusetts State Board of Health, *Third Annual Report* (Boston: Wright and Potter, 1872). In H. Wayne Morgan, *Yesterday's Addicts: American Society and Drug Abuse, 1865–1920* (Norman: University of Oklahoma Press, 1974), 48.

* * *

Further evidence of the different characteristics of the 19th-century drug abuser is provided by historian David Courtwright.

DOCUMENT 6: Characteristics of 19th Century Addicts (David T. Courtwright, 1982)

The outstanding feature of nineteenth-century opium and morphine addiction is that the majority of addicts were women. Orville Marshall's 1878 Michigan survey, Charles Earle's 1880 Chicago survey, and Justin Hull's 1885 Iowa survey indicated that 61.2, 71.9, and 63.4 percent of their respective samples were female. . . .

. . .

. . . studies published between 1871 and 1922 . . . generally support the characterization of opium and morphine addiction as a condition of middle life [i.e., mid-30s to 40s].

With respect to race, whites were overrepresented among opium and morphine addicts, blacks underrepresented.

Source: David T. Courtwright, *Dark Paradise: Opiate Addiction in America Before 1940* (Cambridge, MA: Harvard University Press, 1982), 36–37.

* * *

Brecher cites several possible reasons for the high incidence of opiate addiction among 19th-century women.

DOCUMENT 7: Reasons for High Prevalence of Opiate Use (Edward M. Brecher, 1972)

The widespread medical custom of prescribing opiates for menstrual and menopausal discomforts, and the many proprietary opiates advertised for "female troubles," no doubt contributed to this excess of female opiate users. A 1914 Tennessee survey, which found that two-thirds of the users were women, noted also that two-thirds of the women were between twenty-five and fifty-five. "The first twenty years of this period," the survey report commented, "is about the age when the stresses of life begin to make themselves felt with women, and includes the beginning of the menopause period. [Nineteenth-century women, on the average, reached menopause somewhat earlier than twentieth-century women do.] It appears reasonable, therefore, to ascribe to this part of female life, no small portion of the addiction among women."

The extent to which alcohol-drinking by women was frowned upon may also have contributed to the excess of women among opiate users. Husbands drank alcohol in the saloon; wives took opium at home.

Source: Edward M. Brecher and the Editors of Consumer Reports, *Licit and Illicit Drugs* (Boston: Little, Brown, 1972), 17.

DEVELOPMENT OF HYPODERMIC INJECTION

The development of the hypodermic syringe for injecting liquid solutions of drugs under the skin had important effects on the spread of opiate addiction in the 19th century. Most contemporary accounts place the first common use of the modern hypodermic instruments shortly before the Civil War. However, some historical records indicate that intravenous injection was known as early as 1656, as Charles Terry and Mildred Pellens note in their important work *The Opium Problem*.

DOCUMENT 8: History of Hypodermic Injection (Charles E. Terry and Mildred Pellens, 1928)

Nearly two hundred years before the hypodermic injection of drugs was practiced, Sir Christopher Wren . . . in 1656 first injected drugs intravenously. He employed a quill attached to a small bladder and injected dogs with opium and other drugs and a year later repeated the operation on human beings. . . .

. . . the next advance was made by Lafargue of Saint Emilion in 1836 when he discussed before the Academie de Medecin the administration of morphin and other substances by *inoculation*.

Alexander Wood of Edinburgh quite generally has received credit as the discoverer of the *hypodermatic* method of injecting drugs under the skin in liquid form. Kane [writing about morphine injection in 1880] says that Wood "commenced the practice in 1843 and wrote upon it in 1855. . . ."

Kane also states that Drs. Isaac E. Taylor and Washington claimed to have used practically the same method in 1839. . . .

Commenting further on the development of the hypodermic syringe, Kane states:

"Dr. Wood's syringe-needle was not pointed, and had no lateral opening, it being necessary to incise the skin before introducing it. To Mr. Charles Hunter, of London, is due, however, the highest praise of all. . . . Hunter added the needle point, lateral opening, and made many other small but important improvements."

. . .

According to Kane, Fordyce Barker of New York was the first to employ the "hypodermic syringe proper" in this country. He received one from Professor Simpson while visiting Edinburgh and used it here in May, 1856.

Source: Charles E. Terry and Mildred Pellens, *The Opium Problem* (Bureau of Social Hygiene, 1928; reprint, Montclair, NJ: Patterson Smith Publishing, 1970), 65–66.

* * *

Hypodermic injection became a popular method among physicians for administering opiate drugs in the 1860s. But it also began to be recognized as a cause of chronic opiate intoxication or addiction among addicts who discovered that injection was a quicker and more effective way of getting drugs into their bodies than orally.

DOCUMENT 9: Hypodermic Injection and Addiction (Lawrence Kolb and A. G. Du Mez, 1924)

Among the factors which have operated to increase addiction may be mentioned the advent of the hypodermic method of administration of drugs, which came into general use about the time of the Civil War, and was at first said to be a method of administering morphine without danger of causing addiction. In so far as addiction is concerned, this discovery proved to be a curse rather than a blessing.

Source: Lawrence Kolb and A. G. Du Mez, "The Prevalence and Trend of Drug Addiction in the United States and Factors Influencing It," *Public Health Reports* 39, no. 21 (1924): 1198.

* * *

Because 19th-century physicians viewed hypodermic injection as a way of administering smaller doses of drugs to get the same effect, it was thought that the chances of addiction would be lower using this method. Thus doctors often gave hypodermics to patients, and their use spread rapidly in the latter part of the 1800s.

DOCUMENT 10: Spread of Hypodermic Injection (Charles E. Terry and Mildred Pellens, 1928)

The first record of warning as to the danger of hypodermic administration that we have found was made by Nusbaum who, according to Allbutt [writing in 1905], drew attention to the danger as early as 1864. In 1869 Parrish refers to the growing popularity of this method of administration and cites a case whose chronic use of morphin dated from his introduction to the hypodermic syringe. . . .

. . . we may conclude not only that the hypodermic was used for relief of pain but also that it had become well and favorably known among certain groups for purposes of dissipation to such an extent that the fiction writers of the day adopted it or were employing it much as have certain sensational writers of our own time.

. . .

. . . the medical journals of the day were full of enthusiastic descriptions of new successes in therapeutics through the hypodermic use of morphin and it is very doubtful if any painful condition to which the human race is heir escaped the list of those for whom the drug was recommended.

In America following the Civil War the increase in opiate use was so marked among ex-soldiers as to give rise to the term "army disease" and today in more than one old soldiers' home are cases of chronic opium intoxication which date from this period.

Source: Charles E. Terry and Mildred Pellens, *The Opium Problem* (Bureau of Social Hygiene, 1928; reprint, Montclair, NJ: Patterson Smith Publishing 1970), 68–69.

* * *

One physician, writing in 1877, warned against the risks of hypodermic injection.

DOCUMENT 11: Risks of Hypodermic Method (S. F. McFarland, 1877)

If cases of opium inebriety occur as frequently in the private practice of other physicians as they have in my own, it is coming to be a serious matter, and a few words of caution, against the indiscriminate use of so active a drug, may be pardonable.

Since the introduction of the hypodermic syringe, especially, there has been a noticeable increase in the frequency, as well as the severity, of the cases; and I wish to enter a protest against its imprudent use, and particularly against leaving it in the hands of patients or their friends, to be used at their discretion. . . . It is certainly a most valuable instrument in the hands of the discreet practitioner, and will reach cases which nothing else will, with a certainty and promptness which is very satisfactory; but it is too potent for evil, as well, to be trusted beyond his grasp.

Source: Quoted in Charles E. Terry and Mildred Pellens, *The Opium Problem* (Bureau of Social Hygiene, 1928; reprint, Montclair, NJ: Patterson Smith Publishing, 1970), 70.

SPREAD OF OPIATE USE

A number of journalists and physicians in the latter part of the 19th century chronicled the world of opiate and other drug use. In the following document, excerpted from an 1888 article in *Popular Science Monthly*, the writer describes the results of a survey of prescriptions filled by Boston druggists, and concludes that opium use was on the rise.

DOCUMENT 12: Increase in Opium Use (Virgil G. Eaton, 1888)

For the past year or more I have studied the growth of the opium-habit in Boston. It is increasing rapidly. Not only are there more Chinese "joints" and respectable resorts kept by Americans than there were a year ago, but the number of individuals who "hit the pipe" at home and in their offices is growing very fast. A whole opium "lay-out," including pipe, fork, lamp, and spoon, can now be had for less than five dollars. This affords a chance for those who have acquired the habit to follow their desires in private, without having to reveal their secret to any one. How largely this is practiced I do not know, but, judging from the telltale pallor of the faces I see, I feel sure the habit is claiming more slaves every day.

In order to approximate to [*sic*] the amount of opium in its various forms which is used in Boston, I have made a thorough scrutiny of the physicians' recipes [i.e., prescriptions] left at the drug-stores to be filled. . . .

I was surprised to learn how extensively opium and its alkaloids—particularly sulphate of morphia—are used by physicians. I found them prescribed for every ailment which flesh is heir to. They are used for headache, sore eyes, toothache, sore throat, laryngitis, diphtheria, bronchitis, congestion, pneumonia, consumption, gastritis, liver-complaint, stone in the gall-duct, carditis, aneurism, hypertrophy, peritonitis, calculus, kidney trouble, rheumatism, neuralgia, and all general or special maladies of the body. It is the great panacea and cure-all.

During my leisure time I have looked up more than 10,000 recipes. It has been my practice to go to the files, open the book, or take up a spindle at random, and take 300 recipes just as they come. The first store I visited I found 42 recipes which contained morphine out of the 300 examined. Close by, a smaller store, patronized by poorer people, had 36. Up in the aristocratic quarters, where the customers call in carriages, I found 49 morphine recipes in looking over 300. At the North End, among the poor Italian laborers, the lowest proportion of 32 in 300 was discovered. Without detailing all the places visited, I will summarize by saying that, in 10,200 recipes taken in 34 drug-stores, I found 1,481 recipes which prescribed some preparation of opium, or an average of fourteen and one half per cent of the whole.

This was surprising enough; but my investigations did not end here. Of the prescriptions furnished by physicians I found that forty-two per cent were filled the second time, and of those refilled twenty-three per cent contained opium in some form. Again, twenty-eight per cent of all prescriptions are filled a third time; and of these, sixty-one per cent were of opiates; while of the twenty per cent taken for the fourth filling, seventy-eight per cent were for the narcotic drug, proving, beyond a doubt, that it was the opiate qualities of the medicine that afforded relief and caused the renewal.

From conversation with the druggists, I learned that the proprietary or "patent" medicines which have the largest sales were those containing opiates. One apothecary told me of an old lady who formerly came to him as often as four times a week and purchased a fifty-cent bottle of "cough-balsam." She informed him that it "quieted her nerves" and afforded rest when everything else had failed. After she had made her regular visits for over a year, he told her one day that he had sold out of the medicine required, and suggested a substitute, which was a preparation containing about the same amount of morphine. On trial, the woman found the new mixture answered every purpose of the old. The druggist then told her she had acquired the morphine-habit, and from that time on she was a constant morphine-user.

It was hard to learn just what proportion of those who began by taking medicines containing opiates became addicted to the habit. I should say, from what I learned, that the number was fully twenty-five per cent—perhaps more. The proportion of those who, having taken up the habit in earnest, left it off later on, was very small—not over ten per cent. When a person once becomes an opium-slave, the habit usually holds through life.

Source: Virgil G. Eaton, "How the Opium Habit Is Acquired," *Popular Science Monthly* 33 (September 1888). Reprinted in H. Wayne Morgan, *Yesterday's Addicts: American Society and Drug Abuse, 1865–1920* (Norman: University of Oklahoma Press, 1974), 181.

* * *

Some contemporary observers of the drug scene emphasized the role of physicians in spreading drug use, and recommended more controls on prescriptions. The next document also contains hopeful recommendations for preventing opium addiction.

DOCUMENT 13: Role of Physicians in Spreading the Opium Habit (Virgil G. Eaton, 1888)

At present our clergymen, physicians, and reformers are asking for more stringent laws against the sale of these narcotics. The law compelling every person who purchases opium or other poisons to "register," giving his name and place of residence to the druggist, has been in force in Massachusetts for several years, and all this time the sales have increased. No registration law can control the traffic.

The parties who are responsible for the increase of the habit are the physicians who give the prescriptions. In these days of great mental strain, when men take their business home with them and think of it from waking to sleeping, the nerves are the first to feel the effect of overwork. Opium effects immediate relief, and the doctors, knowing this, and wishing to stand well with their patients, prescribe it more and more. Their design is to effect a cure. The result is to convert their patients into opium-slaves. The doctors are to blame for so large a consumption of of opium, and they are the men who need reforming.

Two means of preventing the spread of the habit suggest themselves to every thoughtful person:

1. Pass a law that no prescriptions containing opium or its preparations can be filled more than once at the druggist's without having the physician renew it. The extra cost of calling on a doctor when the medicine ran out would deter many poor people from acquiring the habit. Such a law would also make the doctors more guarded in prescribing opiates for trivial ailments. With the law in force, and the druggists guarded by strict registration laws, we could soon trace the responsibility

to its proper source, and then, if these safeguards were not enough, physicians could be fined for administering opiates save in exceptional cases.

2. The great preventive to the habit is to keep the body in such a state that it will not require sedatives or stimulants. The young men and women in our cities have too big heads, too small necks, and too flabby muscles. They should forsake medicine, and patronize the gymnasium. Let them develop their muscles and rest their nerves, and the family doctor, who means well, but who can not resist the tendency of the age, can take a protracted vacation. Unless something of the kind is done soon, the residents of our American cities will be all opium-slaves.

Source: Virgil G. Eaton, "How the Opium Habit Is Acquired," *Popular Science Monthly* 33 (September 1888). Reprinted in H. Wayne Morgan, *Yesterday's Addicts: American Society and Drug Abuse, 1865–1920* (Norman: University of Oklahoma Press, 1974), 183–184.

OPIUM SMOKING

The spread of opium smoking, especially among Chinese immigrants, was an important trend in the 19th century, and triggered a national wave of federal and state laws to extend controls over opium use. Beginning in the 1860s, Chinese immigrants arrived in the western United States to work on building the railroads and other large-scale labor projects; they brought with them a cultural acceptance of opium smoking. For much of the 19th century, the spread of opium smoking was of great concern to the Chinese and other Asian governments. Yet it was a major source of revenue for a number of countries. This conflict between the economic benefits of opium cultivation and the social and health consequences of widespread opium smoking was a recurring theme throughout the late 19th and early 20th centuries.

Many of these Chinese laborers settled in San Francisco, and by the 1870s there was considerable attention in that city to the spread of opium smoking from the Chinese to whites, especially women and youth. Much of the smoking took place in "opium dens" in Chinatown and other parts of the city, and lurid tales of rampant drug use and prostitution began to fuel growing hostility against the Chinese. At the same time, a fascination with the exotic appealed to the Victorian mind.

DOCUMENT 14: Opium Smoking in the Late 1800s (H. Wayne Morgan, 1974)

By the 1870's the press reported often on opium smoking, the first form of addiction to attain wide public notoriety. . . . Stories about it usually involved the glamorous West of the gold rush and transcontinental railroad. They often combined the exoticisms of the Orient and rough-and-tumble mining town life. And almost every report carefully described the elaborate "kit" which smokers employed, satisfying a national passion for technology and gadgetry.

A report on smoking in 1881 [by H. H. Kane] carefully noted alleged gradations in styles of opium use. Some authorities held that smoking was less physically injurious, less habit-forming, and easier to cure than use of morphine. Though the public probably equated smoking with western chinatowns, analysts warned that the problem was national in scope. "There was hardly a town of any size in the East, and none in the West, where there is not a place to smoke and Americans [who are] smoking."

Source: H. Wayne Morgan, *Yesterday's Addicts: American Society and Drug Abuse, 1865–1920* (Norman: University of Oklahoma Press, 1974), 5–6.

* * *

In 1875 San Francisco adopted an ordinance that prohibited opium dens and led to a number of raids and arrests. However, the dens continued to flourish.

DOCUMENT 15: San Franciso Law against Opium Smoking, 1875 (Charles E. Terry and Mildred Pellens, 1928)

Shortly before the end of the Civil War the smoking of opium . . . began among the whites. According to Kane, a sporting character by the name of Clendenyn was the first white man to smoke opium in San Francisco in 1868. The second, Kane says, induced to try it by the first, smoked [it] in 1871. . . .

[Quoting Kane:] "The practice spread rapidly and quietly among this class of gamblers and prostitutes until the latter part of 1875, at which time the authorities became cognizant of the fact, and finding, upon investigations, that many women and young girls, as also young men of respectable family, were being induced to visit the dens, where they were ruined morally and otherwise, a city ordinance was passed forbidding the practice under penalty of a heavy fine or imprisonment, or both. Many arrests were made, and the punishment was prompt and thorough. On this account the vice was indulged in much less openly, but none the less extensively, for although the larger smoking-houses were closed, the small dens in Chinatown were well patronized, and the vice grew surely and steadily."

Source: Charles E. Terry and Mildred Pellens, *The Opium Problem* (Bureau of Social Hygiene, 1928; reprint, Montclair, NJ: Patterson Smith Publishing, 1970), 73.

* * *

A number of cities and states began to enact laws prohibiting opium smoking and the operation of opium dens, and by 1914, 27 states had such legislation. Despite increased state and local enforcement efforts, imports of opium for smoking continued to climb in the early part of the 20th century. Federal control during this period was limited to tariffs placed on imported smoking opium. The use of import tariffs to regulate opium and raise tax revenue dates back to 1832, when opium was first placed in the category of drugs and chemicals. In the early 1840s, when opium smuggling into the United States by Chinese laborers began to be noticed, opium was placed in a tariff schedule by itself, subject to an import tax of 15 cents per pound under the Tariff Act of 1842. In 1861 a duty of one dollar a pound was imposed. Later efforts to raise the tariff (in 1883 it was increased to ten dollars a pound) seemed to have little effect on import levels. Legal imports of smoking opium increased threefold between the 1870s and the first decade of the twentieth century.

Finally, in 1887 Congress passed a law banning opium imports by Chinese citizens to the United States, and banning exports by American citizens of smoking opium to China.

DOCUMENT 16: Federal Act Banning Opium Imports and Exports to and from China (February 23, 1887)

Be it enacted, . . . That the importation of opium into any of the ports of the United States by any subject of the Emperor of China is hereby prohibited. Every person guilty of a violation of the preceding provision shall be deemed guilty of a misdemeanor, and, on conviction thereof, shall be punished by a fine of not more than five hundred dollars nor less than fifty dollars, or by imprisonment for a period of not more than six months nor less than thirty days, or by both such fine and imprisonment, in the discretion of the court.

. . .

Sec. 3. That no citizen of the United States shall import opium into any of the open ports of China, nor transport the same from one open port to any other open port, or buy or sell opium in any of such open ports of China, nor shall any vessel owned by citizens of the United States, or any vessel, whether foreign or otherwise, employed by any citizen of the United States, or owned by any citizen of the United in whole or in part, and employed by persons not citizens of the United States, take or carry opium into any of such open ports of China, or transport the same from one open port to any other open port, or be engaged in any traffic therein between or in such open ports or any of them.

Citizens of the United States offending against the provisions of this section shall be deemed guilty of a misdemeanor, and, upon conviction thereof, shall be punished by a fine not exceeding five nor less than fifty dollars, or by both such punishments, in the discretion of the court. The consular courts of the United States in China, concurrently with any district court of the United States in the district in which any offender may be found, shall have jurisdiction to try, and determine all cases arising under the foregoing provisions of this section, subject to the general regulations provided by law.

Source: 49th Congress, Session II, Chapter 210, Statutes of the United States, 1887.

* * *

Imports of opium continued to be a problem, however, and as concern grew over the spread of opium smoking to Americans, proposals were made in Congress either to ban imports of opium completely, or to lower the tariff to reduce the incentive for smuggling. An 1888 memorandum from the Secretary of the Treasury to the Speaker of the House of Representatives made the following recommendation.

DOCUMENT 17: Letter from the Secretary of the Treasury (C. S. Fairchild) to the Speaker of the House (Mr. Carlisle) (1888)

. . . [P]rohibition should, in my opinion, be extended to opium prepared for smoking, on which the rate of duty was increased by the Tariff Act of 1883 from six to ten dollars a pound, presumably with the object of restricting its importation and use. Such has not, however, been the effect of this law, which has served rather to stimulate smuggling, extensively practiced by systematic organizations on the Pacific coast. Recently completed facilities for transcontinental transportation have enabled the opium smugglers to extend their illicit traffic to our Northern border. Although all possible efforts have been made by this Department to suppress this traffic, it is found practically impossible to do so.

If however, Congress is not disposed to prohibit or restrict the importation of opium for smoking, and desires to obtain revenue therefrom, the tax should be materially reduced so that the inducement of smuggling and attendant difficulties and expenses of administering the law may be lessened.

Source: Quoted in Peter D. Lowes, *The Genesis of International Narcotics Control* (Geneva: Librairie Droz, 1966), 95.

* * *

Instead, Congress increased the tariff rate to 12 dollars per pound. Legal imports then declined, and illegal smuggling increased until the tariff was finally lowered to six dollars in 1897. Importation of opium was finally made illegal by the Opium Exclusion Act of 1909 (see Part II).

Despite the great concern over opium smoking by the Chinese and by Americans, and federal legislation to limit importations of opium, perhaps the greatest source of opium addiction in the 19th century was the patent medicine industry. Many over-the-counter preparations contained opium or its various derivatives, and the benefits of the opiates were touted in advertisements as a cure for various ills.

DOCUMENT 18: Opium in Patent Medicines (Charles E. Terry and Mildred Pellens, 1928)

Another influence which operated undoubtedly to extend the use of opium and its derivatives especially during the latter half of the nineteenth century was the patent medicine industry. It would be impossible to form any accurate estimate of the influence exerted by the widespread sale and use of nostrums containing opium, but that this influence was great and contributed in an appreciable degree to the habitual use of the drug is undoubted. It must be remembered that those who employed these secret remedies were for the most part ignorant of drug dangers, sick, frequently in pain, and often suffering from some chronic malady and hence in a mental state which rendered them easy victims to the specious advertisements of the manufacturers. How widespread the custom of self-medication with patent nostrums became in this country is a matter of common knowledge. Newspapers and magazines were filled with fraudulent and misleading but seductive advertisements, while from billboards "pain-killers," "cough mixtures," "soothing syrups," "women's friends," "consumption cures," and a host of others, furnished a constant suggestion that could not fail to have its effect upon a considerable proportion of the population. The peak of the patent medicine industry was reached just prior to the passage of the federal Pure Food and Drugs Act in 1906 [see Part II].

Practically all the remedies advertised . . . contained opium or some of its products and depended principally on these drugs for such virtues as they possessed. It is not surprising that many persons became dependent on these preparations and later turned to the active drug itself when accidentally or otherwise they learned of its presence in the "medicine" they had been taking. Obvious and logical as was the influence of the patent medicine industry, it cannot be measured with any degree of accuracy and therefore must be accepted along with certain other influences such as the counter sales of the drugs themselves—equally immeasurable as a causative factor—as an extremely vicious and probably a very active influence. Many physicians who have treated numbers of cases of chronic opium intoxication in private practice mention instances of cases that owed their origin to the use of opium-containing nostrums.

Source: Charles E. Terry and Mildred Pellens, *The Opium Problem* (Bureau of Social Hygiene, 1928; reprint, Montclair, NJ: Patterson Smith Publishing 1970), 74–75.

COCAINE IN THE 19TH CENTURY

Although most of the attention during the 19th century was directed toward opium and related drugs, other drugs began to be popular. Cocaine, one of the major drugs of abuse in the late 20th century, was generally not considered a problem drug 100 years ago. The use of cocaine has a long tradition in South American cultures, but its usefulness as a local anesthetic was only first discovered in 1884. Among the enthusiasts for cocaine's benefits was Sigmund Freud; he and other physicians felt that cocaine had many benefits, including helping patients overcome opiate addiction. The following description of the uses and benefits of cocaine is from a basic pharmaceutical reference source from the early 1890s. It illustrates that in the 19th century cocaine was accepted as a relatively benign drug with a number of clinical uses.

DOCUMENT 19: Medical Uses of Cocaine (William Martindale, 1892)

Although made known to us soon after the conquest of Peru by Pizarro—more than three centuries ago—the accounts travellers have given of Coca have only received about the same credence, and have been treated with about the same reverence as we pay to a myth. . . . We looked upon its so-called nutritive properties, or rather its hunger and thirst-appeasing effects, as well as its power to ward off fatigue and relieve oppressive respiration during mountain ascents, as superstitions unworthy of more attention than the betel-nut mastication practised in India. The surgical uses of Cocaine as a local anesthetic have, however, to some extent dispelled these illusions, and we have been more ready to receive the accounts of early as well as recent travellers, thinking "there may be something in them." . . .

. . . Coca is classed among the "Narcotics we indulge in," along with Tobacco, Hop, Poppy and Lettuce, Indian Hemp, Areca or Betel-nut, Ava or Kava, Red Thorn Apple *(Datura sanguinea)* fruit, . . . Siberian fungus or Fly Agaric *(Amanita muscaria)*, and Sweet Gale *(Myrica Gale)*. . . . But physiologists have more recently classed it with Tea, Coffee, Mate, Kola Nut, and Cocoa—the Theine- (Methyl-Theobromine) and Theobromine-yielding plants—although Cocaine has no chemical alliance with these principles. As a beverage to substitute for tea or coffee, a decoction or an infusion of Coca is worthy of attention at the present time. The Indian use of it in moderation seems to prolong life, without much need of sleep or food, or even the desire for these although in excess it has, no doubt, a degrading effect. A taste for infusion or decoction of Coca or its pharmaceutical preparations is easily acquired; if a good sample of leaves be used it is not even at first disagreeable.

As the plant admits of easy acclimatisation, and yields annually several crops of leaves, should it come into more extended use it is probable that its cultivation in suitable localities in mountainous parts of India, Ceylon, and Jamaica will prove a profitable enterprise to planters now commencing the growth of it.

Source: William Martindale, *Coca and Cocaine: Their History, Medical and Economic Uses, and Medicinal Preparations*, 2nd ed. (London: H. K. Lewis, 1892), iii–iv.

* * *

Cocaine was also a common ingredient in many patent medicines, tonics, and cures. Its properties as a stimulant were widely advertised as a cure for many real and imagined ills. Joseph Spillane has written an extensive history of cocaine use and distribution in the 19th and early 20th centuries, and the following documents describe the various legal and readily available sources of this drug. First, cocaine was a common ingredient of patent medicines and tonics.

DOCUMENT 20: Cocaine in Patent Medicines (Joseph Spillane, 1994)

In the late-1880s, shortly after cocaine's arrival in the United States, the most common use of coca or cocaine in patent medicines was as an ingredient in various tonic preparations. Soft drinks and coca wines were only the two most common among many such tonics. Long before coca and cocaine appeared in the 1880s, dozens of tonics and "invigorators" filled the cases and shelves of drugstores. In many cases, coca was simply added to an already successful and established line of tonics. . . .

Most patent medicine advertising emphasized cocaine's tonic and stimulant properties. A St. Louis firm which manufactured a product called Cocarettes, made with tobacco and coca leaves, listed "Ten Reasons Why Cocarettes Should Be Used By All Smokers." Included on the list were: "Coca is the finest nerve tonic and exhilarator ever discovered;" "Coca stimulates the brain to great activity and gives tone and vigor to the entire system."

Source: Joseph Spillane, *Modern Drug, Modern Menace* (Santa Monica, CA: RAND Corporation, 1994), 214–215.

* * *

Cocaine was also present in the original formulations of Coca-Cola and similar soft drinks.

DOCUMENT 21: Cocaine in Soft Drinks (Joseph Spillane, 1994)

Coca-Cola not only contained cocaine: its *raison d'etre* was to serve as an appetizing vehicle for both the stimulant and therapeutic properties of coca. John Pemberton, Coca-Cola's creator, was an Atlanta pharmacist who also did some manufacturing for a limited market. Among Pemberton's products was a coca wine, which he called Peruvian Wine Coca. When the city of Atlanta adopted prohibition in 1886, Pemberton was forced to seek an alternative to Peruvian Wine Coca which would contain no alcohol. The syrup which resulted from his experiments he called Coca-Cola. From the beginning, this product was intended to serve a medical market, albeit through a delicious fountain drink. Although the mix of pleasant beverage and medicine seems strange today, it was quite common in the late nineteenth century. In its early advertising, Coca-Cola not only openly acknowledged its coca content, it ardently invoked accepted medical knowledge of coca to make its sales pitch. In 1896, the *National Druggist* . . . ran its first advertisement for Coca-Cola:

"It seems to be a law of nature that the more valuable and efficacious a drug is, the nastier and more unpleasant its taste. It is therefore quite a triumph over nature that the Coca-Cola Co. of Atlanta, Ga., have achieved in their success in robbing both coca leaves and the kola nut of the exceedingly nauseous and disagreeable taste while retaining their wonderful medicinal properties, and the power of restoring vitality and raising the spirits of the weary and debilitated. Not only have they done this, but by some subtle alchemy they have made them the basis of one of the most delightful, cheering, and invigorating of fountain drinks."

The phenomenal success of Coca-Cola gave rise to a host of imitators. This was particularly true in the South. . . . Of the ten soft drinks containing cocaine mentioned in the AMA's *Nostrums and Quackery*, three were manufactured in Atlanta, two in Birmingham AL, one each in Athens, GA, New Orleans, Cincinnati, Canton, OH, and Chicago. Scores of Coca-Cola imitators, with names like Cafe-Coca, Kos-Kola, Kola-Ade, Celery-Cola, Koca-Nola, Wiseola, Rococola, Vani-Kola, and Koke, competed for a part of the lucrative soft drink market.

Source: Joseph Spillane, *Modern Drug, Modern Menace* (Santa Monica, CA: RAND Corporation, 1994), 206–207, 209.

* * *

Finally, coca wine was another popular drink of the late 19th century.

DOCUMENT 22: Popularity of Coca Wine (Joseph Spillane, 1994)

Prior to Coca-Cola's popularization, the most prominent coca/cocaine product was coca wine. . . . Mortimer's survey around the turn of the century revealed that among 276 physicians who employed coca, only fifteen used a solid extract of coca,—twenty used coca leaves, 104 used the fluid extract, and 229 used coca wine. . . . It was also the preparation of choice for the public: the most common form in which cocaine was used in the 1880s and 1890s was as an ingredient in coca wines.

The first and most popular of the coca wines was Vin Mariani. Its manufacturer, Mariani & Company, whose sole business was the manufacture of coca and cocaine products, typified the close relationship between some patent medicine manufacturers and physicians. Mariani claimed that their product was advertised only to physicians, echoing the practices of ethical firms. Like many manufacturers, Mariani promoted their product in many different ways, including the publication of their own periodical called *Mariani's Coca Leaf: An Occasional Review for Physicians Advocating the Rational Uses of Coca,* "mailed free to physicians upon request." Mariani also used an early type of celebrity endorsement; the endorsements they published were clearly designed to appeal to an educated, professional constituency rather than a popular audience. The aggressive pursuit of medical favor resulted in the company being able to boast of having the written endorsement of over seven thousand physicians.

Like Coca-Cola, Vin Mariani inspired a host of imitators. The peak of coca wines' popularity came in the early 1890s, when the catalog of New York wholesale dealer Charles N. Crittenton listed nineteen different brands of coca wine available to the public.

Source: Joseph Spillane, *Modern Drug, Modern Menace* (Santa Monica, CA: RAND Corporation, 1994), 212–213.

* * *

Most of these patent medicines, tonics, and drinks contained relatively small amounts of cocaine, although enough to have a mild stimulant effect. For example, Spillane estimates that with a few exceptions, most of these products contained less than 30 milligrams per ounce of cocaine. The products that may have had a greater impact on the spread of cocaine "habits" were the so-called catarrh cures, marketed as cures for upper respiratory maladies.

DOCUMENT 23: Cocaine Abuse and Patent Medicines (Joseph Spillane, 1994)

Catarrh cures were responsible for nearly all the cocaine abuse connected to patent medicine consumption. At least four factors contributed to this phenomenon. First, even if the products were used as intended, the use of cocaine in treating catarrh and asthma generally required substantial doses of the drug over extended periods of time to provide relief. Moreover, increasing doses usually were necessary to provide the same amount of relief. Second, for recreational cocaine-sniffers, particularly young users, catarrh cures were often the easiest and cheapest method of purchasing cocaine. Druggists reluctant to sell pure cocaine might readily sell a packaged cure.

Third, manufacturers contributed in some respect by encouraging repeated and excessive use. The makers of Az-Ma-Syde recommended that "to cure Asthma use . . . Az-Ma-Syde Atomizer, three times a day, and during each attack." A circular for Ryno's Hay Fever and Catarrh Remedy (which contained nothing but cocaine) advised that for its use in "hay fever, rose col, influenza, or whenever the nose is 'stuffed-up,' red and sore," the remedy should be employed "two to ten times a day, or oftener if really necessary." For "chronic catarrh" Ryno noted that the remedy should be employed two or three times a day, but that "this disease is often very intractable, sometimes requiring several months to cure. . . ."

Fourth, unlike the manufacturers of many low-potency products, catarrh cures seldom revealed that cocaine was an ingredient. Advertising for Ryno's Remedy failed to mention that the product contained any cocaine, despite the fact that it contained nothing but the drug! Birney's Catarrh Cure, perhaps the most well-known of these, also revealed nothing about its cocaine content. While most users fully understood the composition of these cures, some surely did not. Having embarked on a lengthy program of treatment, they may well have found it extremely difficult to break the habit.

Source: Joseph Spillane, *Modern Drug, Modern Menace* (Santa Monica, CA: RAND Corporation, 1994), 227–229.

* * *

By the beginning of the 20th century, government efforts to use legislation to eliminate narcotic and other drugs from patent medicines had begun to pay off. With the increasing publicity about the dangers of patent medicines, fewer over-the-counter medicines contained these drugs, and the public began reducing their consumption of those that did still contain drugs. However, the problem of drug abuse certainly was still prevalent, as shown in this excerpt from a 1908 newspaper article about cocaine use in New York City following enactment of a state law to regulate cocaine sales.

DOCUMENT 24: Cocaine Abuse in the Early 1900s (*New York Times,* 1908)

Since the passage of the Smith Anti-Cocaine bill last year and the crusade of the Department of Health against the drug, which has practically stopped the open sale of "coke" in the city, peddlers, poor, unmoral creatures of the underworld, have sprung up to ply a thriving trade in dispensing the drug among the victims of the habit. Seventh Avenue, between Twenty-eighth and Thirty-third Streets, has come to be known as "Poison Row," for the ease with which the drug can be obtained in the neighborhood and the fact that around these corners the peddlers make their headquarters and send out their agents.

The cocaine habit is pronounced by physicians and neurologists to be the most terrible vice ever acquired by a civilized people, in the havoc that it works upon the mental, moral, and physical life of a person that acquires it. Cocaine, the drug, the discovery of which was hailed by surgeons as an inestimable boon, in making possible local anaesthesia in minor surgical operations, in a very short time proved little less than a curse to a certain class of American society....

...

The "coke peddler" is a familiar figure in the back rooms of saloon dives throughout the country and every "red-light district" has a drug store which caters especially to the "coke" and other "fiends."

...

One result ... has been brought about by the passage of the Smith bill and the crusade against the drug. "Birney's," "Gray's," "The Crown," and the rest are sold no more. Many of these "cures" have gone out of business, others have taken cocaine out of their make-up, and still others cannot obtain a market, some druggists not daring to continue their sale and more refusing it for the most laudable of reasons. A popular soda fountain proprietary drink which a few years ago contained a large percentage of the drug, and was denounced not long ago by Dr. H. W. Wiley, Chief of the Bureau of Chemistry of the Department of Agriculture, is to-day made without cocaine. The makers of an extensively sold "tonic" have taken the same course.

...

Dr. Graeme Monroe Hammond, the neurologist, says that it is absolutely impossible to cure the cocaine fiend, once the habit has become fixed upon him. "There is nothing that we can do for the confirmed user of the drug," says he. "The best thing for the cocaine fiend is to let him die. He is of no use either to himself or to the community. Plenty of energy can be exerted with far more advantage in restricting the habit and preventing new recruits from taking it up. My experience with drug users has been startling. Over 80 per cent of the patients that come to me with this affliction are either physicians or physician's wives. But few of these people are cocaine users. In fact, almost never do I find one unless it is an old, confirmed taker of opium or morphine, who has turned to cocaine as a stronger and more stimulating narcotic. As a rule, however, the habit is found confined to the lower classes of society."

Source: "Brought Within Reach of Its Victims by Secret Means, It Has Become the Most Widespread as It Is the Most Insidious of Deadly Drugs," *New York Times*, August 2, 1908.

DISCOVERY OF HEROIN

Finally, the end of the 19th century saw the discovery of a new opiate drug that was to become one of the primary drugs of abuse of the 20th century. Heroin was first isolated in Germany in 1898, and at first was thought to have many of the same benefits as opium or morphine but without the dangers of addiction or bad side effects.

DOCUMENT 25: Discovery of Heroin in 1898 (Charles E. Terry and Mildred Pellens, 1928)

Dresser in Germany in 1898 produced heroin or diacetylmorphin which was put out as a safe preparation free from addiction-forming properties, possessing many of the virtues and none of the dangers of morphin and codein, and recommended even as an agent of value in the treatment of chronic intoxication to these drugs. Probably no remedy ever was heralded so enthusiastically as was heroin. The prominent place held by opium derivatives in therapeutics, the constant calls on every physician to relieve pain and induce sleep with drugs, and the relative inadequacy of all substitutes for opium combined from the outset to stimulate the use of heroin. It was apparently the ideal preparation—potent analgesic and sedative—at the same time possessing other qualities highly desirable in certain ailments, above all freedom from the dreaded so-called "habit-forming" qualities of the parent drug.

Source: Charles E. Terry and Mildred Pellens, *The Opium Problem* (Bureau of Social Hygiene, 1928; Montclair, NJ: Patterson Smith Publishing 1970), 76–77.

* * *

Citing several late 19th century medical journal articles, Terry and Pellens describe how heroin was used and accepted as a therapeutic agent at the end of the 19th century, despite the recognition by 1906 that it was addictive and could be dangerous.

DOCUMENT 26: Therapeutic Uses of Heroin (Charles E. Terry and Mildred Pellens, 1928)

Floret, in 1898, after six months' use of the drug, . . . states that heroin appears to be unusually useful, prompt, and dependable in coughs and irritations as well as in pains in the chest. . . . He states that in dry bronchitis where codein was not effective heroin was and also that it was valuable in the treatment of tuberculosis and asthma. Nothing was said as to its dangers. . . .

Strube, in 1898 . . . tested [heroin] on 50 patients at the medical University Clinic of Berlin. Most of the material at the clinic were cases of phthisis [a respiratory disease like tuberculosis]. He describes the doses employed to produce sleep and relieve the cough and states that the results were satisfactory. . . .

In 1906 the Council on Pharmacy and Chemistry of the American Medical Association tentatively accepted, for inclusion in the proposed annual "New and Non-Official Remedies," heroin and heroin hydrochloride[,] giving their therapeutic indications as follows:

"When given in small doses heroin hydrochloride has apparently no effect on any of the vital functions except respiration. . . .

In large doses it may produce dizziness, nausea and occasionally constipation and in poisonous amounts, twitching of the extremities, great exhaustion and dimness of vision. . . . The habit is readily formed and leads to most deplorable results. . . . On withdrawing the drug from habitués there is said to be a tendency to respiratory failure. . . .

Heroin and its hydrochloride are recommended chiefly for the treatment of diseases of the air passages attended with cough, difficult breathing and spasm, much as the different forms of bronchitis, pneumonia, consumption, asthma, whooping cough, laryngitis and certain forms of hay fever. It has also been recommended as an analgesic, in the place of morphine in various painful affections."

Source: Charles E. Terry and Mildred Pellens, *The Opium Problem* (Bureau of Social Hygiene, 1928; reprint, Montclair, NJ: Patterson Smith Publishing, 1970), 77–78, 84.

* * *

Like many new drugs, heroin was first thought to be a benign drug that was superior to other opiates; its potential for abuse and addiction was realized only after a number of years.

DOCUMENT 27: Dangers of Heroin Addiction (Lawrence Kolb and A. G. Du Mez, 1924)

In 1898 heroin was put on the market and advertised as an opiate that would not cause addiction. It was soon discovered that this was not the case; but it was nearly 10 years before the medical profession fully appreciated the dangers of the drug. However, the increase in the number of addicts caused by this mistake was more than offset by influences tending to prevent addiction which began to operate before the end of this period.

Source: Lawrence Kolb and A. G. Du Mez, "The Prevalence and Trend of Drug Addiction in the United Sates and Factors Influencing It," *Public Health Reports* 39, no. 21 (1924): 1198–1199.

* * *

At the beginning of the 20th century, then, Americans were becoming more aware of the dangers of drugs, especially their addiction and abuse potential. Although there were some federal laws to limit opium importation, and a number of state and local laws against opium and other drug sale and use, American drug policy was still in its infancy. Opiates and cocaine were still readily available through doctors' prescriptions and some patent medicines. In the first decade of the 20th century, however, important and dramatic changes began to take place in the nation's views toward drugs and the level of government control over their use. The medical profession was gaining in prestige and scientific stature, and the dangers of physician-induced addiction began to be recognized. New concerns over the safety of the nation's food supply and over-the-counter medications led to increasing scrutiny of the patent medicine industry. Finally, increasing problems with the international trafficking in opium and other drugs began to emerge. The result was the development of the first comprehensive federal laws to control drug use, as well as the emergence of stricter and broader state and local anti-drug policies.

Part II

The Early Expansion of Federal Drug Control

The first 15 years of the 20th century were crucial in shaping American drug policy. Together with the increasing concerns about the number of people addicted to opiates and other drugs through patent medicines and doctors' prescriptions, there was a growing recognition on an international level that unchecked opium use in China and other countries and international trafficking in drugs were undermining whatever limited efforts the states and the federal government were making to regulate drugs. Spurred by an influential group of "drug reformers," the United States became involved in several international conferences aimed at developing agreements to place controls on opium trafficking and to reduce drug use. These conferences served to help influence new federal legislation and led directly to the drafting and enactment of the Harrison Act of 1914. This law and its implementation were to shape federal anti-drug policies for the next 50 years.

In addition to the increasing controls placed on opium for smoking and other forms of crude opium, Congress passed the Pure Food and Drug Act in 1906. This was landmark legislation in the federal regulation and protection of the nation's food, as well as in terms of national drug policy. It passed despite strong opposition from the patent medicine industry.

DOCUMENT 28: Passage of Pure Food and Drug Act (Edward M. Brecher, 1972)

A major step forward in the control of opiate addiction was taken in 1906, when Congress passed the Pure Food and Drug Act despite opposition from the patent-medicine interests. The pressures to pass the act were intense—generated by Dr. Harvey W. Wiley and his crusading journalistic followers, notably Samuel Hopkins Adams, who were known as "muckrakers."

. . .

The efforts leading to the 1906 act, the act itself and subsequent amendments, and educational campaigns urging families not to use patent medicines containing opiates, no doubt helped curb the making of new addicts. Indeed, there is evidence of a modest decline in opiate addiction from the peak in the 1890s until 1914.

Source: Edward M. Brecher and the Editors of Consumer Reports, *Licit and Illicit Drugs* (Boston: Little, Brown, 1972), 47.

* * *

The 1906 act was a direct effort to place some federal controls on patent medicines that contained opiates, cocaine, and other drugs. By requiring manufacturers of over-the-counter patent medicines to label their products and to disclose the amount of drugs contained in them, the government hoped to greatly reduce the use of such medicines. Following are the key portions of the Pure Food and Drug Act.

DOCUMENT 29: Pure Food and Drug Act (June 30, 1906)

Be it enacted, . . . That it shall be unlawful for any person to manufacture within any Territory or the District of Columbia any article of food or drug which is adulterated or misbranded, within the meaning of this Act; and any person who shall violate any of the provisions of this section shall be guilty of a misdemeanor, and for each offense shall, upon conviction thereof, be fined not to exceed five hundred dollars or shall be sentenced to one year's imprisonment, or both such fine and imprisonment, in the discretion of the court, and for each subsequent offense and conviction thereof shall be fined not less than one thousand dollars or sentenced to one year's imprisonment, or both such fine and imprisonment, in the discretion of the court.

SEC. 2. That the introduction into any State or Territory or the District of Columbia from any other State or Territory or the District of Columbia, or from any foreign country, or shipment to any foreign country of any article of food or drugs which is adulterated or misbranded, within the meaning of this Act, is hereby prohibited; and any person who shall ship or deliver [such articles] for shipment . . . shall be guilty of a misdemeanor, and for such offense be fined not exceeding two hundred dollars for the first offense, and upon conviction for each subsequent offense not exceeding three hundred dollars or be imprisoned not exceeding one year, or both, in the discretion of the court. . . .

. . .

SEC. 6. That the term "drug," as used in this Act, shall include all medicines and preparations recognized in the United States Pharmacopoeia or National Formulary for internal or external use, and any substance or mixture of substances intended to be used for the cure, mitigation, or prevention of disease of either man or other animals. . . .

. . .

SEC. 8. That the term "misbranded," as used herein, shall apply to all drugs, or articles of food, or articles which enter into the composition of food, the package or label of which shall bear any statement, design, or device regarding such article, or the ingredients or substances contained therein which shall be false or misleading in any particular, and to any food or drug product which is falsely branded as to the State, Territory, or country in which it is manufactured or produced.

That for the purposes of this Act an article shall also be deemed to be misbranded:

In case of drugs:

First. If it be an imitation of or offered for sale under the name of another article.

Second. If the contents of the package as originally put up shall have been removed, in whole or in part, and other contents shall have been placed in such package, or if the package fail to bear a statement on the label of the quantity or proportion of any alcohol, morphine, opium, cocaine, heroin, alpha or beta eucaine, chloroform, cannabis indica, chloral hydrate, or acetanilide, or any derivative or preparation of any such substances contained therein.

Source: Pure Food and Drug Act, Public Law 59–384, 59th Congress, Session I, June 30, 1906.

* * *

Although it was a very important piece of legislation in the evolution of anti-drug policy, the Pure Food and Drug Act, like many subsequent laws, had some unintended consequences. Joseph Spillane described the effect on cocaine use.

DOCUMENT 30: Impact of Federal Laws on Cocaine Use (Joseph Spillane, 1994)

The second result of these regulatory efforts was, ironically, to redirect the flow of powdered cocaine hydrochloride away from medicine manufacturers toward direct sales to consumers. Cocaine itself was not subject to federal regulations, as long as it met national standards for quality and purity. As a consequence, if cocaine manufacturers desired to continue production at high levels, they could do so without attracting much attention. The attack on patent medicines, while the ethical industry was largely ignored, had the unintended result of reinforc[ing] the trend away from popular use of low-potency cocaine preparations toward the use of pure cocaine. In short, the combined efforts of muckrakers, the AMA, and the federal government accelerated the decline in the medical use of coca and cocaine, and increased the importance of pure cocaine hydrochloride in supplying the demands of American consumers.

Source: Joseph Spillane, *Modern Drug, Modern Menace* (Santa Monica, CA: RAND Corporation, 1994), 240–241.

* * *

At the end of the 19th century and the beginning of the 20th century, the opium problem was generally viewed as affecting China and other Asian countries to a much greater degree than the United States. However, as a result of its victory over Spain in the Spanish-American War, the United States acquired the Philippine Islands as a new territory in 1898. Quickly, American diplomats learned that there was a significant opium problem in the Philippines, bringing the issue much closer to home.

DOCUMENT 31: Opium in the Philippines (Arnold Taylor, 1969)

. . . [W]ith the acquisition of the Philippine Islands, the United States acquired a concrete interest in the Far Eastern drug situation. Missionaries called the attention of the government to the opium problem in the islands, and in response to their suggestions, the United States, seeking to demonstrate the beneficence of its rule over dependent peoples, prohibited outright the traffic in and use of the drug except for medical and scientific purposes. It thus became the only Western power with Far Eastern possessions to so restrict the use of the drug, a position which it held until near the end of World War II.

The significance of the Philippine opium situation extended far beyond the islands. Its great importance was in furnishing the United States with ample justification for interceding on behalf of China with the other powers having Oriental possessions. Thus, in 1906, again in response to missionary influence, the United States launched an international campaign to help rid China of the opium menace. Although the movement soon broadened to include most of the world, China remained throughout a major factor in American considerations. And as a result of the great part played by missionaries and other reformers in the inauguration of the movement as well as in carrying it out, American participation in the campaign took on the aura of a moral crusade.

Source: Arnold Taylor, *American Diplomacy and the Narcotics Traffic, 1900–1939* (Durham, NC: Duke University Press, 1969), 328.

* * *

Hamilton Wright was appointed United States Opium Commissioner on July 1, 1906, and was the American delegate to the International Opium Commission, which met at Shanghai in February 1909. He was a respected physician and expert on tropical diseases who had spent several years in China, Japan, and India. Following the adjournment of the International Opium Commission, Wright was at the Department of State, where he became perhaps the most influential individual in the development of early federal drug policy; drug policy historian David Musto called Wright the "father of American narcotic laws." Wright was also the chief U.S. delegate to the 1911 international opium conference at The Hague, which was a key impetus for the first general federal anti-drug law, the Harrison Act.

In connection with the Shanghai International Opium Commission, the federal government banned importation of any form of opium. Thus in 1909 federal curbs on opium joined the prohibitions against opium that already existed in many states and cities. Wright, who spearheaded the drafting of the 1909 anti-opium act, described the rationale for this legislation.

DOCUMENT 32: Hamilton Wright on the 1909 Anti-Opium Act (1928)

Another aspect of the opium question loomed large and was most important to our government, considering that it had convened an International Opium Commission to study and report on the opium problem as it is seen in the Far East. While the diplomatic correspondence proceeded it became apparent to the Department of State that there was a large misuse of opium in the continental United States. When this had been sufficiently demonstrated by the opium commission, it became the bounden duty of our Government to take some steps to clear up the home problem before the American delegates to the International Opium Commission should be brought face to face with the delegations of the other powers. Otherwise the American people stood to be accused of living in a glass house that no doubt would have been shattered on their heads.

Source: Quoted in Charles E. Terry and Mildred Pellens, *The Opium Problem* (Bureau of Social Hygiene, 1928; reprint, Montclair, NJ: Patterson Smith Publishing, 1970), 749.

* * *

Arnold Taylor has traced the political context of America's development of its early narcotics laws in terms of our participation in international efforts to control opium trafficking.

DOCUMENT 33: History of Federal Anti-Opium Laws (Arnold Taylor, 1969)

Aside from the tariff laws, the Act of 1887, and the Excise Act of 1890 placing a tax of $10 a pound on smoking opium manufactured in the United States and restricting its manufacture to American citizens, the only other federal law regulating the sale of narcotics in the United States prior to 1909 was the Pure Food and Drug Act of 1906. . . . To improve America's regulatory system relative to the drugs, the State Department, in cooperation with the Department of Agriculture, set about drafting a bill to regulate the importation and sale of opium and its derivatives in the United States and its dependencies. Some felt that the amendment of the Food and Drug Act would accomplish the desired object. But as the date of the convening of the International Commission neared, it was decided to restrict the bill merely to the prohibition of the importation and manufacture of smoking opium, a prohibition which the importers and manufacturers of opium unanimously favored. A bill touching all aspects of the opium traffic—from importation to consumption—would manifestly be too complicated and controversial for hurried consideration by Congress. The object was to get a law passed before the convening of the Shanghai Commission. Thus Senator Henry Cabot Lodge introduced in the Senate a very simple bill, drafted by the State Department, prohibiting the importation into the United States of opium except for medicinal purposes. To the joy of the American commissioners, the bill was finally passed on February 9, 1909, just a little over a week after the Joint Commission assembled. Thus the American representatives were able to point to this legislative manifestation of the American attitude toward the opium problem as a worthy example for the other nations to follow.

Source: Arnold Taylor, *American Diplomacy and the Narcotics Traffic, 1900–1939* (Durham, NC: Duke University Press, 1969), 58–60.

* * *

In a 1911 magazine interview that painted a dire picture of the current state of the American opium problem, Hamilton Wright described the aftermath of the Shanghai conference and the concern that federal officials had about the amount of opium use in the United States.

DOCUMENT 34: Hamilton Wright on Opium Use (1911)

[DR. WRIGHT:] Of all the nations of the world . . . the United States consumes most habit-forming drugs per capita. Opium, the most pernicious drug known to humanity, is surrounded, in this country, with far fewer safeguards than any nation in all Europe. . . . China now guards it with much greater care than we do; Japan preserves her people from it more intelligently than we do ours, who can buy it, in almost any form, in every tenth one of our drug stores. Our physicians use it recklessly in remedies and thus become responsible for making numberless "dope fiends," and in uncounted nostrums offered everywhere for sale it figures, in habit-making quantities, without restriction. . . . Here physicians often are addicted to the habit, and they continually prescribe opium for insufficient causes or without any real excuse. . . . A proportion of our doctors and a much larger ratio of our druggists regard their liberty to prescribe and sell as license to advise and furnish to its victims the narcotic curse upon demand.

. . .

When Champ Clark, before the Ways and Means Committee, asked me what the effect of the restrictive legislation which I favored would be, I said that it would be to drive out of the business not less than ten per cent, of all the retail druggists in the country, because, in the United States, at least one druggist out of every ten exists by means of profits from the sale of habit-forming drugs, of which, of course, opium and its derivatives are most important. . . . If opium were rightly safeguarded in the United States far more than a full tenth of all the druggists would be immediately forced from business, and many, many a complacent doctor, willing to prescribe the drug upon demand of any patient's hurtful craving for it, would find his practice, now, really, a mere detail of one of the world's most vicious habits, dwindling quickly into nothing.

. . .

Thus, as an outgrowth of the [Shanghai] conference there was begun a movement which has probably been even more important than the conference itself in its results. Starting out to learn the dangers of the foreign opium traffic, we learned that dangers also lie in the home trade, and suggested general domestic investigation by the powers. This was generally agreed to, and the study, it was granted, should include the study of the morphine habit and the vices allied to it. That this would show us as the world's worst sinners few people, if any, suspected, but this has proved to be the case.

. . .

We use more smoking opium per annum than six great European nations put together, nor is this detail of our great consumption of the drug a detail of our Chinese problem, if nowadays we have a Chinese problem. The Chinese may have brought the habit with them to our shores, and many of the Chinese here undoubtedly use opium, but its consumption has grown far beyond the wildest estimate of the capacity of our comparatively small Chinese population. At the coming conference the report of the United States will of sheer necessity be of the nature of a humiliating confession. Russia, Austria-Hungary, Germany, Holland, and Italy have, all put together, a vastly smaller opium consumption than that of the United States, although their total population is 155,000,000 against our 90,000,000.

Every year we manage to consume 500,000 pounds of the drug, while they, in combination use less than 40,000 pounds. Nor are these startling figures the most startling which we must present before that conference and consider carefully ourselves. Our consumption of this greatest curse which humanity has ever known since humanity began is growing constantly, despite the passage of new laws and the continual efforts of the scientists and moralists to teach its dangers. Since 1800 the population of this country has grown 133 per cent, while the amazing fact is plainly on the records that our opium consumption has increased 351 per cent.

Source: Quoted in Edward Marshall, "Uncle Sam Is the Worst Drug Fiend in the World," *New York Times Magazine*, March 12, 1911.

* * *

The prevailing public perception in the United States was that the opium problem was limited, affecting mainly Chinese immigrants. The reality seemed to be that opium use was a much broader issue, according to Arnold Taylor.

DOCUMENT 35: Spread of Opium Problem in the Early 1900s (Arnold Taylor, 1969)

The revelation that the United States had a substantial domestic opium problem came as a surprise to most Americans, who had long viewed the consumption of the drug as a habit peculiar to the Orient. The problem in America stemmed from two main sources: the excessive importation of crude opium from Turkey for manufacture into morphine and other medicinal preparations, and the importation of smoking opium from the Far East, principally from Portuguese Macao, to supply Chinese and other habitual opium smokers in the United States. It was estimated that the maximum annual needs of the American people for opium for medicinal use were 100,000 pounds, whereas the actual annual importation of opium for this purpose was over 500,000 pounds. From 70 to 80 percent of the crude opium imported was used to manufacture morphine, and it was estimated that from 50 to 70 percent of such morphine was used for improper purposes. The remainder of the crude opium was used in medicinal preparations such as laudanum and other extracts which were themselves subject to misuse.

. . . Since 1900 the average annual quantity of smoking opium legally imported was 151,944 pounds. In addition a great deal had been smuggled in, much from Canada, where Chinese firms manufactured it; and some had been surreptitiously manufactured in the United States. Wright estimated that there were in the United States about 52,000 Chinese smokers—about 40 percent of our total Chinese population—and from 100,000 to 150,000 non-Chinese smokers in the American population. He further estimated that of the 650,000 pounds of opium in all forms, imported legally into the United States, 550,000 pounds were used for illegitimate purposes. The revenue derived from the tariff duties on such opium averaged nearly a million and a half dollars annually, constituting one-fifth of 1 percent of America's total revenue.

Source: Arnold Taylor, *American Diplomacy and the Narcotics Traffic, 1900–1939* (Durham NC: Duke University Press, 1969), 58–59.

* * *

On February 9, 1909, Congress passed the act banning importation of opium for nonmedical purposes and providing for fine or imprisonment for violating the act. With its 1914 amendments, the key provisions of this act are presented in the next document.

DOCUMENT 36: Opium Smoking Act, 1909, as Amended (1914)

Be it enacted, . . . That an Act entitled "An Act to prohibit the importation and use of opium for other than medicinal purposes," approved February ninth, nineteen hundred and nine, is hereby amended so as to read as follows:

That after the first day of April, nineteen hundred and nine, it shall be unlawful to import into the United States opium in any form or any preparation or derivative thereof: *Provided*, That opium and preparations and derivatives thereof, other than smoking opium or opium prepared for smoking, may be imported for medicinal purposes only, under regulations which the Secretary of the Treasury is hereby authorized to prescribe, and when so imported shall be subject to the duties which are now or may hereafter be imposed by law.

SECTION 2. That if any person shall fraudulently or knowingly import or bring into the United States, or assist in so doing any opium or any preparation or derivative thereof contrary to law, or shall receive, conceal, buy, sell, or in any manner facilitate the transportation, concealment, or sale of such opium or preparation or derivative thereof after importation, knowing the same to have been imported contrary to law, such opium or preparation or derivative thereof shall be forfeited and shall be destroyed, and the offender shall be fined in any sum not exceeding $5,000 nor less than $50 or by imprisonment for any time not exceeding two years, or both. . . .

. . .

SECTION 4. That any person subject to the jurisdiction of the United States who shall, either as principal or as accessory, receive or have in his possession or conceal on board of or transport on any foreign or domestic vessel or other water craft or railroad car or other vehicle destined to or bound from the United States or any possession thereof, any smoking opium or opium prepared for smoking, or who, having knowledge of the presence in or on any such vessel, water craft, or vehicle of such article, shall not report the same to the principal officer thereof, shall be subject to the penalty provided in section two of this Act. . . . *Provided, however,* That any master of a vessel or other water craft, or person in charge of a railroad car or other vehicle, shall not be liable under this section if he shall satisfy the jury that he had no knowledge and used due diligence to prevent the presence of such article in or on such vessel, water craft, car, or other vessel, and any such article shall be forfeited and shall be destroyed.

. . .

SECTION 6. That no smoking opium or opium prepared for smoking shall be admitted into the United States, or into any territory under the control or jurisdiction thereof, for transportation to another country, nor shall such opium be transferred or transshipped from one vessel to another vessel within any waters of the United States for immediate exportation or any other purpose.

That hereafter it shall be unlawful for any person subject to the jurisdiction of the United States to export or cause to be exported from the United States, or from territory under its control or jurisdiction, or from countries in which the United States exercises extraterritorial jurisdiction, any opium or cocaine, or any salt, derivative, or preparation of opium or cocaine, to any other country: *Provided,* That opium or cocaine, and salts, derivatives, or preparations thereof, except smoking opium or opium prepared for smoking, the exportation of which is hereby absolutely prohibited, may be exported to countries regulating their entry under such regulations as are prescribed by such country for the importation thereof into such country, such regulations to be promulgated from time to time by the Secretary of State of the United States.

SECTION 7. That any person who exports or causes to be exported any of the aforesaid drugs in violation of the preceding section shall be fined in any sum not exceeding $5,000 nor less than $50 or by imprisonment for any time not exceeding two years, or both. And one-half of any fine recovered from any person or persons convicted of an offense under any section of this Act may be paid to the person or persons giving information leading to such recovery, and one-half of any mail forfeited and collected in any proceedings brought under this Act may be paid to the person or persons giving the information which led to the institution of such proceedings, if so directed by the court exercising jurisdiction in the case: *Provided*, That no payment for giving information shall be made to any officer or employee of the United States.

Source: Opium Smoking Act of 1909, as amended (H. R. 1966), 1914.

* * *

Around the same time as the opium importation act was amended, Congress placed additional restrictions on domestic manufacture of smoking opium by levying a tax on its manufacture. This act, passed on January 17, 1914, was a precursor to the much broader Harrison Act, passed later that year (see Part III).

DOCUMENT 37: Federal Tax on Opium for Smoking (1914)

Be it enacted, . . . That an internal-revenue tax of $300 per pound shall be levied and collected upon all opium manufactured in the United States for smoking purposes; and no person shall engage in such manufacture who is not a citizen of the United States and who has not given the bond required by the Commissioner of Internal Revenue. Every person who prepares opium suitable for smoking purposes from crude gum opium, or from any preparation thereof, or from the residue of smoked or partially smoked opium, commonly known as yen shee, or from any mixture of the above, or any of them, shall be regarded as a manufacturer of smoking opium within the meaning of this Act.

. . .

SECTION 3. That all opium prepared for smoking manufactured in the United States shall be duly stamped in such a permanent manner as to denote the payment of the internal-revenue tax thereon.

. . .

SECTION 5. That a penalty of not less than $10,000 or imprisonment for not less than five years, or both, in the discretion of the court, shall be imposed for each and every violation of the preceding sections of this Act relating to opium by any person or persons; and all opium prepared for smoking wherever found within the United States without the stamps required by this Act shall be forfeited and destroyed.

Source: Public Law 63–47, 63rd Congress, January 17, 1914.

* * *

Despite federal laws against opium smoking and an emerging set of state laws, it seemed that existing legislation might be insufficient to control other forms of drug use.

DOCUMENT 38: Inadequacy of Federal Anti-Opium Laws (Arnold Taylor, 1969)

... [P]rior to the Opium Exclusion Act of 1909 the only federal legislation controlling such traffic and use were the Internal Revenue Act of 1890, which placed a tax of $10 per pound on smoking opium manufactured in the United States and restricted such manufacture to American citizens, and the Food and Drug Act of 1906. . . . None of the federal laws controlled the importation and use of narcotic drugs in the United States. The Opium Exclusion Act, however, dealt with only one aspect of the drug problem, that of smoking opium. It did not touch the great excess of medicinal opium imported which was used illicitly, nor did it affect the interstate traffic in the various forms of such opium. The cocaine traffic likewise remained uncontrolled. The situation was compounded by the weakness of many state laws. In some states, habit-forming drugs could be bought without a prescription, some such as laudanum and paregoric and preparations containing opiates being sold in grocery stores. The laws of many states requiring the sale of drugs by prescription only were easily evaded as illegal possession was not considered evidence for conviction, and illegal sale was therefore often hard to prove. Furthermore, in the absence of federal legislation controlling the interstate traffic in narcotics, even the states with stringent laws could not effectively deal with the problem. Thus, even after 1909 there was a pressing need for federal action to meet the domestic situation.

Source: Arnold Taylor, *American Diplomacy and the Narcotics Traffic, 1900–1939* (Durham, NC: Duke University Press, 1969), 126–127.

* * *

In its 1955 report on drug addiction and drug policy, the New York Academy of Medicine described the genesis of the international conferences that spurred the United States to enact major federal legislation to control domestic drug trafficking.

DOCUMENT 39: International Opium Conferences and Federal Legislation (New York Academy of Medicine, 1955)

At the insistence of the United States Government, the conference of the International Opium Commission convened in Shanghai in 1909 in an effort to obtain international action to control the traffic in opium and its products. The Commission recommended that drastic measures be taken by each government in its own territories to control the manufacture, sale and distribution of opium derivatives. Three years later the representatives of twelve world powers met at The Hague to formulate the recommendations of the Commission into an international convention. Here was reached the first important international agreement on the subject, which is known formally as the International Opium Convention of 1912, and popularly as the Hague Convention of 1912. This Convention was designed to bring about the gradual suppression of the abuse of opium, its products and derivatives, and cocaine. The signatory powers contracted to enact effective laws, or regulations, for the control of the production and distribution of raw opium; for prevention of export of raw opium to countries which shall have prohibited its entry; for control of the export of raw opium to countries which restrict its import; and for restricting both import and export of raw opium to that made by duly authorized persons. They further agreed to take measures for the gradual and effective suppression of the manufacture, distribution and use of prepared opium. They also engaged to exert efforts to restrict the import and export of morphine and cocaine preparations to authorized persons and to limit the manufacture, sale and use of these drugs exclusively for medical and scientific purposes.

Source: New York Academy of Medicine, "Report on Drug Addiction," *Bulletin of the New York Academy of Medicine* 31, no. 8 (1955): 592–593.

* * *

In the aftermath of the Hague convention, public awareness and concern about opium and other drugs grew. An emerging new drug problem, heroin, began to take hold as well, as reported in a 1913 article in the *New York Times*.

DOCUMENT 40: Emergence of Heroin Problem (*New York Times*, 1913)

The United States is now second to China and ahead of every other country in the world in the use of opium and the narcotics derived from it, according to a statement today by Dr. B. C. Keister, a specialist of Roanoke, before a meeting of scientists and specialists at the Rittenhouse Hotel. The menace is so great, the speaker said, that there is danger of our "degenerating back to something worse than monkeydom."

Dr. Keister's figures were startling even to his listeners, who are the delegates to the yearly meeting of the Society for the Study of Alcohol and Other Narcotics. The danger of the habit-forming drugs was growing so great, he said, that the only logical course was to cut them out of the pharmacopoeia entirely and prohibit their manufacture.

. . .

Americans addicted to the cocoaine [*sic*] habit consume 150,000 ounces of the drug each year.

Twenty-three per cent of the medical profession, the speaker continued, were now victims of the morphine habit. The medical and criminal records of the country indicated that a complete abolition of the manufacture of the habit-forming drugs, including alcohol, would reduce homicides by fifty per cent, suicides by sixty per cent, and lunacy by thirty-three per cent. The loss to medicine, whatever it might be, from the prohibition of morphine, alcohol, opium and cocaine, would be worth while in view of the possible benefits.

Dr. Keister's statements gained added significance through an address that was delivered immediately afterward by Dr. C. I. Douglas of Boston, who described the ravages of the new drug which, he said, was making victims by the hundred in his own city. This is a new product of opium and its discovery has been so recent that no existing State law may be made to apply against it.

This new chemical is called heroin. Its effects are like those of morphine and it is sold so openly in one district of Boston that the vicinity of the drug store which markets it has become known as "heroin square." The victims, who have increased by the hundreds within the last few months, hold regularly what are known as "sniffing parties," when the drug is passed around occasionally as the chief means of entertainment.

Source: "Say Drug Habit Grips the Nation," *New York Times*, December 5, 1913.

* * *

Opium, heroin, and morphine were not the only drugs that were the focus of attention of those concerned about the impact of drug use at the beginning of the 20th century. The use of cocaine, seen as a relatively benign drug in the latter part of the 19th century, was now being linked to violent behavior, especially among those of the lower classes and members of minority groups. Lurid tales of the violent acts of those high on cocaine became common between 1900 and 1920 and helped to spur increasing calls for more stringent legislation against drugs.

DOCUMENT 41: Cocaine and Violence (Joseph Spillane, 1994)

Clearly, the connection between cocaine and violence presents a complicated historical problem, particularly the task of separating perception from reality. The fear of violent crime committed by cocaine fiends appeared in countless popular accounts of the period. As several historians have argued, there is little doubt that these accounts frequently distorted reality and were sustained through fear and prejudice against cocaine users. On the other hand, historians dare not entirely dismiss the phenomenon as a fiction. Real incidents of violent and erratic behavior resulting directly from cocaine use almost surely did occur. Such incidents must be interpreted in context, however.

In much the same way that the real health costs of cocaine were often grossly exaggerated, so too were the real effects of cocaine on the behavior of its users. Nowhere was this more true than in the South, where police departments in particular rallied to the defense of white communities against cocaine-crazed blacks. No one expressed a more extreme view than [journalist] E. H. Williams. . . . Cocaine, Williams believed, transformed "hitherto inoffensive, law abiding negroes" into "a constant menace to his community. . . ." Under the influence of cocaine, "sexual desires are increased and perverted, peaceful negroes become quarrelsome, and timid negroes develop a degree of 'Dutch courage' that is sometimes almost incredible." The result was that "a large proportion of the wholesale killings in the South during recent years have been the result of cocaine." A black user of cocaine was "absolutely beyond redemption."

. . .

In a summary of seventeen cases of cocaine addiction published in 1893, J. B. Mattison described a wide range of behavioral changes. One young professional "could scarcely restrain himself from assaulting imaginary tormentors, with whom he remonstrated on the street"; another addict assaulted patients at the hospital where he was being treated; and a physician "became violent and vowed to kill himself or others who might try to restrain him." . . .

. . .

As previously noted, police departments were among the most prominent subscribers to theories of a cocaine/violence connection. The following passage from the *Medical Record* was written by E. H. Williams, but illustrates the practical effect which these theories could have on policing:

In the language of the police officer, "the cocaine nigger is sure hard to kill"—a fact that has been demonstrated so often that many of these officers in the South have increased the caliber of their guns for the express purpose of "stopping" the cocaine fiend when he runs amuck.

An experience of the Chief of Police, D. K. Lyerly, of Asheville, N.C., is illustrative. In attempting to arrest a hitherto peaceful negro who had become crazed by cocaine, Lyerly was forced to grapple with the man, who slashed him viciously with a long knife. In self-defence the officer drew his revolver, placed the muzzle over the negro's heart, and fired—"for I knew I had to kill him quick," the chief explained. . . . yet this bullet did not even stagger the crazed negro, and neither did a second bullet which pierced the biceps muscle and entered the thorax. So that the officer had finally to "finish the man with his club." The following day Mr. Lyerly exchanged his .32–20 for a .38 caliber army model, the weapon carried by the men of our army and navy. And a similar exchange has been made by many of our officers in the South who have had experience with the homicidal negro, both before and since the days of cocaine-taking.

In exploring the historical link between cocaine and crime, drug-induced violent behavior accounted for relatively few of the crimes for which cocaine users were formally and informally held responsible. Most users in the urban underground ran afoul of the law fairly regularly but almost entirely for various minor offenses. No doubt, as was widely charged, many users felt compelled to resort to theft or burglary to obtain cocaine. Violent cocaine fiends, however, appear to have been more a terrifying social fiction than an empirical reality, and one with a sharp racial overtone. Especially in the racially tense South, but also in the cities of the North, such fears flourished and shaped the prevalent image of the cocaine user as an unpredictable menace to social order.

Source: Joseph Spillane, *Modern Drug, Modern Menace* (Santa Monica, CA: RAND Corporation, 1994), 310–317.

* * *

Hamilton Wright sounded a similar warning about cocaine and violence in a magazine interview in 1911. Wright also fanned the public's concerns by linking cocaine use to violence by blacks and to prostitution.

DOCUMENT 42: Hamilton Wright on Cocaine Violence (1911)

And opium is not the only habit-forming drug we are called on to fight. . . . Take the question of cocaine, for instance. It is a generally known fact that during the last twenty years cocaine has been diverted from its original use by the surgeon as a local anesthetic for pander to the supposed needs of large numbers of our population. It is estimated after a wide consultation, that 15,000 or 20,000 ounces of this drug are sufficient to satisfy the demands of surgery in the United States. Today there are manufactured in the United States at least 150,000 ounces of the drug, the larger part of which is put to improper uses.

It is the unanimous opinion of every state and municipal organization having to do with the enforcement of State and municipal pharmacy laws that the misuse of cocaine is a direct incentive to crime; that it is perhaps of all factors a singular one in augmenting the criminal ranks. The illicit use of the drug is most difficult to cope with, and the habitual use of it temporarily raises the power of a criminal to a point where in resisting arrest there is no hesitation to murder.

It is really more appalling in its effect than any other habit-forming drug in use in the United States. In the South the use of cocaine among the lower order of working negroes is quite common. It is current knowledge throughout the South that on many public works, levee and railroad construction, and in other working camps where large numbers of negroes congregate, cocaine is peddled pretty openly. In all of our large cities the drug is compounded with low grades of spirit, which make a maddening compound. Inquiries have shown that contractors of labor in the South, under the impression that cocaine stimulates the negro laborers to a greater output of work, wink at the distribution of the drug to them. There is no doubt that this drug, perhaps more than any other, is used by those concerned in the white slave traffic to corrupt young girls, and that when the habit of using the drug has been established, it is but a short time before such girls fall into the ranks of prostitution.

Source: Quoted in Edward Marshall, "Uncle Sam Is the Worst Drug Fiend in the World," *New York Times Magazine*, March 12, 1911.

* * *

By around 1912, then, considerable pressure was building for the United States to enact strong legislation to allow better control over the sale and use of drugs. Similar trends were occurring in the states, which were facing their own political pressures to take a less tolerant stance against opiates and cocaine. In Part III, the development, passage in 1914, and impact of the Harrison Act are discussed. This law was the driving force behind American drug policy for the next 50 years.

Part III

The Harrison Act

In the years surrounding the Shanghai and Hague international narcotic conventions, there was considerable discussion among drug reformers and legislative leaders about the most effective way to combat the drug problem at the federal level. Given the constitutional limits on federal police power in the states, and general concerns over states' rights, federal laws had to focus more narrowly on international controls (imports and exports), interstate transfer, or taxation. The idea to attack the drug problem at the federal level by enacting a taxation act probably came from Dr. Hamilton Wright, according to David Musto.

DOCUMENT 43: Background to the Harrison Act (David F. Musto, 1987)

By late 1909, Wright had a plan for domestic legislation. He decided to seek the control of drug traffic through federal powers of taxation. His bill would require every drug dealer to register, pay a small tax, and record all transactions. The drug container would be required to carry a revenue stamp; interstate traffic would be prohibited between individuals who had not paid the tax. Wright's bill spelled out heavy penal provisions, and possession of drugs other than those specified in the bill would constitute evidence for conviction. . . .

Wright's proposed legislation was eventually introduced on 30 April 1910 by Representative David Foster of Vermont, chairman of the House Committee on Foreign Affairs. The direct antecedent of the Harrison Act, the Foster bill was designed to uncover all traffic in opiates, cocaine, chloral hydrate, and cannabis regardless of the minute quantities that might be involved. Records would be scrupulously kept, bonds given, and reports rendered as required. Violations were to be punished by not less than $500 or more than $5,000 and for no less than one year's imprisonment or more than five. Nothing in the law stipulated any such restrictions on the retail distribution of habit-forming drugs as limiting sales or prescriptions to medical needs. Nor did the bill allow any exemption for patent medicines or household remedies containing relatively small amounts of the controlled drugs.

Source: David F. Musto, *The American Disease: Origins of Narcotic Control*, expanded ed. (New York: Oxford University Press, 1987), 41–42.

* * *

The provisions in the Foster bill that aimed at curtailing retail sales of patent medicines drew considerable opposition from the pharmaceutical and wholesale druggist industries. These interest groups wanted an anti-drug law that exempted proprietary medicines and had less severe penalties for violations. Various trade representatives testified against the bill and lobbied against its passage. The Foster bill died in early 1911.

Two new international conferences on opium (one held in July 1913, the other in June 1914) resulted in renewed and intensified pressure on the United States to enact comprehensive federal legislation controlling drug trafficking and sale.

DOCUMENT 44: International Pressures to Enact Legislation (David F. Musto, 1987)

In January 1912 Wright returned to the United States with two goals: increasing the number of signatories to the [Hague] Convention and dispelling any doubt that this nation would pass the necessary domestic legislation. . . . Representative Francis Burton Harrison . . . agreed to shepherd the antinarcotic legislation through the House. Harrison's task was to assure his colleagues that various trade interests and concerned parties had achieved a generally acceptable narcotic bill or at least one that would engender no unyielding hostility. . . .

Strongly backed by such adamant reformers as Drs. Harvey Wiley, Alexander Lambert, and William Schieffelin, Dr. Wright believed that the legislative goal should be elimination of narcotics except for medical purposes. As a result, the first Harrison bill in the 62nd Congress did not differ greatly from the ill-fated Foster bill of 1910. It contained no provision for exempting small amounts of narcotics on patent medicines. Revenue stamps, record keeping and various details such as bonds, license fees, and severe penalties were retained, although still strongly opposed by the retail druggists.

Source: David F. Musto, *The American Disease: Origins of Narcotic Control*, expanded ed. (New York: Oxford University Press, 1987), 54.

* * *

Beginning in 1913, new legislative efforts began to develop an anti-drug bill that would be acceptable both to Congress and to various special interest groups. The newly elected president, Woodrow Wilson, supported strong federal narcotic laws, and lessons were learned from the defeat of the Foster bill several years earlier. Representative Francis Burton Harrison's 1913 bill contained a number of compromises to appease the medical, pharmaceutical, and druggist industries (e.g., Section 6 allowed medicines to contain small amounts of opiates). It was passed by the House of Representatives on June 26, 1913. However, the Senate did not pass its version of the bill until August 14, 1914. Because this Senate bill contained several amendments that were not acceptable to the House members, a compromise bill was developed and finally passed on December 14, 1914. The Harrison Act of 1914 required anyone who imported, manufactured, sold, gave away, prescribed, or dispensed opiates or coca leaves to register with federal authorities and pay an annual tax or license fee. Those who failed to register or pay the required tax became subject to criminal penalties. The next document presents the key sections of the Harrison Act.

DOCUMENT 45: The Harrison Act (1914)

Be it enacted . . . that on and after the first day of March, nineteen hundred and fifteen, every person who produces, imports, manufactures, compounds, deals in, dispenses, sells, distributes, or gives away opium or coca leaves or any compound, manufacture, salt, derivative, or preparation thereof shall register with the collector of internal revenue of the district his name or style, place of business, and place or places where such business is to be carried on:

. . . At the time of such registry and on or before the first day of July, annually thereafter, every person who produces, imports, manufactures, compounds, deals in, dispenses, sells, distributes, or gives away any of the aforesaid drugs shall pay to the said collector a special tax at the rate of $1 per annum: . . . *Provided further*, That officers of the United States Government who are lawfully engaged in making purchases of the above-named drugs for the various departments of the Army and Navy, the Public Health Service, and for Government hospitals and prisons; and officers of any State government, or of any county or municipality therein, who are lawfully engaged in making purchases of the above-named drugs for State, county, or municipal hospitals or prisons, and officials of any Territory or insular possession or the District of Columbia of the United States who are lawfully engaged in making purchases of the above-named drugs for hospitals or prisons therein shall not be required to register and pay the special tax as herein required.

It shall be unlawful for any person required to register under the terms of this Act to produce, import, manufacture, compound, deal in, dispense, sell, distribute, or give away any of the aforesaid drugs without having registered and paid the special tax provided for in this section.

. . .

That the Commissioner of Internal Revenue, with the approval of the Secretary of the Treasury, shall make all needful rules and regulations for carrying the provisions of this Act into effect.

Sec. 2. That it shall be unlawful for any person to sell, barter, exchange, or give away any of the aforesaid drugs except in pursuance of a written order of the person to whom such article is sold, bartered, exchanged, or given, on a form to be issued in blank for that purpose by the Commissioner of Internal Revenue. Every person who shall accept any such order, and in pursuance thereof shall sell, barter, exchange, or give away any of the aforesaid drugs, shall preserve such order for a period of two years in such a way as to be readily accessible to inspection by any officer, agent, or employee of the Treasury Department duly authorized for that purpose, and the State, Territorial District, municipal, and insular officials named in section five of this Act. . . . Nothing contained in this section shall apply—

(a) To the dispensing or distribution of any of the aforesaid drugs to a patient by a physician, dentist, or veterinary surgeon registered under this Act in the course of his professional practice only: *Provided*, That such physician, dentist, or veterinary surgeon shall keep a record of all such drugs dispensed or distributed, showing the amount dispensed or distributed, the date, and the name and address of the patient to whom such drugs are dispensed or distributed, except such as may be dispensed or distributed to a patient upon whom such physician, dentist or veterinary surgeon shall personally attend; and such record shall be kept for a period of two years from the date of dispensing or distributing such drugs, subject to inspection, as provided in this Act.

(b) To the sale, dispensing, or distribution of any of the aforesaid drugs by a dealer to a consumer under and in pursuance of a written prescription issued by a physician, dentist, or veterinary surgeon registered under this Act: . . . *And provided further*, That such dealer shall preserve such prescription for a period of two years from the day on which such prescription is filled in such a way as to be readily accessible to inspection by the officers, agents, employees, and officials herein before mentioned.

(c) To the sale, exportation, shipment, or delivery of any of the aforesaid drugs by any person within the United States or any Territory or the District of Columbia or any of the insular possessions of the United States to any person in any foreign country, regulating their entry in accordance with such regulations for importation thereof into such foreign country as are prescribed by said country, such regulations to be promulgated from time to time by the Secretary of State of the United States.

(d) To the sale, barter, exchange, or giving away of any of the aforesaid drugs to any officer of the United States Government or of any State, territorial, district, county, or municipal or insular government lawfully engaged in making purchases thereof for the various departments of the Army and Navy, the Public Health Service, and for Government, State, territorial district, county, or municipal or insular hospitals or prisons.

The Commissioner of Internal Revenue, with the approval of the Secretary of the Treasury, shall cause suitable forms to be prepared for the purposes above mentioned, and shall cause the same to be distributed to collectors of internal revenue for sale by them to those persons who shall have registered and paid the special tax as required by section one of this Act in their districts, respectively; and no collector shall sell any of such forms to any persons other than a person who has registered and paid the special tax as required by section one of this Act in his district. . . . Every collector shall keep an account of the number of such forms sold by him, the names of the purchasers, and the number of such forms sold to each of such purchasers. Whenever any collector shall sell any of such forms, he shall cause the name of the purchaser thereof to be plainly written or stamped thereon before delivering the same; and no person other than such purchaser shall use any of said forms bearing the name of such purchaser for the purpose of procuring any of the aforesaid drugs, or furnish any of the forms bearing the name of such purchaser to any person with intent thereby to procure the shipment or delivery of any of the aforesaid drugs. It shall be unlawful for any person to obtain by means of said order forms any of the aforesaid drugs for any purpose other than the use, sale, or distribution thereof by him in the conduct of a lawful business in said drugs or in the legitimate practice of his profession.

. . .

Sec. 3. That any person who shall be registered in any internal-revenue district under the provisions of section one of this Act shall, whenever required so to do by the collector of the district, render to the said collector a true and correct statement or return, verified by affidavit, setting forth the quantity of the aforesaid drugs received by him in said internal-revenue district during such period immediately preceding the demand of the collector, not exceeding three months, as the said collector may fix and determine; the names of the persons from whom the said drugs were received; the quantity in each instance received from each of such persons, and the date when received.

Sec. 4. That it shall be unlawful for any person who shall not have registered and paid the special tax as required by section one of this Act to send, ship, carry, or deliver any of the aforesaid drugs from any State or Territory or the District of Columbia, or any insular possession of the United States, to any person in any other State or Territory or the District of Columbia or any insular possession of the United States: *Provided* That nothing contained in this section shall apply to common carriers engaged in transporting the aforesaid drugs, or to any employee acting within the scope of his employment, of any person who shall have registered and paid the special tax as required by section one of this Act, or to any person who shall deliver any such drug which has been prescribed or dispensed by a physician, dentist, or veterinarian required to register under the terms of this Act, who has been employed to prescribe for the particular patient receiving such drug, or to any United States, State, county, municipal, District, Territorial, or insular officer or official acting within the scope of his official duties.

Sec. 5. That the duplicate order forms and the prescriptions required to be preserved under the provisions of section two of this Act, and the statements or returns filed in the office of the collector of the district, under the provisions of section three of this Act, shall be open to inspection by officers, agents, and employees of the Treasury Department duly authorized for that purpose; and such officials of any State or Territory, or of any organized municipality therein, or of the District of Columbia, or any insular possession of the United States, as shall be charged with the enforcement of any law or municipal ordinance regulating the sale, prescribing, dispensing, dealing in, or distribution of the aforesaid drugs. . . .

Sec. 6. That the provisions of this Act shall not be construed to apply to the sale, distribution, giving away, dispensing, or possession of preparations and remedies which do not contain more than two grains of opium, or more than one-fourth of a grain of morphine, more than one-eighth of a grain of heroin, or more than one grain of codeine, or any salt or derivative of any of them in one fluid ounce, or, if a solid or semisolid preparation, in one avoirdupois ounce; or to liniments, ointments, or other preparations which are prepared for external use only, except liniments, ointments, and other preparations which contain cocaine or any of its salts or alpha or beta eucaine or any of their salts or any synthetic substitute for them: *Provided*: That such remedies and preparations are sold, distributed, given away, dispensed, or possessed as medicines and not for the purpose of evading the intentions and provisions of this Act. The provisions of this Act shall not apply to decocainized coca leaves or preparations made therefrom, or to other preparations of coca leaves which do not contain cocaine.

. . .

Sec. 8. That it shall be unlawful for any person not registered under the provisions of this Act, and who has not paid the special tax provided for by this Act, to have in his possession or under his control any of the aforesaid drugs; and such possession or control shall be presumptive evidence of a violation of this section, and also of a violation of the provisions of section one of this Act: *Provided,* That this section shall not apply to any employee of a registered person, or to a nurse under the supervision of a physician, dentist, or veterinary surgeon registered under this Act, having such possession or control by virtue of his employment or occupation and not on his own account; or to the possession of any of the aforesaid drugs which has or have been prescribed in good faith by a physician, dentist, or veterinary surgeon registered under this Act; or to any United States, State, county, municipal, District, Territorial, or insular officer or official who has possession of any said drugs, by reason of his official duties, or to a warehouseman holding possession for a person registered and who has paid the taxes under this Act; or to common carriers engaged in transporting such drugs. . . .

Sec. 9. That any person who violates or fails to comply with any of the requirements of this Act shall, on conviction, be fined not more than $2,000 or be imprisoned not more than five years, or both, in the discretion of the court.

Sec. 10. That the Commissioner of Internal Revenue, with the approval of the Secretary of the Treasury, is authorized to appoint such agents, deputy collectors, inspectors, chemists, assistant chemists, clerks, and messengers in the field and in the Bureau of Internal Revenue in the District of Columbia as may be necessary to enforce the provisions of this Act.

Source: Public Law 63–223, 63rd Congress, Third Session, December 17, 1914.

EFFECTS OF THE HARRISON ACT ON ADDICTS

One of the key effects of the Harrison Act was to greatly disrupt the availability of drugs to addicts. This occurred in part because the passage of the law made many physicians leery of prescribing drugs, and thus affected the availability of new drug supplies. In addition, a series of internal Treasury Department rulings and procedural decisions led to increased surveillance and prosecution of doctors and pharmacists. Note that the Harrison Act required doctors and druggists to maintain records of their drug prescriptions that were subject to inspection by federal agents. In conjunction with a series of Supreme Court rulings that upheld the constitutionality of the Harrison Act, legal supplies of opiates and other drugs essentially became unavailable to addicts by the early 1920s. The following two articles from the *New York Times*, which appeared shortly after the Harrison Act went into effect, graphically describe the shift from legal to illegal drug sources and the immediate effects on addicts. The first document presents one view, by the influential drug reformer Charles Towns, that the act was not comprehensive enough.

DOCUMENT 46: Shortcomings of the Harrison Act (*New York Times*, 1915)

Neither the Boylan law restricting and regulating the sale of habit-forming drugs in this state, nor the similar Federal law that went into effect on the first of this month, will stop or even seriously interfere with the illicit drug traffic, according to Charles B. Towns, the drug expert who wrote the Boylan law, and assisted in the framing of the Federal statute. . . . Mr. Towns pointed out weaknesses in both laws and their inability to do more than make it harder for drug users to obtain the compounds to which they are addicted.

While both laws require that every legitimate prescription or sale of any compound containing more than a certain amount of opium or cocoa [*sic*] leaves or their derivatives shall be properly registered by competent physicians and druggists, neither law, in the opinion of Mr. Towns, can prevent the smuggling of drugs into the United States from Canada and Mexico. The business of smuggling drugs from these countries, Mr. Towns said yesterday, had increased enormously since the two laws went into effect.

"I am authoritatively informed," said Mr. Towns, that there is one drug store in Juarez, Mexico, from which $300 worth of the forbidden drugs is shipped into this country every day. One patient I have under treatment now obtained his drug from Toronto, whence it was mailed to him in the folds of a newspaper. How can this Government prevent smuggling from these countries as long as Canada and Mexico have little or no regulation of the drug traffic within their own borders and no agreement with the United States? The illicit drug traffic, while it is of course disturbed by the laws, is not stopped; and when illegal drug dealers and users have accustomed themselves to the new conditions, they will be able to sell and receive as much of the drugs as ever."

Mr. Towns also found the State and Federal laws greatly weakened by the exemptions allowed in them.

"The restrictions of the Federal law, for example," he said, "do not apply to preparations which contain two grains or less of opium, one-quarter grain or less of morphine, one eighth or less of heroin, one grain or less of codeine, or any salt or derivative of any of them in one ounce. These exemptions will permit thousands of persons to continue to use habit-forming drugs, and many persons will form the drug habit from using preparations exempted under both the Federal and State laws.

"The spread of the cocaine habit and the enormous consumption of cocaine for other than legitimate medical uses has resulted almost entirely from putting upon the market preparations, under the guise of so-called catarrh cures, that contain from 5 percent to 10 percent only of cocaine. Heroin, which today is the greatest drug menace that this country has to deal with, was first put upon the market fifteen years ago in cough mixtures. The quantity of the drug employed in these mixtures was supposed to be so small that no drug habit would result from its use."

. . .

Mr. Towns said he predicted, when both laws were under discussion, that their passage with the exemption clauses would result in an increased advertisement and sale of preparations containing drugs, within the limits exempted, and yesterday he showed a Times reporter several advertisements in standard magazines of preparations which, he said, were meant to supply the wants of drug users. He also showed a list of several hundred preparations exempt under the laws prepared for distribution by a medical publishing company.

Mr. Towns said, however, that both laws marked a beginning and that great moral good would come from their enactment.

Source: "Drug Smugglers Nullify New Laws," *New York Times*, March 15, 1915.

* * *

The next news story describes the impact of the sudden elimination of legal drug supplies.

DOCUMENT 47: Effect of Laws on Drug Supply (*New York Times*, 1915)

One effect of the Boylan anti-drug law and of the more recently enacted Federal Harrison law, coupled with the activities of police Lieut. Henry Scherb and the sixteen detectives of the "dope squad" under him, has been to deprive hundreds of habitual users of heroin and cocaine of their drugs and reduce them to a pitiful state of craving and suffering. Lieut. Scherb said yesterday that the supply of drugs in the hands of peddlers had about been used up and that, because of the laws and the watchfulness of the police, the peddlers were unable to replenish their stock.

"The result is," Lieut. Scherb said, "that the poor victims who have been getting their dope from peddlers on the street are having a pretty tough time. From every report I get there is a panic among them. Many of them are doubled up in pain at this very minute and others are running to the police and hospitals to get relief. Those who have been getting their drugs from dope doctors and fake-cure places are not so hard hit, because these traffickers have not been touched by the laws, but the poorer people, the men and women we call the 'bums,' who have always bought from street peddlers, are really up against it. The suffering among them is terrible."

Lieut. Scherb said that those who suffered from sudden deprivation of drugs did so either in ignorance or willfully, because anyone absolutely in need of a drug might be treated at any of the city hospitals. This was verified at Bellevue Hospital and the Metropolitan Hospital, on Blackwell's Island, where it was said that everyone suffering from the sudden discontinuance of drugs who had applied for treatment had been received.

. . .

To illustrate the extent to which the illicit supply of drugs had been reduced, Lieut. Scherb said that whereas the trade price of heroin was $6.50 an ounce, the last illicit street sale his men had stopped had been attempted on the basis of $12 for an eighth of an ounce. Also, the Lieutenant said, peddlers who formerly sold drugs are now making quick money selling useless concoctions that have the appearance of drugs with none of their vital characteristics. One man, Lieut. Scherb, said made $111 in one night selling sugar of milk to frantic drug users, who paid for their purchases and allowed the peddler to get away before examining the substance sold them.

Dr. [Perry M.] Lichtenstein expressed the fear yesterday that although the peddlers had been driven out of business, drug users would find a new market in the so-called sanitariums that pretended to cure the drug habit while really existing the purpose of supplying drugs to those who wanted them.

"Prisoners who have come to me recently," Dr. Lichtenstein said, "have told me that these fake sanitariums have begun to spring up everywhere since the Harrison law went into effect. They are allowed to exist by an exemption in the law. According to the law everyone who prescribes a drug must make a record of the prescription, to whom it is given and for what purpose, 'except' the law reads, 'such as may be dispensed or distributed to a patient upon whom such physician, dentist or veterinary surgeon shall personally attend.' "

Source: "Poorer Drug Users in Pitiful Plight," *New York Times*, April 15, 1915.

* * *

Lawrence Kolb and A. G. Du Mez, two senior research scientists for the U.S. Public Health Service (Dr. Kolb was a key figure in drug policy reform through the 1950s), in an important report estimating the number of addicts in the United States, described the immediate impact of the Harrison Act.

DOCUMENT 48: Effects of Harrison Act on Addicts (Lawrence Kolb and A. G. Du Mez, 1924)

The first result of the Harrison law was to cause large numbers of addicts throughout the country to seek treatment. Many who were relieved of their addiction then have no doubt remained cured. The rigid enforcement of the law continues to impel addicts . . . to seek relief. It is common for this type to give as a reason for seeking a cure that they are tired of dodging the police, and occasionally an addict comes for treatment because the peddlers have grown suspicious and refuse to supply him with the drug. The superintendent of the Norfolk [VA] State Hospital reported in 1917, that over 90 per cent of the addicts who applied for treatment did so because they were having difficulty in securing their supplies of narcotics. Most of such cases relapse, but in the course of time those among them who are fairly normal are permanently cured.

. . .

A survey which furnishes an excellent illustration in retrospect of the effect that the Harrison law has had in reducing the extent of addiction is one made by Terry in the city of Jacksonvile [FL] in 1913, two years before the Harrison law became effective. At that time there was a city ordinance which prohibited the dispensing of opium except upon a physician's prescription, and which required all physicians writing prescriptions for any habit-forming narcotics to send a copy of the same together with the name and address of the individual for whom they were intended to the board of health. . . . Apparently no effort was made to discourage addiction or to limit the use of these drugs. The record of duplicate prescriptions and of patients applying at the health department showed 887 habitual users for the year 1913, or 1.31 per cent of the population. . . . Dr. William W. MacDonell, the city health officer at the present time, reports that in 1914 the number of addicts registered had increased to 1,073. Registration of addicts was then discontinued, but a census taken in 1919 showed 111 addicts. In 1920 there were 55 additional cases registered, but some of the 111 had moved away. Addicts are not being registered at the present time, but Doctor MacDonell reports that during the year ending in April, 1924, there were only 20 addicts under treatment in Jacksonville, with 30 additional securing their supplies from peddlers, and a possible 50 more about whom there was no accurate knowledge.

Source: Lawrence Kolb and A. G. Du Mez, "The Prevalence and Trend of Drug Addiction in the United States and Factors Influencing It," *Public Health Reports* 39, no. 21 (1924): 1200–1202.

* * *

In the aftermath of the passage of the Harrison Act, the Treasury Department continued to actively monitor drug distribution and use and to assess whether the Harrison Act was having the desired impacts. Four years after the Harrison Act became law the department decided to conduct a study of the drug problem. Arnold Taylor described the conclusions of the report.

DOCUMENT 49: 1918 Treasury Department Study of Drug Problem (Arnold Taylor, 1969)

In 1918 the Secretary of the Treasury appointed a special narcotics committee to investigate the drug problem in the United States and to recommend remedial measures and administrative changes in the narcotic laws. Their report confirmed previous statements that there was a very serious narcotics problem in the United States. Their findings were very largely based on information received from police officials, physicians, and local and state public health officials. . . . They estimated the number of addicts at about 1,000,000. The committee found that addiction was acquired primarily in two ways: by association with drug addicts, in which case the principal drugs used were heroin and cocaine, and through physicians' prescriptions, in which case the principal drugs used were morphine and opium preparations. Drugs used by addicts, in order of their frequency, were morphine, heroin, the various forms of opium, and cocaine. Codeine, laudanum, and paregoric were used in equal amounts. Addiction cut across all racial, social, and economic barriers and was discovered to be equally prevalent among both sexes.

An interesting feature of the report was the prominence given to liquor prohibition as a cause of drug addiction. In the responses from police officials, prohibition stood third behind physicians' prescriptions and association with other addicts as a cause of drug addiction. In reports of state and local health officials it stood third in order of frequency behind physicians' prescriptions and use of drugs for chronic diseases. The prohibition referred to was that on the state and local level, since nationwide [alcohol] prohibition had not yet come into effect. Without committing themselves on the matter, the committee held that the increased sales of narcotics and patent medicines containing opiates in the Southern states, where liquor prohibition had been long in effect, supported the consensus of opinion that nationwide prohibition would result in an increase of drug addiction. This was an argument that the "wets" could well use, and they did. . . .

In its recommendations the Committee urged (1) the enactment of legislation on the national, state, and local levels providing care and treatment of addicts; (2) that the State Department urge the signatories of the Hague Opium Convention to enact enforcement measures; (3) that the cooperation of Mexico and Canada be secured to suppress smuggling; (4) that an educational campaign against the drug traffic be initiated throughout the country; (5) that research be undertaken by both public and private medical organizations into the nature of drug addiction and the means of treatment; and (6) that there be absolute prohibition of the use of heroin and the traffic in it, as its evil effects far outweighed its medical benefits.

Source: Arnold Taylor, *American Diplomacy and the Narcotics Traffic, 1900–1939* (Durham, NC: Duke University Press, 1969), 124.

* * *

News coverage of the Treasury Department committee report emphasized that the nation still had a very serious drug problem, suggesting that "dope peddlers" now controlled the distribution and sale of illegal drugs. The Treasury Department's estimate of 1 million addicts was most likely a gross exaggeration. The most scholarly analysis of the number of addicts conducted during this era, by U.S. Public Health Service scientists Kolb and Du Mez, estimated the number of addicts at perhaps one-quarter of that number.

DOCUMENT 50: Estimated Number of Addicts (Lawrence Kolb and A. G. Du Mez, 1924)

The 1918 Treasury Department survey showing 237,655 addicts apparently contains an indeterminate error of exaggeration, as already pointed out. The highest estimate based on any unrevised survey is 269,000; the lowest, exclusive of the Army survey, is 104,300. These figures may therefore be accepted as the maximum and minimum numbers for the period 1915 to 1922; but from what has been brought out relative to the surveys it would seem that somewhat less than 215,000 is more nearly correct for the beginning, and about 110,000 the approximate number for the end of the period.

. . .

All the evidence shows that there has been a still further reduction in the number of addicts since the surveys were made. This assertion is made with full knowledge that the number of addicts in our penal institutions has greatly increased in recent years. There is nothing in this to cause alarm. One of the recently enacted laws has made it a crime for unlicensed persons to have narcotics in their possession. This law is being rigidly enforced, and addicts, who formerly were unmolested, are now being sent to jail.

. . .

It is believed that the trend of addiction in this country for the past six decades has paralleled very closely the quantities of narcotics available, as represented by the average annual importations, in proportion to the population. This being true, it follows that the trend of addiction was upward until about the year 1900, when it took a downward course, which it has maintained up to the present time.

Source: Lawrence Kolb and A. G. Du Mez, "The Prevalence and Trend of Drug Addiction in the United States and Factors Influencing It," *Public Health Reports* 39, no. 21 (1924): 1189, 1197–1198.

ENFORCEMENT OF THE HARRISON ACT

Once the Supreme Court upheld the provisions of the Harrison Act (see Part IV), those in the Internal Revenue Bureau responsible for its enforcement set out on a campaign to enforce its provisions.

DOCUMENT 51: Report on Federal Crackdown on Drugs (*New York Times*, 1920)

Plans for a national campaign against the drug habit by the most stringent enforcement of the Harrison Anti-Narcotic Act yet attempted are being formed by officers of the Internal Revenue Bureau, it was announced today by Charles Rogers, Assistant Supervising Collector at Washington. . . .

"In the hue and cry against liquor, the public apparently has forgotten that more sinister social menace, the drug habit," Mr. Rogers said. "Just as soon as our bureau has the income tax work off its hands, we are going to roll up our sleeves and go after 'dope' tooth and nail."

Mr. Rogers said the bureau had reports of an alarming increase of the number of drug victims and in the smuggling traffic.

Source: "Plan National Drive Against Drug Traffic," *New York Times*, March 7, 1920.

* * *

Kolb and Du Mez cite a physicians' survey as evidence that many fewer physicians were prescribing narcotics to addicts in the aftermath of the Harrison Act.

DOCUMENT 52: Harrison Act Curtailed Physicians' Prescriptions of Opiates (Lawrence Kolb and A. G. Du Mez, 1924)

An illustration of the effect produced by the tremendous drive against narcotic addiction which has been going on in recent years is given by the answers to the questionnaire sent out by [Dr. Carleton] Simon in 1923 to the physicians of New York State, asking how many addicts they had treated in 1922. The 51.6 per cent who replied treated only 775 cases of addiction; and from the information furnished it seems that these were mostly old people or persons suffering from incurable diseases. In the Treasury Department survey, made in 1918, 37 per cent of physicians in New York State were treating 12,365 addicts.

The increasing difficulties of an addict's career since 1918 ha[ve] compelled many of them to seek cure, but the difference in the two surveys just discussed is too great to be attributed to this factor alone. Most of it is no doubt due to a change in the viewpoint and practice of physicians. Responding to the temper of court rulings [Supreme Court decisions regarding Harrison; see Part IV], physicians no longer prescribe narcotics merely to satisfy addiction, and some of them are loath to prescribe for an addict at all, even when his physical condition would seem to require a continuation of addiction, although there is nothing in the law or rulings of the Bureau of Internal Revenue which justifies this attitude. In 1918, physicians probably reported transients and other addicts not regularly treated by them. The changing attitude toward the narcotic problem was sufficient to reverse this by 1923.

Source: Lawrence Kolb and A. G. Du Mez, "The Prevalence and Trend of Drug Addiction in the United States and Factors Influencing It," *Public Health Reports* 39, no. 21 (1924): 1202.

* * *

In response to the 1918 Treasury Department report, Congress passed additional laws over the next few years designed to ameliorate some of the consequences of the Harrison Act. These included 1924 legislation that specifically made heroin importation illegal.

With passage of the Harrison Act in 1914, the medical role in treating addicts became much more problematic. The federal investigation and prosecution of physicians and clinics that dispensed drugs to addicts, and the series of Supreme Court decisions that upheld the Harrison Act's constitutionality and supported the law's restrictions on dispensing illegal drugs to addicts and other patients, made most physicians shy away from dealing with addicts in their regular medical practice. In this context, it is not surprising that the ambulatory (or outpatient) treatment of addicts became a controversial issue in the early 1920s.

Terry and Pellens describe how the enforcement of the Harrison Act by the Treasury Department discouraged physicians and druggists from prescribing and selling drugs to patients. Coupled with the Treasury Department's crackdown on the narcotics clinics (see Part IX), it was inevitable that a newly expanded black market in heroin, morphine, cocaine, and the other drugs would become the chief source of drugs for chronic users beginning in the early 1920s.

DOCUMENT 53: Enforcement of the Harrison Act (Charles E. Terry and Mildred Pellens, 1928)

The passage of the Harrison Narcotic Act and the adoption of regulations relating thereto have also contributed to the creation of the present attitude of the medical profession. It must be remembered that prior to this time counter sales of these drugs had been the rule in most states and thus the user secured his accustomed amount. With the enforcement of the new law limiting the distribution to one channel physicians were appealed to by hosts of patients who previously had bought directly from the retail druggist or by mail order from the wholesaler. His adjustment was not too difficult, however, and while it somewhat increased the cost to the drug user and added inconvenience it doubtless had a beneficial effect as it brought these cases into the hands of the physician and led to an increase in professional interest that stimulated study and inevitably would have led to many cures and improvements in methods of treatment. The enforcement of the regulations, however, in some cases called into question the judgment and integrity of physicians and druggists and indictments were brought against members of these professions. Whether conviction followed or not mattered little as the effects of press publicity dealing with what were supposedly willful violations of a beneficent law were most disastrous to those concerned. Such occurrences caused both physicians and druggists everywhere to fear such actions. This attitude may or may not have been justified but it was a very natural outgrowth of the law's administration. . . .

The interest of physicians in these cases thus was checked and they even began to refuse to prescribe. Pharmacists also refused to fill prescriptions and chronic users wandered from one to another and finally were forced to secure their drug to seek it wherever it could be gotten—from the peddler at his own price. Thus was an illegal substitute for the legal channels of supply created by the law because the law was so interpreted and administered as to render the registered distributors uncertain of their status.

Source: Charles E. Terry and Mildred Pellens, *The Opium Problem* (Bureau of Social Hygiene, 1928; reprint, Montclair, NJ: Patterson Smith Publishing, 1970), 90–91.

* * *

As discussed later in this book, the Harrison Act had far-reaching consequences for the ability of physicians to treat addicts by giving them maintenance dosages of a drug.

DOCUMENT 54: Prohibitions Against Prescribing Drugs to Addicts (New York Academy of Medicine, 1955)

Under the law . . . the medical and allied professions are charged with the responsibility of prescribing narcotics under restrictions. Physicians may prescribe narcotics to patients for the relief of pain and discomfort associated with disease. They may attempt to treat an addict to free him of this habit, but only in a manner dictated by the Federal regulations. They may not prescribe a narcotic drug to keep comfortable a confirmed addict who refuses withdrawal but who might under regulated dosage lead a useful life and later might agree to withdrawal. These prohibitions are specifically set forth in the Federal regulations:

> . . . This bureau [Federal Bureau of Narcotics] has never sanctioned or approved the so-called reductive ambulatory treatment of addiction, however, for the reason that where the addict controls the dosage he will not be benefited or cured.
>
> This bureau cannot under any circumstances sanction the treatment of mere addiction where the drugs are placed in the addict's possession, nor can it sanction the use of narcotics to cover a period in excess of thirty days, when personally administered by the physician to a patient either in a proper institution or unconfined. If a physician, pursuant to the so-called reductive ambulatory treatment, places narcotic drugs in the possession of the addict who is not confined, such action will be regarded as showing lack of good faith in the treatment of addiction and that the drugs were furnished to satisfy the cravings of the addict.
>
> An order purporting to be a prescription issued to an addict or habitual user of narcotics, not in the course of professional treatment in an attempted cure of the habit, but for the purpose of providing the user with narcotics sufficient to keep him comfortable by maintaining his customary use is not a prescription within the meaning and intent of the act; and the persons filling and receiving drugs under such an order, as well as the person issuing it, will be regarded as guilty of violation of the law.

It should be added that a verdict of guilty carries a prison sentence. All things considered it is small wonder that most physicians would prefer not to have addicts appear as patients in their offices.

Source: New York Academy of Medicine, "Report on Drug Addiction," *Bulletin of the New York Academy of Medicine* 31, no. 8 (1955): 595.

* * *

The Harrison Act was the first federal attempt to place general restrictions on the prescribing of opiates and cocaine (although many states already had laws that made sale or possession of these drugs illegal). Although its interpretation caused some difficulties, and it underwent several revisions, this act remained one of the statutory bases for federal anti-drug policy for nearly 60 years.

Part IV

Supreme Court Decisions on the Harrison Act

The 1914 Harrison Act was the key watershed in the shift in federal drug policy. Nonetheless, the Harrison Act was vaguely written in some respects, and the interpretation of its meaning and of Congress' true intent when it passed the law quickly became areas of controversy. Sections 2 and 8, particularly, were subject to various interpretations. Section 2 made it lawful for a doctor or a druggist to dispense or distribute drugs "in the course of his professional practice only." Section 8 made it illegal for anyone to possess drugs who had not registered under the, act, and who had not paid the special tax required to be paid by those who were registered. What was not clear was who was required to register, what "in the course of his professional practice" really meant in terms of the prescription of drugs, and whether those who could not register under the act (e.g., addicts) would be in violation of Section 8. Because of these interpretive difficulties, a series of important Supreme Court decisions between 1916 and 1928 attempted to resolve the application of the Harrison Act to the prescribing and dispensing of drugs to addicts, and to determine whether the act was in fact constitutional (given that police powers are reserved to the states).

A review of these decisions is important because (1) they helped shape how the federal government carried out the provisions of the Harrison Act; (2) they illustrate how Supreme Court decisions can be inconsistent and controversial; and (3) they help us to understand how the federal government was able to use the Court's decisions selectively to justify its interpretations of the Harrison Act and how it was enforced.

The first Supreme Court test of the constitutionality of the Harrison Act came about nine months after the act became law. The federal government appealed an opinion by the U.S. District Court of Western Pennsylvania concerning an indictment against a Pittsburgh physician for conspiring with an individual not registered under the Harrison Act to possess morphine. The physician, Jin Fuey Moy, who had a reputation as a "dope doctor," had supplied an unregistered addict named Willie Martin with one dram (about 600 grains or 3.9 grams or .14 ounce) of morphine. The district court had held that the penalty provisions of the Harrison Act, as a revenue measure, only applied to those required to register under the act (e.g., physicians, druggists) and not to all U.S. citizens. Thus, an opium user might legally possess the drug. The Supreme Court, in a 7–2 decision, affirmed this opinion in the following decision written by Oliver Wendell Holmes.

DOCUMENT 55: *United States v. Jin Fuey Moy* (1916)

This is an indictment under § 8 of the act of December 17, 1914 [Harrison Act]. It was quashed by the District Court on the ground that the statute did not apply to the case. The indictment charges a conspiracy with Willie Martin to have in Martin's possession opium and salts thereof, to wit, one dram of morphine sulphate. It alleges that Martin was not registered with the collector of internal revenue of the district, and had not paid the special tax required; that the defendant for the purpose of executing the conspiracy issued to Martin a written prescription for the morphine sulphate, and that he did not issue it in good faith, but knew that the drug was not given for medicinal purposes but for the purpose of supplying one addicted to the use of opium. The question is whether the possession conspired for is within the prohibitions of the act.

. . .

By § 8 it is declared unlawful for "any person" who is not registered and has not paid the special tax to have in his possession or control any of the said drugs and "such possession or control" is made presumptive evidence of a violation of this section and of § 1. . . . The district judge considered that the act was a revenue act and that the general words "any person" must be confined to the class of persons with whom the act previously had been purporting to deal. The Government on the other hand contends that this act was passed with two others in order to carry out the International Opium Convention; that Congress gave it the appearance of a taxing measure in order to give it a coating of constitutionality, but that it really was a police measure that strained all the powers of the legislature and that § 8 means all that it says, taking its words in their plain literal sense.

A statute must be construed, if fairly possible, so as to avoid not only the conclusion that it is unconstitutional but also grave doubts upon that score. If we could know judicially that no opium is produced in the United States the difficulties in this case would be less, but we hardly are warranted in that assumption when the act itself purports to deal with those who produce it. Congress, at all events, contemplated production in the United States and therefore the act must be construed on the hypothesis that it takes place. If opium is produced in any of the States obviously the gravest question of power would be raised by an attempt of Congress to make possession of such opium a crime. The Government invokes Article VI of the Constitution, that treaties made under the authority of the United States shall be the supreme law of the land. But the question arises under a statute not under a treaty. The statute does not purport to be in execution of a treaty but calls itself a registration and taxing act. The provision before us was not required by the Opium Convention, and whether this section is entitled to the supremacy claimed by the Government for treaties is, to say the least, another grave question, and, if it is reasonably possible, the act should be read so as to avoid both.

The foregoing consideration gains some additional force from the penalty imposed by § 9 upon any person who violates any of the requirements of the act. It is a fine of not more than $2,000 or imprisonment for not more than five years, or both, in the discretion of the court. Only words from which there is no escape could warrant the conclusion that Congress meant to strain its powers almost if not quite to the breaking point in order to make the probably very large proportion of citizens who have some preparation of opium in their possession criminal or at least *prima facie* criminal and subject to the serious punishment made possible by § 9. It may be assumed that the statute has a moral end as well as revenue in view, but we are of opinion that the District Court, in treating those ends as to be reached only through a revenue measure and within the limits of a revenue measure, was right.

Approaching the issue from this point of view we conclude that "any person not registered" in § 8 cannot be taken to mean any person in the United States but must be taken to refer to the class with which the statute undertakes to deal—the persons who are required to register by § 1. It is true that the exemption of possession of drugs prescribed in good faith by a physician is a powerful argument taken by itself for a broader meaning.... This exemption stands alongside of one that saves employees of registered persons as do §§ 1 and 4, and nurses under the supervision of a physician &c., as does § 4, and is so far vague that it may have had in mind other persons carrying out a doctor's orders rather than the patients. The general purpose seems to be to apply to possession exemptions similar to those applied to registration. Even if for a moment the scope and intent of the act were lost sight of the proviso is not enough to overcome the dominant considerations that prevail in our mind.

Judgment affirmed.

Source: 241 *U.S. Reports* 394, decided June 5, 1916.

* * *

As a result of this ruling, the Treasury Department began efforts to convince Congress to amend the Harrison Act to make it more difficult for doctors to prescribe drugs to addicts (i.e., persons who did not register under the Harrison Act). For example, in the Bureau of Internal Revenue Annual Report for 1917, the commissioner stated the following.

DOCUMENT 56: Bureau of Internal Revenue Annual Report (1917)

This decision makes it practically impossible to control the illicit traffic in narcotic drugs by unregistered persons, as the mere possession of any quantity of the drugs is not evidence of violation, and therefore the government is forced to prove in every case, even where the circumstances indicate sale and dispensing, actual sales by this class of offenders, which it has been found difficult to do.

Source: Quoted in David F. Musto, *The American Disease: Origins of Narcotic Control*, expanded ed. (New York: Oxford University Press, 1987), 130.

* * *

Of course, despite the commissioner's concerns, the Jin Fuey Moy decision did not preclude the regulation of drug possession under state law; by 1916 most states had laws making the possession and sale of opiates and cocaine illegal.

Three years later, two key Supreme Court decisions (both handed down on March 3, 1919) bolstered the federal government's use of the Harrison Act. The first decision, *United States v. Doremus*, upheld the constitutionality of the act by overruling a district court decision that the Harrison Act was unconstitutional because it was really a policing measure, not a revenue act. In the second decision, *Webb et al. v. United States*, the Supreme Court responded to questions from the Sixth Circuit Court of Appeals regarding whether the issuing of prescriptions for large amounts of morphine to an addict, in order to keep him comfortable, was legitimate practice of medicine and therefore allowable under the Harrison Act. The Supreme Court decided that such indiscriminate provision of morphine without an intent to cure was prohibited under the act. The division of the Court on these important constitutional questions was clear from the narrow 5–4 majority decisions on both cases.

The Doremus case involved a Texas doctor who had been indicted for prescribing 500 one-sixth grain tablets (about 5,400 mg) of heroin to a known addict. The U.S. District Court quashed the indictment in ruling that the policing of Dr. Doremus' practice was irrelevant to a revenue measure, and exceeded the allowable powers of the federal government. The majority of the Supreme Court reversed the district court opinion.

DOCUMENT 57: *United States v. Doremus* (1919)

Opinion of the Court (Delivered by MR. JUSTICE DAY):

Doremus was indicted for violating § 2 of the so-called Harrison Narcotic Drug Act. . . . Upon demurrer to the indictment the District Court held the section unconstitutional for the reason that it was not a revenue measure, and was an invasion of the police power reserved to the States. . . .

There are ten counts in the indictment. The first two were treated by the court below as sufficient to raise the constitutional question decided. The first count in substance charges that: Doremus, a physician, duly registered, and who had paid the tax required by the first section of the act, did unlawfully, fraudulently, and knowingly sell and give away and distribute to one Ameris a certain quantity of heroin, to wit, five hundred one-sixth grain tablets of heroin, a derivative of opium, the sale not being in pursuance of a written order on a form issued on the blank furnished for that purpose by the Commissioner of Internal Revenue.

The second count charges in substance that: Doremus did unlawfully and knowingly sell, dispense and distribute to one Ameris five hundred one-sixth grain tablets of heroin not in the course of the regular professional practice of Doremus, and not for the treatment of any disease from which Ameris was suffering, but as was well known by Doremus, Ameris was addicted to the use of the drug as a habit, being a person popularly known as a "dope fiend," and that Doremus did sell, dispense, and distribute the drug, heroin, to Ameris for the purpose of gratifying his appetite for the drug as an habitual user thereof.

. . .

It is made unlawful [by Harrison] for any person to obtain the drugs by means of the order forms for any purpose other than the use, sale or distribution thereof by him in the conduct of a lawful business in said drugs, or the legitimate practice of his profession.

It is apparent that the section makes sales of these drugs unlawful except to persons who have the order forms issued by the Commissioner of Internal Revenue, and the order is required to be preserved for two years in such way as to be readily accessible to official inspection. But it is not to apply (a) to physicians, etc., dispensing and distributing the drug to patients in the course of professional practice, the physician to keep a record thereof, except in the case of personal attendance upon a patient; and (b) to the sale, dispensing, or distributing of the drugs by a dealer upon a prescription issued by a physician, etc., registered under the act.

. . .

This statute purports to be passed under the authority of the Constitution, Article I, § 8, which gives the Congress power "To lay and collect taxes, duties, imposts and excises, to pay the debts and provide for the common defence and general welfare of the United States; but all duties, imposts and excises shall be uniform throughout the United States."

The only limitation upon the power of Congress to levy excise taxes of the character now under consideration is geographical uniformity throughout the United States. This court has often declared it cannot add others. Subject to such limitation Congress may select the subjects of taxation, and may exercise the power conferred at its discretion . . . Of course Congress may not in the exercise of federal power exert authority wholly reserved to the States. Many decisions of this court have so declared. And from an early day the court has held that the fact that other motives may impel the exercise of federal taxing power does not authorize the courts to inquire into that subject. If the legislation enacted has some reasonable relation to the exercise of the taxing authority conferred by the Constitution, it cannot be invalidated because of the supposed motives which induced it. . . .

Nor is it sufficient to invalidate the taxing authority given to the Congress by the Constitution that the same business may be regulated by the police power of the State.

The act may not be declared unconstitutional because its effect may be to accomplish another purpose as well as the raising of revenue. If the legislation is within the taxing authority of Congress—that is sufficient to sustain it.

The legislation under consideration was before us in a case concerning § 8 of the act, and in the course of the decision we said: "It may be assumed that the statute has a moral end as well as revenue in view, but we are of opinion that the District Court, in treating those ends as to be reached only through a revenue measure and within the limits of a revenue measure, was right." (*United States v. Jin Fuey Moy*, 241 U.S. 394, 402). Considering the full power of Congress over excise taxation the decisive question here is: Have the provisions in question any relation to the raising of revenue? That Congress might levy an excise tax upon such dealers, and others who are named in § 1 of the act, cannot be successfully disputed. The provisions of § 2, to which we have referred, aim to confine sales to registered dealers and to those dispensing the drugs as physicians, and to those who come to dealers with legitimate prescriptions of physicians. Congress, with full power over the subject, short of arbitrary and unreasonable action which is not to be assumed, inserted these provisions in an act specifically providing for the raising of revenue. Considered of themselves, we think they tend to keep the traffic aboveboard and subject to inspection by those authorized to collect the revenue. They tend to diminish the opportunity of unauthorized persons to obtain the drugs and sell them clandestinely without paying the tax imposed by the federal law. This case well illustrates the possibility which may have induced Congress to insert the provisions limiting sales to registered dealers and requiring patients to obtain these drugs as a medicine from physicians or upon regular prescriptions. Ameris, being . . . an addict, may not have used this great number of doses for himself. He might sell some to others without paying the tax, at least Congress may have deemed it wise to prevent such possible dealings because of their effect upon the collection of the revenue.

We cannot agree with the contention that the provisions of § 2, controlling the disposition of these drugs in the ways described, can have nothing to do with facilitating the collection of the revenue, as we should be obliged to do if we were to declare this act beyond the power of Congress acting under its constitutional authority to impose excise taxes. It follows that the judgment of the District Court must be reversed.

Reversed.

Source: 249 *U.S. Reports* 86, decided March 3, 1919.

* * *

Webb et al. v. United States arose from the case of a Memphis doctor and a druggist who had been indicted for conspiring to violate the Harrison Act by providing morphine to addicts for the sole purposes of maintaining an addiction. Dr. Webb and the pharmacist had regularly sold morphine prescriptions for 50 cents apiece. The key question for the Supreme Court was whether this type of prescribing of drugs without clear medical justification was allowable under the Harrison Act.

DOCUMENT 58: *Webb et al. v. United States* (1919)

Opinion of the Court (Delivered by Mr. Justice Day):

This case involves the provisions of the Harrison Narcotic Drug Act, considered in No. 367, just decided, *ante*, 86 [*United States v. Doremus*]. The case comes here upon a certificate from the Circuit Court of Appeals for the Sixth Circuit. From the certificate it appears that Webb and Goldbaum were convicted and sentenced in the District Court of the United States for the Western District of Tennessee on a charge of conspiracy to violate the Harrison Narcotic Law. While the certificate states that the indictment is inartificial, it is certified to be sufficient to support a prosecution upon the theory that Webb and Goldbaum intended to have the latter violate the law by using the order blanks (§ 1 of the act) for a prohibited purpose.

The certificate states: "If §2, rightly construed, forbids sales to a non-registrable user, and if such prohibition is constitutional, we next meet the question whether such orders as Webb gave to applicants are 'prescriptions,' within the meaning of exception (b) in §2.

"We conclude that the case cannot be disposed of without determining the construction and perhaps the constitutionality of the law in certain particulars, and for the purpose of certification, we state the facts as follows . . . :

"Webb was a practicing physician and Goldbaum a retail druggist, in Memphis. It was Webb's regular custom and practice to prescribe morphine for habitual users upon their application to him therefor. He furnished these 'prescriptions,' not after consideration of the applicant's individual case, and in such quantities and with such direction as, in his judgment, would tend to cure the habit or as might be necessary or helpful in an attempt to break the habit, but without such consideration and rather in such quantities as the applicant desired for the sake of continuing his accustomed use. Goldbaum was familiar with such practice and habitually filled such prescriptions. Webb had duly registered and paid the special tax as required by §1 of the act. Goldbaum had also registered and paid such tax and kept all records required by the law. Goldbaum had been provided with the blank forms contemplated by §2 of the act for use in ordering morphine, and, by the use of such blank order forms, had obtained from the wholesalers, in Memphis, a stock of morphine: It had been agreed and understood between Webb and Goldbaum that Goldbaum should, by using such order forms, procure a stock of morphine, which morphine he should and would sell to those who desired to purchase and who came provided with Webb's so-called prescriptions. It was the intent of Webb and Goldbaum that morphine should thus be furnished to the habitual users thereof by Goldbaum and without any physician's prescription issued in the course of a good faith attempt to cure the morphine habit. In order that these facts may have their true color, it should also be stated that within a period of eleven months Goldbaum purchased from wholesalers in Memphis, thirty times as much morphine as was bought by the average retail druggist doing a larger general business, and he sold narcotic drugs in 6,500 instances; that Webb regularly charged fifty cents for each so-called prescription, and within this period had furnished, and Goldbaum had filled, over 4,000 such prescriptions, and that one Rabens, a user of the drug, came from another state and applied to Webb for morphine and was given at one time ten so-called prescriptions for one drachm [dram] each, which prescriptions were filled at one time by Goldbaum upon Rabens' presentation, although each was made out in a separate and fictitious name."

Upon these facts the Circuit Court of Appeals propounds to this court three questions:

"1. Does the first sentence of §2 of the Harrison Act prohibit retail sales of morphine by druggists to persons who have no physician's prescription, who have no order blank therefor and who cannot obtain an order blank because not of the class to which such blanks are allowed to be issued?

"2. If the answer to question one is in the affirmative, does this construction make unconstitutional the prohibition of such sale?

"3. If a practicing and registered physician issues an order for morphine to an habitual user thereof, the order not being issued by him in the course of professional treatment in the attempted cure of the habit, but being issued for the purpose of providing the user with morphine sufficient to keep him comfortable by maintaining his customary use, is such order a physician's prescription under exception (b) of §2?

"If question one is answered in the negative, or question two in the affirmative, no answer to question three will be necessary; and if question three is answered in the affirmative, questions one and two become immaterial."

What we have said of the construction and purpose of the act in [*United States v. Doremus*] plainly requires that question one should be answered in the affirmative. Question two should be answered in the negative for the reasons stated in the opinion in [*United States v. Doremus*]. As to question three—to call such an order for the use of morphine a physician's prescription would be so plain a perversion of meaning that no discussion of the subject is required. That question should be answered in the negative.

Source: 249 *U.S. Reports* 96, decided March 3, 1919.

* * *

The dissenting opinions in both the Doremus and Webb cases were based on the conclusion that the district court's decision was correct, in that Section 2 of the Harrison Act was unconstitutional because it dealt with matters reserved for the police powers of the states.

The Doremus and Webb decisions had important effects on the availability of drugs and the willingness of physicians to prescribe them to addicts. The Treasury Department was quick to use these decisions to support its contentions that the Harrison Act disallowed the ongoing dispensing of drugs to addicts for the purposes of keeping them physically comfortable or maintaining their addiction.

DOCUMENT 59: Effects of Webb Decision on Physicians (David T. Courtwright, 1982)

These laws and decisions [referring to the Supreme Court decisions up to *Webb*] had a marked impact on the addict in the street and on the kinds of drugs he used. After the Harrison Act went into effect addicts, as unregistered persons, had to obtain a prescription for their drugs. Increasingly these prescriptions were written by "dope doctors," licensed physicians who would for a fee provide the necessary service. During a single month one New York City doctor "wrote scrip" for 68,282 grains of heroin, 54,097 grains of morphine, and 30,280 grains of cocaine. Although addicts might grumble at being gouged by the dope doctors, their only alternative was the black market. Black market prices were up sharply, however, since unregistered dealers ran significant risks of prosecution and since it was now much more difficult to obtain sizable shipments from legitimate manufacturers.

The situation deteriorated further during 1919 to 1921, in the wake of the Webb decision and the closure of many of the hastily organized narcotic clinics. Some addicts, particularly those in rural areas and those suffering from chronic and incurable diseases, were still able to obtain morphine on a legal or quasi-legal basis. But a growing number of other users, particularly nonmedical addicts living in large cities, were forced to rely on illegal purchases.

Source: David T. Courtwright, *Dark Paradise: Opiate Addiction in America Before 1940* (Cambridge, MA: Harvard University Press, 1982), 107.

* * *

One year after these key decisions, a second case involving Dr. Jin Fuey Moy was decided by the Supreme Court. In this case Jin Fuey Moy had been convicted of violating the Harrison Act by indiscriminately selling morphine prescriptions to addicts for the purpose of maintaining their addiction. In this decision, delivered without dissent, the Court upheld the conviction, holding that such dispensing of morphine was "not in the course of his professional practice."

DOCUMENT 60: *Jin Fuey Moy v. United States* (1920)

Opinion of the Court (Delivered by Mr. Justice Pitney)

. . .

The indictment contained twenty counts. . . . Defendant was convicted upon eight counts, acquitted upon the others. Each count averred that on a date specified, at Pittsburgh, in the County of Allegheny, in the Western District of Pennsylvania, and within the jurisdiction of the court, defendant was a practicing physician, and did unlawfully, willfully, knowingly, and feloniously sell, barter, exchange, and give away certain derivatives and salts of opium, to-wit, a specified quantity of morphine sulphate, to a person named, not in pursuance of a written order from such person on a form issued in blank for that purpose by the Commissioner of Internal Revenue under the provisions of §2 of the act . . . and that said person "was not then and there a patient of the said Jin Fuey Moy, and the said morphine sulphate was dispensed and distributed by the said Jin Fuey Moy not in the course of his professional practice only; contrary to the form of the Act of Congress," etc.

It is objected that the act of selling or giving away a drug and the act of issuing a prescription are so essentially different that to allege that defendant sold the drug by issuing a prescription for it amounts to a contradiction of terms, and the repugnance renders the indictment fatally defective. The Government suggests that the clause as to issuing the prescription may be rejected as surplusage; but we are inclined to think it enters so intimately into the description of the offense intended to be charged that it cannot be eliminated, and that unless defendant could "sell," in a criminal sense, by issuing a prescription, the indictment is bad. If "selling" must be confined to a parting with one's own property there might be difficulty. But by §332 of the Criminal Code, "Whoever directly commits any act constituting an offense defined in any law of the United States, or aids, abets, counsels, commands, induces, or procures its commission, is a principal." Taking this together with the clauses quoted from §2 of the Anti-Narcotic Act, it is easy to see, and the evidence in this case demonstrates, that one may take a principal part in a prohibited sale of an opium derivative belonging to another person by unlawfully issuing a prescription to the would-be purchaser. Hence there is no necessary repugnance between prescribing and selling, and the indictment must be sustained.

The evidence shows that defendant was a practicing physician in Pittsburgh, registered under the act so as to be allowed to dispense or distribute opium and its derivatives without a written order in official form, "in the course of his professional practice only"; that he was in the habit of issuing prescriptions for morphine sulphate without such written order and not in the ordinary course of professional practice; that he issued them to persons not his patients and not previously known to him, professed morphine users, for the mere purpose, as the jury might find, of enabling such persons to continue the use of the drug, or to sell it to others; in some cases he made a superficial physical examination, in others none at all; his prescriptions called for large quantities of morphine—8 to 16 drams at a time—to be used "as directed," while the directions left the recipient free to use the drug virtually as he pleased. His charges were not according to the usual practice of medical men, but according to the amount of the drug prescribed, being invariably one dollar per dram. All the prescriptions were filled at a single drug store in Pittsburgh, the recipients being sent there by defendant for the purpose; and persons inquiring at that drug store for morphine were sent to defendant for a prescription. The circumstances strongly tended to show cooperation between defendant and the proprietors of the drug store. At and about the dates specified in the indictment—the spring of the year 1917—and for more than two years before, the number of prescriptions issued by defendant and filled at this drug store ran into the hundreds each month, all calling for morphine sulphate or morphine tablets in large quantities. In one case a witness who had procured from defendant two prescriptions—one in his own name for 10 drams, the other, in the name of a fictitious wife for 6 drams—and had been directed by defendant to the specified drug store in order to have them filled, asked defendant to confirm the prescriptions by telephone so there would be no trouble; to which defendant replied: "Oh, never mind; we do business together; we understand each other." On another occasion the same witness, having received from defendant two prescriptions for 8 drams each, one in his own name, the other in the name of the supposed wife, stating in one case a Cleveland address, in the other a Pittsburgh address, presented them at the drug store to be filled, and was told by the manager that he would not fill any more prescriptions under a Pittsburgh address; "they were taking too big a chance, and I must go back to the Chinaman and tell him what he told me, and he would understand—the Chinaman would understand." Witness returned the two prescriptions to defendant, told him what the manager had said, and defendant retained those prescriptions and issued to the witness a new one for 16 drams in place of them, with which the witness returned to the drug store and procured the specified quantity of the drug.

In each case where defendant was found guilty the evidence fully warranted the jury in finding that he aided, abetted, and procured a sale of morphine sulphate without written order upon a blank form issued by the Commissioner of Internal Revenue; and that he did this by means of a prescription issued not to a patient and not in the course of his professional practice, contrary to the prohibition of §2 of the act. Manifestly the phrases "to a patient" and "in the course of his professional practice only" are intended to confine the immunity of a registered physician, in dispensing the narcotic drugs mentioned in the act, strictly within the appropriate bounds of a physician's professional practice, and not to extend it to include a sale to a dealer or a distribution intended to cater to the appetite or satisfy the craving of one addicted to the use of the drug. A "prescription" issued for either of the latter purposes protects neither the physician who issues it nor the dealer who knowingly accepts and fills it. *Webb* v. *United States*, 249 U.S. 96.

. . .

The judgment under review is *Affirmed.*

Source: 254 *U.S. Reports* 189, decided December 6, 1920.

* * *

A key 1922 Supreme Court case addressed whether the Harrison Act allowed a physician to prescribe doses of drugs that might allow an addict to maintain his or her habit. In this case, Dr. Morris Behrman of New York City had been arrested for prescribing large amounts of heroin, morphine, and cocaine at the same time to a known addict, with the understanding that the patient would self-administer the drugs over a period of time. In a 6–3 decision, the Court upheld Dr. Behrman's indictment on the grounds that the dispensing of such large amounts of drugs could only result in the maintenance of an addiction or the illegal diversion of these drugs to others. This decision bolstered the government's stance against maintaining addicts on drugs.

DOCUMENT 61: *United States v. Behrman* (1922)

Opinion of the court (Delivered by Mr. Justice Day):

. . .

The indictment charges that the defendant did unlawfully sell, barter, and give to Willie King a compound, manufacture, and derivative of opium, to wit, 150 grains of heroin and 360 grains of morphine, and a compound, manufacture, and derivative of coca leaves, to wit, 210 grains of cocaine, not in pursuance of any written order of King, on a form issued for that purpose by the commissioner of internal revenue of the United States; that the defendant was a duly licensed physician and registered under the act, and issued three written orders to the said King in the form of prescriptions, signed by him, which prescriptions called for the delivery to King of the amount of drugs above described; that the defendant intended that King should obtain the drugs from the druggist upon the said orders; that King did obtain upon said orders drugs of the amount and kind above described, pursuant to the said prescriptions; that King was a person addicted to the habitual use of morphine, heroin, and cocaine, and known by the defendant to be so addicted; that King did not require the administration of either morphine, heroin, or cocaine by reason of any disease other than such addiction; that defendant did not dispense any of the drugs for the purpose of treating any disease or condition other than such addiction; that none of the drugs so dispensed by the defendant was administered to or intended by the defendant to be administered to King by the defendant or any nurse, or person acting under the direction of the defendant; nor were any of the drugs consumed or intended to be consumed by King in the presence of the defendant, but that all of the drugs were put in the possession or control of King with the intention on the part of the defendant that King would use the same by self-administration in divided doses over a period of several days, the amount of each of said drugs dispensed being more than sufficient or necessary to satisfy the craving of King therefor if consumed by him all at one time; that King was not in any way restrained or prevented from disposing of the drugs in any manner he saw fit; and that the drugs so dispensed by the defendant were in the form in which said drugs are usually consumed by persons addicted to the habitual use thereof to satisfy their craving therefor, and were adapted for such consumption.

The question is: Do the acts charged in this indictment constitute an offense within the meaning of the statute? As we have seen, the statute contains an exception to the effect that it shall not apply to the dispensing or distribution of such drugs to a patient by a registered physician, in the course of his professional practice only, nor to the sale, dispensing, or distribution of the drugs by a dealer to a consumer under a written prescription by a registered physician. The rule applicable to such statutes is that it is enough to charge facts sufficient to show that the accused is not within the exception.

The district judge who heard this Case was of the opinion that prescriptions in the regular course of practice did not include the indiscriminate doling out of narcotics in such quantity to addicts as charged in the indictment, but, out of deference to what he deemed to be the view of a local district judge in another case, announced his willingness to follow such opinion until the question could be passed upon by this court, and sustained the demurrer. In our opinion the district judge who heard the case was right in his conclusion, and should have overruled the demurrer.

Former decisions of this court have held that the purpose of the exception is to confine the distribution of these drugs to the regular and lawful course of professional practice, and that not everything called a prescription is necessarily such. *Webb v. United States,* 249 U.S. 96; *Jin Fuey Moy v. United States,* 254 U.S. 189.

. . .

It may be admitted that to prescribe a single dose, or even a number of doses, may not bring a physician within the penalties of the act; but what is here charged is that the defendant physician, by means of prescriptions, has enabled one, known by him to be an addict, to obtain from a pharmacist the enormous number of doses contained in 150 grains of heroin, 360 grains of morphine and 210 grains of cocaine. As shown by Wood's United States Dispensatory, a standard work in general use, the ordinary dose of morphine is one fifth of a grain, or cocaine one eighth to one fourth of a grain, of heroin one sixteenth to one eighth of a grain. By these standards more than three thousand ordinary doses were placed in the control of King. Undoubtedly doses may be varied to suit different cases, as determined by the judgment of a physician. But the quantities named in the indictment are charged to have been intrusted to a person known by the physician to be an addict, without restraint upon him in its administration or disposition by anything more than his own weakened and perverted will. Such so-called prescriptions could only result in the gratification of a diseased appetite for these pernicious drugs, or result in an unlawful parting with them to others, in violation of the act as heretofore interpreted in this court, within the principles laid down in the Webb and Jin Fuey Moy cases, supra.

We hold that the acts charged in the indictment constituted an offense within the terms and meaning of the act. The judgment of the District Court to the contrary should be reversed.

Reversed.

Source: 258 *U.S. Reports* 280, decided March 27, 1922.

* * *

In the dissenting opinion, Justice Oliver Wendell Holmes writes that no matter how implausible, the prescription could have been written by Dr. Behrman according to his professional judgment. Without a trial on that issue, the act should not be considered a crime.

DOCUMENT 62: Dissenting Opinion by Justice Holmes et al., *United States v. Behrman* (1922)

If this case raised a question of pleading, I should go far in agreeing to disregard technicalities that were deemed vital a hundred or perhaps even fifty years ago. But we have nothing to do with pleading as such, and as the judge below held the indictment bad, it can be sustained only upon a construction of the statute different from that adopted below.

The indictment, for the very purpose of raising the issue that divides the court, alleges in terms that the drugs were intended by the defendant to be used by King in divided doses over a period of several days. The defendant was a licensed physician and his part in the sale was the giving of prescriptions for the drugs. In view of the allegation . . . and the absence of any charge to the contrary, it must be assumed that he gave them in the regular course of his practice, and in good faith. Whatever ground for skepticism we may find in the facts, we are bound to accept the position knowingly and deliberately taken by the pleader, and evidently accepted by the court below.

It seems to me impossible to construe the statute as tacitly making such acts, however foolish, crimes, by saying that what is in form a prescription, and is given honestly, in the course of a doctor's practice, and therefore, so far as the words of the statute go, is allowed in terms, is not within the words, is not a prescription, and is not given in the course of practice, if the court deems the doctor's faith in his patient manifestly unwarranted. It seems to me wrong to construe the statute as creating a crime in this way without a word of warning. Of course, the facts alleged suggest an indictment in a different form; but the government preferred to trust to a strained interpretation of the law rather than to the finding of a jury upon the facts. I think that the judgment should be affirmed.

Mr. Justice McReynolds and Mr. Justice Brandeis concur in this Opinion.

Source: 258 *U.S. Reports* 280, decided March 27, 1922.

* * *

In his important book tracing the history of the legal system's control of drug addiction, *The Addict and the Law,* Alfred Lindesmith concluded that the Behrman decision made it virtually impossible for doctors to prescribe drugs to addicts, no matter what the medical need.

DOCUMENT 63: Effects of Behrman Decision (Alfred R. Lindesmith, 1965)

The Behrman case in 1922 gave further support to the idea that it was not legitimate for a physician to prescribe drugs for an addict, for in it the court ruled that such prescriptions were illegal regardless of the purpose the doctor may have had. The decision in this case seemed to deprive physicians of the defense that they had acted in good faith, for Dr. Behrman was convicted despite the fact that the prosecution stipulated that he had prescribed drugs in order to treat and cure addicts.

After the Behrman case the legal position of the addict seemed quite clear. He was simply denied all access to legal drugs. The rulings by the Supreme Court seemed to be moving toward the idea that the physician could not legally prescribe drugs to relieve the addict's withdrawal distress or to maintain his habit, but could provide drugs only to an addict undergoing institutional withdrawal and then only in diminishing doses. However, criticism of the law from medical sources may have shaken the Court's confidence, for even before the Linder decision in 1925, a note of doubt crept into some decisions. For example, in the Behrman case, in which vast quantities of drugs had been prescribed, the Court suggested that a single dose or even a number of doses might not bring a physician within the penalties of the law.

The Supreme Court decisions up to 1922 made it impossible for doctors to treat addicts in any way acceptable to law enforcement officials. The ambulatory method of treatment had been condemned, and since addicts were not accepted in hospitals, the doctor's right to administer diminishing doses during an institutional cure was mainly theoretical. The danger of arrest and prosecution was clearly recognized after 1919, when the first of the important doctor cases had been decided by the Supreme Court. Most doctors simply stopped having anything to do with addicts and the few who did not do this found themselves threatened with prosecution. The illicit traffic burgeoned during these years as addicts who had formerly obtained legal supplies turned to it in increasing numbers.

Source: Alfred R. Lindesmith, *The Addict and the Law* (Bloomington, IN: Indiana University Press, 1965), 6–7.

* * *

In the view of reformer Rufus King, whose book *The Drug Hang-up* criticized the history of American drug policy, the Berhman decision triggered a crackdown by Treasury Department agents against physicians and addicts.

DOCUMENT 64: Effects of Behrman Decision (Rufus King, 1972)

[After the] Behrman decision . . . the Narcotics Division launched a reign of terror, threatening doctors who had anything further to do with drug addicts, and sending a goodly number of recalcitrant practitioners off to prison with the Behrman formula. Any prescribing of drugs for an addict, unless he had some other ailment that called for treatment with narcotics, was likely to mean trouble with the Treasury agents. The addict patient vanished; the addict-criminal emerged in his place. And so instead of policing a small domain of petty stamp-chiselers, Treasury was able to expand its drug-law enforcement until the prison population began to swell with thousands of felony drug convictions each year.

Far more than the parallel campaign against liquor, the typical victim of this war on drug users often tended to be a respected member of his community until the T-men caught him. In cases that went all the way to trial, the ratio between arrests and convictions remained notably low, indicating abusive use of the indictment process: in 1920, 3,477 arrests produced 908 convictions; in 1921, 4,014 arrests produced 1,583; at the peak, in 1925, 10,297 federal arrests produced 5,600 convictions. . . . [I]n a 1928 census of federal prisoners (in federal institutions), in the very heyday of Prohibition, there were two prisoners serving sentences for narcotic offenses for every one incarcerated for liquor-law violations. Drug offenders constituted one-third of the total federal prison population.

Source: Rufus King, *The Drug Hang-up* (New York: W. W. Norton, 1972), 43–44.

* * *

In the next key Supreme Court case, *Linder v. United States,* the Court again considered the legality of maintaining an addict without the immediate intent of a cure, but reached a different conclusion than in the Behrman case. Charles Linder, a Spokane, Washington, physician, was convicted of selling one morphine tablet and three cocaine tablets to an addict who was working as an informer for the U.S. Treasury Department. The Court unanimously overturned Linder's conviction, ruling that the doctor had the right to prescribe small amounts of drugs to addicts for self-administration as long as he was acting in good faith as part of sound medical practice, in this case to relieve the suffering caused by withdrawal.

DOCUMENT 65: *Linder v. United States* (1925)

Opinion of the court (Delivered by Mr. Justice McReynolds):

The court below affirmed the conviction of petitioner by the district court, eastern district of Washington, under the following count of an indictment returned therein June 26, 1922. As to all other counts the jury found him not guilty.

Count II. . . . the grand jurors . . . present: That Charles O. Linder, . . . hereinafter in this indictment called the defendant, late of the county of Spokane, state of Washington, heretofore, to wit; on or about the 1st day of April, 1922, at Spokane, in the northern division of the eastern district of Washington, and within the jurisdiction of this court, did then and there violate the Act of December 17, 1914 . . . in that he did then and there knowingly, wilfully, unlawfully sell, barter, and give to Ida Casey, a compound, manufacture, derivative of opium, to wit: one (1) tablet of morphine and a compound, manufacture, and derivative of coca leaves, to wit: three (3) tablets of cocaine, not in pursuance of any written order of Ida Casey on a form issued for that purpose by the Commissioner of Internal Revenue of the United States; that the defendant was a duly licensed physician and registered under the act: that Ida Casey was a person addicted to the habitual use of morphine and cocaine and known by the defendant to be addicted; that Ida Casey did not require the administration of either morphine or cocaine by reason of any disease other than such addiction; that the defendant did not dispense any of the drugs for the purpose of treating any disease or condition other than such addiction; that none of the drugs so dispensed by the defendant was administered to or intended by the defendant to be administered to Ida

Casey by the defendant or any nurse, or person acting under the direction of the defendant; nor were any of the drugs consumed or intended to be consumed by Ida Casey in the presence of the defendant, but that all of the drugs were put in the possession or control of Ida Casey with the intention on the part of the defendant that Ida Casey would use the same by self-administration in divided doses over a period of time, the amount of each of said drugs dispensed being more than sufficient or necessary to satisfy the cravings of Ida Casey therefor if consumed by her all at one time; that Ida Casey was not in any way restrained or prevented from disposing of the drugs in any manner she saw fit; and that the drugs so dispensed by the defendant were in the form in which said drugs are usually consumed by persons addicted to the habitual use thereof to satisfy their craving therefor, and were adapted for consumption.

. . .

Manifestly, the purpose of the indictment was to accuse petitioner of violating § 2 of the Narcotic Law, and the trial court so declared. . . .

Petitioner maintains that the facts stated are not sufficient to constitute an offense. The United States submit that, considering *United States v. Behrman*, 258 U.S. 280, the sufficiency of the indictment is clear.

The trial court charged:

"If you are satisfied beyond a reasonable doubt that defendant knew that this woman was addicted to the use of narcotics, and if he dispensed those drugs to her for the purpose of catering to her appetite or satisfying her cravings for the drug, he is guilty under the law. If, on the other hand, you believe from the testimony that the defendant believed in good faith this woman was suffering from cancer or ulcer of the stomach, and administered the drug for the purpose of relieving her pain, or if you entertain a reasonable doubt upon that question, you must give the defendant the benefit of the doubt and find him not guilty."

In effect, the indictment alleges that the accused, a duly registered physician, violated the statute by giving to a known addict four tablets containing morphine and cocaine with the expectation that she would administer them to herself in divided doses, while unrestrained and beyond his presence or control, for the sole purpose of relieving conditions incident to addiction and keeping herself comfortable. It does not question the doctor's good faith nor the wisdom or propriety of his action according to medical standards. It does not allege that he dispensed the drugs otherwise than to a patient in the course of his professional practice, or for other than medical purposes. The facts disclosed indicate no conscious design to violate the law, no cause to suspect that the recipient intended to sell or otherwise dispose of the drugs, and no real probability that she would not consume them.

The declared object of the Narcotic Law is to provide revenue, and this court has held that whatever additional moral end it may have in view must "be reached only through a revenue measure and within the limits of a revenue measure." *United States V. Jin Fuey Moy,* 241 U.S. 394. Congress cannot, under the pretext of executing delegated power, pass laws for the accomplishment of objects not intrusted to the Federal government. And we accept as established doctrine that any provision of an act of Congress ostensibly enacted under power granted by the Constitution, not naturally and reasonably adapted to the effective exercise of such power, but solely to the achievement of something plainly within power reserved to the states, is invalid, and cannot be enforced. . . . In the light of these principles and not forgetting the familiar rule that "a statute must be construed, if fairly possible, so as to avoid not only the conclusion that it is unconstitutional, but also grave doubts upon that score," the provisions of this statute must be interpreted and applied.

Obviously, direct control of medical practice in the states is beyond the power of Federal government. Incidental regulation of such practice by Congress through a taxing act cannot extend to matters plainly inappropriate and unnecessary to reasonable enforcement of a revenue measure. The enactment under consideration levies a tax, upheld by this court, upon every person who imports, manufactures, produces, compounds, sells, deals in, dispenses, or gives away opium or coca leaves or derivatives therefrom, and may regulate medical practice in the states only so far as reasonably appropriate for or merely incidental to its enforcement. It says nothing of "addicts" and does not undertake to prescribe methods for their medical treatment. They are diseased and proper subjects for such treatment, and we cannot possibly conclude that a physician acted improperly or unwisely or for other than medical purposes solely because he has dispensed to one of them, in the ordinary course and in good faith, four small tablets of morphine or cocaine for relief of conditions incident to addiction. What constitutes bona fide medical practice must be determined upon consideration of evidence and attending circumstances. Mere pretense of such practice, of course, cannot legalize forbidden sales, or otherwise nullify, valid provisions of the statute, or defeat such regulations as may be fairly appropriate to its enforcement within the proper limitations of a revenue measure.

United States v. Jin Fuey Moy, supra, points out that the Narcotic Law can be upheld only as a revenue measure. It must be interpreted and applied accordingly. Further, grave constitutional doubts concerning § 8 cannot be avoided unless limited to persons who are required to register by § 1. Mere possession of the drug creates no presumption of guilt as against any other person.

In *United States v. Doremus,* 249 U.S. 86 . . . [t]he trial court held Par. 2 invalid because it invaded the police power of the state. This court declared: "Of course Congress may not in the exercise of Federal power exert authority wholly reserved to the states. . . . If the legislation enacted has some reasonable relation to the exercise of the taxing authority conferred by the Constitution, it cannot be invalidated because of the supposed motives which induced it. . . . We cannot agree with the contention that the provisions of § 2, controlling the disposition of these drugs in the ways described, can have nothing to do with facilitating the collection of the revenue, as we should be obliged to do if we were to declare this act beyond the power of Congress acting under its constitutional authority to impose excise taxes." The sharp division of the court in this cause and the opinion in Jin Fuey Moy's case clearly indicated that the statute must be strictly construed and not extended beyond the proper limits of a revenue measure.

Webb v. United States, 249 U.S. 96, came here on certified questions. . . . The third inquired whether a regular physician's order for morphine issued to an addict, not in the course of professional treatment with design to cure the habit, but in order to provide enough of the drug to keep him comfortable by maintaining his customary use, is a "physician's prescription." . . . The narrated facts show, plainly enough, that physician and druggist conspired to sell large quantities of morphine to addicts under the guise of issuing and filling orders. . . . The answer thus given must not be construed as forbidding every prescription for drugs, irrespective of quantity, when designed temporarily to alleviate an addict's pains, although it may have been issued in good faith and without design to defeat the revenues. This limitation of the reply is confirmed by Behrman's Case, 258 U.S. 280 (infra), decided three years later, which suggests at least that the accused doctor might have lawfully dispensed some doses.

In *Jin Fuey Moy v. United States* 254 U.S. 189, doctor and druggist conspired to sell opiates. The prescriptions were not issued in the course of professional practice. The doctor became party to prohibited sales. "Manifestly the phrases 'to a patient' and 'in the course of his professional practice only' are intended to confine the immunity of a registered physician, in dispensing the narcotic drugs mentioned in the act, strictly within the appropriate bounds of a physician's professional practice, and not to extend it to include a sale to a dealer or a distribution intended to cater to the appetite or satisfy the craving of one addicted to the use of the drug. A 'prescription' issued for either of the latter purposes protects neither the physician who issues it, nor the dealer who knowingly accepts and fills it."

. . .

United States v. Balint, 258 U.S. 250, holds: "It is very evident from a reading of it [§2 of the Harrison Act] that the emphasis of the section is in securing a close supervision of the business of dealing in these dangerous drugs by the taxing officers of the government, and that it merely uses a criminal penalty to secure recorded evidence of the disposition of such drugs as a means of taxing and restraining the traffic."

. . . And replying, this court said [in *United States v. Behrman*, 258 U.S. 280]:

"The district judge who heard this case was of the opinion that prescriptions in the regular course of practice did not include the indiscriminate doling out of narcotics in such quantity to addicts as charged in the indictment. . . . In our opinion the district judge who heard the case was right in his conclusion. . . . Former decisions of this court have held that the purpose of the exception is to confine the distribution of these drugs to the regular and lawful course of professional practice, and that not everything called a prescription is necessarily such. . . ."

This opinion related to definitely alleged facts and must be so understood. The enormous quantity of drugs ordered [in *Behrman*], considered in connection with the recipient's character, without explanation, seemed enough to show prohibited sales and to exclude the idea of bona fide professional action in the ordinary course. The opinion cannot be accepted as authority for holding that a physician who acts bona fide and according to fair medical standards may never give an addict moderate amounts of drugs for self administration in order to relieve conditions incident to addiction. Enforcement of the tax demands no such drastic rule, and if the act had such scope it would certainly encounter grave constitutional difficulties.

The Narcotic Law is essentially a revenue measure, and its provisions must be reasonably applied with the primary view of enforcing the special tax. We find no facts alleged in the indictment sufficient to show that petitioner had done anything falling within definite inhibitions or sufficient materially to imperil orderly collection of revenue from sales. Federal power is delegated, and its prescribed limits must not be transcended even though the end seems desirable. The unfortunate condition of the recipient certainly created no reasonable probability that she would sell or otherwise dispose of the few tablets intrusted to her; and we cannot say that by so dispensing them the doctor necessarily transcended the limits of that professional conduct with which Congress never intended to interfere.

The judgment below must be reversed. The cause will be remanded to the District Court for further proceedings in harmony with this opinion.

Source: 268 *U.S. Reports* 5, decided April 13, 1925.

* * *

In the Linder decision, there were two important departures from earlier Supreme Court decisions, according to Lindesmith.

DOCUMENT 66: Comment on Linder Decision (Alfred R. Lindesmith, 1965)

The two new elements in this decision are (a) the Court's explicit espousal of the view that addiction is a disease and (b) the rule that a physician acting in good faith and according to fair medical standards may give an addict moderate amounts of drugs to relieve withdrawal distress without necessarily violating the law.

This opinion, which is still the controlling doctrine of the federal courts, seems to make nonsense of what had gone before, for it said that the addict who had been denied medical care by earlier decisions was a diseased person entitled to such care. More important still, it clearly implies that the question of what constitutes proper medical care is a medical issue and therefore, presumably, one to be settled, not by legislators, judges, juries, or policemen, but by the medical profession. Certainly the federal courts in particular cannot legally tell doctors what to do with addicts if addiction is viewed as a disease.

The logical consequences which seem to follow from the acceptance of the Linder opinion were spelled out by Federal Judge L. R. Yankwich in 1936:

"I am satisfied therefore, that the Linder case, and the cases which interpret it, lay down the rule definitely that the statute does not say what drugs a physician may prescribe to an addict. Nor does it say the quantity which a physician may or may not prescribe. Nor does it regulate the frequency of prescription. Any attempt to so interpret the statute, by an administrative interpretation, whether that administrative interpretation be oral, in writing, or by an officer or by a regulation of the department, would be not only contrary to the law, but would also make the law unconstitutional as being clearly a regulation of the practice of medicine."

Source: Alfred R. Lindesmith, *The Addict and the Law* (Bloomington: Indiana University Press, 1965), 9–10.

* * *

Despite the potential opening that the Linder decision gave for doctors to prescribe reasonable amounts of drugs to addicts, it did not appear to have much effect on either federal policy as carried out by the Treasury Department or on the continuing reluctance of physicians to prescribe drugs to addicts. The Federal Bureau of Narcotics interpreted the Linder decision as allowing the continued enforcement of the Harrison Act against physicians who prescribed drugs to addicts.

DOCUMENT 67: Federal Bureau of Narcotics Interpretation of Linder Decision (c. 1925)

It seems, therefore, that the substance of the holding was that, in the absence of an averment in the indictment that the sale was not in the course of professional practice only, the Court could not find as a matter of law that the sale of the tablets by Dr. Linder "necessarily transcended" the limits of professional practice.

We submit that the Linder case did not lay down the rule that a doctor acting in good faith and guided by proper standards of medical practice may give an addict moderate amounts of drugs in order to relieve conditions incident to addiction. What the Court stated in the Linder case was that the opinion [in the Behrman case] "cannot be accepted as authority for holding that a physician, who acts bona fide and according to fair medical standards, may never give an addict moderate amounts of drugs for self-administration in order to relieve conditions incident to addiction." This is not an affirmative declaration that a physician may continue to dispense narcotic drugs to an addict to gratify addiction.

Source: Quoted in Alfred R. Lindesmith, *The Addict and the Law* (Bloomington: Indiana University Press, 1965), 16.

* * *

Lindesmith offers other reasons why the Linder decision did not result in measurable changes in enforcement of the Harrison Act.

DOCUMENT 68: Lack of Effect of Linder Decision (Alfred R. Lindesmith, 1965)

There are a number of reasons for the impotence of the Linder doctrine and prominent among them is the legal confusion in the subsequent cases. Since the Linder decision appeared in 1925, the Supreme Court has not had the opportunity to expand and clarify it by ruling on other similar cases. Reasons for this lack of opportunity are probably that few reputable physicians care to play Russian roulette with their careers by challenging existing enforcement practices, and second, that the government has been careful about prosecuting certain types of cases so as not to give the Supreme Court a chance to expand and emphasize the precedent of the Linder case.

. . .

The lower federal courts were no doubt reluctant to follow the logical implications of the Linder case, for this would have meant upsetting an established enforcement policy vigorously supported by police propaganda and to some extent by popular opinion and by part of the medical profession. In 1925 this policy had been in operation for a decade. Apathy in the medical and legal professions, based in large part upon the addict's low social status, his lack of funds, and the fact that he is a difficult and troublesome person, contributed heavily to the reluctance to change the status quo.

Source: Alfred R. Lindesmith, *The Addict and the Law* (Bloomington: Indiana University Press, 1965), 12–13.

* * *

Shortly after the Linder decision, the Supreme Court invited a new test of the constitutionality of the Harrison Act. This finally came about in a 1928 case, *Nigro v. United States*, in which the Court upheld the act's constitutionality by a 6–3 decision. This case was a result of questions posed by the Eighth Circuit Court of Appeals in considering the conviction of Frank Nigro for selling one ounce of morphine without registering with the transaction forms required by the Commissioner of Internal Revenue, and paying the required tax, under Section 2 of the Harrison Act.

DOCUMENT 69: *Nigro v. United States* (1928)

Opinion of the Court (Delivered by MR. CHIEF JUSTICE TAFT)

This case comes here by certificate of the Circuit Court of Appeals of the Eighth Circuit, and is intended to submit to us, for answer, certain questions concerning the validity and proper construction of the Anti-Narcotic Act of December 17, 1914, as amended in the Revenue Act of 1918, February 24, 1919.

The Circuit Court of Appeals bases its questions on issues arising in its consideration on error of a judgment of conviction on the second count of an indictment drawn under § 2 of the Act. The count charged that one Frank Nigro and one Roy Williams unlawfully sold to one A. L. Raithel one ounce of morphine, not being sold in pursuance of a written order of A. L. Raithel on a form issued in blank for that purpose by the Commissioner of Internal Revenue. Roy Williams was not apprehended. Frank Nigro was tried and convicted, and sentence was imposed of five years' imprisonment at the Leavenworth penitentiary. The Circuit Court of Appeals expressed the opinion that the case could not be disposed of without determining the construction and possibly the constitutionality of the first provision of § 2 of the Act. . . .

A summing up of the evidence, tending to show the sale of an ounce of morphine by the defendants as charged in the second count, is contained in the certificate by the court.

The questions submitted for our consideration are as follows:

QUESTION I.

Is the provision which is contained in the first sentence of section 2 of the Act limited in its application to those persons who by section 1 are required to register and pay the tax?

QUESTION II.

If a broader construction is given to said provision, is the provision as so construed, constitutional?

If question I is answered in the affirmative, then we ask,

QUESTION III.

Is it necessary for the Government in prosecuting under said provision, to allege and prove that defendant was a person required by section 1 to register and pay the tax?

If question III is answered in the affirmative, then we ask,

QUESTION IV.

Is the allegation that defendant made the sale not in pursuance of a written order of the buyer on a form issued in blank for that purpose by the Commissioner of Internal Revenue of the United States, sufficient to charge that defendant was a person required to be registered and to pay the tax under section 1?

. . .

The present case relates to the validity of the second section of the law; but, before considering this, we must answer the first question and construe the meaning of the first sentence of § 2 quoted above. The controversy is whether the words "any person" in that sentence include all persons or apply only to persons who are required to register and pay the tax under the first section of the act.

. . .

In interpreting the Act, we must assume that it is a taxing measure, for otherwise it would be no law at all. If it is a mere act for the purpose of regulating and restraining the purchase of the opiate and other drugs, it is beyond the power of Congress and must be regarded as invalid. . . . Everything in the construction of § 2 must be regarded as directed toward the collection of the taxes imposed in § 1 and the prevention of evasion by persons subject to the tax. If the words can not be read as reasonably serving such a purpose, § 2 can not be supported.

The importation, preparation and sale of the opiate, or other like drugs, and their transportation and concealment in small packages, are exceedingly easy and make the levy and collection of a tax thereon correspondingly difficult. More than this, use of the drug for other than medicinal purposes leads to addiction and causes the addicts to resort to so much cunning, deceit and concealment in the procurement and custody of the drug, and to be willing to pay such high prices for it that, to be efficient, a law for taxing it needs to make thorough provision for preventing and discovering evasion of the tax—as by requiring that sales, purchases and other transactions in the drug be so conducted and evidenced that any dealing in it where the tax has not been paid, may be detected and punished and that opportunity for successful evasion may be lessened as far as may be possible.

The literal meaning of "any person," in the first line of the first sentence of § 2, includes all persons within the jurisdiction. The word "persons" is given expressly the meaning of a partnership, association or corporation, as well as that of a natural person. Why should it not be given its ordinary comprehensive significance? The argument to the contrary in favor of limiting it to exclude all but those who are required to register and pay the tax is that it would be superfluous to include persons selling opium who are not registered, because they are denounced as criminals by the first section for selling without registration. That is no reason why they may not be included under a second reasonable restriction enforceable by punishment.

. . .

There is nothing in the language of the section itself that would reduce the significance of the words "any person" from the meaning of "all persons" to that of those persons only who are required to register and pay the tax, as there was in *United States v. Jin Fuey Moy*, 241 U.S. 394. . . . It was held that § 8 applied only to persons required to register under § 1 and pay the . . . tax. The language of § 8 is more restricted than § 2. It reads: "That it shall be unlawful for any person not registered under the provisions of this Act, and who has not paid the special tax provided for by this Act, to have in his possession or under his control any of the aforesaid drugs." The words "any person" in § 2 are not linked with those who have not registered and have not paid the tax, but ought to do so, as are the same words in § 8. The narrow construction of § 8 in the *Jin Fuey Moy* case was reached, in part certainly, because of the juxtaposition of the words.

. . .

We are of opinion, therefore, that the provision which is contained in the first sentence of § 2 of the Act is not limited in its application to those persons who by § 1 are required to register and pay the tax. We answer the first question in the negative.

This brings us to the second question, which is ". . . is the provision as so construed, constitutional?" It was held to be constitutional in *United States v. Doremus*, 249 U.S. 86. . . . The inquiry was whether § 2, in making sales of the drugs unlawful except to persons giving orders on forms issued by the Commissioner of Internal Revenue, . . . and forbidding any person to obtain the drugs by means of such order forms for any other purpose than use, sale or distribution in the conduct of a lawful business, or in the legitimate practice of his profession, bore a reasonable relation to the enforcement of the tax provided by § 1 and did not exceed the power of Congress. It was held that § 2 aimed to confine sales to registered dealers, and to those dispensing the drugs as physicians, and to those who come to dealers with legitimate prescriptions of physicians; that Congress, with full power over the subject, inserted these provisions in an Act specifically providing for the raising of revenue.

. . .

Four members of the Court dissented in the *Doremus* case, because of opinion that the court below had correctly held the Act of Congress, in so far as it embraced the matters complained of, to be beyond its constitutional power, and that the statute, in § 2, was a mere pretext as a tax measure and was in fact an attempt by Congress to exercise the police power reserved to the States and to regulate and restrict the sale and distribution of dangerous and noxious narcotic drugs. Since that time, this Court has held that Congress by merely calling an Act a taxing act can not make it a legitimate exercise of taxing power under § 8 of Article I of the Federal Constitution, if in fact the words of the act show clearly its real purpose is otherwise. . . . By the Revenue Act of 1918, the Anti-Narcotic Act was amended so as to increase the taxes under § 1. . . . Thus the income from the tax for the Government becomes substantial. Under the Narcotic Act, as now amended, the tax amounts to about one million dollars a year, and since the amendment in 1919 it has benefited the Treasury to the extent of nearly nine million dollars. If there was doubt as to the character of this Act—that it is not, as alleged, a subterfuge—it has been removed by the change whereby what was a nominal tax before was made a substantial one. It is certainly a taxing act now. . . .

It may be true that the provisions of the Act forbidding all but registered dealers to obtain the order forms has the incidental effect of making it more difficult for the drug to reach those who have a normal and legitimate use for it, by requirement of purchase through order forms or by physician's prescription. But this effect, due to the machinery of the Act, should not render the order form provisions void as an infringement on state police power where these provisions are genuinely calculated to sustain the revenue features. Section 2 was once sustained by this Court some nine years ago, with more formidable reason against it than now exists under the amended statute. Its provisions have been enforced for those years. Whatever doubts may have existed respecting the order form provisions of the Act have been removed by the amendment made in 1919.

. . .

In this case, the qualification of the right of a resident of a State to buy and consume opium or other narcotic without restraint by the Federal Government, is subject to the power of Congress to lay a tax by way of excise on its sale. Congress does not exceed its power if the object is laying a tax and the interference with lawful purchasers and users of the drug is reasonably adapted to securing the payment of the tax. Nor does it render such qualification or interference with the original state right an invasion of it because it may incidentally discourage some in the harmful use of the thing taxed. . . .

This leads to an answer to the second question in the affirmative, and makes it unnecessary for us to answer the remaining third and fourth questions.

Source: 276 *U.S. Reports* 332, decided April 9, 1928.

* * *

There were two separate dissents in the *Nigro* decision, with Justice McReynolds concluding that the main intent of the Harrison Act was to regulate drug traffic within the states, and thus was unconstitutional.

Document 70: Dissenting Opinions, *Nigro v. United States* (1928)

The separate opinion of MR. JUSTICE McREYNOLDS.

. . .

It is maintained, first, that § 2 applies to all sales, including, of course, those made by one who is not registered, to a purchaser who cannot possibly secure an order form; and, secondly, that so construed, it is constitutional. Both propositions, I think, are wrong.

Section 1 of the Act imposes a definite tax. . . . All who are subject to the tax are required to register. . . .

Section 2. declares—

"That it shall be unlawful for any person to sell, barter, exchange, or give away any of the aforesaid drugs [opium, &c.] except in pursuance of a written order of the person to whom such article is sold, bartered, exchanged, or given, on a form to be issued in blank for that purpose by the Commissioner of Internal Revenue. . . .

. . ."

Obviously, no one who has not registered and paid the special tax laid by § 1 can obtain "suitable forms."

. . .

I can discover no adequate ground for thinking Congress could have supposed that collection of the prescribed tax would be materially aided by requiring those who engage in selling surreptitiously to consumers to do an impossible thing—receive an order upon a blank which the purchaser could not obtain. The plain intent is to control the traffic within the States by preventing sales except to registered persons and holders of prescriptions, and this amounts to an attempted regulation of something reserved to the States. The questioned inhibition of sales has no just relation to the collection of the tax laid on dealers. The suggestion to the contrary is fanciful. Although disguised, the real and primary purpose is not difficult to discover and it is strict limitation and regulation of the traffic.

. . .

The habit of smoking tobacco is often deleterious. Many think it ought to be suppressed. The craving for diamonds leads to extravagance and frequently to crime. Silks are luxuries and their use abridges the demand for cotton and wool. Those who sell tobacco, or diamonds, or silks may be taxed by the United States. But, surely, a provision in an act laying such a tax which limited sales of cigars, cigarettes, jewels, or silks to some small class alone authorized to secure official blanks would not be proper or necessary in order to enforce collection. The acceptance of such a doctrine would bring many purely local matters within the potential control of the Federal Government. The admitted evils incident to the use of opium cannot justify disregard of the powers "reserved to the States, respectively, or to the people."

MR. JUSTICE BUTLER, dissenting.

Section 1 was originally enacted December 17, 1914. It was amended by the Revenue Act of 1918 passed February 24, 1919. It contains the following: "It shall be unlawful for any person required to register under the provisions of this Act to . . . sell . . . any of the aforesaid drugs without having registered and paid the special tax as imposed by this section."

Section 2 appeared in its present form in the original Act. The pertinent provision is: "It shall be unlawful for any person to sell . . . any of the aforesaid drugs except in pursuance of a written order of the person to whom such article is sold . . . on a form to be issued in blank for that purpose by the Commissioner of Internal Revenue."

The effect of these two provisions is to prohibit sale by any person who has not registered and to permit sale by a registered person upon a written blank issued by the Commissioner. That conclusion is so plain that discussion cannot affect it.

Question 1 should be answered Yes.
Question 2 need not be answered.
Question 3 should be answered Yes.
Question 4 should be answered No.

MR. JUSTICE SUTHERLAND concurs in this opinion.

Source: 276 *U.S. Reports* 332, decided April 9, 1928.

* * *

The Nigro decision was the last test of the constitutionality of the Harrison Act. Since 1928, the constitutionality of federal laws regulating drug use and sale has not been successfully challenged. However, as anti-drug laws developed following World War II, other aspects of drug policy have faced legal questions that have resulted in Supreme Court review. For example, several court cases have involved the legality of "no-knock" searches by law enforcement officers. Such provisions had first been written into federal anti-drug laws in 1970. Another seminal Supreme Court case in 1962 struck down a California law that made it a crime to be an addict, even if no drugs were found in the person's possession. The latter decision had an important impact on the nature of anti-drug laws and the legal status of being an addict. These decisions are reviewed later in this book.

Part V

Overview of State Anti-Drug Laws

EARLY STATE ANTI-DRUG LAWS

American drug policy experts and political leaders had recognized early on that effective controls against drugs would require both federal and state laws and policies. Because of the constitutional limitations of federal police and legislative powers in the states, it was important that states supplement federal laws with their own legislation and policies to limit drug sale and use. Most obviously, with state and local law enforcement primarily responsible for controlling crime and illegal drug dealing, state and local laws were required to set guidelines for legal and illegal behaviors.

In the late 19th and early 20th centuries, state laws against drugs generally were contained within broader laws regulating the use and sale of poisons, intoxicants, and similar substances considered to be injurious to health. The first state to include drugs as part of its anti-poison laws was Pennsylvania, which included morphine in its 1860 law. In 1885 Ohio became one of the first states to regulate opium in a law against opium smoking. The first state to make cocaine illegal was Illinois, whose 1897 law made it illegal to sell or give away cocaine except on a doctor's prescription. By 1912 most states had passed laws regulating the sale of opium, cocaine, and their derivatives and preparations, requiring an original doctor's prescription. The early state laws varied in their provisions and their effectiveness, as the following 1912 document by Martin Wilbert and Murray Motter suggests; this document also is an early recognition of the need for states to have uniform anti-drug laws. Wilbert was a pharmacist with the U.S. Public Health Service and a member of the American Medical Association

Council on Pharmacy and Chemistry. In the latter role, he was an important figure in the development of the Harrison Act.

DOCUMENT 71: Shortcomings of State Anti-Drug Laws (Martin Wilbert and Murray Motter, 1912)

In many of the States antinarcotic laws are so comprehensive that practically every retail druggist would be subject to fine or imprisonment were an attempt made to enforce the legislation ostensibly in force, while in other States the laws are so burdened with exceptions and provisos as practically to nullify every effort to control the traffic in narcotic drugs.

The present-day form of legislation designed to prevent the misbranding of drugs and of foods is of comparatively recent origin, though many of the States have long had laws requiring that the contents of a package of medicine be true to label and making the druggist responsible for damages accruing from the use of a wrongly labeled medicine. The differences in the requirements for the method of labeling drug . . . clearly show the need for greater uniformity in the several State laws.

Source: Martin Wilbert and Murray Motter, "Digest of Laws and Regulations in Force in the United States Relating to the Possession, Use, Sale, and Manufacture of Poisons and Habit-Forming Drugs," *Public Health Bulletin* No. 56 (Washington, DC: Office of the Surgeon General, U.S. Public Health Service, November 1912), 15.

* * *

The following documents are excerpts from examples of early state laws against sale and possession of opiates, cocaine, and other drugs. They illustrate the variety of approaches and concerns and the range of punishments that were developed by states in these early attempts to control drug use. For example, the West Virginia law allowed doctors to prescribe opiates (but not cocaine) to addicts as part of their "treatment."

DOCUMENT 72: Nevada State Law (1881)

From and after the last day of March, 1881, it shall be unlawful for any person or persons, as principals or agents, to have in his, her or their possession any opium pipe, or part thereof, or to smoke opium, or to sell or give away for such purpose, or otherwise dispose of any opium in this state, except druggists and apothecaries; and druggists and apothecaries shall sell it only on the prescriptions of legally practicing physicians.

Source: Cited in Compiled Laws of 1899, Nevada.

DOCUMENT 73: West Virginia State Law (1909)

Sec. 4433a20. No person, firm or corporation shall dispense or sell at retail any of the poisons enumerated in the following schedule except as hereinafter provided.

SCHEDULE C: Cocaine . . . opium, morphine, herione [*sic;* meaning heroin], chloral hydrate or any salt or compound of any of the foregoing substances or any preparations or compound containing any of the foregoing substances or their salts or compounds, except on the original written order or prescription of a lawfully authorized practitioner of medicine, dentistry or veterinary medicine, which order shall be dated and contain the name of the person for whom prescribed. . . .

Sec. 4433a27. It shall be unlawful for any practitioner of medicine, dentistry or veterinary medicine to furnish or prescribe for the use of any habitual user of the same any cocaine, heroin, opium, morphine, chloral hydrate or any salt or compound of any of the foregoing substances or their salts or compounds . . . provided, however, that the provisions of this section shall not be construed to prevent any lawfully authorized practitioner of medicine from furnishing or prescribing in good faith for the use of any habitual user of narcotic drugs, who is under his professional care, such substances as he may deem necessary for his treatment, when such prescriptions are not given or substances furnished for the purpose of evading the provisions of this act.

Sec. 1. That no person shall sell, give away or otherwise dispense cocaine, . . . except on the prescription of a licensed physician in good standing in his profession, not of intemperate habits or addicted to the use of any drug, and any person violating the provisions of this section shall be guilty of a felony. . . .

Sec. 2. If any person, except a licensed physician, dentist or veterinary surgeon, manufacturing pharmacist or chemist, or wholesale or retail pharmacist or druggist, have in his possession cocaine . . . with intent to sell, give away or otherwise dispense the same, he shall be deemed guilty of a felony. . . . Provided, that nothing herein contained shall be construed to apply to any hospital, college or scientific public institution.

Source: West Virginia Code of Laws: Supplement, 1909.

DOCUMENT 74: New Hampshire State Law (1909)

Sec. 1. It shall be unlawful for any person, firm or corporation to manufacture any so-called catarrh powder or catarrh cure, or any patent or proprietary preparation containing cocaine, or any of its salts, or alpha or beta eucaine, or any of their salts, or any synthetic substitute for the aforesaid.

Sec. 2. (as amended by Laws of 1911, chapter 7). It shall be unlawful for any person, firm or corporation to sell, exchange, deliver, expose for sale, give away or have in his possession or custody with intent to sell, exchange, deliver, or give away, in any street, way, square, park or other public place, or in any hotel, restaurant, liquor saloon, bar-room, public hall, place of amusement, or public building any cocaine or any of its salts, or any synthetic substitute for the aforesaid, or any preparation containing any of the same, *provided, however*, that the foregoing provisions shall not apply to sales to apothecaries, druggists, physicians, veterinaries and dentists, or to sales by apothecaries or druggists upon the original prescriptions of a physician, *provided* the prescription is retained and kept on file as authority for the sale and not refilled.

Source: New Hampshire Laws of 1909, Chapter 162.

* * *

In addition to similar laws against selling cocaine or opiates without a physician's prescription, Indiana's law contained a provision that was quite unique for the early 1900s: a requirement that public school teachers be trained about drugs and alcohol and educate their students about the effects of drugs.

DOCUMENT 75: Indiana State Law (1908)

Sec. 2494. It shall be unlawful for any druggist or druggist's clerk to sell, barter, trade or give any opium, morphine or cocaine, to any person addicted to the habitual use of opium, morphine or cocaine, unless such person secure a written prescription therefore, from a licensed physician. Any person violating any provisions of this section shall, upon conviction, be fined.

. . .

Sec. 6586. Provides for teaching "the nature of alcoholic drinks and narcotics and their effect on the human system in connection with the subjects . . . regularly taught in the common schools of the state, and in all educational institutions supported wholly or in part by money received from the state.

Sec. 6587. Requires that teachers in the common schools be qualified to teach the above subjects.

Source: Indiana Annotated Statutes, 1908.

* * *

Not only did most states have anti-drug laws on the books in the early 1900s, but a number of large cities did as well. Some of these laws were part of health or sanitary codes, as in the following example of an early New York City law prohibiting the sale of opiates or cocaine without a doctor's prescription.

DOCUMENT 76: Opiate and Cocaine Prohibitions (New York City Sanitary Code, 1910)

No cocain or salts of cocain . . . and no opium or official preparations of opium, and no morphine or salts of morphine, or the derivatives of either of them, shall be sold at retail by any person in the City of New York except upon the written prescription of a licensed physician, duly authorized to practice as such or other person duly authorized by law to practice medicine and administer drugs, or perform surgery with the use of instruments.

Nothing hereinbefore mentioned, however, shall apply to compounded mixtures containing opium or morphine or their derivatives the formulas for which are given in the latest Dispensatory or National Formulary, in which said mixtures the maximum dose, as plainly stated on the label of the package as dispensed does not contain in excess of one-half a grain of powdered opium or the equivalent of its alkaloids; or to preparations for external use only, in the form of liniments, ointments, or oleates. The last-mentioned preparations shall be labeled "For External Use Only," and marked "Poison."

Source: Section 182, New York City Sanitary Code, 1910.

* * *

As of December 31, 1914, the New York City Sanitary Code was revised to add marijuana to the "habit-forming" drugs being regulated.

In a news story announcing this pending revision, the *New York Times* stressed that although marijuana use was not a large problem at the time, the increasing controls over opiate use might lead to a rise in the number of marijuana or hashish users.

DOCUMENT 77: Fear of Increasing Marijuana Use (*New York Times,* 1914)

. . . [T]he inclusion of Cannabis indica among the drugs to be sold only on prescription is only common sense. Devotees of hashish are now hardly numerous enough here to count, but they are likely to increase as other narcotics become harder to obtain.

Source: *New York Times,* July 30, 1914.

* * *

Between 1910 and 1914, there was growing concern in many urban areas about the proliferation of cocaine and opiate use. In New York City, which at that time as in the present day had the largest concentration of addicts in the nation, there was increasing pressure to enact legislation to help control the growing drug problem. Although laws already existed to control cocaine trafficking, opiate use was becoming more problematic. Led by Charles Towns and other individuals and organizations, new legislation was proposed and enacted by the New York State legislature in 1914. Called the Boylan Act after its main legislative sponsor, State Senator John Boylan, this was one of the key state laws of the time. The Boylan Act was aimed mainly at placing more controls on the dispensing of opiates and other drugs by physicians to their patients. In addition, Section 249a of the law contains one of the nation's first "civil commitment" provisions, allowing a magistrate to commit an addict to a hospital for treatment.

DOCUMENT 78: Boylan Anti-Drug Act, New York State (1914)

Sec. 245. No pharmacist, druggist or other person shall sell, have or offer for sale or give away any chloral, opium or any of its salts, alkaloids or derivatives or any compound or preparation of any of them except upon the written prescription of a duly licensed physician, veterinarian or dentist, provided that the provisions of this article shall not apply to the sale of domestic and proprietary remedies, actually sold in good faith as medicines and not for the purposes of evading the provisions of this article and provided further that such remedies and preparations do not contain more than two grains of opium, or one-fourth grain of morphine or one-fourth grain of heroin or one grain of codeine, or ten grains of chloral or their salts in one fluid ounce or if a solid preparation, in one avoirdupois ounce, nor to plasters, liniments and ointments for external use only.

Sec. 246. It shall be unlawful for any person to sell at retail or give away any of the drugs, their salts, derivatives or preparations mentioned in section 245 of this chapter except as herein provided without first receiving a written prescription signed by a duly licensed physician, veterinarian or dentist. . . . It shall be unlawful . . . to issue any such prescription . . . except after a physical examination of any person for the treatment of disease, injury or deformity. . . . Any person, other than a manufacturer of any of the drugs mentioned in section 245 or a wholesale dealer in drugs or a licensed pharmacist, licensed druggist, duly registered practicing physician, licensed veterinarian or a licensed dentist, who shall possess any of the drugs . . . shall be guilty of a misdemeanor, unless said possession is authorized by the certificate described in this section.

. . .

Sec. 249. It is unlawful for any person to sell at retail or furnish to any person other than a duly licensed physician, dentist or veterinarian, an instrument commonly known as a hypodermic syringe or an instrument commonly known as a hypodermic needle, without the written order of a duly licensed physician or veterinarian. . . . Any person or persons who sell, dispose of or give away [such an] instrument, . . . except in the manner prescribed in this section, shall be guilty of a misdemeanor.

Sec. 249a. The constant use by any person of any habit-forming drug, except under the direction and consent of a duly licensed physician, is hereby declared to be dangerous to the public health. Whenever a complaint shall be made to any magistrate that any person is addicted to the use of any habit-forming drug, without the consent of a duly licensed physician, such magistrate, after due notice and hearing, is satisfied that the complaint is founded and that the person is addicted to the use of a habit-forming drug, shall commit the person to a state, county or city hospital or institutions licensed under the state lunacy commission. Whenever the chief medical officer of such an institution shall certify to any magistrate that any person so committed has been sufficiently treated or give any other reason which is deemed adequate and sufficient, he may discharge the person so committed.

Sec. 249b. Any license . . . issued to any physician, dentist, veterinarian, pharmacist or registered nurse may be revoked by the proper officers or boards . . . upon proof that the licensee is addicted to the use of any habit-forming drug or drugs. . . . Whenever it shall appear after one year from date of revocation . . . that such licensee has fully recovered and is no longer an addict . . . such board may grant a rehearing and in its discretion reissue the license. . . .

Sec. 249c. Whenever any physician, dentist, veterinarian, pharmacist or registered nurse is convicted in a court having jurisdiction of any of the violations of this article, any officer or board having power to issue licenses . . . may, after giving such licensee reasonable notice and opportunity to be heard, revoke the same.

Sec. 249d. Any violation of any of the provisions of this article shall be deemed a misdemeanor.

Source: Chapter 363, Article 11-a, Laws of New York, enacted April 14, 1914.

* * *

News coverage on the Boylan Act stressed that it was expected that the law would result in an increased number of arrests, which indeed is what occurred. In addition, the Department of Health would be responsible for maintaining prescription records.

DOCUMENT 79: Expected Impact of Boylan Act (*New York Times*, 1914)

Commissioner of Corrections Katharine B. Davis anticipates a great increase in the number of prisoners committed to city institutions after the new law gets to work. These institutions are now full, and the Commissioner may ask for a room in a city owned building near the Criminal Court Building for male prisoners caught in the anti-drug net. At the Workhouse there is a room where women may be put, but it will be necessary to evict a number of very old women who occupy that room. These women will be allowed to stay in the chapel.

Assistant District Attorney Floyd H. Wilmot, who has charge of the prosecution of drug cases, said yesterday that the police would enforce the new law. It seemed to be the opinion in the office that the duty of the Board of Health extended beyond the mere distribution of blanks. There is the keeping of records of blanks given out and the inquiry as to sales and prescriptions. . . .

. . .

Charles B. Towns, . . . who framed the law, believes that for the time being it will not affect habitual drug users, who have secret channels in the underworld for obtaining supplies. It will, however, cut off the supply of those who in the past have broken no law to obtain drugs. Persons wanting the drugs will still be able to purchase outside of New York, and for this reason Mr. Towns believes there should be national legislation to restrict the traffic.

Source: "New Anti-Drug Law Is in Effect Today," *New York Times*, July 1, 1914.

* * *

However, the Boylan Act apparently did not control the illegal narcotics trade as successfully as the act's proponents would have hoped, as the following news report indicated two years later. Drugs were still readily available, and the addicts seemed to be getting younger, suggesting that new users were becoming addicted. This *New York Times* article quotes Dr. Ernest Bishop, an important figure from the early 20th century in promoting the view that drug addiction was a disease that required medical intervention rather than punishment.

DOCUMENT 80: Drug Problems Persist Despite New Laws (*New York Times*, 1916)

The drug evil has now reached into every corner of the city with amazing rapidity, according to testimony given at the City Hall yesterday afternoon at the first hearing of the Joint Legislative Committee appointed last Spring to investigate the habit-forming drug traffic, with a view to remedial legislation. In spite of the Boylan law, which, it was admitted, had produced many good results, it was the belief of District Attorney Francis J. Martin of the Bronx, Assistant District Attorney Albert B. Unger of Manhattan, Howard Clark Barber, Superintendent of the Society for the Prevention of Crime, and Dr. Ernest C. Bishop, in charge of the narcotic wards of the workhouse on Blackwell's island, that the number of drug addicts in this city had been increased to 200,000.

. . . Mr. Unger asserted that the present law regulating the sale of narcotics acted as a bulwark and protection for unscrupulous physicians and druggists. . . .

Mr. Unger said it generally was believed that most of the habit-forming drugs that were sold in this city were exported from this country to either Canada or Mexico and then smuggled back into the United States. District Attorney Martin of the Bronx concurred in this view.

Howard Clark Barbour suggested that the committee investigate the methods and results of the treatment of drugs victims in the hospitals where, he said he was reliably informed, a substantial number of addicts died under treatment either because of incompetence or ignorance.

"The number of addicts is increasing all the time," said Dr. Bishop. "I remember when victims sent to us were men, some of them aged, but now they are chiefly young men and boys. These victims are divided into addicts of the upper world, and addicts of the lower world.

"The addicts of the upper world are legion. They include judges, physicians, lawyers, and ministers. You have no idea of the tremendous number of addicts, and most of them have tried any number of treatments. Withdrawal of narcotic drugs is not a cure."

Dr. Bishop, when asked by Chairman Whitney if he believed narcotics should be prescribed for a man, for instance, 60 years old who had been using drugs for twenty-five years, answered in the affirmative.

"I believe a good deal of the increase in the underworld addicts," he added, "is a result of scared physicians. I believe it would be a measure of relief if you would open a supply of drugs from which an addict who is honest may get needed drugs his physician is afraid to prescribe for him. You will at least cut off the underworld. An honest man who has become an addict must have drugs to keep in condition to work and support his family, if his physician will not prescribe it for him he will surely get it through the underworld."

Dr. Bishop said the drug evil was in all our institutions, such as the Tombs and Workhouse. As long as there were men in agony because of the drug need they would get the drug if it was obtainable.

Source: "Finds Drug Evil Pervades City," *New York Times*, December 5, 1916.

* * *

Up through the 1920s, most state anti-drug laws provided that violations of the laws were misdemeanors, with fines or relatively short jail or prison terms allowed. According to the analysis of state laws contained in the 1928 review of the opium problem by Terry and Pellens, convictions under the anti-drug laws in only ten states at that time were deemed felonies.

UNIFORM OR MODEL STATE DRUG LAWS

Because of the importance of having consistent state laws, given the ease of traveling between states, it was also recognized that the enforcement of drug laws would be facilitated if all states had similar provisions. Beginning in the early 1920s and up to the present day, there have been a number of efforts to draft and recommend uniform state drug laws.[1]

Longtime Federal Bureau of Narcotics Commissioner Harry Anslinger, in the 1953 book *The Traffic in Narcotics*, described from the federal perspective the rationale for uniform state laws before and after the Harrison Act was enacted. In Anslinger's view, model uniform state laws were necessary because some state laws were not adequate for controlling drug problems.

DOCUMENT 81: Need for Uniform State Drug Laws (Harry J. Anslinger and William F. Tompkins, 1953)

At a meeting of the National Conference of Commissioners on Uniform State Laws, held in Washington, D.C., in 1932, the fifth tentative draft submitted by the subcommittee on Uniform State Laws was approved and adopted by the Conference as a model Uniform State Narcotic Act. This Act has been enacted into law, substantially as drafted, by forty-three States and the territories of Alaska, Hawaii, and Puerto Rico, and the District of Columbia. Of the five States which have not adopted the Uniform Narcotic Law, two—Pennsylvania and California—have in effect, State narcotic laws which are considered to be of comparable efficacy.

. . . it is important that we understand the reasons for uniform legislation. Unfortunately, in the twenty years which have passed since this Act was drafted, the reasons for its enactment have become obscured. As a result, despite the fact that most of the States have enacted it, the obligations of the various States under the terms of the Act have not always been fulfilled as the legal authorities who framed this Act had intended.

Prior to the enactment of any Federal statute the States which legislated against the use of narcotic drugs were impelled to do so in order to secure their citizens against injury to their health, morals, and general welfare. The very early laws were designed to eradicate the evils of opium smoking and the maintenance of opium dens. Later, however, some of the States enacted laws covering other narcotic drugs and providing various penalties for their violation, but so little knowledge of the traffic was possessed by the framers of the various acts that an examination of them revealed such a varied expression of ideas on a single subject that it could only be classed as chaotic and absurd.

When the Harrison Act was enacted by the Federal Government, it was contemplated that the authorities of the several States would accept and discharge the responsibility of investigating, detecting, and preventing the local illicit traffic conducted by the retail peddler, together with the institutional care and treatment of drug addicts within their respective jurisdictions. The expectation, however, proved to be totally unfounded. Instead, notwithstanding the limited power of the Federal Government, State officers became imbued with the erroneous impression that the problem of preventing the abuse of narcotic drugs was one exclusively cognizable by the United States Government and that the Federal law, alone, should represent all the control necessary over the illicit narcotic drug traffic. During the years from 1914 to 1932 the situation was such that very few States made any attempt to accept a just part of the burden of enacting and enforcing adequate laws to control the traffic.

. . .

This illogical, indifferent attitude not only prevented the passage of adequate laws of inestimable benefit to the State's own citizens, but it resulted in a number of the States in an almost complete failure to enforce the laws already on the statute books, even in those aspects of the crime with which only the State itself could deal. Federal courts became flooded with cases of a minor character which should have been handled in the State courts but which were not thus handled, either from lack of adequate laws or because the duties and responsibilities appeared burdensome, expensive, or distasteful. . . .

. . .

. . . the States, having supreme police power within their own boundaries to enact and enforce all laws necessary to the peace, health, morals, and general welfare of their citizens, are not hampered by the narrow limitations that restrict the Federal Government in its fight to control the illicit narcotic drug traffic. In other words, there were gaps in the Federal law which the States could and should plug. For example, the Federal law did not directly prohibit self-administration by a physician, and the Federal Government could not deprive him of his right to purchase narcotic drugs until the State had first deprived him of his license to practice his profession.

. . .

In brief, it can readily be seen that the reasons for and the need for a Uniform State Narcotic Act were both cogent and obvious. . . . This [1932] law was not perfect, nor did it present a complete solution of the narcotic problem, but it did represent a very important step toward uniformity in the laws as well as in the cooperation between the States and the Federal Government. In drafting the Uniform Act the committee had to take into consideration two Federal laws—the Harrison Act and the Narcotic Drugs Import and Export Act. While it was a fact that without these

Federal laws on the subject, the individual States would have been greatly handicapped in combating the distribution of narcotic drugs within their borders, it is important to remember that these acts were not for the purpose of exercising any police power, which is a prerogative of the State. Their validity was predicated on the power of the Federal Government to tax, to regulate interstate and foreign commerce, and to make treaties.

. . .

Provisions [of the 1932 Uniform Narcotic Drug Act] with regard to care and treatment of addicts, and search and seizure were omitted from the Act. Since it was felt that each State could better legislate on those subjects individually, and recognizing that the question of care and treatment was of vital and paramount importance and that the cure of addicts was as much a duty of the State as was the care of its insane, the committee recommended that no State delay in making an immediate and complete study of this problem. In connection therewith, the experts were in almost unanimous agreement on two points: (1) that the treatment of drug addiction was a medical and not a penal problem, and (2) that treatment looking toward the cure of addiction, without confinement in a drug-free atmosphere, was uniformly unsuccessful.

Source: Harry J. Anslinger and William F. Tompkins, *The Traffic in Narcotics* (New York: Funk and Wagnalls, 1953), 155–161.

* * *

One of the early recommendations for uniform state drug laws came from the medical establishment. In 1921 the American Medical Association (AMA) recommended that a committee be established to adopt a model state law to supplement the Harrison Act.

DOCUMENT 82: Recommendation for Uniform State Drug Laws (Committee on Narcotic Drugs of the Council on Health and Public Instruction, American Medical Association, 1921)

6. Your committee recommends that the Harrison Law be supplemented . . . by uniform state laws, in harmony with and supplemental to the Harrison law, which shall base their control of any medical abuse of narcotic drugs on those powers possessed by the states to punish crime as well as to revoke the license to practice medicine, dentistry, pharmacy or veterinary medicine.

The committee recommends . . . that it be . . . authorized to request the appointment of a Committee on Uniform State Narcotic Law by the National Conference of Commissioners on Uniform State Laws, and to cooperate with such committee . . . in preparation of such a law; it further recommends that state narcotic laws should follow the general principles set forth below:

—A model state law need not be a tax law; and in fact, the taxing feature should be abolished. Its clear purpose, like that of the federal statute, should be definitely the control of distribution of the narcotic drugs, limiting to the utmost every possible abuse. . . .

—Unnecessary duplication of records under federal and state laws should be eliminated, the state accepting the records kept under the Harrison Law. . . .

—A state law should embrace recognition of the clear purpose and intent of the Harrison Law . . . to prohibit distribution of narcotic drugs through physicians prescribing or dispensing them to addicts for self-administration. . . .

—Unlawful possession of narcotic drugs should be made "prima facie evidence" of violation of the narcotic law, as in the Harrison Law.

—Legal commitment of addicts on their own application, as well as their penal commitment, should be made equally effective in order to insure complete control of them while under treatment for the cure of their addiction.

—Provision should be made . . . for the treatment of those addicted to the use of narcotic drugs, in suitable institutions, existing or proposed for that purpose, or by private physicians . . . under the most rigid regulations.

Source: Report of the Committee on Narcotic Drugs of the Council on Health and Public Instruction, *Journal of the American Medical Association* 76, no. 24 (June 11, 1921): 1669–1671.

* * *

In March 1922 a conference was held in New York City sponsored by the committee of the AMA Council on Health and Public Instruction to discuss the development of the model state drug laws suggested the year before in the above document. Also at this conference were representatives of the American Drug Trade Conference, the American Veterinary Medical Association, the Narcotic Drug Control League, and various pharmaceutical associations.

DOCUMENT 83: Description of 1922 Meeting on Uniform State Drug Laws (Charles E. Terry and Mildred Pellens, 1928)

The purpose of the meeting . . . was "to see whether we can come to an agreement in respect to uniform State laws which shall supplement the Harrison Act in order that there may be unanimity of professional and trade cooperation back of the narcotic law."

The "model" law which was considered at this conference, followed in the main the provisions of the Harrison Act and certain regulations thereunder. The chief points of difference are included in what follows: . . .

Section 6, (2), provided that prescriptions containing codein or a preparation containing codein, could be refilled. . . .

Section 10 required a physical examination to be made by a physician, dentist, or veterinarian, prior to the prescribing or dispensing of habit-forming drugs.

Source: Charles E. Terry and Mildred Pellens, *The Opium Problem* (Bureau of Social Hygiene, 1928; reprint, Montclair, NJ: Patterson Smith Publishing, 1970), 904–905.

STATE MARIJUANA LAWS

Prior to the passage of the Marihuana Tax Act of 1937, the federal government was more interested in leaving enforcement of marijuana sale and use to the states. In the early 1930s, in lobbying for passage of a uniform narcotics law for the states, the Federal Bureau of Narcotics used the supposed marijuana "menace" to help convince states to pass the legislation.

DOCUMENT 84: Federal Bureau of Narcotics and State Marijuana Laws (Jerome Himmelstein, 1983)

. . . [T]he bureau in the 1930s attempted to limit its responsibility for day-to-day narcotics enforcement and resist proposals for federal marihuana legislation. . . . Its strategy was to have the states handle marihuana and deal with small-time narcotics offenders, while it made general policy and took care of large-scale trafficking.

The bureau sought to accomplish this governmental division of labor by getting the states to pass the Uniform Narcotic Drugs Act. The act had been under consideration for some seven years by a committee appointed by the National Conference of Commissioners on Uniform State Laws, when Commissioner Anslinger led the newly created FBN into the drafting process in 1931. He initially urged the inclusion of marihuana in the act but backed down in response to opposition from pharmaceutical companies, physicians, and the hemp industry. A final draft of the act, with a marihuana provision included only as a supplement, was approved in late 1932.

The bureau immediately began to lobby for state adoption of the act by sending its agents directly to legislators and by enlisting the help of sympathetic organizations—the Women's [*sic*] Christian Temperance Union, the World Narcotic Defense Association, the General Federation of Women's Clubs, and the Hearst press. Its efforts met with little success initially. By the end of 1934, only ten states had passed the act; opponents effectively pointed to its expense, its red tape, and its pretensions to control the medical profession and the pharmaceutical industry.

In response to this impasse, the bureau changed the thrust of its arguments and reversed its stand on the marihuana problem: Rather than insisting that the extent of marihuana use was exaggerated, it began to publicize the marihuana "menace" in its arguments for the Uniform Narcotic Drugs Act. . . . The emphasis on the marihuana menace appears to have been successful. Within a year, eighteen additional states had adopted the act, and those without previous legislation included the marihuana provision. At the same time, however, it undermined the bureau's effort to deflect pressure for federal controls. The modest increase in the attention given to marihuana as a result of the bureau's propaganda stimulated new demands for federal legislation and broke down bureaucratic resistance.

Source: Jerome Himmelstein, *The Strange Career of Marihuana* (Westport, CT: Greenwood Press, 1983), 57–58.

* * *

State laws and policies concerning marijuana have varied widely over the past 50 years, ranging from extremely punitive laws, even for marijuana possession, to those that are quite lenient. Examples of such laws are presented in subsequent parts of this book.

STATE LAWS IN THE 1950s

One of the effects of the 1951 Boggs Act, the federal law that increased penalties for drug crimes (see Part VIII), was to encourage states to pass laws that also increased penalties for drug sale and possession. At the federal level, drug policy makers understood that federal laws were not sufficient by themselves to control drug trafficking at the local level. As he had done in the early 1930s with the Uniform State Drug Laws, Commissioner Anslinger continued to urge states to replicate some of the punitive features of the Boggs Act.

DOCUMENT 85: Call for Stronger State Anti-Drug Laws (Harry J. Anslinger and William F. Tompkins, 1953)

Strong laws, good enforcement, stiff sentences, and a proper hospitalization program are the necessary foundations upon which any successful program must be predicated. . . . Probably the greatest reason for an increase in drug addiction has been the failure on the part of legislators, of police, and of other officials to observe these important fundamentals. Most important, good results can be attained by perfecting the framework of the present Federal and State laws, which are fundamentally sound.

First of all, there is no excuse for any State to have a law which is in any way weaker than the Boggs Act. . . . Several States have enacted laws duplicating the Boggs Act, with New Jersey providing a wider range in its penalties, i.e., two to fifteen years for the first offense, five to twenty-five years for the second, and ten to life for the third, with an added provision of two years to life for any offense where a minor is involved.

Source: Harry J. Anslinger and William F. Tompkins, *The Traffic in Narcotics* (New York: Funk and Wagnalls, 1953), 295–296.

* * *

It should be pointed out that Anslinger's praise for New Jersey's law in the above document was not surprising given that his co-author, William Tompkins, was the U.S. attorney for New Jersey and chairman of the Legislative Commission to Study Narcotics of the New Jersey General Assembly. In addition to New Jersey, Ohio also enacted one of the so-called "Little Boggs Acts" that provided for sentences of 2 to 15 years for a first drug possession offense, with mandatory penalties for drug sales ranging from 10 to 20 years for a first offense to 30 years to life for a third offense.

In 1956 the New Jersey legislature passed an even more stringent anti-drug law, providing for mandatory minimum sentences of 20 years for sales by an adult (over 21) to a minor (under 18) or using a youth under 18 to assist with drug distribution, and a 10-year mandatory minimum for a first sale offense.

STATE LAWS SINCE THE 1970s

The next major revision of the uniform state laws was made in response to the federal Comprehensive Drug Abuse Prevention and Control Act of 1970 (see Part X). Because that act represented a consolidation of the existing federal laws and a recodification of illegal drugs into different "schedules," it became important for states to make their anti-drug laws consistent. The following document, from the preface of the final report of the National Conference of Commissioners on Uniform State Laws, describes the goals and rationale for this 1970 set of uniform state drug laws.

DOCUMENT 86: Preface to Final Report, National Conference of Commissioners on Uniform State Laws (1970)

This Uniform Act was drafted to achieve uniformity between the laws of the several states and those of the Federal government. It has been designed to complement the new Federal narcotic and dangerous drug legislation and provide an interlocking trellis of Federal and State law to enable government at all levels to control more effectively the drug abuse problem.

. . .

Much of this major increase in drug use and abuse is attributable to the increased mobility of our citizens and their affluence. As modern America becomes increasingly mobile, drugs clandestinely manufactured or illegally diverted from legitimate channels in one part of a State are easily transported for sale to another part of that State or even to another State. . . . It becomes critical to approach not only the control of illicit and legitimate traffic in those substances at the national and international levels, but also to approach this problem at the State and local level on a uniform basis.

A main objective of this Uniform Act is to create a coordinated and codified system of drug control, similar to that utilized at the Federal level, which classifies all narcotics, marihuana, and dangerous drugs subject to control into five schedules. . . .

. . .

The Uniform Act updates and improves existing State laws and insures legislative and administrative flexibility to enable the States to cope with both present and future drug problems.

Source: Uniform Controlled Substances Act, National Conference of Commissioners on Uniform State Laws, Chicago, IL, August 1970, 3–4.

* * *

At the same time President Richard Nixon and his Department of Justice under Attorney General John Mitchell were developing the legislation that resulted in the 1970 act, federal officials were urging the National Conference of Commissioners on Uniform State Laws to adopt similar legislation for the states.

DOCUMENT 87: Need for New Uniform State Drug Laws in 1970 (Rufus King, 1972)

While comprehensive federal law was being pushed on Capitol Hill, the Department of Justice also pushed the other project promised in President Nixon's 1969 message, drafting a virtually identical measure for adoption by the states and pressuring the National Conference of Commissioners on Uniform State Laws to sponsor it. . . .

It will be recalled that a Uniform Narcotic Drug Act was promulgated by the Commissioners in 1932, approved by the American Bar Association the same year, and quickly adopted all over the nation. Subsequently, this Act was modified from time to time by innovations such as the addition of a prohibition against marijuana, and in 1966 the Commissioners sponsored a separate Model State Drug Abuse Control Act to bring local jurisdictions into line with the then-new federal campaign against so-called dangerous drugs.

. . .

In August 1970 the Commissioners approved and recommended the new Uniform Act. . . . The American Bar Association officially approved the state measure in February 1971. . . . [The Uniform Act] follows the fedeal provisions and subordinates state activities to federal policies at every important juncture.

Source: Rufus King, *The Drug Hang-up* (New York: W. W. Norton, 1972), 320–321.

* * *

An important development in the history of state drug policy was passage of the so-called Rockefeller Drug Laws in New York State in

1973. At the urging of Governor Nelson Rockefeller, the New York State legislature passed some of the most punitive state laws in the nation. These laws greatly increased penalties for the sale and possession of drugs, including a maximum life sentence for selling more than a few ounces of heroin or cocaine. Sale of any amount of these drugs was subject to a mandatory prison sentence of up to 20 years. In his annual message to the state legislature urging passage of this law, Governor Rockefeller painted a dire picture of the impact of drugs.

DOCUMENT 88: Statement on New Drug Law (Governor Nelson Rockefeller, January 3, 1973)

Virtually every poll of public concerns documents that the number one growing concern of the American people is crime and drugs coupled with an all-pervasive fear for the safety of their person and their property.

This reign of fear cannot be tolerated.

The law-abiding people of this State have the right to expect tougher and more effective action from their elected leaders to protect them from lawlessness and crime.

People are terrorized by the continued prevalence of narcotic addiction and the crime and human destruction it breeds.

People are outraged by the existence of corruption within the very law enforcement system itself.

People have lost patience with courts that dally and delay in bringing criminal elements to justice.

People are baffled and disheartened by revolving-door criminal justice and a correctional system that doesn't seem to correct. . . .

. . .

We have this choice:

—Either we can go on as we have been, with little real hope of changing the present trend;

—Or we must take those stern measures that, I have become convinced, common sense demands.

We must create an effective deterrent to the pushing of the broad spectrum of hard drugs.

In my opinion, society has no alternatives.

I therefore am proposing the following program for dealing with the illegal pushers of drugs including heroin, amphetamines, LSD, hashish and other dangerous drugs.

(1) Life Prison Sentences for All Pushers

. . .

(2) Life Sentence for Violent Crimes by Addicts

. . .

(3) Removal of Youthful Offender Protections

. . .

(4) Payment for Information on Hard Drug Pushers

. . .

(5) 100 Percent Tax on Drug Pusher Assets

Source: Governor Nelson Rockefeller, Annual Message to the New York State Legislature, January 3, 1973.

* * *

Most recently, as part of the Anti-Drug Abuse Act of 1988, Congress called for the creation of a presidential commission to develop model legislation for the states to reduce drug-related problems. The President's Commission on Model State Drug Laws was named in November 1992. Its goals were broader than just enforcing anti-drug laws and punishing drug law violators, as described in the following document.

DOCUMENT 89: Goal Statement (President's Commission on Model State Drug Laws, 1993)

. . . The Commissioners included state legislators, treatment service providers, an urban mayor, police chiefs, state attorneys general, a housing specialist, district attorneys, a state judge, prevention specialists, attorneys, and other experts.

The Commissioners developed the following mission statement:

"Our mission is to develop comprehensive model state laws to significantly reduce, with the goal to eliminate, alcohol and other drug abuse in America through effective use and coordination of prevention, education, treatment, enforcement, and corrections."

Source: President's Commission on Model State Drug Laws, *Executive Summary* (Washington, DC: The White House, December 1993), 2.

* * *

Treatment and prevention were important aspects of the commission's final report; it was meant to go beyond the usual punitive anti-drug approach.

DOCUMENT 90: Emphasis on Treatment and Prevention (President's Commission on Model State Drug Laws, 1993)

Acknowledging that alcohol and other drug abuse pervades all levels of society, this report will be strikingly different from other efforts that have urged a holy war on drug abusers. The legislative remedies offered within do not rely exclusively on punishment and deterrence to "solve" drug problems. Instead, the goal of this report is to establish a comprehensive continuum of responses and services, encompassing prevention, education, detection, treatment, rehabilitation, and law enforcement to allow individuals and communities to fully address alcohol and other drug problems. Tough sanctions are used to punish those individuals who refuse to abide by the law. More importantly, the recommended sanctions are designed to be constructive, attempting to leverage alcohol and other drug abusers into treatment, rehabilitation, and ultimately, recovery.

Source: President's Commission on Model State Drug Laws, *Executive Summary* (Washington, DC: The White House, December 1993), 1–2.

* * *

The 1993 commission developed 44 model state drug laws that tried to address many aspects of drug policy. The model laws covered such areas as asset forfeiture, eviction of drug dealers from housing, control of chemical precursors to illegal drugs, reducing illegal diversion of prescription drugs, laws on driving while intoxicated, drug-free schools and workplaces, and expanding criminal justice–based drug treatment. The commission's report was unusual in the history of American drug policy in recognizing the importance of a comprehensive and integrated approach that was not limited to law enforcement and punishment. The following document is from the conclusion of the *Executive Summary*.

DOCUMENT 91: Concluding Statement (President's Commission on Model State Drug Laws, 1993)

This final report represents a blueprint for states to address their alcohol and other drug problems in a truly comprehensive manner. This report, though comprehensive, is not offered to the states as the sole answer to all alcohol and other drug problems. A single report cannot solve every problem involving alcohol and other drugs. However, the legislation included within this final report represents a portfolio of responses that work. States are encouraged to consider the model legislation, to select from the portfolio of legislation those model statutes that might remedy a particular problem, to tailor those needed model statutes to the particular subtleties of that state, and, finally, to enact the spirit that these model statutes encompass. In most instances, the Commission is not tied to specific legislative language, but rather, it embraces the ideas, reasoning, and experience behind the recommended model state statutes.

The Commission has sought to reflect the interrelated nature of alcohol and other drug problems in its legislative responses. For example, in the nuisance abatement statute, fines against negligent property owners can be waived if the owner agrees to transfer the title of the property to a community anti-drug group or a treatment organization. In the model safe schools legislation, cooperative working agreements between school officials and law enforcement are developed to govern those instances when law enforcement is needed to address drug problems found within schools. The model criminal justice treatment statute redesigns the way in which the criminal justice and treatment systems interact to address drug-abusing offenders.

This comprehensive, interrelated approach to addressing the problems of drugs is not an exercise in simple rhetoric, but a well-seasoned basis for alcohol and other drug policy.

Source: President's Commission on Model State Drug Laws, *Executive Summary* (Washington, DC: The White House, December 1993), 18.

* * *

Part V has provided an overview of the basic development and structure of state anti-drug laws. Throughout the remainder of this book, examples of other state legislative and policy initiatives are presented as they are relevant for understanding the evolution of American drug policies.

NOTE

1. This approach is not unique to drug policy. Several commissions over the years have created model state laws in a number of policy areas.

Part VI

Marijuana Policy: The Early Years

Marijuana is one of the oldest drugs known to be used for intoxicating purposes. References to its use as a "medicine" go back several thousand years. Although there are several varieties of cannabis, it is the species *Cannabis sativa* that generally has been used for medicinal or intoxication purposes. Other species, such as *Cannabis indica,* have lower levels of the active ingredient delta-9-tetrahydrocannabinol (THC).

DOCUMENT 92: Early History of Marijuana Use (Edward M. Brecher, 1972)

. . . [M]arijuana, hemp, or cannabis is in fact a highly useful plant cultivated throughout recorded history and perhaps much earlier as well. There is only one species—its scientific name is *Cannabis sativa*—which yields both a potent drug and a strong fiber long used in the manufacture of fine linen as well as canvas and rope. The seeds are valued as birdseed and the oil, which resembles linseed oil, is valuable because paints made with it dry quickly.

. . .

A Chinese treatise on pharmacology attributed to the Emperor Shen Nung and alleged to date from 2737 B.C. contains what is usually cited as the earliest reference to marijuana. According to one tradition, it was Shen Nung who first taught his people to value cannabis as a medicine. Shen Nung, however, was a mythical figure, and the treatise was compiled much later than 2737 B.C.

The first known reference to marijuana in India is to be found in the Atharva Veda, which may date as far back as the second millennium B.C. Another quite early reference appears on certain cuneiform tablets unearthed in the Royal Library of Ashurbanipal, an Assyrian king . . . about 650 B.C.; but the cuneiform descriptions of marijuana in his library "are generally regarded as obvious copies of much older texts," says Dr. Robert P. Walton, an American physician and authority on marijuana who assembled much of the historical data here reviewed. This evidence "serves to project the origin of hashish back to the earliest beginnings of history." . . .

The ancient Greeks used alcohol rather than marijuana as an intoxicant; but they traded with marijuana-eating and marijuana-inhaling peoples. . . . Certainly Herodotus was referring to marijuana when he wrote in the fifth century B.C. that the Scythians cultivated a plant that was much like flax but grew thicker and taller; this hemp they deposited upon red-hot stones in a closed room—producing a vapor, Herodotus noted, "that no Grecian vapor-bath can surpass. The Scythians, transported with the vapor, shout aloud."

Herodotus also described people living on islands in the Araxes River, who "meet together in companies," throw marijuana on a fire, then "sit around in a circle; and by inhaling the fruit that has been thrown on, they become intoxicated by the odor, just as the Greeks do by wine; and the more fruit is thrown on, the more intoxicated they become, until they rise up and dance and betake themselves to singing." . . .

The date on which marijuana was introduced into western Europe is not known. . . . An urn containing marijuana leaves and seeds, unearthed near Berlin, Germany, is believed to date from 500 B.C.

. . .

The use of marijuana as an intoxicant also spread quite early to Africa. In South Africa, Dr. Frances Ames of the University of Cape Town reports, marijuana "was in use for many years before Europeans settled in the country and was smoked by all the non-European races, i.e. Bushmen, Hottentots and Africans. It was probably brought to the Mozambique coast from India by Arab traders and the habit, once established, spread inland."

Source: Edward M. Brecher and the Editors of Consumer Reports, *Licit and Illicit Drugs* (Boston: Little, Brown, 1972), 397–398.

* * *

Marijuana also has a long history of cultivation in the Western Hemisphere, mainly as a source of hemp fiber or rope. The extent to which the plant was also used as an intoxicant before the mid-19th century is not clear.

DOCUMENT 93: Early Marijuana History in the New World (Edward M. Brecher, 1972)

The first definite record of the marijuana plant in the New World dates from 1545 A.D., when the Spaniards introduced it into Chile. . . .

There is no record that the Pilgrims brought marijuana with them to Plymouth—but the Jamestown settlers did bring the plant to Virginia in 1611, and cultivated it for its fiber. Marijuana was introduced into New England in 1629. From then until after the Civil War, the marijuana plant was a major crop in North America. . . . In 1762, "Virginia awarded bounties for hempculture and manufacture, and imposed penalties upon those who did not produce it."

George Washington was growing hemp at Mount Vernon three years later—presumably for its fiber, though it has been argued that Washington was also concerned to increase the medicinal or intoxicating potency of his marijuana plants.

. . . At various times in the nineteenth century large hemp plantations flourished in Mississippi, Georgia, California, South Carolina, Nebraska, and other states, as well as on Staten Island, New York. The center of nineteenth-century production, however, was in Kentucky, where hemp was introduced in 1775.

Source: Edward M. Brecher and the Editors of Consumer Reports, *Licit and Illicit Drugs* (Boston: Little, Brown, 1972), 403–405.

MARIJUANA IN THE 19TH CENTURY

Marijuana has always been a controversial drug, and it has had an interesting policy history in the United States. It was a widely used medicine in the 19th century. It was the last major drug to be regulated by the federal government. As use spread in the early 1920s state and federal officials became alarmed and passed stringent anti-marijuana laws, while demonizing the drug as dangerous. At various points in the 20th century, it has been tolerated, scorned, revered, and feared. During the 1960s and 1970s there was a great increase in marijuana use and new acceptance of it as a relatively benign drug; this view spurred the enactment of various laws that decriminalized possession of marijuana for personal use. The recent passage of "medical marijuana" laws in California, Arizona, and other states has renewed the debate about the relative dangers and efficacy of marijuana.

A good overview of the early social and commercial history of marijuana in the United States through the mid-20th century was provided in the 1944 LaGuardia Committee report on the marijuana problem in New York City.

DOCUMENT 94: Beginning of Marijuana Smoking (LaGuardia Committee Report, 1944)

At the present time it can be found growing either wild or cultivated, legally or illegally, in practically all our States. Lawful cultivation is confined principally to the states of Kentucky, Illinois, Minnesota and Wisconsin. It has been estimated that not more than ten thousand acres are devoted to its legal production. . . .

Since the history of hemp cultivation in America dates back to the seventeenth century, it is exceedingly interesting, but difficult to explain, that the smoking of marihuana did not become a problem in our country until approximately twenty years ago, and that it has become an acute problem associated with a great deal of publicity only in the past ten years.

. . . The introduction into the United States of the practice of smoking marihuana has been the subject of a great deal of speculation. The most tenable hypothesis at the present time is that it was introduced by Mexicans entering our country.

Source: Mayor's Committee on Marihuana, *The Marihuana Problem in the City of New York* (Lancaster, PA: Cattell Press, 1944), 2–3.

* * *

Although marijuana was grown mostly as a source of hemp for rope fiber, the intoxicating properties of the plant's extract were widely known during the 19th century, and indeed marijuana was a widely recognized medicine for a number of purposes through the early part of the 20th century. In the following passage from his 1938 book about the history of marijuana, Dr. Robert Walton, a professor of pharmacology at the University of Mississippi School of Medicine, indicates that potent hashish was extracted from hemp fiber grown in Kentucky in the mid-19th century.

DOCUMENT 95: Extraction of Marijuana from Hemp (Robert Walton, 1938)

Hemp grown for fiber in Kentucky has been shown to contain a substantial degree of . . . potency. H. C. Wood, in 1869, prepared an alcoholic extract of hemp grown near Lexington and proceeded to test the product himself. A large dose (20 to 30 grains) produced marked effects and, on subsequent occasions, milder but definite effects were obtained with doses as low as ¼ grain. This latter dose is lower than the usual dose of the Indian extract [Indian hemp was thought to be more potent medicinally than the domestically produced plant] and was probably the result of a more than usually selective extraction. Houghton and Hamilton in 1908 concluded from animal experiments that the Kentucky hemp was fully as active as the best imported Indian product. In any event, it is clear that the potentiality of hashish abuse has always existed with this type of hemp production.

Source: Robert Walton, *Marijuana, America's New Drug Problem* (Philadelphia: J. B. Lippincott, 1938), 44.

* * *

Marijuana was widely dispensed by physicians and pharmacists during the 19th century for a variety of ills, and was listed in standard pharmaceutical reference works until 1942.

DOCUMENT 96: Early Use of Marijuana as a Medicine (Edward M. Brecher, 1972)

Between 1850 and 1937, marijuana was quite widely used in American medical practice for a wide range of conditions. The *United States Pharmacopeia* . . . admitted marijuana as a recognized medicine in 1850 under the name *Extractum Cannabis* or Extract of Hemp, and listed it until 1942. The *National Formulary* and United States *Dispensatory*, less selective, also included monographs on marijuana and cited recommendations for its use for numerous illnesses. In 1851 the United States *Dispensatory* reported:

Extract of hemp is a powerful narcotic [here meaning sleep-producing drug], causing exhilaration, intoxication, delirious hallucinations, and, in its subsequent action, drowsiness and stupor, with little effect upon the circulation. It is asserted also to act as a decided aphrodisiac, to increase the appetite, and occasionally to induce the cataleptic state. In morbid states of the system, it has been found to cause sleep, to allay spasm, to compose nervous disquietude, and to relieve pain. In these respects it resembles opium; but it differs from that narcotic in not diminishing the appetite, checking the secretions, or constipating the bowels. It is much less certain in its effects, but may sometimes be preferably employed, when opium is contraindicated by its nauseating or constipating effects, or its disposition to produce headache, and to check the bronchial secretion. The complaints in which it has been specially recommended are neuralgia, gout, rheumatism, tetanus, hydrophobia, epidemic cholera, convulsions, chorea, hysteria, mental depression, delirium tremens, insanity, and uterine hemorrhage.

Many eminent British and American physicians recommended marijuana as an effective therapeutic agent. Dr. J. Russell Reynolds, Fellow of the Royal Society and Physician in Ordinary to Her Majesty's (Queen Victoria's) Household, reported in *Lancet* in 1890, for example, that he had been prescribing cannabis for thirty years and that he considered it one of the most valuable medicines we possess.

Source: Edward M. Brecher and the Editors of Consumer Reports, *Licit and Illicit Drugs* (Boston: Little, Brown, 1972), 405.

* * *

Other distinguished physicians such as Sir William Osler (the Johns Hopkins and University of Oxford medical schools) praised marijuana for its medicinal value. Bonnie and Whitebread, in their history of marijuana control in the United States, found that the medical literature of the 19th century contained numerous reports extolling the benefits of marijuana.

DOCUMENT 97: Medical Benefits of Marijuana in the 19th Century (Richard J. Bonnie and Charles H. Whitebread, 1974)

Over one hundred articles recommending cannabis use were published in medical journals between 1840 and 1900. . . . Pharmaceutical houses soon developed preparations of cannabis and extracts, tinctures, and herb packages were readily available at any pharmacy. [However] . . . there is no evidence that these pharmaceutical preparations of cannabis, most of them imported, were used for intoxicant purposes here during the nineteenth century.

Source: Richard J. Bonnie and Charles H. Whitebread, *The Marihuana Conviction: A History of Marihuana Prohibition in the United States* (Charlottesville: University Press of Virginia, 1974), 4.

* * *

Nonetheless, the nonmedicinal use of marijuana to intoxication, although not as widespread as the use of opiates in the 19th century, was clearly known, as suggested in a *Scientific American* report from 1869.

DOCUMENT 98: Early Report of Intoxication (*The Scientific American*, 1869)

The drug hashish, the cannabis indica of the U.S. Pharmacopeia, the resinous product of hemp, grown in the East Indies and other parts of Asia, is used in those countries to a large extent for its intoxicating properties and is doubtless used in this country for the same purpose to a limited extent.

Source: The Scientific American, September 18, 1869, 183.

* * *

The following document is an excerpt from a colorful description of a hashish house, published in November 1883. This article, written by the author of an 1880 medical textbook on morphine, suggests that such smoking dens were common in large cities. The author describes his adventures smoking hashish in Victorian splendor, and the article illustrates how 19th-century drug-taking was often a middle- and upper-class phenomenon.

DOCUMENT 99: Description of a Hashish House (H. H. Kane, 1883)

"And so you think that opium-smoking as seen in the foul cellars of Mott Street and elsewhere is the only form of narcotic indulgence of any consequence in this city, and that hashish, if used at all, is only smoked occasionally and experimentally by a few scattered individuals?"

"That certainly is my opinion, and I consider myself fairly well informed."

"Well, you are far from right. . . . There is a large community of hashish smokers in this city, who are daily forced to indulge their morbid appetites, and I can take you to a house up-town where hemp is used in every conceivable form, and where the lights, sounds, odors, and surroundings are all arranged so as to intensify and enhance the effects of this wonderful narcotic."

. . .

"You will probably be greatly surprised at many things you will see to-night," he said, "just as I was when I was first introduced into the place by a friend. I have travelled over most of Europe, and have smoked opium in every joint in America, but never saw anything so curious as this, nor experienced any intoxication so fascinating yet so terrible as that of hashish."

"Are the habitués of this place of the same class as those who frequent the opium-smoking dives?"

"By no means. They are about evenly divided between Americans and foreigners; indeed, the place is kept by a Greek, who has invested a great deal of money in it. All the visitors, both male and female, are of the better classes, and absolute secrecy is the rule. The house has been opened about two years, I believe, and the number of regular habitués is daily on the increase."

"Are you one of the number?"

"I am, and find the intoxication far pleasanter and less hurtful than that from opium. . . ."

We paused before a gloomy-looking house, entered the gate, and passed up the steps. The windows were absolutely dark, and the entranceway looked dirty and desolate. Four pulls at the bell, a pause, and one more pull were followed by a few moments' silence, broken suddenly by the sound of falling chain, rasping bolt, and the grinding of a key in the lock. The outer door was cautiously opened, and at a word from my companion we passed into the vestibule. The outer door was carefully closed by some one whom I could not distinguish in the utter darkness. A moment later the inner door was opened, and never shall I forget the impression produced by the sudden change from total darkness to the strange scene that met my eyes. The dark vestibule was the boundary line separating the cold, dreary streets and the ordinary world from a scene of Oriental magnificence.

. . .

"Hashish eaters and smokers in the East . . . always, prior to indulging in the drug, surrounded themselves with the most pleasing sounds, faces, forms, etc."

"I see," I answered, dreamily. "But what is there behind those curtains that I see moving now and again?" The heavy curtains just opposite where we lay seemed to shut in an alcove.

"There are several small rooms there," said my companion, "shut off from this room by the curtains you see move. Each is magnificently fitted up, I am told. They are reserved for persons, chiefly ladies, who wish to avoid every possibility of detection, and at the same time enjoy their hashish and watch the inmates of this room."

"Are there many ladies of good social standing who come here?"

"Very many. Not the cream of the *demi-monde*, understand me, but *ladies*. Why, there must be at least six hundred in this city alone who are habitués. Smokers from different cities, Boston, Philadelphia, Chicago, and especially New Orleans, tell me that each city has its hemp retreat, but none so elegant as this."

Source: H. H. Kane, "A Hashish-House in New York," *Harper's Monthly* 67 (November 1883): 944–949. Reprinted in H. Wayne Morgan, *Yesterday's Addicts: American Society and Drug Abuse, 1865–1920* (Norman: University of Oklahoma Press, 1974).

THE EARLY 20TH CENTURY

During the first part of the 20th century, so-called tea-pads continued to be a favored means of distributing and smoking marijuana in New York City. The 1944 LaGuardia Committee report described these pads in terms similar to those used by Kane.

DOCUMENT 100: Settings of Marijuana Smoking (LaGuardia Committee Report, 1944)

There are two channels for the distribution of marihuana cigarettes—the independent peddler and the "tea-pad." From general observations, conversations with "pad" owners, and discussions with peddlers, the investigators estimated that there were about 500 "tea-pads" in Harlem and at least 500 peddlers.

A "tea-pad" is a room or an apartment in which people gather to smoke marihuana. . . . It is our impression that the landlord, the agent, the superintendent or the janitor is aware of the purposes for which the premises are rented.

The "tea-pad" is furnished according to the clientele it expects to serve. Usually, each "tea-pad" has comfortable furniture, a radio, victrola or, as in most instances, a rented nickelodeon. The lighting is more or less uniformly dim, with blue predominating. An incense burner is considered part of the furnishings. The walls are frequently decorated with pictures of nude subjects suggestive of perverted sexual practices. The furnishings, as described, are believed to be essential as a setting for those participating in smoking marihuana.

Most "tea-pads" have their trade restricted to the sale of marihuana. Some places did sell marihuana and whisky, and a few places also served as houses of prostitution. Only one "tea-pad" was found which served as a house of prostitution, and in which one could buy marihuana, whisky and opium.

The marihuana smoker derives greater satisfaction if he is smoking in the presence of others. His attitude in the "tea-pad" is that of a relaxed individual, free from the anxieties and cares of the realities of life. The "tea-pad" takes on the atmosphere of a very congenial social club. The smoker readily engages in conversation with strangers, discussing freely his pleasant reactions to the drug and philosophizing on subjects pertaining to life in a manner which, at times, appears to be out of keeping with his intellectual level. A constant observation was the extreme willingness to share and puff on each other's cigarettes. A boisterous, rowdy atmosphere did not prevail and on the rare occasions when there appeared signs indicative of a belligerent attitude on the part of a smoker, he was ejected or forced to become more tolerant and quiescent. One of the most interesting setups of a "tea-pad," which was clearly not along orthodox lines from the business point of view, was a series of pup tents arranged on a roof-top in Harlem. Those present proceeded to smoke their cigarettes in the tents. When the desired effect of the drug had been obtained they all emerged into the open and engaged in a discussion of their admiration of the stars and beauties of nature.

Because of the possibility of spreading disease, note should be taken of what seems to be a custom known as "pick-up" smoking. It is an established practice whereby a marihuana cigarette is lit and after one or two inhalations is passed on to the next person. This procedure is repeated until all present have had an opportunity to take a puff or two on the cigarette.

Occasionally a "tea-pad" owner may have peddlers who sell their wares in other localities and at the same time serve as procurers for those who wish to smoke marihuana on the premises.

Source: Mayor's Committee on Marihuana, *The Marihuana Problem in the City of New York* (Lancaster, PA: Cattell Press, 1944), 9–11.

* * *

Brecher describes the easy commercial availability of the drug in Baltimore in the late 19th century.

DOCUMENT 101: Easy Availability of Marijuana (Edward M. Brecher, 1972)

The ready availability of hashish in candy form in Baltimore was reported in 1894 by Dr. George Wheelock Grover in his book, *Shadows Lifted or Sunshine Restored in the Horizon of Human Lives: A Treatise on the Morphine, Opium, Cocaine, Chloral, and Hashish Habits*: "Once while passing down the leading business street in Baltimore, I saw upon a sign above my head, Gungawalla Candy, Hashish Candy. I purchased a box of the candy and, while waiting with two or three medical friends, . . . determined that I would experiment upon myself [and] test the power of this drug. I took a full dose at 11 o'clock in the forenoon." Hashish taken orally is much slower-acting than smoked hashish, and Dr. Grover felt nothing for about three hours. Then the drug "manifested its peculiar witchery with scarcely prelude or warning."

Source: Edward M. Brecher and the Editors of Consumer Reports, *Licit and Illicit Drugs* (Boston: Little, Brown, 1972), 409.

* * *

It was during the period 1910–1920 that marijuana began to emerge as a more popular drug and to cause concern among law enforcement and other government agencies. Two circumstances appear to have driven the growing attention toward marijuana. First, an influx of marijuana smuggling from Mexico and Cuba into some southern states, notably Texas and Louisiana, began to arouse much concern. Second, passage of the Eighteenth Amendment prohibiting the sale of alcohol and the Volstead Act of 1920 made it much more difficult and expensive to obtain alcoholic beverages. This served to increase the popularity of the relatively inexpensive marijuana. Through the 1920s and up to passage of the Marihuana Tax Act of 1937, the first federal antimarijuana legislation, media and government attention toward marijuana began to center on its use by Mexican laborers and the fears that they would spread the drug to youth and other vulnerable populations. Between 1914 and 1931, 29 states passed laws banning the nonmedical sale and use of marijuana.

DOCUMENT 102: Spread of Marijuana Use Through the 1920s (Richard J. Bonnie and Charles H. Whitebread, 1974)

Druggists in Houston reported in 1917 that their marihuana purchasers were no longer predominantly Mexican, but increasingly white—"sporting" women (prostitutes), gamblers, pimps, and "hop heads," some of whom were allegedly "having difficulty in obtaining their usual supply of dope." In Galveston the story was much the same. One druggist characterized his marihuana clientele as "Mexicans, a low class of whites, and East Indians coming off the boats." Another referred to "Mexicans, Negroes, and chauffeurs, and a low class of whites such as those addicted to the use of habit-forming drugs, and hangers-on of the underworld."

Source: Richard J. Bonnie and Charles H. Whitebread, *The Marihuana Conviction: A History of Marihuana Prohibition in the United States* (Charlottesville: University Press of Virginia, 1974), 43.

* * *

Concern over marijuana smuggling and use in New Orleans was exacerbated by a series of newspaper articles in the mid-1920s about the influx of large amounts of marijuana from Mexico and Cuba. In his 1938 book, Robert Walton characterized New Orleans as a center for the spread of marijuana use among the local population, and marijuana was a major social problem for the local authorities. There was particular concern about the use of this drug among school children.

DOCUMENT 103: Marijuana Problems in New Orleans (Robert Walton, 1938)

Verifications came in by the hundreds from harassed parents, teachers, neighborhood pastors, priests, welfare workers and club women. Warrington House for boys was full of children who had become habituated to the use of cannabis. The superintendent of the Children's Bureau reported that there were many problem children there who had come under the influence and two who had run away because they couldn't get their "muggles" at the Bureau. The Director of Kingsley House for boys received many pleas from fathers of boys who had come under the influence and were charged with petty crimes. After personally seeing these boys in an hysterical condition or on the well-known "laughing jags," the director termed the situation decidedly grave. The Waif's Home, at this time, was reputedly full of children, both white and colored, who had been brought in under the influence of the drug. Marihuana cigarettes could be bought almost as readily as sandwiches. Their cost was two for a quarter. The children solved the problem of cost by pooling pennies among the members of a group and then passing the cigarettes from one to another, all the puffs being carefully counted.

The result of these investigations ended in a wholesale arrest of more than 150 persons. Approximately one hundred underworld dives, soft-drink establishments, night clubs, grocery stores, and private homes were searched in the police raid. Addicts, hardened criminals, gangsters, women of the streets, sailors of all nationalities, bootleggers, boys and girls—many flashily dressed in silks and furs, others in working clothes—all were rounded up in the net which Captain Smith and his squad had set.

. . . Notwithstanding the thoroughness with which this police roundup was carried out, it did not entirely eradicate in one stroke a vice which had already become so well-established. During the next few years New Orleans experienced a crime wave which unquestionably was greatly aggravated by the influence of this drug habit. . . . Dr. W. B. Graham, State Narcotic Officer, declared in 1936 that 60 per cent of the crimes committed in New Orleans were by marihuana users.

Source: Robert Walton, *Marijuana, America's New Drug Problem* (Philadelphia: J. B. Lippincott, 1938).

* * *

Various exposés led to the passing of fairly stringent anti-marijuana legislation in Louisiana in 1924. During the next ten years, many arrests were made for marijuana sale or possession in New Orleans, and local officials continued to blame marijuana for much of the local crime.

DOCUMENT 104: Louisiana Anti-Marijuana Law (1924)

Section 1. Be it enacted by the Legislature of Louisiana, That no person shall possess, sell, dispose of, transport, deliver, in any form whatever in the State of Louisiana, the plant known as Marajuana [*sic*], or any of its derivatives, either dried, or in the form of cigarettes, tobacco or any other way whatsoever.

Section 2. No person shall possess, sell, deliver, dispose of or manufacture any cigarette, tobacco, or other smoking or chewing or snuffing article which either in whole or part contains any plant either in the dried form or otherwise of the Mexican plant known as Marajuana.

Section 3. That any person who shall violate any of the provisions of this act shall be guilty of a misdemeanor, and upon conviction shall be fined not less than fifty dollars, nor more than one thousand dollars and imprisoned in the Parish jail for not less than thirty days nor more than six months.

Section 4. The provisions of this act shall not be construed to apply to the sale, distribution, giving away, dispensing or possession of preparations or remedies which do not contain more than one-half grain of the solid extract of Cannabis Indica, Cannabis America or Marajuana or its equivalent to one fluid ounce, or to liniments, ointments or other preparations which are prepared for external use only; provided that such remedies and preparations are prescribed, sold, distributed, given away, dispensed or possessed as medicines and not to evade the purpose of this act.

Source: Act No. 41, House Bill No. 275, Louisiana Legislature, July 8, 1924.

* * *

The genesis of increased attention toward marijuana can also be traced to the influx of Mexican immigrants and farm workers into the West during the early 1900s. Marijuana was readily available in many areas of Texas, New Mexico, and Arizona after 1910, and as a large influx of Mexican farm laborers began to settle in the Rocky Mountain states, newspaper stories about the dangers of marijuana smoking appeared. Between 1915 and 1930, most of the western states passed laws banning the use or sale of marijuana. In general, the public image of the Mexican immigrant smoking marijuana and committing crimes was clearly a driving force behind passage of these laws.

DOCUMENT 105: Fears about Marijuana Use by Mexicans (LaGuardia Committee Report, 1944)

It is accepted that in Mexico marihuana smoking is an old, established practice. Therefore, it would appear logical to assume that Mexican laborers crossing our border into the Southwest carried this practice with them. Having used marihuana in their native land, they found it natural to continue smoking it in the new country, and planted it for personal consumption. Once available, it was soon made use of by our citizens. . . .

Believing that marihuana smoking might be deleterious, and knowing it to be widespread, federal and municipal governments, private individuals, and such agencies as the Opium Advisory Association, the International Narcotic Education Association and others investigated the subject. These investigative organizations have contributed a great deal of data and pertinent information to the knowledge of the use of marihuana.

The mass of information so obtained when untangled can be summed up with the general statement that a majority of investigators are of the opinion that marihuana smoking is deleterious, although a minority maintain that it is innocuous. The majority believe that marihuana smoking is widespread among school children; that the dispensers of the drug are organized to such an extent that they encourage the use of marihuana in order to create an ever-increasing market; that juvenile delinquency is directly related to the effects of the drug; that it is a causative factor in a large percentage of our major crimes and sexual offenses; and that physical and mental deterioration are the direct result of the prolonged habit of smoking marihuana.

As a result of these official and semi-official conclusions in regard to the disastrous effects produced by this habit, the newspapers and magazines of our country have given it wide publicity.

Source: Mayor's Committee on Marihuana, *The Marihuana Problem in the City of New York* (Lancaster, PA: Cattell Press, 1944), 3.

* * *

Marijuana smoking was of particular concern along the Rio Grande border of Texas, where its use was popular among Mexicans, racial minorities, and lower-class whites. As early as 1914 El Paso, Texas, passed a law making sale and possession of marijuana illegal. In 1919 and then 1923, the Texas state legislature passed laws prohibiting the nonmedical transfer and possession of marijuana. An El Paso police captain attributed violent behavior to the use of marijuana.

DOCUMENT 106: Quote from Texas Police Captain (1923)

I have had almost daily experience with the users of [marijuana] for the reason that when they are addicted to the use they become very violent, especially when they become angry and will attack an officer even if a gun is drawn on him, they seem to have no fear, I have also noted that when under the influence of this weed they have abnormal strength and that it will take several men to handle one man where under ordinary circumstances one man could handle him with ease. [Marijuana produces a] lust for blood, [the user is] insensitive to pain . . . [and has] superhuman strength when detained or hindered from doing whatever he is attempting to do.

Source: Quoted in Richard J. Bonnie and Charles H. Whitebread, *The Marihuana Conviction: A History of Marihuana Prohibition in the United States* (Charlottesville: University Press of Virginia, 1974), 34.

* * *

This lurid account of the effects of marijuana is quite similar to earlier descriptions by law enforcement officers of blacks under the influence of cocaine (see Part I). In most western states during this period, anti-marijuana laws were passed with very little publicity or debate. However, by the early 1930s, concern over marijuana had heightened. The *San Antonio Light* reported on the passage of a new Texas law in 1931 prohibiting possession of marijuana.

DOCUMENT 107: News Report on New Marijuana Law (*San Antonio Light*, 1931)

At last the state legislature had taken a definitive step toward suppression of traffic in a dangerous and insanity-producing narcotic easily compounded of a weed (marihuana) indigenous to this section. . . . This newspaper has urged the passage of prohibitory legislation and is gratified that the solons at Austin have acted, even if tardily, in the suppression of traffic in a drug which makes the addict frequently a dangerous or homicidal maniac.

Source: *San Antonio Light* editorial, May 4, 1931, quoted in Richard J. Bonnie and Charles H. Whitebread, *The Marihuana Conviction: A History of Marihuana Prohibition in the United States* (Charlottesville: University Press of Virginia, 1974), 40.

* * *

By the late 1920s anti-marijuana legislation had been passed in a number of midwestern and eastern states as well, largely in response to fears about spread of the drug among the underclass and immigrant groups. By 1927, 15 states had enacted laws against the sale or possession of marijuana (in contrast, 47 states had laws against opium, 37 against cocaine, 36 against morphine, and 30 against heroin by 1927 [Terry and Pellens, Appendix VI]). These laws tended to treat marijuana sale and possession equally. Examples of two of these state laws follow.

DOCUMENT 108: New Mexico Anti-Marijuana Law (1923)

Sec. 1. It shall be unlawful to import into the State of New Mexico cannibas indica, also known as hashish and mariguana [*sic*] in any form or any preparation or derivative thereof; Provided, That cannabis indica . . . may be imported for medicinal purposes only, and then only by licensed pharmacists and licensed physicians of the State of New Mexico.

Sec. 2. That if any person shall fraudulently or knowingly import or bring into the State of New Mexico, or assist in so doing, any cannabis indica or any preparation or derivative thereof contrary to law, or shall receive, conceal or in any manner facilitate the transportation or concealment of such cannabis indica or preparation or derivative thereof, after importation, . . . the offender shall be fined in any sum not exceeding $500 and not less than $100, or by imprisonment for any time not exceeding three years and not less than one year, or both. . . .

Sec. 3. It shall be unlawful for any person, association or corporation. . . . to plant, cultivate, produce, sell, barter or give any cannabis indica, be it known by whatever name, or preparation or derivative thereof, or offer any such cannabis indica, or preparation or derivative thereof for sale, gift, barter or trade; Provided, nothing in this section shall be held to apply to such sale, gift, barter or trade of cannabis indica by licensed physicians, or licensed pharmacists upon the written prescription of regular licensed physicians, when the same is intended for medicinal or scientific purposes only.

Sec. 4. Any person violating any of the provisions of the preceding section shall, for the first offense, be imprisoned for a period of not less than one year nor more than three years, and for the second and any subsequent offense shall be imprisoned for not less than three years and not more than five years.

Sec. 5. That it is necessary for the preservation of the public peace and safety of the inhabitants of the State of New Mexico that the provisions of this Act shall become effective at the earliest possible time; therefore, an emergency is hereby declared to exist and this act shall take effect and be in full force and effect from and after its passage and approval.

Source: H.B. No. 56, Ch. 42, New Mexico, March 7, 1923.

* * *

The Colorado law, like the earlier Louisiana law (Document 104), still allowed small amounts of marijuana to be sold in patent medicines.

DOCUMENT 109: Colorado Anti-Marijuana Law (1927)

Sec. 1. That Cannabis Indica, or Cannabis Sativa, commonly known as Indian Hemp, Hasheesh, or Marijuana, is hereby found and declared to be a habit-forming drug, the unrestricted use of which is injurious to the wellbeing of the users.

Sec. 2. That from and after the passage of this Act the growing, possession, sale or gift of Cannabis Indica or any derivative thereof, in any form or compound, shall be prohibited, Provided that the production, possession and sale of Cannabis Indica may be permitted under the following conditions:

FIRST: Cannabis Indica may be grown and the product sold by the grower alone, under rules and regulations consistent with this Act, to be formulated by the Board of Health of the State of Colorado, the sale by the grower to be restricted to regularly established manufacturing or wholesale druggists.

SECOND: Wholesale and manufacturing druggists may sell Cannabis Indica and the derivatives and compounds thereof to retail druggists who either are or who regularly employ licensed or registered pharmacists under the laws of the State of Colorado.

THIRD: Retail druggists may sell Cannabis Indica and derivatives and compounds thereof only upon original prescription of a physician regularly licensed to practice medicine in the State of Colorado, and such prescription may not be refilled or used a second time.

PROVIDED, FURTHER, that nothing herein contained shall prohibit the sale of Cannabis Indica or derivatives thereof when compounded with other drugs or medicines in which the amount of Cannabis Indica or any derivative thereof shall not exceed one half grain solid extract or its equivalent to one fluid ounce of solution in which it is contained or when it shall not exceed one half grain solid extract or its equivalent to one ounce, avoirdupois weight, of total with which it is included, in solid or semi-solid form, and only such fluids, solids, and semi-solid substances containing Cannabis Indica or a derivative thereof, are prepared for and by reason of their composition suitable for external use only.

Sec. 3. Any person who violates the terms of this Act shall be guilty of a misdemeanor and on conviction thereof shall be punished by a fine of not less than Fifty Dollars or more than Three Hundred Dollars, or by imprisonment in the County jail for not less than one month nor more than six months or by both fine and imprisonment, in the discretion of the Court.

. . .

Sec. 5. The General Assembly hereby finds and declares this Act to be necessary for the immediate preservation of the public peace, health and safety.

Sec. 6. In the opinion of the General Assembly an emergency exists wherefor this Act shall take effect and be in force from and after its passage.

Source: H.B. No. 477, Ch. 95, Colorado, March 21, 1927.

* * *

The substantial influx of Mexican laborers into the industrial cities of the Midwest in the 1920s was often accompanied by law enforcement crackdowns against these groups, discrimination, and newspaper stories linking crime and marijuana smoking.

DOCUMENT 110: Comments of Illinois Law Enforcement Official (1927)

There are about 7,000 Mexicans in Gary, 10,000 in Indiana Harbor, and 8,000 in South Chicago. . . . The Mexicans depend on the steel mills, railroads, and construction gangs for employment. Many are drifters when slack labor conditions prevail. . . . Twenty-five percent of these Mexicans smoke marijuana. In fact, many of them make their living by raising and peddling the drug.

Source: Memo from Arthur E. Paul (Chief, Chicago Office of U.S. Department of Agriculture, Food, Drug, and Insecticide Administration) to Chief, Central District, June 27, 1927, quoted in Richard J. Bonnie and Charles H. Whitebread, *The Marihuana Conviction: A History of Marihuana Prohibition in the United States* (Charlottesville: University Press of Virginia, 1974), 46.

* * *

Within a short time, editorials in the *Chicago Tribune* were pushing the Illinois state legislature to enact anti-marijuana legislation. A June 1929 article in the newspaper reported the following.

DOCUMENT 111: *Chicago Tribune* Article on Marijuana Problem (1929)

The number of addicts is growing alarmingly according to authorities, because of the ease with which marihuana can be obtained. The habit was introduced a dozen years ago or so by Mexican laborers . . . but it has become widespread among American youths . . . even among school children. . . . There being no legal ban such as makes other drugs scarce, "loco weed" is cheap. The rush of its popularity in Chicago and all over the country since the coming of Prohibition is partly explained by the price of cigarettes, 3 for 50 cents or at most 30 cents apiece.

Source: Quoted in Richard J. Bonnie and Charles H. Whitebread, *The Marihuana Conviction: A History of Marihuana Prohibition in the United States* (Charlottesville: University Press of Virginia, 1974), 47.

* * *

By the late 1920s, sensational tales of the effects of marijuana were becoming common. The following news story appeared in the *New York Times* on July 6, 1927.

DOCUMENT 112: Report about Marijuana Tragedy (*New York Times,* 1927)

A widow and her four children have been driven insane by eating the Marijuana plant, according to doctors, who say that there is no hope of saving the children's lives and that the mother will be insane for the rest of her life.

The tragedy occurred while the body of the father, who had been killed, was still in a hospital.

The mother was without money to buy other food for the children, whose ages ranged from 3 to 15, so they gathered some herbs and vegetables growing in the yard for their dinner. Two hours after the mother and children had eaten the plants, they were stricken. Neighbors, hearing outbursts of crazed laughter, rushed to the house to find the entire family insane. Examination revealed that the narcotic Marijuana was growing among the garden vegetables.

Source: New York Times, July 6, 1927.

* * *

By the early 1920s federal officials were beginning to take note of the use of marijuana by Mexicans in the southwestern United States and among the "criminal class" and youth in New Orleans.

DOCUMENT 113: Federal Concern about Marijuana in the 1920s (Jerome Himmelstein, 1983)

Reports on marihuana by the U.S. Department of Agriculture in 1917 and the U.S. Canal Zone authorities in 1925 cite numerous accounts by law enforcement officials and newspapers in the Southwest regarding the connections between marihuana, Mexicans, and violence. The brief legislative discussions that preceded the passage of antimarihuana legislation in numerous southwestern and western states often made pointed references to the Mexican origins and violent effects of the drug. California crime studies in the 1920s noted the high rates of crime and delinquency among Mexicans, and the state's narcotics reports identified marihuana as a Mexican drug. . . .

. . .

It was the New Orleans–Southwest stereotype that insinuated itself into the perceptions of federal narcotics officials. The Wickersham study [a 1931 national report on crime that found high rates of crime among Mexicans, including violent crime] and the 1917 Department of Agriculture investigation made their way into the bureau's [Federal Bureau of Narcotics] files, and a New Orleans FBN agent forwarded Stanley's article [a 1920s report by the New Orleans district attorney that blamed marihuana for violent crime] to his superiors in Washington. FBN Commissioner Harry Anslinger reported that his first perceptions of marihuana were based on reports from southwestern and western states where there was concern about the behavior of Mexicans who "sheriffs and local police departments claimed got loaded on the stuff and caused a lot of trouble, stabbings, assaults, and so on."

Source: Jerome Himmelstein, *The Strange Career of Marihuana* (Westport, CT: Greenwood Press, 1983), 51–52, 53–54.

FEDERAL OFFICIALS TAKE NOTICE: THE 1937 MARIHUANA TAX ACT

Despite the considerable attention paid to marijuana by the local media in cities, it was not until the mid-1930s that the U.S. government began to identify this drug as a major problem requiring federal intervention. Congress eventually passed the Marihuana Tax Act of 1937. This law, modeled after the Harrison Act of 1914, required physicians or pharmacists who prescribed or dispensed marijuana to register with federal authorities and pay an annual tax or license fee. Anyone who grew, imported, prescribed, or dispensed marijuana was also required to register with federal tax authorities, and those who did not register or pay the required tax became subject to criminal penalties. Indeed, the 1931 annual report on drugs of the U.S. Treasury Department played down the dangers of marijuana use.

DOCUMENT 114: U.S. Treasury Department Annual Report (1931)

A great deal of public interest has been aroused by newspaper articles appearing from time to time on the evils of the abuse of marijuana, or Indian hemp, and more attention has been focused on specific cases reported of the abuse of the drug than would otherwise have been the case. This publicity tends to magnify the extent of the evil and lends color to the inference that there is an alarming spread of the improper use of the drug, whereas the actual increase in such use may not have been inordinately large.

Source: U.S. Treasury Department, *Traffic in Opium and Other Dangerous Drugs for the Year Ended December 31, 1931* (Washington, D.C.: U.S. Government Printing Office, 1932), 51.

* * *

Interestingly, this perspective did not seem to hold at the Treasury Department for very long, and soon its Bureau of Narcotics began using anecdotes of particularly egregious drug-related events to convince legislators and the public that the problem had worsened. Consider these rather dramatic passages from a 1937 article by Bureau Commissioner Harry Anslinger, written to coincide with Congressional debate over the new anti-marijuana legislation during the summer of 1937, and widely distributed.

DOCUMENT 115: Dangers of Marijuana (Harry Anslinger and Courtney Cooper, 1937)

The sprawled body of a young girl lay crushed on the sidewalk the other day after a plunge from the fifth story of a Chicago apartment house. Everyone called it suicide, but actually it was murder. The killer was a narcotic known to America as marijuana, and to history as hashish. It is a narcotic used in the form of cigarettes, comparatively new to the United States and as dangerous as a coiled rattlesnake.

How many murders, suicides, robberies, criminal assaults, holdups, burglaries, and deeds of maniacal insanity it causes each year, especially among the young, can be only conjectured. The sweeping march of its addiction has been so insidious that, in numerous communities, it thrives almost unmolested largely because of official ignorance of its effects.

Here indeed is the unknown quantity among narcotics. No one can predict its effect. No one knows, when he places a marijuana cigarette to his lips, whether he will become a philosopher, a joyous reveler in a musical heaven, a mad insensate, a calm philosopher, or a murderer.

That youth has been selected by the peddlers of this poison as an especially fertile field makes it a problem of serious concern to every man and woman in America.

[Descriptions follow of other horrible incidents linked to smoking marijuana.]

. . .

. . . there has been a race between the spread of marijuana and its suppression. Unhappily, so far, marijuana has won by many lengths. The years 1935 and 1936 saw its most rapid growth in traffic. But at least we now know what we are facing. We know its history, its effects, and its potential victims. Perhaps with the spread of this knowledge the public may be aroused sufficiently to conquer the menace. Every parent owes it to his children to tell them of the terrible effects of marijuana to offset the enticing "private information" which these youths may have received. There must be constant enforcement and equally constant education against this enemy which has a record of murder and terror running through the centuries.

. . .

It began with the whispering of vendors in the Southwest that marijuana would perform miracles for those who smoked it, giving them a feeling of physical strength and mental power, stimulation of the imagination, the ability to be "the life of the party." The peddlers preached also of the weed's capabilities as a "love potion." Youth, always adventurous, began to look into these claims and found some of them true, not knowing that this was only half the story. They were not told that addicts may often develop a delirious rage during which they are temporarily and violently insane; that this insanity may take the form of a desire for self-destruction or a persecution complex to be satisfied only by the commission of some heinous crime.

. . .

But to crush this traffic we must first squarely face the facts. Unfortunately while every state except one has laws to cope with the traffic, the powerful right arm which could support these states has been all but impotent. I refer to the United States government. There has been no national law against the growing, sale, or possession of marijuana.

As this is written a bill to give the federal government control over marijuana has been introduced in Congress by Representative Robert L. Doughton of North Carolina, Chairman of the House Ways and Means Committee. . . .

The passage of such a law, however, should not be the signal for the public to lean back, fold its hands, and decide that all danger is over. America now faces a condition in which a new, although ancient, narcotic has come to live next door to us, a narcotic that does not have to be smuggled into the country. This means a job of unceasing watchfulness by every police department and by every public-spirited civic organization. It calls for campaigns of education in every school, so that children will not be deceived by the wiles of peddlers, but will know of the insanity[,] the disgrace, the horror which marijuana can bring to its victim. . . .

Source: Harry Anslinger and Courtney Cooper, "Marijuana: Assassin of Youth," *American Magazine* (July 1937): 19, 150.

* * *

In the several years leading up to passage of the 1937 Marihuana Tax Act, Commissioner Anslinger and the Federal Bureau of Narcotics began expressing increasing concern over marijuana and pressed legislation against its sale and possession at the state and federal levels. Because marijuana was still legal under federal law, Anslinger made it a priority to convince states to enact stronger laws against the drug, and to adopt uniform state laws. By 1935 the bureau was now identifying marijuana as a major problem in need of strong state enforcement.

It is interesting that 20 years later, Anslinger seemed to have softened his views somewhat. In Congressional hearings preceding the enactment of the 1956 Narcotic Control Act, Anslinger's testimony before Senator Price Daniel's Subcommittee on Improvements in the Federal Criminal Code of the Committee on the Judiciary seemed to play down somewhat the dangers of marijuana relative to opiates.

DOCUMENT 116: Congressional Testimony by Harry Anslinger (1956)

When Mr. Anslinger appeared before the Senate subcommittee which was investigating the illicit drug traffic in 1955 under the guidance of Senator Price Daniel, there were only a few offhand discussions of marihuana. Mr. Anslinger observed that the Bureau in its national survey was "trying to keep away from the marihuana addict, because he is not a true addict." The real problem, he said, was the heroin addict. Senator Daniel thereupon remarked:

"Now, do I understand it from you that, while we are discussing marihuana, the real danger there is that the use of marihuana leads many people eventually to the use of heroin, and the drugs that do cause complete addiction; is that true?"

Mr. Anslinger agreed: "That is the great problem and our great concern about the use of marihuana, that eventually if used over a long period, it does lead to heroin addiction."

Senators Welker and Daniel pursued the subject, and Mr. Anslinger, when prompted, agreed that marihuana was dangerous. Senator Welker finally asked this question:

"Is it or is it not a fact that the marihuana user has been responsible for many of our most sadistic, terrible crimes in this nation, such as sex slayings, sadistic slayings, and matters of that kind?"

Mr. Anslinger hedged: "There have been instances of that, Senator. We have had some rather tragic occurrences by users of marihuana. It does not follow that all crime can be traced to marihuana. There have been many brutal crimes traced to marihuana, but I would not say that it is a controlling factor in the commission of crimes."

Source: Quoted in Alfred R. Lindesmith, *The Addict and the Law* (Bloomington: Indiana University Press, 1965), 23.

* * *

As has occurred periodically with other drugs, the federal government began framing the legislative and policy debate to emphasize the dangers of marijuana to youth. During the hearings on the 1937 Marihuana Tax Act, one speaker made the following statement.

DOCUMENT 117: From Hearings on Marihuana Tax Act (1937)

[Marihuana] is now being used extensively by high school children. . . . The fatal marihuana cigarette must be recognized as a deadly drug and American children must be protected against it. . . . The great majority of indulgers are ignorant and inexperienced youngsters. . . . We have had numerous reports of school children and young people using cigarettes made from this weed. . . . The National Congress of Parents and Teachers . . . is deeply concerned with increasing use of marihuana by children and youth.

Source: Quoted in Jerome Himmelstein, *The Strange Career of Marijuana* (Westport, CT: Greenwood Press, 1983), 66.

* * *

Although the media gave marijuana little publicity during the late 1920s and early 1930s, the emerging importance placed by the Bureau of Narcotics on anti-marijuana legislation resulted in intensified magazine coverage in the two years preceding passage of the Tax Act. Many of these articles were prompted or assisted by the Bureau of Narcotics as it intensified its campaign for federal legislation.

In one example, Richmond Hobson, founder of various "narcotics education" associations and one of the most virulent and widely published prohibitionists, joined the anti-marijuana crusade.

DOCUMENT 118: Dangers of Marijuana (Richmond Hobson, 1936)

Marihuana is a most virile and powerful stimulant. The physiological effect of this drug produces a peculiar psychic exaltation and derangement of the central nervous system. The stage of exaltation and confusion, more marked in some addicts than in others, is generally followed by a stage of depression.

Sometimes the subject passes into a semi-conscious state, experiencing vivid and extravagant dreams which vary according to the individual character and mentality. In some the stage is one of self-satisfaction and well-being. In others, it is alarming, presenting the fear of some imminent and indefinite danger or of impending death. Later the dreams are sometimes followed by a state of complete unconsciousness. Sometimes convulsive attacks and acute mania are developed.

The narcotic content in marihuana decreases the rate of heart beat and causes irregularity of the pulse. Death may result from the effect upon the heart.

Prolonged use of marihuana frequently develops a delirious rage which sometimes leads to high crimes, such as assault and murder. Hence marihuana has been called the "killer drug." The habitual use of this narcotic poison always causes a very marked mental deterioration and sometimes produces insanity. Hence marihuana is frequently called "loco weed." (Loco is the Spanish word for crazy.)

While the marihuana habit leads to physical wreckage and mental decay, its effects upon character and morality are even more devastating. The victim frequently undergoes such degeneracy that he will lie and steal without scruple; he becomes utterly untrustworthy and often drifts into the underworld where, with his degenerate companions, he commits high crimes and misdemeanors. Marihuana sometimes gives man the lust to kill unreasonably and without motive. Many cases of assault, rape, robbery and murder are traced to the use of marihuana.

Source: Richmond Hobson, *Marihuana or Indian Hemp and Its Preparations*, Washington, D.C.: International Narcotic Education Association, 1936.

* * *

During the 1930s, any publication or report that refuted the notion that marijuana was a menace was essentially ignored by federal and state narcotics officials, and most of the media coverage drew on the reports or views of the Federal Bureau of Narcotics or other law enforcement officials that emphasized the dangers of marijuana.

DOCUMENT 119: Bureau of Narcotics Emphasis of Marijuana's Dangers (Jerome Himmelstein, 1983)

The pervasive belief that marihuana use in America was dangerous, violent, and a threat to youth was decisively shaped by the Federal Bureau of Narcotics. . . . Studies by the Indian Hemp Commission in 1894, the U.S. Canal Zone Committee in 1926 and 1933, and Walter Bromberg in 1934, all of which distinctly downplayed the dangers of marihuana use, were rarely mentioned during the period. . . . This may seem odd, since the three studies not only were available and obviously known but also constituted the most systematic work done on marihuana use to that time. The bureau, however, found their findings uncongenial to its own position and was able to drown them with silence. It never mentioned either the Indian or the Canal Zone study.

Source: Jerome Himmelstein, *The Strange Career of Marihuana* (Westport, CT: Greenwood Press, 1983), 69–70.

* * *

Some opposition to the Tax Act came from the American Medical Association, even though the proposed legislation maintained the physician's right to prescribe marijuana. An editorial in the May 1, 1937 issue of the *Journal of the American Medical Association* questioned the need for the law and its ability to control nonmedical use of marijuana.

DOCUMENT 120: Editorial Against Federal Marijuana Law (*Journal of the American Medical Association,* 1937)

The medical profession today seldom dispenses the drug. Many physicians will, however, probably feel it necessary to preserve their right to use it if and when circumstances make it advisable to do so and accordingly will feel compelled to pay the tax. . . . The million dollars to be collected annually . . . will no doubt be charged as a part of the cost of practising medicine, dentistry, and pharmacy. So also will the expense of record keeping and reporting, called for under the bill. All this will in the end be paid for by the patient and thus will go to swell the cost of sickness. Thus the sick and injured must contribute toward federal efforts to suppress a habit that has little or no relation to the use of cannabis for medicinal purposes and that is already within the jurisdiction of the several states. . . .

After more than twenty years of federal effort and the expenditure of millions of dollars, the opium and cocaine habits are still widespread. The best efforts of an efficient bureau of narcotics, supplemented by the efforts of an equally efficient bureau of customs, have failed to stop the unlawful flow of opium and coca leaves and their compounds and derivatives, on which the continuance and spread of narcotic addiction depends. The best efforts of the Public Health Service to find means for the prevention and cure of narcotic addiction have not yet accomplished that end. Two federal narcotic farms . . . cannot yet guarantee the cure of narcotic addiction [see Part VII]. What reason is there, then, for believing that any better results can be obtained by direct federal efforts to suppress a habit arising out of the misuse of such a drug as cannabis? Certainly it is almost as easy to smuggle into the country and to distribute as are opium and coca leaves. Moreover it can be cultivated in many parts of the United States and grows wild in field and forest and along the highways in many places.

Source: "Federal Regulation of thc Medicinal Use of Cannabis," *Journal of the American Medical Association* 108 (May 1, 1937): 1543. Copyright 1937, American Medical Association.

* * *

In June 1937, at the annual convention of the AMA, its Committee on Legislative Activities minimized the addictive potential of the medicinal use of marijuana.

DOCUMENT 121: Marijuana Is Not Addictive (AMA Committee on Legislative Activities, 1937)

There is positively no evidence to indicate the abuse of cannabis as a medicinal agent or to show that its medicinal use is leading to the development of cannabis addiction. Cannabis at the present time is slightly used for medicinal purposes, but it would seem worth while to maintain its status as a medicinal agent for such purposes as it now has. There is a possibility that a restudy of the drug by modern means may show other advantages to be derived from its medicinal use. Your committee also recognizes that in the border states the extensive use of the marijuana weed by a certain type of people would be hard to control.

Source: Report of the AMA Committee on Legislative Activities, *Journal of the American Medical Association* 108 (June 26, 1937): 2214. Copyright 1937, American Medical Association.

* * *

The Marihuana Tax Act was passed by the 75th Congress on August 2, 1937, the first federal regulation of that drug. In comparison to previous and subsequent federal anti-drug legislation, the committee hearings on the bill were brief and there was relatively little public discussion or debate. The act was a revenue measure modeled after the Harrison Act; following are some key passages.

DOCUMENT 122: Marihuana Tax Act (1937)

SECTION 2.

(a) Every person who imports, manufactures, produces, compounds, sells, deals in, dispenses, prescribes, administers, or gives away marihuana shall . . . pay the following special taxes respectively:

(1) Importers, manufacturers, and compounders of marihuana, $24 per year.

(2) Producers of marihuana . . . $1 per year, or fraction thereof. . . .

(3) Physicians, dentists, veterinary surgeons, and other practitioners who distribute, dispense, give away, administer, or prescribe marihuana to patients upon whom they in the course of their professional practice are in attendance, $1 per year. . . .

(4) Any person not registered as an importer, manufacturer, producer, or compounder who obtains and uses marihuana in a laboratory for the purpose of research, instruction, or analysis, or who produces marihuana for any such purpose, $1 per year. . . .

(5) Any person who is not a physician, dentist, veterinary surgeon, or other practitioner and who deals in, dispenses, or gives away marihuana, $3 per year: *Provided*, That any person who has registered and paid the special tax as an importer, manufacturer, compounder, or producer, as required by subdivisions (1) and (2) of this subsection, may deal in, dispense, or give away marihuana imported, manufactured, compounded, or produced by him without further payment of the tax imposed by this section.

. . .

(e) Any person subject to the tax imposed by this section shall, upon payment of such tax, register his name or style and his place or places of business with the collector of the district in which such place or places of business are located.

. . .

SECTION 4.

(a) It shall be unlawful for any person required to register and pay the special tax under the provisions of section 2 to import, manufacture, produce, compound, sell, deal in, dispense, distribute, prescribe, administer, or give away marihuana without having so registered and paid such tax.

. . .

SECTION 6.

(a) It shall be unlawful for any person, whether or not required to pay a special tax and register under section 2, to transfer marihuana, except in pursuance of a written order of the person to whom such marihuana is transferred, on a form to be issued in blank for that purpose by the Secretary.

(b) Subject to such regulations as the Secretary may prescribe, nothing contained in this section shall apply—

(1) To a transfer of marihuana to a patient by a physician, dentist, veterinary surgeon, or other practitioner registered under section 2, in the course of his professional practice only: *Provided*, That such physician, dentist, veterinary surgeon, or other practitioner shall keep a record of all such marihuana transferred, showing the amount transferred and the name and address of the patient to whom such marihuana is transferred. . . .

(2) To a transfer of marihuana, made in good faith by a dealer to a consumer under and in pursuance of a written prescription issued by a physician, dentist, veterinary surgeon, or other practitioner registered under section 2: . . . *Provided further*, That such dealer shall preserve such prescription for a period of two years from the day on which such prescription is filled so as to be readily accessible for inspection by the officers, agents, employees, and officials mentioned in section 11.

. . .

SECTION 7.

(a) There shall be levied, collected, and paid upon all transfers of marihuana which are required by section 6 to be carried out in pursuance of written order forms taxes at the following rates:

(1) Upon each transfer to any person who has paid the special tax and registered under section 2 of this Act, $1 per ounce of marihuana or fraction thereof.

(2) Upon each transfer to any person who has not paid the special tax and registered under section 2 of this Act, $100 per ounce of marihuana or fraction thereof.

. . .

SECTION 10.

(a) Every person liable to any tax imposed by this Act shall keep such books and records, render under oath such statements, make such returns, and comply with such rules and regulations as the Secretary may from time to time prescribe.

(b) Any person who shall be registered under the provisions of section 2 in any internal-revenue district shall, whenever required so to do by the collector of the district, render to the collector a true and correct statement or return, verified by affidavits, setting forth the quantity of marihuana received or harvested by him during such period immediately preceding the demand of the collector, not exceeding three months, as the said collector may fix and determine. If such person is not solely a producer, he shall set forth in such statement or return the names of the persons from whom said marihuana was received, the quantity in each instance received from such persons, and the date when received.

SECTION 11.

The order forms and copies thereof and the prescriptions and records required to be preserved under the provisions of section 6, and the statements or returns filed in the office of the collector of the district under the provisions of section 10 (b) shall be open to inspection by officers, agents, and employees of the Treasury Department duly authorized for that purpose, and such officers of any State, or Territory, or of any political subdivision thereof, or the District of Columbia, or of any insular possession of the United States as shall be charged with the enforcement of any law or municipal ordinance regulating the production, sale, prescribing, dispensing, dealing in, or distributing of marihuana. . . .

SECTION 12.

Any person who is convicted of a violation of any provision of this Act shall be fined not more than $2,000 or imprisoned not more than five years, or both, in the discretion of the court.

Source: Public Law No. 75–238 (Marihuana Tax Act), August 2, 1937.

* * *

Press coverage of the passage of the Tax Act stressed the alleged dangers of the drug as well as its ready availability, relatively inexpensive price, and popularity among marginal and immigrant groups in American society. The following *Newsweek* article appeared two weeks after passage of the Marihuana Tax Act; some of its content seems to have been adapted from the writings of Commissioner Anslinger.

DOCUMENT 123: Dangers of Marijuana (*Newsweek*, 1937)

Cannabis sativa, scraggly tramp of the vegetable world, grows with equal ease alongside Chinese railroad tracks, in Indianapolis' vacant lots, and on Buenos Aires ash dumps. Birdseed manufacturers harvest the mature plant, thresh out the seeds, and use them to restore molting pigeons to health. The plant's fiber is twisted into rope and woven into cheap cloth.

It was neither of these legitimate uses that impelled Representative Robert L. Doughton of North Carolina to introduce a bill imposing a transaction tax on commerce in the weed; he was interested in *Cannabis sativa* because it is a dangerous and devastating narcotic known to the Orient as hashish, to the Occident as marihuana.

Through Turkish water pipes Indians and other Orientals for centuries have inhaled the acrid, tarry smoke of hashish. About a decade ago Negro musicians in New Orleans began drying and crushing the plant's leaves and rolling them into cigarettes. Known variously as bennys, reefers, Mary Warners, and muggles, these cigarettes spread over the United States; shoestring peddlers market them for a dime apiece. Recently, Negro bandmen have introduced them to London's smart Mayfair.

Nearly every State has enacted legislation curbing production, and enforcement agents have discovered cultivated plots growing in Maryland, in Brooklyn, N.Y., and even in the San Quentin prison lot. But curbing the traffic without Federal aid has proved all but impossible. Since few policemen know enough botany to recognize the weed, arrests for cultivation and sale are made almost entirely by narcotics squads of big-city police forces. Doughton's measure—which became law last week when President Roosevelt signed it—imposes a tax on all transactions; since no peddler would be foolish enough to pay such a tax, he is instantly liable to a $2,000 fine or a five-year jail term, or both.

Inhaling the smoke—which is held in the lungs as long as possible—impels some users to lassitude, others to violence. Generally, however, subjective reactions stick to one well-defined track:

Half an hour after smoking a reefer, the subject becomes jovial, carefree, and capable of rare feats of strength. Hallucinations follow: space expands and time slows down; a minute seems like a day and a room looks like a place viewed from the large end of a pair of binoculars. This phase is valuable to hot-band players—time distortion slows down everything and gives opportunity to crowd in a dozen cornet notes where previously there was only time for one. The third stage of intoxication is the dangerous one. The weed acts as a powerful aphrodisiac and renders users capable of various acts of violence; a California man decapitated his best friend, while under the violent spell of the smoke, and a Florida youngster put the ax to his mother and father.

No one can guess how widespread use of the narcotic is. Sensational press stories about its use in grade and high schools generally prove unfounded.

Source: "Marihuana: New Federal Tax Hits Dealings in Potent Weed." From *Newsweek*, August 14, 1937

* * *

Several months later, the national magazine *Literary Digest* printed a transcription of a radio broadcast by the attorney general of Kansas, Clarence Beck, containing similar inflammatory themes.

DOCUMENT 124: Dangers of Marijuana (Clarence Beck, 1938)

The dangerous narcotic drug marijuana grows wild in almost every state in the Union and therefore is easily obtainable. . . . Because it grows in so many different places, it has become the cheapest of all drugs.

It is estimated the Narcotic Bureau of the New York Police Department in 1936 alone destroyed almost 40,000 pounds of marijuana plants, found growing within the city limits. Because of its rapidly increasing use, marijuana demands a price as high as $60 a pound.

While city officials have destroyed hundreds of thousands of plants, those parasitic criminals who traffic in the drug plant the seed in open lots, where it grows without the need of cultivation. Then, under cover of darkness, the weed is harvested, dried and its leaves made into cigarettes. These cigarettes are sometimes called reefers and are also known as "goof butts," "muggles," "tea," or "gage." They are bootlegged at prices ranging from 5 to 50 cents.

The drug is considered more dangerous than cocaine or opium, neither of which will grow in this country.

While medical men and scientists have disagreed as to the properties of marijuana and some have been inclined to minimize its harmfulness, records offer ample evidence that it has a disastrous effect on many of its users.

. . . The natives of the Malay Peninsula, while under its effect, have been known to engage in violent and bloody deeds with complete disregard for their personal safety.

Source: "Marijuana Menace," *Literary Digest*, January 1, 1938, 26–27.

* * *

In 1940 Mayor Fiorello LaGuardia of New York City sought the assistance of the scientific community in understanding the extent of the marijuana problem in that city. An expert committee was established with the guidance of the New York Academy of Medicine, and it issued its final report in 1944. In the foreword to that report, Mayor LaGuardia stated that although there was considerable concern about the impact of the marijuana problem, its use and distribution were localized and its negative effects on society exaggerated.

DOCUMENT 125: Marijuana Problem Exaggerated (LaGuardia Committee Report, 1944)

As Mayor of the City of New York, it is my duty to foresee and take steps to prevent the development of hazards to the health, safety, and welfare of our citizens. . . . rumors were recently circulated concerning the smoking of marihuana by large segments of our population and even by school children. . . .

. . .

I am glad that the sociological, psychological, and medical ills commonly attributed to marihuana have been found to be exaggerated insofar as the City of New York is concerned. I hasten to point out, however, that the findings are to be interpreted only as a reassuring report of progress and not as encouragement to indulgence, for I shall continue to enforce the laws prohibiting the use of marihuana until and if complete findings may justify an amendment to existing laws. The scientific part of the research will be continued in the hope that the drug may prove to possess therapeutic value for the control of drug addiction.

. . .

[The key conclusions of the committee were:]

1. Marihuana is used extensively in the Borough of Manhattan but the problem is not as acute as it is reported to be in other sections of the United States.
2. The introduction of marihuana into this area is recent as compared to other localities.
3. The cost of marihuana is low and therefore within the purchasing power of most persons.
4. The distribution and use of marihuana is centered in Harlem.
5. The majority of marihuana smokers are Negroes and Latin-Americans.
6. The consensus among marihuana smokers is that the use of the drug creates a definite feeling of adequacy.
7. The practice of smoking marihuana does not lead to addiction in the medical sense of the word.
8. The sale and distribution of marihuana is not under the control of any single organized group.
9. The use of marihuana does not lead to morphine or heroin or cocaine addiction and no effort is made to create a market for these narcotics by stimulating the practice of marihuana smoking.

10. Marihuana is not the determining factor in the commission of major crimes.
11. Marihuana smoking is not widespread among school children.
12. Juvenile delinquency is not associated with the practice of smoking marihuana.
13. The publicity concerning the catastrophic effects of marihuana smoking in New York City is unfounded.

Source: Mayor's Committee on Marihuana, *The Marihuana Problem in the City of New York* (Lancaster, PA: Cattell Press, 1944), v, 24–25.

* * *

Like the Harrison Act, the constitutionality of the Marihuana Tax Act was ultimately tested and upheld by the U.S. Supreme Court, although it took thirteen years for a case to reach the nation's highest court. In a U.S. district court case from the Northern District of Illinois, the defendant (Sanchez) moved to dismiss a suit brought by the United States to collect taxes owed under the Marihuana Tax Act. Sanchez claimed that the act was a penalty for marijuana transfer, not a tax, and was therefore unconstitutional. The district court agreed and dismissed the case. In reversing this decision, the Supreme Court decided that the tax was a legitimate use of federal taxing power even though an additional effect may be to regulate and punish the transfer of marijuana. The key passages of the Supreme Court's opinion follow.

DOCUMENT 126: *United States v. Sanchez et al.* (1950)

MR. JUSTICE CLARK delivered the opinion of the Court:

This is a direct appeal, 28 U.S.C. § 1252, from dismissal by the District Court of a suit for recovery of $8701.65 in taxes and interest alleged to be due under § 7 (a) (2) of the Marihuana Tax Act, 50 Stat. 551, now § 2590 (a) (2) of the Internal Revenue Code. 26 U.S.C. § 2590 (a) (2). In their motion to dismiss, which was granted without opinion, defendants attacked the constitutionality of this subsection on the ground that it levied a penalty, not a tax. The validity of this levy is the issue here.

In enacting the Marihuana Tax Act, the Congress had two objectives: "First, the development of a plan of taxation which will raise revenue and at the same time render extremely difficult the acquisition of marihuana by persons who desire it for illicit uses and, second, the development of an adequate means of publicizing dealings in marihuana in order to tax and control the traffic effectively."

. . .

It is obvious that § 2590, by imposing a severe burden on transfers to unregistered persons, implements the congressional purpose of restricting traffic in marihuana to accepted industrial and medicinal channels. Hence the attack here rests on the regulatory character and prohibitive burden of the section as well as the penal nature of the imposition. But despite the regulatory effect and the close resemblance to a penalty, it does not follow that the levy is invalid.

First. It is beyond serious question that a tax does not cease to be valid merely because it regulates, discourages, or even definitely deters the activities taxed. . . . The principle applies even though the revenue obtained is obviously negligible . . . or the revenue purpose of the tax may be secondary. . . . Nor does a tax statute necessarily fall because it touches on activities which Congress might not otherwise regulate. . . .

From the beginning of our government, the courts have sustained taxes although imposed with the collateral intent of effecting ulterior ends which, considered apart, were beyond the constitutional power of the lawmakers to realize by legislation directly addressed to their accomplishment.

These principles are controlling here. The tax in question is a legitimate exercise of the taxing power despite its collateral regulatory purpose and effect.

Second. The tax levied by § 2590 (a) (2) is not conditioned upon the commission of a crime. The tax is on the transfer of marihuana to a person who has not paid the special tax and registered. Such a transfer is not made an unlawful act under the statute. Liability for the payment of the tax rests primarily with the transferee; but if he fails to pay, then the transferor, as here, becomes liable. It is thus the failure of the transferee to pay the tax that gives rise to the liability of the transferor. Since his tax liability does not in effect rest on criminal conduct, the tax can be properly called a civil rather than a criminal sanction. The fact Congress provided civil procedure for collection indicates its intention that the tax be treated as such. . . .

Nor is the civil character of the tax imposed by § 2590 (a) (2) altered by its severity in relation to that assessed by § 2590 (a) (1). The difference has a rational foundation. Unregistered persons are not likely to procure the required order form prior to transfer or pay the required tax. Free of sanctions, dealers would be prone to accommodate such persons in their unlawful activity. The imposition of equally severe tax burdens on such transferors is reasonably adapted to secure payment of the tax by transferees or stop transfers to unregistered persons, as well as to provide an additional source from which the expense of unearthing clandestine transfers can be recovered.

The judgment below must be reversed and the cause remanded for further proceedings in conformity with this opinion.

Source: 340 *U.S. Reports* 42, *United States v. Sanchez et al.*, decided November 13, 1950.

* * *

The 1950s marked the end of a phase of American drug policy against marijuana. For the most part, marijuana policy evolved during the first half of the 20th century from one of limited concern about the drug to a set of fairly punitive policies. Under both federal and state laws, possession or sale of marijuana was treated similarly to that of other illegal drugs such as heroin and cocaine. With the great spread of marijuana use in the 1960s, however, came a new era in policy toward this drug that resulted in much more tolerance for individual use and a substantial reduction in penalties for possession or individual use. These policies and trends will be discussed in Part XI.

Part VII

American Drug Policy to World War II

Although passage and enforcement of the Harrison Act (See Documents 45, 47–48, 51–53) helped to initiate expanded federal and state control over the sale and distribution of narcotics, ongoing problems remained that were not addressed by that law. For example, in the years leading up to 1920, there was growing concern that Japan was shipping large amounts of drugs to China (particularly opium), and that this could affect America's ability to increase trade with China. With the economic depression in the United States following World War I, there was concern that continuing opium problems in China would have a negative economic impact on a potential new and large market. The China Club, based in Seattle, was a strong and effective lobbying force for increasing economic ties to China and played an important role in urging Congress to enact new legislation to curb international drug traffic.

DOCUMENT 127: Genesis of Import-Export Act (David F. Musto, 1987)

In autumn 1920, as the postwar economic depression worsened, members of the China Club met with Representative John Miller and Senator Homer Jones to prepare a simple amendment to the narcotic laws which would ban all exportation of narcotics from the United States, whether of domestic origin or in transit.

Hearings were held on Miller's bill . . . in December 1920 and January 1921. . . . Witnesses provided considerable information on the current problem of American narcotic control. Provision of morphine for Chinese addicts was only one danger that arose from our loose import-export laws. Closer to home, American narcotic exports to Canada showed a great increase after the Harrison Act. The consensus among the witnesses and the subcommittee was that most of the drugs illegally used in the United States were not of foreign origin but were domestic manufactures smuggled back after legal export. The proposed act would plug this loophole and attempt to prevent transshipment of foreign products for the economic exploitation of China.

. . .

In February 1921 . . . Representative Rainey submitted a revision of the Jones-Miller proposal, which would permit narcotic exports . . . upon assurance that the nation to which the materials were exported would monitor the use and disposition of the drugs.

Source: David F. Musto, *The American Disease: Origins of Narcotic Control*, expanded ed. (New York: Oxford University Press, 1987), 194–195.

NARCOTIC DRUGS IMPORT AND EXPORT ACT

It became clear to federal officials that despite the Harrison Act and its enforcement, large quantities of drugs were still being brought into the United States and supplying the black market. The Narcotic Drugs Import and Export Act of 1922 strengthened existing laws against international drug smuggling.

DOCUMENT 128: Overview of Import-Export Act (New York Academy of Medicine, 1955)

In growing recognition that there was need for a more comprehensive measure of control over import and export of narcotic drugs than was provided by the [opium import] Act of 1909, as amended in 1914, an extensively revised form of this older statute was re-enacted by Congress in 1922 as the Narcotic Drugs Import and Export Act. It authorized the importation of only such quantities of opium and coca leaves as the then Federal Narcotics Control Board found to be necessary to meet medical needs. With this legitimate exception, importation of any form of narcotic drug was prohibited. Exportation of manufactured narcotic drugs and preparations was permitted under a system of control designed to assure their use for medical purposes only in the country of destination. Under the special amendment to this statute in 1924, the legal manufacture of heroin in the United States ceased.

Source: New York Academy of Medicine, "Report on Drug Addiction," *Bulletin of the New York Academy of Medicine* 31, no. 8 (1955): 593.

* * *

The 1922 act placed tight restrictions on importation and exportation of drugs, and expanded the 1909 opium import act to include cocaine and its derivatives.

DOCUMENT 129: Narcotic Drugs Import and Export Act (1922)

. . . [S]ections 1 and 2 of the Act entitled "An Act to prohibit the importation and the use of opium for other than medicinal purposes," approved February 9, 1909, as amended, are amended to read as follows:

That when used in this Act—

(a) The term "narcotic drug" means opium, coca leaves, cocaine, or any salt, derivative, or preparation of opium, coca leaves, or cocaine;

Sec. 2. (a) That there is hereby established a board to be known as the "Federal Narcotics Control Board" and to be composed of the Secretary of State, the Secretary of the Treasury, and the Secretary of Commerce. Except as otherwise provided in this Act or by other law, the administration of this Act is vested in the Department of the Treasury.

(b) That it is unlawful to import or bring any narcotic drug into the United States or any territory under its control or jurisdiction; except that such amounts of crude opium and coca leaves as the board finds to be necessary to provide for medical and legitimate uses only, may be imported and brought into the United States or such territory under such regulations as the board shall prescribe. All narcotic drugs imported under such regulations shall be subject to the duties which are now or may hereafter be imposed upon such drugs when imported.

(c) That if any person fraudulently or knowingly imports or brings any narcotic drug into the United States or any territory under its control or jurisdiction, contrary to law, or assists in so doing, or receives, conceals, buys, sells, or in any manner facilitates the transportation, concealment, or sale of any such narcotic drug after being imported or brought in, knowing the same to have been imported contrary to law, such person shall upon conviction be fined not more than $5,000 and imprisoned for not more than ten years.

(d) Any narcotic drug imported or brought into the United States or any territory under its control or jurisdiction, contrary to law, shall (1) if smoking opium or opium prepared for smoking, be seized and summarily forfeited to the United States Government without the necessity of instituting forfeiture proceedings of any character; or (2), if any other narcotic drug, be seized and forfeited to the United States Government, without regard to its value....

(e) Any alien who at any time after his entry is convicted under subdivision (c) shall, upon the termination of the imprisonment imposed by the court upon such conviction and upon warrant issued by the Secretary of Labor, be taken into custody and deported in accordance with the provisions of sections 19 and 20 of the Act of February 5, 1917, entitled "An Act to regulate the immigration of aliens to, and the residence of aliens in, the United States," or provisions of law hereafter enacted which are amendatory of, or in substitution for, such sections.

...

That sections 5 and 6 of such Act of February 9, 1909, as amended, are amended to read as follows:

Sec. 5. That no smoking opium or opium prepared for smoking shall be admitted into the United States or into any territory under its control or jurisdiction for transportation to another country, or be transferred or transshipped from one vessel to another vessel within any waters of the United States for immediate exportation or for any other purpose; and except with the approval of the board, no other narcotic drug may be so admitted, transferred, or transshipped.

Sec. 6. (a) That it shall be unlawful for any person subject to the jurisdiction of the United States Government to export or cause to be exported from the United States, or from territory under its control or jurisdiction, or from countries in which the United States exercises extraterritorial jurisdiction, any narcotic drug to any other country: *Provided,* That narcotic drugs (except smoking opium and opium prepared for smoking, the exportation of which is hereby absolutely prohibited) may be exported to a country only which has ratified and become a party to the convention and final protocol between the United States Government and other powers for the suppression of the abuses of opium and other drugs, commonly known as the International Opium Convention of 1912, and then only if (1) such country has instituted and maintains, in conformity with that convention, a system, which the board deems adequate, of permits or licenses for the control of imports of such narcotic drugs; (2) the narcotic drug is consigned to an authorized permittee; and (3) there is furnished to the board proof deemed adequate by it, that the narcotic drug is to be applied exclusively to medical and legitimate uses within the country to which exported, that it will not be reexported from such country, and that there is an actual shortage of and a demand for the narcotic drug for medical and legitimate uses within such country.

Sec. 3. That section 8 of such Act of February 9, 1909, as amended, is amended to read as follows:

Sec. 8. (a) That a narcotic drug that is found upon a vessel arriving at a port of the United States or territory under its control or jurisdiction and is not shown upon the vessel's manifest, or that is landed from any such vessel without a permit first obtained from the collector of customs for that purpose, shall be seized, forfeited, and disposed of in the manner provided in subdivision (d) of section 2, and the master of the vessel shall be liable (1) if the narcotic drug is smoking opium, to a penalty of $25 an ounce, and (2) if any other narcotic drug, to a penalty equal to the value of the narcotic drug.

Source: Public Law 67–227 (Narcotic Drugs Import and Export Act), May 26, 1922.

* * *

As with other major anti-drug laws before and after it, passage of the Import-Export Act raised expectations about its effects on drug use and availability. The following magazine article about the act illustrates the unrealistic hopes that often accompanied new legislation in this era.

DOCUMENT 130: News Report on Passage of Import-Export Act (*Literary Digest*, 1922)

"Snow parties," which are said to have become so prevalent as to menace American civilization, will be made impossible by the Jones-Miller bill governing the manufacture, importation and exportation of habit-forming drugs, which has been passed by Congress and made law by the signature of President Harding. By striking at the source of supply, the bill goes to the root of the evil, and, in time, will eliminate it altogether. . . .

[Quoting Representative Miller, one of the bill's sponsors:] . . . "The illicit use of morphine and cocaine is spreading to such an alarming extent in the United States and in other countries as to cause deep concern for our civilization. The number of drug addicts in this country is now alarming, and reports from every locality indicate these unfortunates are on the increase. It is our duty first to protect our own people from the illicit use of these drugs and we should in all good conscience assist the Chinese and other nationals who are now attempting to heal themselves not only of the use of opium, prepared for smoking but other narcotic drugs equally deleterious. . . .

By the enactment of this bill the two principal producing nations of the world will have united in stamping out the illicit use of narcotic drugs the world over, and especially will this legislation be of more assistance to the people of China than of any other foreign country. . . . It will in a greater respect, however, save our own people from the activities of the smuggler and the illegitimate trafficker. In our judgment there never has been a more important measure touching the general welfare of our people than this bill."

Source: "Ending the Narcotic Menace," *Literary Digest*, June 10, 1922, 34.

NARCOTIC FARMS

During the 1920s, enforcement of the Harrison Act led to substantial increases in the number of addicts incarcerated in federal prisons. This increase brought pressure on Congress to do something about prison overcrowding. For example, in 1926 it was estimated that about 35 percent of the nearly 7,000 federal prisoners were serving sentences for drug law violations.

One of the key Congressional leaders on narcotics matters during the 1920s was Representative Stephen Porter of Pittsburgh, who led the American delegation to the second Geneva Conference on drugs in 1924–1925. Representative Porter had been advocating for federal narcotics hospitals to house addicts for several years, working with staff of the Department of Justice to draft legislation that would allow prisoners to be detained in alternative institutions. Others, including wardens from several federal prisons who cited severe overcrowding, pressured Congress to provide some alternative to incarceration for convictions of addicts under the Harrison Act. Although on a much greater scale, this concern about prisons overcrowded with drug addicts continues to the present day. As in the 1920s, the growth of the prison population in the late 1990s has spurred calls for increased access to drug treatment and alternatives to incarceration for drug-involved offenders.

In conjunction with the U.S. Department of Justice, Porter drafted a bill to create the first federal narcotic treatment centers for addicts, called narcotic "farms." The bill was passed by Congress on January 19, 1929, although the first farm (located in Lexington, Kentucky) did not open until 1935. A second opened in Fort Worth, Texas, in 1938. The bill received widespread support from federal and state officials as well as citizen groups such as the American Civic Reform Union, led by Reverend Albert Gregg. In the following document, Gregg writes in support of the Porter bill. The document shows two common and somewhat conflicting themes that have long been part of the drug policy debate: a humanitarian approach emphasizing treatment, and the punitive emphasis on isolating addicts from society.

DOCUMENT 131: Support for Narcotic Farms Law (Albert Sidney Gregg, 1928)

The Porter bill [that created the narcotic farms] is the culmination of various lines of influence that have been in active operation for some time, due to an imperative demand for more prison room. On several occasions Warden John W. Snook, of the U.S. penitentiary in Atlanta, has called attention to the overcrowded condition of that prison, and recommended to the Attorney General that a separate institution be erected to take care of the addicts. One-third of the prisoners in Atlanta have been sent there for violating the drug act [the Harrison Act], mainly the "possession" of drugs. The same proportion holds good in the other U.S. penal institutions. . . .

On April 26, 27, 28, 1928, hearings were held by the Judiciary Committee, in which a score of officials and experts were heard in favor of the bill, and numerous communications read by Mr. Porter. There was no opposition.

A very fine humanitarian spirit characterized the discussions. Practically all agreed that a drug addict is a sick man, and not essentially a criminal, and that he should be put in an institution where he could be cured, in place of in a prison where the dominant idea is repression, restriction and punishment. . . .

This is a gigantic undertaking, and of far-reaching importance. It is a direct blow at the terrible drug menace which is debauching so many young people, and causing so much misery and crime throughout the United States. . . .

The importance of this legislation lies chiefly in the segregation of drug addicts from other prisoners, and in keeping them under strict custodial control.

Drug addicts now confined in Federal penitentiaries are mostly drug peddlers also, and have been committed for violations of the Harrison Act.

It is improbable that the Government can do much with this type of prisoner in the way of rehabilitation, and he must not be confused with the non-criminal type of drug addict.

To sum up, the chief benefits to be gained by the enactment of the Porter bill, will be—

1. The keeping in custody of criminal drug addicts for a longer period, preventing them from preying upon the public.

2. Prevention of the spread of drug addiction to other prisoners, it

being a well known fact that few prisons or penitentiaries are entirely free from narcotics.

3. Relieving the congestion and overcrowding of our U.S. penitentiaries, which has become a scandal to the nation, chiefly due to the large number of persons committed for violations of the Harrison Act, in many cases for short terms, only to be released, to again corrupt the public.

Source: Rev. Albert Sidney Gregg, "United States Narcotic Farms," *Narcotic Education* 2 (1928): 9–10.

* * *

The idea of creating narcotic farms received wide support in Congress, which wanted to avoid having to pay for new federal prisons.

DOCUMENT 132: Congressional Support for Narcotic Farms Law (David F. Musto, 1987)

The need for the farms was obvious to Congress. Representative John J. Cochran, who had earlier prepared a similar measure, told his colleagues on the day the Porter bill passed the House without opposition, "Notice has been served on the Congress that the great increase in the population at the Federal penitentiaries makes it imperative that either the Porter bill be enacted into law or two additional penitentiaries constructed." Yet this practical reason was overcast with a humanitarian sentiment which had previously failed to persuade Congress to make federal provision for the general treatment of addicts: Representative Cochran went so far as to claim for the farms that "2,000 or 3,000 men and women, slaves to habit-forming drugs, will be placed on these farms and be subject to treatment and eventually cured." Everyone associated with the narcotic farm proposal enthusiastically endorsed it—except the Surgeon General of the Public Health Service, who would have the responsibility to operate the institutions.

Source: David F. Musto, *The American Disease: Origins of Narcotic Control*, expanded ed. (New York: Oxford University Press, 1987), 205.

* * *

The narcotic farms legislation was enacted into law on January 19, 1929. The next document includes the key sections of the law.

DOCUMENT 133: Act to Create Narcotic Farms (1929)

Section 222

The Attorney General, the Secretary of the Treasury and the Secretary of War are authorized and directed to select sites for two institutions for the confinement and treatment of persons who have been or shall be convicted of offenses against the United States, including persons convicted by general courts-martial and consular courts, and who are addicted to the use of habit-forming narcotic drugs, and for the confinement and treatment of addicts who voluntarily submit themselves for treatment.

. . .

Section 225

The control and management of the United States narcotic farms shall be vested in the Secretary of the Treasury, who shall have power to appoint competent superintendents, assistant superintendents, physicians, pharmacists, psychologists, nurses, and all other officers and employees necessary for the safe-keeping, care, protection, treatment, and discipline of the inmates. There is hereby created in the office of the Surgeon General of the Bureau of the Public Health Service, in the Department of the Treasury, a division to be known as the Narcotics Division, which shall be in charge of a physician trained in the treatment and care of narcotic addicts, and which division shall have charge of the management, discipline, and methods of treatment of said United States narcotic farms under the rules and regulations promulgated by the Secretary of the Treasury.

Section 226

The care, discipline, and treatment of the persons admitted to or confined in a United States narcotic farm shall be designed to rehabilitate them, restore them to health, and where necessary train them to be self-supporting and self-reliant. For this purpose the Secretary of the Treasury shall have authority to promulgate all necessary rules and regulations for the government of the officers and inmates of said United States narcotic farms. The Surgeon General of the Bureau of Public Health Service shall also give the authorized representatives of each State the benefit of his experience in the administration of said United States narcotic farms and the treatment of persons confined therein through the publication and dissemination of information on methods of treatment and research in this field, together with individual and group case histories, to the end that each State may be encouraged to provide similar facilities for the care and treatment of narcotic addicts within their own jurisdiction.

Section 227

The authority vested with the power to designate the place of confinement of a prisoner is hereby authorized and directed to transfer to the United States narcotic farms, as accommodations become available, all addicts, as herein defined, who are now or shall hereafter be sentenced to confinement in or be confined in any penal, correctional, disciplinary, or reformatory institution of the United States . . . : *Provided,* That no addict shall be transferred to a United States narcotic farm who, in the opinion of the officer authorized to direct the transfer, is not a proper subject for confinement in such an institution either because of the nature of the crime he has committed, or his apparent incorrigibility.
. . .

Section 230

Any inmate of said narcotic farms or any narcotic addict confined in any institution convicted of an offense against the United States shall not be eligible for parole . . . or receive any commutation allowance for good conduct . . . unless and until the Surgeon General of the Bureau of the Public Health Service shall have certified that said inmate is no longer a narcotic addict as defined by this chapter. When such certificate shall have been made, the board of parole of the penal correctional, disciplinary, or reformatory institution from which such former addict was transferred may authorize his release on parole without transfer back to such institution.

Section 231

Not later than one month prior to the expiration of the sentence of any addict confined in a United States narcotic farm, he shall be examined by the Surgeon General of the Bureau of the Public Health Service, or his authorized representative. If he believes the person to be discharged is still an addict within the meaning of this chapter and that he may by further treatment in a United States narcotic farm be cured of his addiction, the addict shall be informed, under such rules and regulations as the Secretary of the Treasury may promulgate, of the advisability of his submitting himself to further treatment. The addict may then apply in writing to the Secretary of the Treasury for further treatment in a United States narcotic farm for a period not exceeding the maximum length of time considered necessary by the Surgeon General of the Bureau of the Public Health Service. Upon approval of the application by the Secretary of the Treasury or his authorized agent, the addict may be given such further treatment as is necessary to cure him of his addiction: *Provided*, That if any addict voluntarily submits himself to treatment he may be confined in a United States narcotic farm for a period not exceeding the maximum amount of time estimated by the Surgeon General of the Bureau of the Public Health Service as necessary to effect a cure or until he ceases to be an addict within the meaning of this chapter.

Section 232

Any person, except an unconvicted alien, addicted to the use of habit-forming narcotic drugs, whether or not he shall have been convicted of an offense against the United States, may apply to the Secretary of the Treasury, or his authorized representative, for admission to a United States narcotic farm.

Any such addict shall be examined by the Surgeon General of the Bureau of the Public Health Service or his authorized agent, who shall report to the Secretary of the Treasury whether the applicant is an addict within the meaning of this chapter; whether he believes he may by treatment in a United States narcotic farm be cured of his addiction and the estimated length of time necessary to effect a cure, and any further pertinent information bearing on the addiction, habits or character of the applicant. The Secretary of the Treasury may, in his discretion, admit the applicant to a United States narcotic farm. No such addict shall be admitted unless he voluntarily submits to treatment for the maximum amount of time estimated by the Surgeon General of the Bureau of the Public Health Service as necessary to effect a cure, and unless suitable accommodations are available after all eligible addicts convicted of offenses against the United States have [been] admitted. The Secretary of the Treasury may require any such addict voluntarily applying to pay the cost of his subsistence, care, and treatment. . . . *Provided*, That if any addict voluntarily submits himself to treatment he may be confined in a United States narcotic farm for a period not exceeding the maximum amount of time estimated by the Surgeon General of the Bureau of the Public Health Service as necessary to effect a cure of the addiction or until he ceases to be an addict within the meaning of this chapter: *And provided further*, That any person who voluntarily submits himself for treatment at a United States narcotic farm not forfeit or abridge thereby any of his rights as a citizen of the United States; nor shall such submission be used against him in any proceeding in any court, and that the record of his voluntary commitment shall be confidential and not divulged.

Source: 45 Stat. 1085 (Act to Create Narcotics Farms), January 19, 1929.

* * *

As the next document suggests, news coverage of the passage of the Porter narcotic farms bill and the opening of the first farm in Lexington stressed the importance of isolating addicts and keeping them under close supervision for a lengthy period of time, as well as expressing hope that the farms would help cure addicts.

DOCUMENT 134: Opening of the Federal Narcotic Farms (*New York Times*, April 14, 1929)

Two Federal prison farms are soon to be established where scientific methods of cure and treatment of drug addicts will be studied and tested. Their location will be determined by a commission which will include the Attorney General, the Secretary of the Treasury and the Secretary of War. . . .

Treatment of drug patients in the past has been hampered because the afflicted were allowed to leave the hospitals whenever they pleased, whether they were cured or not, and those who were committed to State institutions could leave after their short sentences were served. For this reason many cures have not been permanent. The new narcotic farms will receive only prisoners committed by Federal courts, and they will be kept under supervision as rigid as that of a penitentiary. . . .

The work of the public health service will include three lines of endeavor. First, the effort will be directed toward the "withdrawal symptoms"—such as sneezing, cramps, collapse, restlessness and delirium. The second consideration will be the building up of will power and desire for improvement and a strengthened muscular and nervous system. The third will be custodial service, including the work of psychiatrists and medical work after the cure seems assured.

Source: New York Times, April 14, 1929.

* * *

The Lexington narcotic farm opened with a $4 million budget and 350 employees, with a capacity for 1,400 inmates. Although there was much hope for their success, most studies of the outcomes for addicts treated at the Lexington or Fort Worth hospitals found discouraging results. Relapse rates were quite high, and few patients treated at these farms appeared to achieve long-term abstinence. By the early 1970s, both facilities had been converted to federal prisons.

THE FEDERAL BUREAU OF NARCOTICS

During the 1920s important changes were beginning to take place in the federal administration and enforcement of anti-drug laws. The enforcement of alcohol prohibition and drug prohibition both rested within the Treasury Department but had different administrative structures and priorities. Alcohol prohibition generally received more attention, but the Prohibition Unit was beset by political patronage and scandal. For most of the decade, the Narcotic Division was under the direction of pharmacist Levi Nutt, who oversaw the division's successful campaigns against narcotics clinics (see Part IX). By the end of the 1920s, however, ongoing concerns about the relationship between alcohol and narcotics enforcement, as well as internal problems within the Narcotic Division, helped push Congress to restructure the nation's anti-drug enforcement efforts. David Musto describes the transition in the following document.

DOCUMENT 135: Federal Drug Control Structure in the 1920s (David F. Musto, 1987)

Levi Nutt, a registered pharmacist who joined the Treasury Department in 1901, had been an official of the Alcohol Tax Unit, which administered the Harrison Act. Enforcement of the Harrison Act had been, until 1920, a difficult task because the Bureau of Internal Revenue [where enforcement was originally placed] rapidly acquired immense new responsibilities for income taxes and other sources of revenue to prepare for and prosecute World War I, while congressional provision for increased personnel and reorganization lagged behind.

. . .

The head of the Narcotic Division [of the Prohibition Unit of the Treasury Department], Levi G. Nutt, remained in his post from 1920 until early 1930, outlasting several Prohibition commissioners who succeeded one another as the enforcement of dry laws failed under widespread dishonesty and public contempt. One reason for the poor quality of prohibition enforcement was that jobs were openly filled by political patronage. . . . The Narcotic Division, however, was under civil service.

. . .

As soon as the [narcotic] farms were authorized, [Congressman] Porter began to work for the establishment of a separate government agency to enforce the Harrison Act and represent the nation in foreign conferences. . . .

The right moment for a separate agency came in 1929. Friends of the Harrison Act had long regretted the close association between narcotic and liquor law enforcement. . . . But Nutt had stayed on in narcotics through Democratic and Republican administrations, trying to catch erring physicians, peddlers, and smugglers; he was becoming a permanent bureaucratic fixture.

Then misconduct in the operation of the federal narcotics office in New York City and the questionable actions of members of Nutt's family led to his transfer from the Narcotic Division and his replacement by Harry J. Anslinger, then Assistant Commissioner of the Prohibition Bureau with responsibility for foreign control. . . .

. . .

Nutt became field supervisor of the Prohibition agents and then head of the Alcohol Tax Unit in Syracuse until his retirement. Anslinger became Acting Commissioner of Narcotics upon the creation of the Federal Bureau of Narcotics on 1 July 1930 and was appointed Commissioner of narcotics by President Hoover on 25 September, serving until his retirement in 1962.

Source: David F. Musto, *The American Disease: Origins of Narcotic Control*, expanded ed. (New York: Oxford University Press, 1987), 183, 207–208.

* * *

In his position as Commissioner of Narcotics, Harry Anslinger became the driving force behind many of America's drug policies for the next 30 years. He had great influence in Congress, and as a skilled politician was adept at convincing Congress and other policy makers about the need for tough enforcement of anti-drug laws and the dangers of drug use. His visibility, power, and influence on the development of uniform state drug laws extended his reach to state-level drug policy as well.

The 1930 federal law that established the Bureau of Narcotics within the Treasury Department set the structure for federal anti-drug policy until the 1960s, after which several restructurings took place.

DOCUMENT 136: Establishment of Bureau of Narcotics (New York Academy of Medicine, 1955)

Originally the Federal Narcotics Control Board had the responsibility of control over narcotic drug imports and exports. The duty of enforcing the Harrison Narcotic Law was assumed by the Bureau of Internal Revenue through its field officers engaged in enforcing all internal revenue laws. There was no separate, specialized group of officers bound exclusively to the duty of enforcing this statute. With a growing realization of the inadequacy of such an arrangement for law enforcement to cope with the control of narcotic drug traffic, the Congress in 1930 established the Bureau of Narcotics in the Treasury Department. To this Bureau were transferred all functions and duties of control over narcotic drug imports and exports and enforcement of the narcotic law which were previously exercised by the Federal Narcotics Control Board and the Bureau of Internal Revenue, respectively. The Federal Narcotics Control Board was thereby abolished. The policy of the new Bureau was to cut off the supply of the illicit drug traffic at the source. Steps were taken to curb the smuggling of large quantities of contraband narcotics. At the same time the Bureau attacked the illicit domestic traffic.

Source: New York Academy of Medicine, "Report on Drug Addiction," *Bulletin of the New York Academy of Medicine* 31, no. 8 (1955): 594.

* * *

The 1930 act gave the Bureau of Narcotics and its commissioner considerable power to enforce federal drug laws, including the import and export laws and the determination of the amount of drugs that could be legally imported. The commissioner was also authorized to advise states on their own drug policies and the drafting of anti-drug laws.

DOCUMENT 137: Act to Create Federal Bureau of Narcotics (1930)

Be it enacted . . . That there shall be in the Department of the Treasury a bureau to be known as the Bureau of Narcotics and a Commissioner of Narcotics who shall be at the head thereof. The Commissioner of Narcotics shall be appointed by the President, by and with the advice and consent of the Senate, and shall receive a salary at the rate of $9,000 per annum. The commissioner shall make an annual report to Congress.

Sec. 2. . . .

(b) In order to aid in the detection and prevention of the unlawful importation of narcotic drugs into the United States, and under such regulations as the Secretary of the Treasury may prescribe, the Commissioner of Narcotics may confer or impose upon such officers and employees of the Bureau of Narcotics, as he may designate any of the rights, privileges, powers, or duties of customs officers and employees, and may assign any of such officers and employees of the Bureau of Narcotics to duty at ports of entry or other places specified by such commissioner.

Sec. 3. (a) The Federal Narcotics Control Board established by the Narcotic Drugs Import and Export Act, as amended, . . . is hereby abolished, and all the authority, powers, and functions exercised by such board are hereby transferred to and shall be vested in and exercised and performed by the Commissioner of Narcotics.

. . .

(e) All orders, rules, and regulations in respect of any laws relating to narcotic drugs which have been issued by the Commissioner of Prohibition or the Federal Narcotics Control Board and which are in effect on the date this Act takes effect shall, after such date, continue in effect as though this Act had not been enacted or until modified, superseded, or repealed by the Commissioner of Narcotics, with the approval of the Secretary of the Treasury.

Sec. 4. (a) The Narcotics Division in the office of the Surgeon General of the United States Public Health Service in the Treasury Department, as created by the Act entitled "An Act to establish two United States narcotic farms for the confinement and treatment of persons addicted to the use of habit-forming narcotic drugs who have been convicted of offenses against the United States, and for other purposes," approved January 19, 1929 (U.S.C., Supp. III, title 21, ch. 8), shall be known as the Division of Mental Hygiene. The authority, powers, and functions exercised by such Narcotics Division are hereby transferred to the Division of Mental Hygiene. . . .

(b) The Surgeon General of the Public Health Service is authorized and directed to make such studies and investigations, as may be necessary, of the abusive use of narcotic drugs; of the quantities of crude opium, coca leaves, and their salts, derivatives, and preparations, together with such reserves thereof, as are necessary to supply the normal and emergency medicinal and scientific requirements of the United States; and of the causes, prevalence, and means for the prevention and treatment of mental and nervous diseases. The Surgeon General shall report to the Secretary of the Treasury not later than the 1st day of September each year the results of such studies and investigations. The results of such studies and investigations of the quantities of crude opium, coca leaves, or other narcotic drugs, together with such reserves thereof, as are necessary to supply the normal and emergency medicinal and scientific requirements of the United States, shall be made available to the Commissioner of Narcotics, to be used at his discretion in determining the amounts of crude opium and coca leaves to be imported under the Narcotic Drugs Import and Export Act, as amended.

. . .

Sec. 6. In addition to the amount of coca leaves which may be imported under section 2 (b) of the Narcotic Drugs Import and Export Act, the Commissioner of Narcotics is authorized to permit, in accordance with regulations issued by him, the importation of additional amounts of coca leaves: *Provided*, That after the entry, thereof into the United States all cocaine, ecgonine, and all salts, derivatives, and preparations from which cocaine or ecgonine may be synthesized or made, contained in such additional amounts of coca leaves, shall be destroyed under the supervision of an authorized representative of the Commissioner of Narcotics. All coca leaves imported under this section shall be subject to the duties which are now or may hereafter be imposed upon such coca leaves when imported.

. . .

Sec. 8. That the Secretary of the Treasury shall cooperate with the several States in the suppression of the abuse of narcotic drugs in their respective jurisdictions, and to that end he is authorized (1) to cooperate in the drafting of such legislation as may be needed, if any, to effect the end named, and (2) to arrange for the exchange of information concerning the use and abuse of narcotic drugs in said States and for cooperation in the institution and prosecution of cases in the courts of the United States and before the licensing boards and courts of the several States. The Secretary of the Treasury is hereby authorized to make such regulations as may be necessary to carry this section into effect.

Source: Public Law 71–357 (Act to Create Federal Bureau of Narcotics), June 14, 1930.

CONTROLLING OPIUM PRODUCTION

Notwithstanding the Harrison Act, the Narcotic Drugs Import and Export Act, and other federal and state legislation, it was still legal to grow opium poppies in the United States as World War II began. As the war got under way, the disruption of normal shipping and trade routes led to a shortage of imported heroin. Concerns that domestic opium production would increase as a result, along with the need to assure that a sufficient supply of legal opiates (especially morphine) would be available for medicinal purposes during the war, led Congress to pass an act placing domestic opium production under strict federal controls. The Opium Poppy Control Act of 1942 required opium poppy growers in the United States to obtain licenses, and limited the amount of opium production to that estimated to fulfill domestic medical and scientific needs. The key provisions of this act are as follows.

DOCUMENT 138: Opium Poppy Control Act (1942)

Be it enacted . . . That it is the purpose of this Act (1) to discharge more effectively the obligations of the United States under the International Opium Convention of 1912, and the Convention for Limiting the Manufacture and Regulating the Distribution of Narcotic Drugs of 1931; (2) to promote the public health and the general welfare; (3) to regulate interstate and foreign commerce in opium poppies; and (4) to safeguard the revenue derived from taxation of opium and opium products.

. . .

Sec. 3. It shall be unlawful for any person who is not the holder of a license authorizing him to produce the opium poppy, duly issued to him by the Secretary of the Treasury in accordance with the provisions of this Act, to produce or attempt to produce the opium poppy, or to permit the production of the opium poppy in or upon any place owned, occupied, used, or controlled by him.

Sec. 4. (a) Except as otherwise provided in section 7: (1) it shall be unlawful for any person who is not the holder of a license authorizing him to produce the opium poppy or to manufacture opium or opium products, duly issued to him by the Secretary of the Treasury in accordance with the provisions of this Act, to purchase or in any other manner obtain the opium poppy; and (2) it shall be unlawful for any person to sell, transfer, convey any interest in, or give away the opium poppy to any person not so licensed.

(b) It shall be unlawful for any person who is not the holder of a license authorizing him to manufacture opium or opium products, duly issued to him by the Secretary of the Treasury in accordance with the provisions of this Act, to manufacture, compound, or extract opium or opium products from the opium poppy.

Sec. 5. It shall be unlawful for any person who is not the holder of a license authorizing him to produce the opium poppy or to manufacture opium or opium products, duly issued to him by the Secretary of the Treasury in accordance with the provisions of this Act, to send, ship, carry, transport, or deliver any opium poppies within any State, Territory, the District of Columbia, the Canal Zone, or insular possession of the United States, or from any State, Territory, the District of Columbia, the Canal Zone, or insular possession of the United States, into any other State, Territory, the District of Columbia, the Canal Zone, or insular possession of the United States: *Provided,* That nothing contained in this section shall apply to any common carrier engaged in transporting opium poppies pursuant to an agreement with a person duly licensed under the provisions of this Act as a producer of the opium poppy, or as a manufacturer of opium or opium products, or to any employee of any person so licensed while acting within the scope of his employment.

Sec. 6. . . .

(b) A license to procure the opium poppy shall be issued only to a person who, in the opinion of the Secretary of the Treasury, is determined to be a person (1) of good moral character; (2) of suitable financial standing and farming experience; (3) who owns or controls suitable farm land to be used as a production area . . . ; and (4) who complies with such additional requirements as the Secretary of the Treasury shall deem and prescribe as reasonably necessary for the controlled production and distribution of the opium poppy. Each such license shall be nontransferable and shall be valid only to the extent of the production area and maximum weight of opium poppy yield specified in the license, shall state the locality of the production area, and shall be effective for a period of one year from the date of issue and may be renewed, in the discretion of the Secretary of the Treasury, for a like period.

(c) A license to manufacture opium or opium products shall be issued only to a person who, in the opinion of the Secretary of the Treasury, is determined to be a person (1) of good moral character; (2) who possesses a method and facilities, deemed satisfactory to the Secretary of the Treasury, for the efficient and economical extraction of opium or opium products; (3) who has such experience in manufacturing and marketing other medicinal drugs as to render reasonably probable the orderly and lawful distribution of opium or opium products of suitable quality to supply medicinal and scientific needs; and (4) who complies with such additional requirements as the Secretary of the Treasury shall deem and prescribe as reasonably necessary for the controlled production, manufacture, and distribution of the opium poppy, opium, or opium products. Such license shall be nontransferable, shall state the maximum quantity of opium poppies purchasable or obtainable thereunder, and shall be effective for a period of one year from the date of issue and may be renewed, in the discretion of the Secretary of the Treasury, for a like period.

(d) All licenses issued under this Act shall be limited to such number, localities, and areas as the Secretary of the Treasury shall determine to be appropriate to supply medicinal and scientific needs of the United States for opium or opium products, with due regard to provision for reasonable reserves. . . .

(e) The Secretary of the Treasury may revoke or refuse to renew any license issued under this Act, if, after due notice and opportunity for hearing, he finds such action to be in the public interest, or finds that the licensee has failed to maintain the requisite qualifications.

Sec. 7. It shall be unlawful for any person to sell, transfer, convey any interest in, or give away, except to a person duly licensed under this Act, or for any unlicensed person to purchase or otherwise obtain, opium poppy seed for the purpose of opium poppy production: *Provided, That* the seed obtained from opium poppies produced by licensed producers may be sold or transferred by such producers to unlicensed persons, and may thereafter be sold or transferred, for ultimate consumption as a spice seed or for the manufacture of oil.

Sec. 8. (a) Any opium poppies which have been produced or otherwise obtained heretofore, and which may be produced or otherwise obtained hereafter in violation of any of the provisions of this Act, shall be seized by and forfeited to the United States.

(b) The failure upon demand by the Secretary of the Treasury, or his duly authorized agent, of the person in occupancy or control of land or premises upon which opium poppies are being produced or stored to produce an appropriate license, or proof that he is the holder thereof, shall constitute authority for the seizure and forfeiture of such opium poppies.

(c) The Secretary of the Treasury, or his duly authorized agent, shall have the authority to enter upon any land (but not a dwelling house, unless pursuant to a search warrant issued according to law) where opium poppies are being produced or stored, for the purposes of enforcing the provisions of this Act.

. . .

(e) The Secretary of the Treasury is hereby directed to destroy any opium poppies seized by and forfeited to the United States under this section, or to deliver for medical or scientific purposes such opium poppies to any department, bureau, or other agency of the United States Government. . . .

Sec. 9. . . .

(b) Nothing in this Act shall be construed to repeal any provision of the Narcotic Drugs Import and Export Act, as amended . . . : Provided, That the Secretary of the Treasury is hereby authorized to limit further or to prohibit entirely the importation or bringing in of crude opium, to the extent that he shall find the medical and scientific needs of the United States for the opium poppies reduced in accordance with this Act.

. . .

Sec. 13. (a) Any person who violates any provision of this Act shall be guilty of a felony and upon conviction thereof, be fined not more than $2,000, or imprisoned not more than five years, or both, in the discretion of the court.

(b) Any person who willfully makes, aids, or assists in the making of, or procures, counsels, or advises in the preparation or presentation of, a false or fraudulent statement in any application for a license under the provisions of this Act shall (whether or not such false or fraudulent statement is made by or with the knowledge or consent of the person authorized to present the application) be guilty of a misdemeanor, and, upon conviction thereof, be fined not more than $2,000 or imprisoned for not more than one year, or both.

Source: Public Law 78–797 (Opium Poppy Control Act), December 11, 1942.

* * *

Commissioner Anslinger, taking credit for passage of this law, described the origins and purposes of the Opium Poppy Control Act in the next document.

DOCUMENT 139: Opium Poppy Control Act (Harry J. Anslinger and William F. Tompkins, 1953)

Due to the shortage of supplies of imported poppy seed after the beginning of World War II, certain persons in the United States commenced to grow the opium poppy, ostensibly for seed yield, ignoring friendly warnings communicated by the Commissioner of Narcotics that the seed pods contained morphine which could and would be readily extracted, even in impure form, by peddlers with the inevitable result of spreading drug addiction. The Commissioner sought and obtained the enactment of special legislation—the Opium Poppy Control Act of 1942—which prohibited the growth of the opium poppy in the United States except under a special license issuable only upon a demonstrated need for domestic production of the opium poppy to supply opium derivatives for medical and scientific uses. No such need has arisen nor is it likely under modern developments that such need will ever arise, and no licenses have been issued. The few crops of opium poppies that were growing were seized, and those who had planted them in defiance of the statute, sought an injunction against the seizure on the ground that the statute was unconstitutional. After a thorough hearing, a three-judge Federal Court in California held the statute constitutionally valid as the execution of an international obligation under the 1912 Convention, and the crops were destroyed.

Source: Harry J. Anslinger and William F. Tompkins, *The Traffic in Narcotics* (New York: Funk and Wagnalls, 1953), 137–138.

* * *

With the passage of the Opium Poppy Act of 1942, federal anti-drug policies, as well as state policies, were basically set until the early 1950s. With the end of World War II came new concerns about the spread of drug abuse, especially among youth, the spread of heroin use, and renewed efforts to strengthen and toughen anti-drug policies.

Part VIII

Drug Policy from World War II Through the 1950s: The Escalation of Punishment

The end of World War II through the 1950s was an important time in the history of American drug policy. In the beginning of that period, renewed fears about the spread of addiction and the emergence of attention toward the "Communist menace" helped spur federal legislation that greatly escalated the range of penalties that could be imposed on drug offenders. Later on, the emergence and growth of the mental health field, and new research on the psychological and medical processes of drug addiction, led to competing calls for decriminalization of drug addiction and the development of new treatment methods.

THE PROBLEMS OF DRUG SMUGGLING AND TEEN DRUG ABUSE

With the end of World War II, government officials feared that the reopening of merchant shipping routes and international trade would increase the smuggling of drugs that had largely remained under control during the war. In addition, they feared an epidemic of addiction among returning soldiers, as had occurred following World War I. At the same time, the appearance of the perceived Communist threat provided a scapegoat to blame for increased drug trafficking. As anti-Communist fervor grew through the late 1940s and early 1950s, drug smuggling was increasingly linked to Chinese and other "subversive" Communist groups. Also, increasing attention was being paid to organized crime: the hearings on organized crime held by Senator Estes Kefauver of Tennessee during the early 1950s provided the first public scrutiny of the Mafia. The Special Senate Committee to Investigate Organized Crime in Interstate Commerce illuminated the role of the Mafia in drug trafficking, especially heroin. In its final report, the Kefauver Committee summarized its views about the Mafia's involvement in drugs.

DOCUMENT 140: Kefauver Committee Final Report (1952)

Experienced enforcement officers believe that the present influx of heroin from abroad is managed by the Mafia. . . . Worldwide in scope, the Mafia is believed to derive the major source of its income from the distribution and smuggling of narcotics.

Source: Quoted in Rufus King, *The Drug Hang-up* (New York: W. W. Norton, 1972), 117.

* * *

Harry Anslinger, the powerful and influential commissioner of the Federal Bureau of Narcotics, was instrumental in placing responsibility for the spread of drug addiction on the Mafia and on China, as is evident in the next document.

DOCUMENT 141: Drugs and the Mafia (Harry J. Anslinger and Will Oursler, 1961)

The professional narcotic mobsters are the most ruthless criminals in the world. . . . I warn the American public—and urge them—not to let irresponsible statements by misinformed people weaken our position on narcotic controls. Because of America's leading role in building these controls, any weakening of our stand would open the doors to world disaster. Only the organized underworld—and the Communists—would cheer. . . .

I warn America to stand firm against the encroaching power of the syndicate. . . . I believe that the organized syndicate in America, with its strong Mafia influence, presents an immediate and present danger to our society. When we curtail their people-to-people dope pushing, they turn to other outlets for criminal cash. . . .

I believe especially that we must be on guard against the use of drugs as a political weapon by the Communist forces in China and elsewhere in the Orient, Europe, and Africa. There is every possibility that some of the Commies and fellow travelers may join hands with the world-wide syndicate—for profits and subversive politics combined. There is every possibility that they may try to make narcotics a new "sixth" column to weaken and destroy selected targets in the drive for world domination.

Source: Harry J. Anslinger and Will Oursler, *The Murderers* (New York: Farrar, Straus and Cudahy, 1961), 294–295.

* * *

Following World War II, there was considerable media coverage about the smuggling of drugs into the United States, which often played up the role of Communists and organized smuggling rings. The next two documents are illustrative.

DOCUMENT 142: Drug Smuggling in the 1940s (*New York Times*, 1948)

Customs officers will increase their vigilance in searching ships coming here from France and Mediterranean ports to frustrate attempts to smuggle narcotics, Herman Lipski, deputy surveyor in charge of the service's enforcement division, said yesterday.

A group of officers from the division uncovered about fifteen pounds of pure morphine here Monday on the transport Marine Marlin. The cache was said to be worth $500,000 in the illicit drug market.

Six crew members were said to be "under suspicion" and an investigation by customs investigators was said last night to be continuing. No arrests have been reported.

Mr. Lipski and other Customs spokesmen said that the morphine had been brought aboard the Marine Marlin by members of an international smuggling ring.

They expressed the belief that the ring was the same one that hid large narcotics shipments aboard the French freighter St. Tropez and the Government-owned liner John Ericsson last year. On Feb. 4, 1947, Customs men seized heroin valued in the illicit market at $250,000 on the Ericsson. On March 18, 1947, operatives of the service uncovered heroin valued at $1,147,500 on the St. Tropez.

. . .

Mr. Lipski said that there had been narcotics seizures almost daily since a drive against the illicit traffic began about a year ago. In addition to the morphine seized on the Marine Marlin, a small quantity of marijuana was confiscated on the ship. Another small marijuana seizure was made on the freighter Spitfire Monday. She arrived here from the Far East Saturday.

Source: "Customs Tightens Vigil on Narcotics," *New York Times*, March 10, 1948.

DOCUMENT 143: China's Role in Drug Smuggling (*New York Times*, 1954)

The United States accused the Foreign Ministry of Communist China today of directing a campaign to spread drug addiction in the Western world.

The charge was made by Harry J. Anslinger, Federal Narcotics Commissioner. He declared that Peiping Government officials had assumed overall control of the illicit narcotics traffic, both to reap profits and also to "demoralize the people of the free world."

Mr. Anslinger made the accusation in furnishing up-to-date evidence on the illegal drug trade to the United Nations Commission on Narcotic Drugs. . . .

The Commissioner's remarks on Red China brought an almost instant protest from the Soviet and Polish members of the commission, both complaining that the United States was slandering an absent government and also dragging in political issues.

. . .

Mr. Anslinger reminded the members that he had warned for several years that the illegal drug trade on the Chinese mainland was growing. But the new element, he declared, is that the Foreign Ministry now has taken over the direction of drug exports and distribution through the National Trading Company, which has its headquarters in Peiping.

In the last year, he said, 800 tons of opium, heroin and morphine, valued at $60,000,000, was shipped out. . . .

This spreading of narcotic addiction for profit and political motive is not the work of one man in the Communist regime, Mr. Anslinger charged. "It is the policy of the entire Communist regime in mainland

China." It is part of a continuing twenty-year plan, he continued, to spread addiction among free peoples. . . .

Mr. Anslinger also made these other charges:

. . .

—There has been a threefold increase in some land areas devoted to opium cultivation in Communist China and the establishment of new heroin factories.

In his account of the smashing of the San Francisco narcotic ring Mr. Anslinger told the commission that eight prominent Chinese had been arrested and that Judah Isaac Ezra, a Hong Kong supplier of morphine, had been indicted. Federal agents seized six pounds of heroin—sufficient to supply 1,000,000 addict doses.

The drugs, he reported, were carried into this country by merchant seamen, or sometimes smuggled in ornately carved camphorwood chests with special compartments.

Source: "U.S. Charges China Spurs Drug Habit," *New York Times*, May 5, 1954.

* * *

In a late 1940s article in a popular, widely circulated magazine, another foreign threat was described: the smuggling of opium and marijuana across the Mexican border.

DOCUMENT 144: Drug Smuggling from Mexico (Peter Packer, 1948)

Heroin, morphine, opium—products of Mexico's red poppy—are today moving in a hundred cunning ways across the Mexican border into the United States. With marijuana, they developed into an illicit business amounting to an estimated $40,000,000 in 1947. Most of the dope went to the United States. A determined effort to stop this traffic is engaging the full time of hundreds of American and Mexican customs officers and narcotic agents. . . .

. . .

In the past few months co-operation between U.S. and Mexican authorities in the capture of smugglers and the seizure of narcotics has become more effective than it had been hitherto. Behind this cooperation lie the efforts of Dr. Harry J. Anslinger, dynamic chief of the U.S. Treasury's Narcotics Division and his associates in the U.S. Customs. . . .

The Treasury report for 1947 on seizures of illicit narcotics shows a substantial increase over the previous year. During last year 7,388 ounces of opium and its derivatives were seized, as compared with 5,464 ounces in 1946. . . .

Relentlessly the battle of the border against the thugs and runners of the dope rings goes on. . . . An alarming result of such smuggling was the arrest . . . of a sixteen-year-old student in Manhattan. He produced long lists of customers among the children of the high school he attended.

"It's mighty serious when that stuff coming up from below the border finds its way into our high schools," said one narcotics agent. "That's why this war against the scum who are running this traffic is an all-out war!"

Source: Peter Packer, "The War Against Dope Runners," *Collier's Magazine*, July 31, 1948, 14–15, 47.

* * *

The other area of concern in the postwar debate about drug problems was the notion that drug sales to and addiction among teenagers were increasing. This idea paralleled the attention paid to young drug abusers (especially of heroin) in the 1920s. The media and policy makers gave considerable coverage to the questions about drug problems in schools and among youth.

DOCUMENT 145: Spread of Teenage Addiction (Harry J. Anslinger and Will Oursler, 1961)

Wherever extensive teenage addiction erupts, as it did in American communities in the years following World War II, we face an extraordinary enforcement problem. . . . The ruthlessness of this business is hard to believe.

Source: Harry J. Anslinger and Will Oursler, *The Murderers* (New York: Farrar, Straus and Cudahy, 1961), 187.

DOCUMENT 146: Postwar Increase in Addiction (*New York Times*, 1950)

A "substantial rise" in narcotics addiction since the end of World War II was reported yesterday by Garland H. Williams, district supervisor of the Federal Narcotics Bureau.

However, the Police Department asserted that addiction had risen about 10 per cent, with virtually all of the increase among teenagers in the Bronx.

. . .

Information uncovered is expected to lead this week to important wholesale distributors, who are held responsible for the heavy flow of heroin and marijuana, the most popular narcotics, and are reported to be financing the centers where the teenagers congregate, he added.

Known as "pad joints," because all windows and doors are sealed tightly with cotton wadding or newspapers, to prevent the tell-tale odor of "junk" from seeping out into the street, the dimly illuminated places feature juke boxes and shoddy oriental-type decorations.

. . .

Lieutenant Boylan and Mr. Williams agreed that the post-war increase in narcotic addiction was normal. They attributed it to easier sources of supply of raw materials from foreign countries and better shipping facilities. A similar rise in narcotic distribution followed the first World War.

Mr. Williams also declared that addiction could be cut down materially if a law were passed to force users to take a cure. Attempts to pass measures against illegal addiction have failed so far, he noted.

Source: "10% Post-war Rise in City Narcotic Addicts Laid by Police Chiefly to Bronx Teen-agers," *New York Times*, April 11, 1950. Copyright © 1950 by The New York Times. Reprinted by permission.

* * *

One year later a national news magazine published the following report suggesting that large numbers of students were using drugs.

DOCUMENT 147: Increased Drug Use among Students (*Newsweek*, 1951)

Last week, New York City school teachers were studying a little pamphlet hastily issued by the Police Department. Its contents: a description of various types of narcotics, the methods used by addicts to get their "lift," and a list of the "more common symptoms of drug addiction."

The teachers were alerted to be on the lookout for furtive glances, watery eyes, marked restlessness and body movement, stooped shoulders, unusual and abnormal ideas, and frequent yawning. Once upon a time, the average schoolmarm faced these classroom manifestations as part of the job; now, New York City teachers were being warned that they often were symptoms of drug addiction. Behind the warning lay an ugly fact. The organized dope trade has established a steady, tragic market in the city's school system. It had mushroomed into a citywide affliction, with an estimated 2,000 peddlers feeding about 30,000 users, half of whom, according to New York police, were teen-agers.

The average New Yorker took one look at this fact and screamed: How long has this been going on? Last week, as official agencies, aroused citizens' organizations, and newsmen dug into the problem, it was obvious that there was no one, clear-cut, answer. In New York, the dope traffic had always been a tough problem because of the city's natural position as leading port of entry for illegal imports. And since the second world war, the problem had been getting worse.

. . .

Official reports showed plainly that the time for action had come. Police blotters had become veritable charts of the dope traffic. More and more teenagers, arrested for assault and armed robbery, had said they were trying to get money for more dope.

Meanwhile, social agencies reported that record numbers of teen-agers were appealing to them for help in breaking the habit. One official said: "Why, we've been forced to send them to the House of Detention or Rikers Island for 'cold turkey' [sudden and complete] withdrawal [of drugs]. There's no more ghastly sight than a child addict undergoing this ordeal."

City Councilwoman Bertha Schwartz, completing a personal study, noted a shocking increase in addiction cases, from the age of 13 up. "Teenagers," she said, "pawn the clothes off their backs. Girl addicts become prostitutes. . . . [They] admit they would kill their own father or mother if the parent stands between me and a fix."

The World-Telegram & Sun, one of the prime movers in the current expose, pointed out that addiction deaths in New York City in 1950 totaled 58; 23 of the victims were less than 25 years of age. One recent case, reported by the paper, concerned a 17-year-old who was found in a drug induced coma. He "literally slept his ebbing life away under the influence of dope." Authorities were unable to discover whether the youngster had taken an overdose by accident, or was trying to commit suicide with the needle, a common "way out" for despondent addicts.

Last week, after months of careful work, the Police Department opened its drive on the teen-agers—and the men and women behind them. Headquarters announced that the roundup would take months. It would take that long to stamp out primary drug sources, search out new ones, and retrace steps to stamp out any buds which might have developed on the remains of the old ones.

Source: "New York Wakes Up to Find 15,000 Teen-age Dope Addicts." From *Newsweek*, January 29, 1951

* * *

That same year, another popular magazine article colorfully described the impact of drug addiction on youth and called for enhanced penalties against drug traffickers who sell to teenagers, a policy that was adopted in later federal and state legislation during the 1950s. Similar concerns about selling drugs to youth during the 1980s led to the enactment of enhanced penalties for selling drugs to minors in federal and state laws.

DOCUMENT 148: Fighting Teen Drug Addiction (Howard Whitman, 1951)

We can stop teen-age drug addiction now. To do it, we must recognize this dread new curse for what it is. It is not just another form of delinquency. It is the deliberate exploitation of naive boys and girls by drug traffickers who aim to open up a rich new market, to raise a huge new crop of addicts.

What crime is worse, more villainous than addicting teen-age boys and girls to narcotics? "You might as well shoot them in the back," remarked Senator Estes Kefauver in Washington. "It might even be kinder."

The teen-age victims themselves call it the "white death." I have seen their rueful faces and probed into the wreckage of young lives ruined—possibly for good—at sixteen, seventeen, eighteen. They call it "white death" because of the powdered white opiate with which the drug merchants have enslaved them.

What are we going to do about it?

Are we going to sit back and accept it? Are we going to wring our hands in surrender and admit that henceforth one of the hazards of growing up—even for our own children—may be enslavement to narcotic drugs?

Or are we ready to beat the dope merchants at their own game, to make the teen-age drug traffic (as we once made kidnapping) too hot to handle? Do we have the vitality, the determination to stamp out this curse here and now?

. . .

Today the racketeers, their peddlers and "pushers," have infiltrated the school neighborhoods and the drugstore counters. They do not blatantly hawk their wares. They don't have to. Boys and girls already in enslavement to drugs will seek them out, even if they have to walk miles or wait hours to make, as they say "a connection." . . .

. . .

As it is now, our federal narcotics laws do not make a single distinction between selling drugs to innocent children . . . and selling drugs to old hands who have been addicted for years. The crime is legally the same.

Moreover, though we have arrested plenty of peddlers, scores have gone scot-free and the bulk have been given ridiculously inadequate sentences. The average sentence has been eighteen months. This is no overhead at all to a racketeer. The peddlers' own contempt for such wrist-slapping is summed up in what one of them said to a federal agent—"I can do a rap like that standing on my head."

. . .

What effect would stiffer sentences have? We already have a convincing example. Memphis, Tennessee, was full of dope peddlers during the 1920's. It was a distribution point between north and south. When caught, peddlers got off with sixty-day sentences and the traffic flourished. Then Memphis got a new district judge, the late J. Will Ross. He meted out sentences of ten to twelve and even seventeen years.

The drug traffic cleared out of Memphis like a squealing pig. It has never come back. To this day, in the penitentiaries, the word is still heard among inveterate junkies, "Keep out of Memphis. It's hot."

. . .

The fight against teen-age drug traffic adds up to two simple steps. They are easy for the federal government as well as the states to take. They involve no rigmarole. They cost not one cent.

Recognize the selling of drugs, directly or indirectly, to teen-agers as a separate crime. . . . A simple law, a simple amendment to an existing law, can meet it point-blank by defining as a separate crime the peddling of narcotics to minors. Then—2. *Triple the penalties*. Instead of the five- and ten-year maximum sentences under federal narcotics laws, and similar penalties under state laws, triple the sentences when teen-agers have been victimized. . . . Make this the third great instance in which a virile society draws a line on the ground and resolutely says, "This far—but no farther!"

This is society's one-two punch which will send the teen-age drug traffic reeling. It is the only action the dope merchants fear, the only language they understand. . . .

The big stick will knock them out just as it knocked out white slavery and kidnapping. They will keep their leprous hands off our boys and girls.

Source: Howard Whitman, "How We Can Stop Narcotic Sales," *Woman's Home Companion*, June 1951.

* * *

It is interesting that Bureau of Narcotics Commissioner Anslinger sometimes tried to play down the seriousness of the nation's drug problems when it suited his or the bureau's needs. When he wanted to demonstrate what a good job his bureau was doing, he would cite statistics showing that there were fewer addicts. When lobbying for more funding before Congress, Anslinger often emphasized the dire state of drug addiction across the United States.

DOCUMENT 149: Teenage Addiction Problem Overstated (John Gerrity, 1952)

In contrast to the horrifying spectacle splashed across the nation of "hundreds of thousands of dope fiends," there are at the moment, the Federal Bureau of Narcotics insists, only 50,000 to 60,000 drug addicts in the United States. And most of these, along with the peddlers who serve them, are clustered in seven major cities—New York, Baltimore, Philadelphia, Detroit, Chicago, New Orleans, and Washington, D.C. . . .

Contrariwise, except for a rare case in Boston, New England has no addictions. From Virginia as far south as Florida and as far west as New Orleans, not a single teen-age addict is known to exist. There are other parts of the country with very favorable records; the rate of addiction in Minnesota, Kansas, Montana, the Dakotas, and Wyoming, for instance, is one out of 25,000 as opposed to the national rate of one in 3,000.

. . .

"Why," asks Harry J. Anslinger, U.S. Narcotics Commissioner, "would a business man and drug peddlers are business men desert a proven market for the hazards of an unproved one, like teen-age high-school students?

"Peddlers might branch out and expand their operations," Mr. Anslinger continues, "if they had a surplus after taking care of old customers. But, if for only two reasons, we are certain that the wholesale supply is diminishing, not increasing. The purity of heroin has dropped in three years from 75 percent to slightly more than 3 per cent, indicating that a little must now satisfy where much more once did. And during this time the price of diluted heroin has risen from $1,000 an ounce to $3,000 an ounce."

Mr. Anslinger claims that nearly all high school addicts are in New York City and Chicago. And reports of addiction there, he claims, are vastly exaggerated. "Shortly after the Kefauver expose," he says, "the New York City Mayor's Committee announced that there were 90,000 addicts in the metropolitan area, many of these being in high schools.

"Another source claimed that among 15,000 parochial and Yeshiva school students they found not one addict. The city authorities began to revise their estimates when we asked them to explain why peddlers had singled out public school students and ignored parochial school students."

A similar story, related by police chief Robert V. Murray, illustrates the magnification of the menace in Washington. "Here the members of the school board ran the test themselves. Every one of 15,000 public and parochial high school students underwent thorough physical examinations," he said. "They found three students sufficiently addicted to heroin to require hospital and psychiatric care."

More recently it was disclosed that a two-year investigation of the high schools of Westchester County, New York, discovered no evidence of drug addiction among pupils; and that one investigator who tried to buy marijuana cigarettes or other narcotics from students succeeded only in obtaining cigarettes made from cut-plug tobacco which pupils attempted to pass off as marijuana.

. . .

Meanwhile the most awkward problem which faces the Federal Narcotics Bureau and intelligent police officials within the United States today grows out of the very hysteria which the crime investigations have caused. Apparently we persist in being a nation of calamity-howlers whose violent surges of zeal for reform sometimes hinder, rather than help, the organizations that could do some genuine good. . . .

There will always be some illegal drug traffic. A few doctors will continue to write illegal prescriptions. Still fewer pharmacists will illegally renew prescriptions for morphine and barbiturates. And thieves will always rob drug stores.

But as for the widely publicized "drug menace" which is supposed to be threatening the future of teen-agers by the hundreds of thousands, it simply doesn't exist, and the sooner we realize this, the easier it will be for our expert officials to combat the scattered drug traffic that does exist.

Source: John Gerrity, "The Truth About the 'Drug Menace,' " *Harper's Magazine*, February 1952.

* * *

Finally, Dr. Lawrence Kolb, a former Public Health Service official who was a key crusader for the medical model of addiction, suggested that the post–World War II teenage drug problem had been exaggerated.

DOCUMENT 150: Teenage Addiction Problem Overstated (Lawrence Kolb, 1956)

After World War II, it was found that some teen-agers in a few large American cities were becoming addicted to heroin and marijuana. Although the addiction was not widespread—it was found mostly among deprived classes in neighborhood gangs—there was a loud outcry. A statewide survey conducted by Pennsylvania officials, reported in the January, 1952, issue of Pennsylvania Health, disclosed no positive case of teen-age addiction in Pennsylvania schools. The "upsurge" was a myth; there are actually fewer teen-age addicts in the United States now than there were in the '20's.

Source: Lawrence Kolb, "Let's Stop This Narcotics Hysteria!," *Saturday Evening Post*, July 28, 1956.

THE BOGGS ACT AND THE EISENHOWER COMMITTEE

Within this climate of concern over increasing numbers of young addicts, the role of drug exportation and trafficking by Communist and organized crime groups, and the lack of viable treatment alternatives, it is not surprising that Congress responded with new, tougher legislation against drugs. A new law, sponsored by Representative Hale Boggs of Louisiana, modified the 1922 Import and Export Act and for the first time established mandatory minimum sentences of two years in prison for any violation of federal drug trafficking laws. The Kefauver Committee included the proposed bill as one of its recommendations. Popularly known as the Boggs Act, this 1951 law also allowed longer prison sentences for repeat offenses and disallowed a suspended sentence or probation for such repeat offenders.

DOCUMENT 151: Boggs Act (1951)

. . . [S]ection 2 (c) of the Narcotic Drugs Import and Export Act, as amended (U.S.C., title 21, sec. 174), is amended to read as follows:

(a) Whoever fraudulently or knowingly imports or brings any narcotic drug into the United States or any territory under its control or jurisdiction, contrary to law, or receives, conceals, buys, sells, or in any manner facilitates the transportation, concealment, or sale of any such narcotic drug after being imported or brought in, knowing the same to have been imported contrary to law, or conspires to commit any of such acts in violation of the laws of the United States, shall be fined not more than $2,000 and imprisoned not less than two or more than five years. For a second offense, the offender shall be fined not more than $2,000 and imprisoned not less than five or more than ten years. For a third or subsequent offense, the offender shall be fined not more than $2,000 and imprisoned not less than ten or more than twenty years. Upon conviction for a second or subsequent offense, the imposition or execution of sentence shall not be suspended and probation shall not be granted. . . .

. . .

Sec. 2. Section 2557 (b) (1) of the Internal Revenue Code is amended to read as follows:

(1) Whoever commits an offense or conspires to commit an offense described in this subchapter, subchapter C of this chapter, or parts V or VI of subchapter A of chapter 27 for which no specific penalty is otherwise provided, shall be fined not more than $2,000 and imprisoned not less than two or more than five years. For a second offense, the offender shall be fined not more than $2,000 and imprisoned not less than five or more than ten years. For a third or subsequent offense, the offender shall be fined not more than $2,000 and imprisoned not less than ten or more than twenty years. Upon conviction for a second or subsequent offense, the imposition or execution of sentence shall not be suspended and probation shall not be granted.

Source: Public Law 82–255 (Boggs Act), November 2, 1951.

* * *

Despite the assumption that the Boggs Act, in toughening federal anti-drug laws, would help reduce the problems of drug addiction, it was apparent within several years that the concern about the effects of drugs was not going to go away. In 1954 President Dwight Eisenhower decided to launch another "war" on drug addiction, and convened a special cabinet committee to examine the current fight against drugs and to recommend new solutions. The idea that treatment and rehabilitation were part of the fight against drugs began to emerge.

DOCUMENT 152: Announcement of New Presidential Study (*New York Times*, 1954)

President Eisenhower called today for a new war on narcotic addiction at the local, national and international level.

He appointed a special Cabinet committee of five members to coordinate the campaign against illegal narcotics and enjoined them to "omit no practical step to minimize and stamp out narcotic addiction." . . .

James C. Hagerty, White House press secretary, said that new legislation might be asked from the next Congress to step up the drive against the narcotics traffic and to aid the rehabilitation of those who have become addicts. . . .

. . .

"In order to define more clearly the scope of the problems which we face and to promote effective cooperation among Federal, state and local agencies, a comprehensive up-to-date survey on the extent of narcotic addiction is urgently needed and should be made by the committee," President Eisenhower said in a letter to the committee members.

"A determination of what the states and local agencies have accomplished and what they are equipped to do in the field of law enforcement and in the rehabilitation of the victims of the scourge should also be included in the survey."

. . .

"I know that devoted and strenuous attention is being given to the problem on a number of fronts; but we should omit no practical step to minimize and stamp out narcotic addiction."

Source: "President Launches Drive on Narcotics," *New York Times*, November 28, 1954. Copyright © 1954 by The New York Times. Reprinted by permission.

* * *

The final report of the Eisenhower Committee was released in February 1956 and called for increased federal-state coordination, adequate treatment resources, commitment of addicts to hospitals for treatment, and more severe penalties for nonusing drug sellers. The committee also noted that the problem of addiction among youth appeared to have been exaggerated. The report's recommendations were summarized as follows.

DOCUMENT 153: Eisenhower Committee Final Report (*New York Times,* 1956)

Heavier punishment, more enforcement officers and better Federal-State coordination were among steps recommended today to combat the narcotic evil.

. . .

The [Eisenhower] committee, while it remarked that "the existence of one addict is one addict too many, found it some comfort that an estimate of 60,000 addicts in the country was not as high as had been expected."

It added that "unofficial reports of a problem of serious dimensions among young people of school age have been exaggerations." It noted that of 24,043 addicts reported by various agencies in 1953–54 only 13 per cent were under 21 years old and that 3,145 of these, or 87.6 per cent, were 18 or over.

The committee made fourteen recommendations. . . .

1. The Federal Government should encourage and help state and municipal studies related to the special circumstances of the communities.
2. Federal assistance to states and cities should include courses of instructions for both public health and enforcement officers.
3. In each state and in each city having a narcotics problems [*sic*] one senior law enforcement official should be specifically charged with fighting the evil.
4. In states and municipalities there should be, if justified by the number of addicts, adequate facilities for treatment and rehabilitation of addicts. . . .
5. States should give consideration to establishing, or using more frequently, legal procedures for committing addicts to institutions for treatment.
6. Pending full availability in the States of treatment facilities, legislation should be passed permitting states to commit addicts to Federal hospitals for treatment.
7. The Surgeon General of the Public Health Service should be permitted to disclose "information on voluntary patients" where, in his opinion, "physicians and recognized welfare agencies will be enabled to act in the interests of the patients in further treatment for their addiction."
8. The Government should keep up its close cooperative effort in the

United Nations and other international organizations to foster the "highly encouraging" progress toward international controls of narcotics.

9. There should be further study of the advisability of teaching about narcotics in schools. Warning was sounded that such programs might only attract attention and "arouse curiosity over experimentation with the drugs."

10. There should be more severe maximum sentences for both first and repeating offenders against the narcotics laws, particularly for the seller of drugs who does not use them himself. . . .

11. Increase in the agent force of the Federal Bureau of Narcotics should be considered.

12. There should be a study of possible Federal legislation to establish controls over the manufacture and distribution of "synthetic drugs with properties similar to the narcotics."

13. Enforcement problems arising from court decision[s] limiting "the procurement and presentation of evidence" should receive "thorough and careful consideration from the standpoint of the optimum in law enforcement."

14. A study similar to that covering narcotics should be made of the extent and effects of improper use of such other drugs as marijuana, amphetamines, barbiturates and others that "affect emotional behavior," the study to be used to determine "the appropriate scope of Federal, state and local regulatory controls."

Source: "U.S. Report Spurs Drive on Narcotics," *New York Times*, February 6, 1956.

THE DEBATE OVER PUNITIVE DRUG LAWS AND THE 1956 NARCOTIC CONTROL ACT

In the early 1950s some important competing views emerged about the direction that government drug control policy should take. At the national level, the powerful American Bar Association (ABA) created a special Committee on Narcotics in 1954, and in early 1955 the ABA passed a resolution urging Congress to review federal drug policy. In addition, the medical establishment was becoming somewhat uneasy about the trend toward ever-increasing penalties for drug law violations. In the early 1950s both the American Medical Association (AMA) and the New York Academy of Medicine began investigations into the efficacy of existing drug policies and the development of possible alternative, more medically oriented policies.

The New York Academy of Medicine's Committee on Public Health, Subcommittee on Drug Addiction, released a major report of its findings in 1955. Reviewing the history of American drug policy from the Harrison Act to the mid-1950s, the academy was fairly critical of the current trend toward more punitive federal laws, and urged the government to view addiction as a disease and to support new research on treatment and addiction. Its most controversial recommendations related to allowing physicians to dispense narcotic drugs to addicts under a maintenance clinic model (see Document 246). The report concluded that the emphasis on punishment in the Boggs Act might worsen the drug problem.

DOCUMENT 154: Boggs Act Too Punitive (New York Academy of Medicine, 1955)

The punitive approach is no deterrent to the non-addict dealer or to the addict. The threat of stiff penalties in the form of jail sentences has not prevented the non-addict dealer or the addict from taking the risk. Furthermore, the serving of sentences in jail has not proved the solution of drug addiction. For one thing, the record of repeat jail sentences for addicts is so large that the procedure has been called "the revolving door policy." For another, confinement in jails succeeds in thoroughly instructing in the ways of the underworld those addicts who had not yet engaged in criminal activity. Particularly in the case of young addicts the jail sentence is a dangerous approach to a medical problem. During incarceration the young addict, who had perhaps not even finished school because of his subjection to narcotics, learns from other prisoners not a skill with which he can support himself, but how to get along without working at all, even less desirable ways of maintaining his drug habit, and a complete course in drug addiction. . . .

In view of the enormously magnified economic aspects of drug traffic, perhaps the punitive approach may not be the most effective way to bring about substantial reduction in drug addiction.

. . .

The present Federal regulations control the practice of medicine in relation to drug addiction to such an extent, and so look upon the physician as a potential criminal, that he prefers not to include the treatment of drug addiction in his practice.

. . .

Judged by the criteria of abstinence from narcotics, and of accession to a gainful occupation in society, the rehabilitation of the drug addict in our present state of knowledge is a highly expensive, exceedingly slow and prolonged procedure necessitating repetitive efforts.

As a means of stamping out drug addiction, prevention remains the most practical and essential step. The crux of any program aimed to rid society of drug addiction is to stop the formation of new addicts.

The program of the past has also been inadequate in two approaches which hold promise of contributing to the diminution of drug addiction: research and education.

Source: New York Academy of Medicine, "Report on Drug Addiction," *Bulletin of the New York Academy of Medicine* 31, no. 8 (1955): 601.

* * *

At the federal level, the Bureau of Narcotics vigorously defended their policies in a series of publications including Commissioner Anslinger's 1953 book, *The Traffic in Narcotics*. And on March 18, 1955, the U.S. Senate passed a resolution introduced by Senator Price Daniel of Texas to have the Senate Judiciary Committee conduct a broad review of federal drug policy and draft new legislation.

Under the chairmanship of Senator Daniel, the special Subcommittee on Improvements in the Federal Criminal Code began hearings on June 2, 1955. In addition to those in Washington, D.C., hearings were held in a number of cities where drug problems were of great concern, such as New York, Philadelphia, Chicago, San Francisco, Dallas, Los Angeles, and Detroit. A statement by Senator Daniel at one of the hearings, responding to testimony by doctors from the Public Health Service who had expressed some support for ambulatory treatment of addicts, set the tone for the hearings and the resulting legislation.

DOCUMENT 155: Statement by Senator Price Daniel (1955)

Gentlemen, I tell you that, after sitting through two more days of hearings here, I am convinced that we are never going to lick this problem of the drug traffic until we get the addicts off the streets of this country. . . . Some of the enforcement officers think it is best to get them in the jails temporarily, and the different States have passed those kind of laws. I would like to see us at the same time that we set up our laws to take them off the streets, set up some place to have them go and get a chance for treatment, and then if they won't take it, and you cannot do anything with them, then, it seems to me, it is just humane to put them in some kind of colony or some kind of farm or institution like you do mental patients. . . .

I think you see that what this Committee is driving at and what kind of information we would like to have now has been brought out in the discussion, and I am sure you have some papers, studies, and other things that would be of help to us; and if we have not asked for them specifically, we will appreciate your volunteering them or any other information that would be helpful to the Committee.

Source: Quoted in Rufus King, *The Drug Hang-up* (New York: W. W. Norton, 1972), 133.

* * *

In its preliminary report to the Senate after the hearings were concluded, the Daniel Committee expressed its view about the seriousness of the drug problem.

DOCUMENT 156: Preliminary Report to the Senate Judiciary Committee (1956)

We were surprised and shocked at the extent and far-reaching effect of the illicit drug traffic in the United States and have concluded that narcotic addiction and the dope traffic constitutes one of the most serious problems facing the nation.

Source: Senate Judiciary Committee Hearings, pursuant to Senate Resolution 67, January 23, 1956, 2.

* * *

The tone of the Daniel Committee's report on the national hearings was clearly designed to convey a deep concern about the effects of drug addiction and drug trafficking on American society in the 1950s. A report on the committee's findings in a national news magazine painted a grim picture. Interestingly, the same figure of 60,000 drug addicts that was reassuringly low to the Eisenhower Committee was an alarming number to the Daniel Committee.

DOCUMENT 157: Report on Daniel Committee Findings (*Time*, January 16, 1956)

In Washington this week Texas' Senator Price Daniel reported on the findings of a seven month scrutiny by a Senate Judiciary Subcommittee into narcotics addiction and illicit drug traffic in the U.S. It was the first nationwide investigation of the problem and the Daniel subcommittee heard 345 witnesses, including many addicts and smugglers, for a total of 8,667 pages of testimony. The subcommittee dredged up some hideous and alarming facts. Items:

The U.S. now has more drug addicts (60,000) than all other Western nations combined. In the past three years the Federal Bureau of Narcotics has compiled a list of names and addresses of 30,000 known addicts, and the list is growing at the rate of 1,000 a month.

Illegal dope traffic has trebled since World War II. At the end of the war, there was one addict to every 10,000 persons in the U.S., in 1955 there was one to every 3,000. Thirteen percent of all addicts in the country are under 21.

Approximately 50% of all crime in U.S. cities, and 25% of all crime in the nation, is attributable to drug addiction.

Daniel and his colleagues proposed a detailed program of controls, which they are drafting into specific legislation. Among the recommendations:

. . . The death penalty, he added, should be imposed only in an extreme case, such as that of a peddler who made addicts out of 40 high-school students in San Antonio.

At least 50 new agents should be added to the Federal Bureau of Narcotics staff. The bureau now has only 227 agents—fewer than the narcotics control staff of the New York City Police Department.

Source: "Drug Addiction," *Time*, January 16, 1956.

* * *

Out of the Daniel hearings came the Narcotic Control Act of 1956, which increased maximum allowable penalties beyond those enacted in the 1951 Boggs Act. For example, the maximum sentence for a first possession offense was increased from 5 to 10 years, and for a second offense from 10 to 20 years. Penalties for importing drugs (including marijuana) were also increased to a minimum of 5 years and a maximum of 20 years in prison. And, for the first time, this federal legislation provided for the death penalty for a drug offense: at the discretion of a jury, a person 18 or older could be sentenced to death for selling heroin to a youth under age 18. In addition, the 1956 act authorized narcotics agents to carry guns and to arrest suspected drug violators without a warrant (Section 7607), and required that addicts, drug users, and those previously convicted of drug offenses under federal or state laws must register and obtain a certificate from the Treasury Department upon leaving the United States (Section 1407).

The special penalties against heroin in the 1956 act reflected particular concern about this drug in the early 1950s. In the Daniel Committee's report, the following statement was made about heroin.

DOCUMENT 158: Preliminary Report to the Senate Judiciary Committee (1956)

Heroin smugglers and peddlers are selling murder, robbery, and rape, and should be dealt with accordingly. Their offense is human destruction as surely as that of the murderer. In truth and in fact, it is "murder on the installment plan," leading not only to the final loss of one's life but to others who acquire this contagious infection through association with the original victim.

Source: Senate Judiciary Committee Hearings, pursuant to Senate Resolution 67, January 23, 1956, 7.

* * *

Key sections of the 1956 Narcotic Control Act are presented in the following document. The original document includes newly enacted sections of federal law that are numbered in the 100s and 200s; the other numbers are revisions of sections of previously enacted laws.

DOCUMENT 159: Narcotic Control Act (1956)

Sec. 7237. VIOLATION OF LAWS RELATING TO NARCOTIC DRUGS AND TO MARIHUANA.

(a) . . . Whoever commits an offense, or conspires to commit an offense, described in part I or part II of subchapter A of chapter 39 for which no specific penalty is otherwise provided, shall be imprisoned not less than 2 or more than 10 years and, in addition, may be fined not more than $20,000. For a second offense, the offender shall be imprisoned not less than 5 or more than 20 years and, in addition, may be fined not more than $20,000. For a third or subsequent offense, the offender shall be imprisoned not less than 10 or more than 40 years and, in addition, may be fined not more than $20,000.

(b) . . . Whoever commits an offense, or conspires to commit an offense, . . . shall be imprisoned not less than 5 or more than 20 years and, in addition, may be fined not more than $20,000. For a second or subsequent offense, the offender shall be imprisoned not less than 10 or more than 40 years and, in addition, may be fined not more than $20,000. If the offender attained the age of 18 before the offense and—

(1) the offense consisted of the sale, barter, exchange, giving away, or transfer of any narcotic drug or marihuana to a person who had not attained the age of 18 at the time of such offense, or

(2) the offense consisted of a conspiracy to commit an offense described in paragraph (1), the offender shall be imprisoned not less than 10 or more than 40 years and, in addition, may be fined not more than $20,000.

. . .

Sec. 7607. ADDITIONAL AUTHORITY FOR BUREAU OF NARCOTICS AND BUREAU OF CUSTOMS.

The Commissioner, Deputy Commissioner, Assistant to the Commissioner, and agents, of the Bureau of Narcotics of the Department of the Treasury, and officers of the customs . . . may—

(1) carry firearms, execute and serve search warrants and arrest warrants, and serve subpoenas and summonses issued under the authority of the United States, and

(2) make arrests without warrant for violations of any law of the United States relating to narcotic drugs . . . or marihuana . . . where the violation is committed in the presence of the person making the arrest or where such person has reasonable grounds to believe that the person to be arrested has committed or is committing such violation.

. . .

Sec. 107. SALE OF HEROIN TO JUVENILES—PENALTIES.

Section 2 of the Narcotic Drugs Import and Export Act, as amended, is further amended by adding at the end thereof the following:

(1) Not withstanding any other provision of law, whoever, having attained the age of eighteen years, knowingly sells, gives away, furnishes, or dispenses, facilitates the sale, giving, furnishing, or dispensing, or conspires to sell, give away, furnish, or dispense, any heroin unlawfully imported or otherwise brought into the United States, to any person who has not attained the age of eighteen years, may be fined not more than $20,000, shall be imprisoned for life, or for not less than ten years, except that the offender shall suffer death if the jury in its discretion shall so direct.

. . .

Sec. 1407. BORDER CROSSINGS—NARCOTIC ADDICTS AND VIOLATORS.

(a) In order further to give effect to the obligations of the United States pursuant to the Hague convention of 1912, proclaimed as a treaty on March 3, 1915, and the limitation convention of 1931, proclaimed as a treaty on July 10, 1933, and in order to facilitate more effective control of the international traffic in narcotic drugs, and to prevent the spread of drug addiction, no citizen of the United States who is addicted to or uses narcotic drugs . . . (except a person using such narcotic drugs as a result of sickness or accident or injury and to whom such narcotic drug is being furnished, prescribed, or administered in good faith by a duly licensed physician in attendance upon such person, in the course of his professional practice) or who has been convicted of a violation of any of the narcotic or marihuana laws of the United States, or of any State thereof, the penalty for which is imprisonment for more than one year, shall depart from or enter into or attempt to depart from or enter into the United States, unless such person registers, under such rules and regulations as may be prescribed by the Secretary of the Treasury with a customs official, agent, or employee at a point of entry or a border customs station. Unless otherwise prohibited by law or Federal regulation such customs official, agent or employee shall issue a certificate to any such person departing from the United States; and such person shall, upon returning to the United States, surrender such certificate to the customs official, agent, or employee present at the port of entry or border customs station.

(b) Whoever violates any of the provisions of this section shall be punished for each such violation by a fine of not more than $1,000 or imprisonment for not less than one nor more than three years, or both.

Source: Public Law 84–728 (Narcotic Control Act), July 18, 1956.

* * *

Other provisions of the 1956 act include (1) a requirement that any heroin lawfully possessed prior to the passage to this act be surrendered to the federal government, for compensation, and (2) provisions for the Bureau of Narcotics to share information and data with the states, including the names of drug addicts, and to conduct training programs for state and local narcotics enforcement personnel.

Reaction to the 1956 act was mixed. Hard-line anti-drug advocates applauded the increased penalties, feeling that they would help deter drug use and drug selling. Given the growing countermovement (starting in the early 1950s) to recognize drug addiction as a medical problem and to increase the availability of treatment, others felt that the 1956 act should have been more balanced.

DOCUMENT 160: Call for More Balanced Policies (*New York Times*, 1956)

Now that Congress has passed and sent to the President a bill drastically increasing penalties for illegal sale and possession of narcotics—

even up to and including the death penalty—we urge that it devote equal attention to the other side of the coin: medical treatment and rehabilitation procedures.

Severe punishment of the drug peddler is necessary as a deterrent, but punishment alone is not the answer to the drug problem. For forty years the emphasis in combating illicit narcotics in this country has been on punishment; and today we are believed to have more dope addicts than all the other nations of the West combined.... These are truly appalling figures. The economic rewards of this traffic are so great (an ounce of heroin that costs $5 in Communist China may be sold for several thousand dollars in New York City) that it should be clear that even the most stringent penalties, necessary as they are, will not abolish the purchase and sale of illegal drugs. This is especially true because in many cases the seller is himself an addict who pushes the sale to provide funds to keep himself supplied.

Addicts are sick, as sick as alcoholics or the mentally ill or people afflicted with dread diseases. Some excellent work is being done by the Federal Government, and by state and private agencies, to cope with the problem in medical terms, with efforts directed toward rehabilitation. But a great deal more is needed, in terms of money and effort and psychological approach....

There is still plenty of work left for Congress to do in the field of narcotics control, even more important than that which has just been done. The problem has by no means been solved by the bill that is now awaiting the President's signature.

Source: Editorial, *New York Times*, July 11, 1956.

* * *

Dr. Lawrence Kolb also thought the 1956 act was too punitive, and that drug addiction should be treated as an illness.

DOCUMENT 161: 1956 Narcotic Act Too Punitive (Lawrence Kolb, 1956)

As an example, one prominent official has said that illegal heroin traffic is more vicious than arson, burglary, kidnapping or rape, and should entail harsher penalties. Last May thirty-first the United States Senate went even further, in passing the Narcotic Control Act of 1956. In this measure, third-offense trafficking in heroin becomes the moral equivalent of murder and treason; death is the extreme penalty....

In my opinion, the lawmakers completely missed the point. Most drug addiction is neither menace nor mortal sin, but a health problem—indeed, a minor health problem when compared with such killers as alcoholism, heart disease and cancer.

. . .

Distorted news has prepared the public to support extreme measures to suppress imagined evils. When legislators undertook last spring to do something about the so-called drug menace, Federal law provided two years in prison for a first-time narcotic-law offender. The minimum for a second offense was five years, and for a third, ten years, with no probation or suspension of sentence for repeaters. The Narcotic Control Act of 1956 proposed increasing penalties for heroin trafficking to a minimum of five years for the first offense, ten years for the second offense, life imprisonment or death for the third offense.

What happens under such laws? In one case, under the old law, a man was given ten years for possessing three narcotic tablets. Another man was given ten years for forging three narcotic prescriptions—no sale was involved. And another ten year sentence was imposed on a man for selling two marijuana cigarettes, which are just about equal in intoxicating effect to two drinks of whisky. Extremists have gone on to demand the death penalty. They would do away with suspended sentences, time off for good behavior, the necessity for a warrant before search. They want wire tapping legalized in suspected narcotic cases, and they would make the securing of bond more difficult.

Existing measures and those which are advocated defy common sense and violate sound principles of justice and penology. There is nothing about the nature of drug addicts to justify such penalties. They only make it difficult to rehabilitate offenders who could be helped by a sound approach which would take into account both the offense and the psychological disorders of the offender.

Drug addiction is an important problem which demands the attention of health and enforcement officials. However, the most essential need now is to cure the United States of its hysteria, so that the problem can be dealt with rationally. A major move in the right direction would be to stop the false propaganda about the nature of drug addiction and present it for what it is—a health problem which needs some police measures for adequate control. Our approach so far has produced tragedy, disease and crime.

Source: Lawrence Kolb, "Let's Stop This Narcotics Hysteria!," *Saturday Evening Post*, July 28, 1956.

* * *

The New York Academy of Medicine also criticized the act's punitive approach and expressed doubt that it would have any effect on reducing drug addiction.

DOCUMENT 162: 1956 Narcotic Act Too Punitive (New York Academy of Medicine, 1955)

The Academy's principal objections to the Payne Bill [the 1956 act] are its punitive approach and excessive penalties. In its opinion, the bill would have been no more successful in stamping out addiction than the present laws which it would have amended. Indeed it might have brought an even greater degree of failure to the extent that its penalties were unreasonably excessive.

In short, the Payne Bill contained several commendable provisions, but these were more than offset by its continued punitive approach with fantastically severe penalties.

Source: New York Academy of Medicine, "Report on Drug Addiction," *Bulletin of the New York Academy of Medicine* 31, no. 8 (1955): 602.

* * *

The close of the 1950s saw the end of one phase of a long era of American drug policy, an era in which the reach and breadth of anti-drug policies continued to grow. Although there were interim periods in which concern over drug abuse and drug trafficking lessened, the general direction of drug policy in the first half of the 20th century was to increase punishments for violations of drug laws. Beginning in the 1960s, however, there was considerable social upheaval triggered by the Vietnam War, including student protests, the "hippie" and civil rights movements, and increasing drug use among the middle class. Coupled with an emerging mental health and substance abuse treatment movement, the focus of American drug policy over the next 20 years shifted to a greater tolerance for drug use, and a greater distinction between the drug seller and drug user.

Part IX

The Medicalization of Addiction: Drug Treatment and Anti-Drug Policy

Tracing the history of attempts by the medical profession to treat drug addiction is helpful for understanding the context in which drug policy developed beginning in the latter part of the 19th century. The fears about the effects of drug addiction on individuals, the labeling of addicts as drug "fiends," and the lack of effective treatment all fueled public and political concerns. In the era in which the Harrison Act and similar state anti-drug laws appeared, relatively little was known about the basis of addiction or the ways in which it could be cured. At a time when the opium or cocaine addict began to be viewed as incurable and a danger to society, it is not surprising that federal and state lawmakers began passing ever more stringent and punitive laws. Indeed, it was not until the 1950s that advances in the mental health and medical fields led to a more general acceptance of the psychosocial and physiological factors associated with addiction, and the development and government funding of more clinically appropriate treatment methods.

A review of the myriad "cures" for drug addiction from the late 1800s through the 1920s is instructive for several reasons. First, it illustrates the rather primitive state of knowledge about the physical and psychological dynamics of addiction (and physiology in general) at that time. Second, some of these cures were similar to the quack cures for other ills fostered by the patent medicine industry. In the early 1900s, the medical profession was only beginning to emerge from an era of loose professional standards and to develop more rigorous science-based practices. Third, a description of these cures and treatment methods shows the lack of distinction between short-term abstinence and long-term elimination of drug use. Finally, although the early attempts to cure addiction may sometimes seem humorous today, they do in fact illustrate the seriousness with which opiate and cocaine addiction began to be viewed in the early part of the 20th century. Physicians were willing to try almost anything to cure addiction.

ADDICTION "CURES" IN THE 19TH CENTURY

"Cures" for opiate addiction in the late 19th and early 20th centuries were not really methods of treatment per se. Most methods included various forms of detoxification in which addicts were weaned from the drug. This was sometimes done abruptly, by reducing doses over a relatively short period of time, or using a gradual reduction in dose over a more extended period. Most methods incorporated attempts to soften the sometimes severe opiate withdrawal symptoms by giving the patient various medicines, nutrients, or vitamins. The following documents illustrate some of the treatments for opium addiction noted in the medical literature of the late 19th century that incorporate variations on the detoxification "cure." Most of these were compiled by Charles Terry and Mildred Pellens in their seminal work *The Opium Problem,* originally published in 1928. First is an early description of the gradual withdrawal method described by a physician in 1856.

DOCUMENT 163: "A Treatise on Therapeutics and Pharmacology or Materia Medica" (George B. Wood, 1856)

It is satisfactory to know that this evil habit may be corrected, without great difficulty, if the patient is earnest; and, as the disorders induced by it are mainly functional, that a good degree of health may be restored. It will not answer to break off suddenly. No fortitude is sufficient to support the consequent misery, and life may be sacrificed in the effort. . . . Dr. B. H. Coates . . . states that he has seen well-characterized cases in which delirium tremens occurred; and this result might reasonably be anticipated. The proper method of correcting the evil is by gradually withdrawing the cause; a diminution of the dose being made every day, so small as to be quite imperceptible in its effects. Supposing, for example, that a fluid ounce of laudanum is taken daily, the abstraction of a minim every day would lead to a cure in somewhat more than a year; and the process might be much more rapid than this. Time, however, must be allowed for the system gradually to regain the healthy mode of action, which it had gradually lost.

Source: Reprinted in Charles E. Terry and Mildred Pellens, *The Opium Problem* (Bureau of Social Hygiene, 1928; reprint, Montclair, NJ: Patterson Smith Publishing 1970), 518.

* * *

The importance of exercise and physical heath was described in a standard textbook on opium addiction published in 1872. This document also compares the gradual and sudden withdrawal methods.

DOCUMENT 164: "The Opium Habit" (Horace Day, 1872)

Certain conditions . . . seem to be the almost indispensable preliminaries to success in relinquishing opium by those who have been long habituated to its use. The first and most important of these is a firm conviction on the part of the patient that the task can be accomplished. . . . A second condition necessary to success, is sufficient physical health, with sufficient firmness of character to undergo . . . the inevitable suffering of the body. . . . With a very moderate share of vigor of constitution, and with a will, capable under the circumstances of strenuous and sustained exertion, there is no occasion to anticipate a failure here.

This effort should be made with the advice and under the eye of an intelligent physician. So far as I have had the opportunity to know, the profession generally is not well informed on the subject.

. . .

The amount of time which should be devoted to the experiment must depend very greatly upon these considerations—the condition of the patient, the length of time which has elapsed since the habit was formed, and the quantity habitually taken. When the habit is of recent date, and the daily dose has not been large . . . if the patient has average health, his emancipation from the evil may be attained in a comparatively short period, though not without many sharp pangs and many wakeful nights which call for the exercise of all his resolution.

The question will naturally suggest itself to others, as it has often done to myself, whether a less sudden relinquishment of opium would not be preferable as being attended with less present and less subsequent suffering. Numerous cases have come under my notice where a very gradual reduction was attempted, but which resulted in failure. . . .

The general directions I should be disposed to suggest for the observance of the confirmed opium-eater would be something as follows:

1. To diminish the daily allowance as rapidly as possible to one-half. A fortnight's time should effect this without serious suffering, or anything more than slight irritation and some other inconveniences that will be found quite endurable to one who is in earnest in his purpose.
2. For the first week, if the previous habit has been to take the daily dose in a single portion, or even in two portions, morning and night, it will be found advisable to divide the diminished quantity into four parts.

In the third week a further gain of ten grains can the more easily be made by still further dividing the daily portion into an increased number of parts, say ten. The feeling of restlessness and irritability by this time will have become somewhat annoying, and the actual struggle will be seen to have commenced. It will doubtless require at some point some persistence of character to bear up against the increased impatience, both of body and spirit, which marks this stage of the descent. . . .

I have not ventured to say in how short a time confirmed habits of opium-eating may be abandoned. In my own case it was 39 days, but with my present experience I should greatly prefer to extend the time to at least sixty days; and this chiefly with reference to the violent effects upon the constitution produced by the suddenness of the change of habit.

Source: Reprinted in Charles E. Terry and Mildred Pellens, *The Opium Problem* (Bureau of Social Hygiene, 1928; reprint, Montclair, NJ: Patterson Smith Publishing, 1970), 520–521.

* * *

The substitution of other "tonics" to ease the symptoms of opium withdrawal was a common practice in the late 19th century. In the following example, one of these recommended tonics is cannabis (marijuana).

DOCUMENT 165: "Therapeutics and Materia Medica" (A. Stille, 1874)

It may not be without profit to mention that the most successful means which have been employed to cure the habit of opium-eating consist in the gradual substitution for it of aromatic and stimulant tonics. Ginger, black pepper colombo and quassia may be employed successively for this purpose. If this plan cannot be carried out, it is far better, for the sake of the patient, to insist upon an abrupt cessation of his habit than to attempt to win him from it by degrees.... If he passes safely through the terrible trial of total abstinence, his cure may be counted upon as probable. But he must meanwhile be not only encouraged morally, but physically sustained....

At bedtime there is given, to promote sleep, tincture of cannabis, 30 or 40 minims.... The food should at first consist of milk and beef-tea, for which, as the appetite improves, more solid aliment may be substituted. Alcoholic stimulants should, if possible, be avoided. Zinc, quinia, and iron, under various forms, must afford strength to the nervous system and a due body to the blood and both must be improved by stimulating the skin by means of baths, friction, active exercise, and whatever will tend to withdraw the patient from those habits of solitude and self-contemplation in which his vice has immured him.

Source: Reprinted in Charles E. Terry and Mildred Pellens, *The Opium Problem* (Bureau of Social Hygiene, 1928; reprint, Montclair, NJ: Patterson Smith Publishing, 1970), 522.

* * *

Other recommended treatments allowed the use of alcohol when the abrupt withdrawal method was being used. In the following document, the care with which the physician describes the need for safe surroundings for the patient during withdrawal illustrates the difficulties and dangers of the process.

DOCUMENT 166: "Morbid Craving for Morphia" (E. Levinstein, 1878)

As soon as the patient has consented to give up his personal liberty, and the treatment is about to commence, he is to be shown the rooms set apart for him for a period of eight to fourteen days, all opportunities for attempting suicide having been removed from them. Doors and windows must . . . [be] so constructed that the patients can neither open nor shut them. Hooks for looking glasses, for clothes and curtains must be removed. The bedroom, for the sake of control, is to have only the most necessary furniture; a bed, devoid of protruding bedposts, a couch, an open washstand, a table furnished with alcoholic stimulants (champagne, port wine, brandy), ice in small pieces, and a tea urn with the necessary implements. In the room which is to serve as a residence for the medical attendant for the first three days, the following drugs are to be kept under lock and key: a solution of morphia of 2 per cent., chloroform, ether, ammonia, . . . mustard, an ice bag, and an electric induction apparatus. . . . During the first four or five days of the abstinence, the patient must be constantly watched by two female nurses. Male attendants are of no use in cases of morbid craving for morphia, as they are generally more accessible to bribing, and are less to be relied upon and less capable of self-sacrifice. They are, however, wanted for the coarser manipulations, for attending to the bath of male patients, and may then be admitted under supervision.

During the first four or five days, the nurses must be changed every twelve hours, as the service requires mental and physical ability, and is very fatiguing.

. . .

The greatest care during treatment is to be bestowed upon the diet, from the commencement of the withdrawal of the drug. During the first three days, food is only to be given in a fluid form; strong wines and, according to individual susceptibility, pure alcoholic liquors are to be resorted to. They are best given in the same manner as a medicine, every hour or two hours.

Many people have an intense craving for alcoholic beverages, others greatly objecting to them. The first-mentioned patients may be allowed to drink wine in unlimited quantities, without any ill effects, as by doing so they pass over the first days of abstinence in a less distressing manner; should, however, there be reluctance and distaste for alcohol a light milk diet (2 ounces of milk every hour, or two hours) may be ordered. This agrees well even with persons who are greatly troubled with vomiting.

Source: Reprinted in Charles E. Terry and Mildred Pellens, *The Opium Problem* (Bureau of Social Hygiene, 1928; reprint, Montclair, NJ: Patterson Smith Publishing, 1970), 522–523.

* * *

In the late 19th century cocaine was sometimes considered useful in assisting in withdrawal from opium addiction. However, the following is one of the earliest descriptions of dangers of the use of coca in that way.

DOCUMENT 167: Use of Cocaine in Opiate Withdrawal (Charles E. Terry and Mildred Pellens, 1928)

Earle [*The Opium Habit*, 1880] advocates rapid withdrawal reporting that he used fluid extract of coca in three or four cases in all of which it proved of great service although he believes that it is by no means a specific and has no power to disgust the patient with the desire for his favorite drug. He also calls attention to the danger of opium patients becoming addicted to the coca habit and cites one of his cases as an example concluding that "while we have in coca an agent which is of undoubted value, its indiscriminate use should be interdicted."

Source: Charles E. Terry and Mildred Pellens, *The Opium Problem* (Bureau of Social Hygiene, 1928; reprint, Montclair, NJ: Patterson Smith Publishing, 1970), 527–528.

* * *

In 1883 the German physician A. Erlenmeyer, a prominent advocate of the "rapid withdrawal" method, described gradual withdrawal as the oldest method but one that was unsatisfactory. Its problems included difficulty in controlling access to drugs, the prolonging of abstinence symptoms, and the need for a long recuperation period. Abrupt withdrawal had some advantages, according to Erlenmeyer, including "certainty" and speed of success, but several disadvantages, including the expense, danger to the patient, and the lack of suitable space in many hospitals. However, some physicians reported high cure rates using the gradual withdrawal method.

DOCUMENT 168: Benefits of Gradual Withdrawal (R. Burkart, 1884)

Since 1872 I have treated the cases of morphinism intrusted to me exclusively by the gradual withdrawal method. . . . To carry out successfully this method of treatment it is advisable to have the patient in a hospital where continuous medical supervision, a good nursing staff, bathing facilities, etc. are available. Here it is unnecessary to keep the morphinist in detached rooms for the sake of the other inmates as is required in abrupt withdrawal, because it rarely happens that the patients during gradual withdrawal disturb their neighbors by their restlessness and loud noise. Usually my method of treatment for chronic morphine poisoning averts the delirium and excitement which are usually the result of abrupt withdrawal. . . .

I have been able to bring about 71 per cent cures in the treatment of morphinists under these conditions. This number means that among my "not cured" morphinists, there were many patients who it is true sought treatment but were not quite ready to stand much suffering and who immediately decided again to give up the cure, as soon as any noteworthy discomfort of withdrawal appeared. . . .

In general, even my method of treatment . . . is not free of disagreeable and annoying secondary symptoms; sometimes the patients during withdrawal . . . are for a day at a time in a very distressing and deplorable state.

Usually the period which I have found necessary for withdrawal varies between 14 and 21 days, according to the size of the daily dose. In especially weak cases sometimes I require an even longer period, 4–7 weeks.

Source: Reprinted in Charles E. Terry and Mildred Pellens, *The Opium Problem* (Bureau of Social Hygiene, 1928; reprint, Montclair, NJ: Patterson Smith Publishing, 1970), 534–535.

* * *

Abrupt withdrawal certainly had its dangers, as it does now.

DOCUMENT 169: "Considerations on the Treatment of Morphinism" (B. Ball and D. Jennings, 1887)

Abrupt suppression . . . practiced by a great number of other physicians, has in its favor one great advantage: it causes the patient to suffer for a much shorter time. Once the crisis [is] over . . . the patient no longer feels the peculiar distress of the morphine dipsomaniac; he no longer has the painful sense of depression and of down-heartedness which makes him long for another injection. But, on the other hand, by sudden suppression, we run the risk of producing the serious results already described. The patient may be taken with delirium tremens; he may be attacked with acute mania; he may finally (and this is the most serious danger) fall into collapse, which . . . is sometimes followed by death. It is therefore impossible to carry through a sudden suppression outside of an asylum or hospital.

Source: Reprinted in Charles E. Terry and Mildred Pellens, *The Opium Problem* (Bureau of Social Hygiene, 1928; reprint, Montclair, NJ: Patterson Smith Publishing, 1970), 536–537.

DRUG TREATMENT FROM 1900 TO 1930

The early part of the 20th century saw a continued proliferation of "cures," often hospital-based, that were based on withdrawing from the drug. One of the most publicized cures was that developed by Charles Towns and Dr. Alexander Lambert in 1908. Towns was considered one of the nation's experts on drug addiction and treatment in the early part of the 20th century. A former insurance salesman, he became interested in cures for opiate addiction. His business and sales skills, as well as his passionate interest in addiction and its treatment, helped establish him as an expert in the field. Towns was instrumental in developing and proposing one of the nation's first comprehensive statewide anti-drug laws in 1913 (see Part V). He developed a prototype for what later became the Towns-Lambert cure, traveling to China to test it on opium addicts. Towns' ability to interest Alexander Lambert in the "cure" was a large factor in its popularity. Lambert was a professor at the Cornell University Medical School and personal physician to Theodore Roosevelt. His prominence in the medical field and his political connections helped to interest the American delegates to the Shanghai Opium Commission in the Towns cure and to provide substantial credibility to Towns' claims of success. David Musto described the origins of this treatment.

DOCUMENT 170: Origins of the Towns-Lambert Cure (David F. Musto, 1987)

Towns later related that he was approached by a fellow who whispered, "I have got a cure for the drug habit, morphine, opium, heroin, codeine—any of 'em. We can make a lot of money out of it." Towns was skeptical and sought the advice of his personal physician, who said that the claim was ridiculous. With this opinion challenging him, Towns began investigating the cure by putting advertisements in the paper to locate drug fiends who wanted to be helped. Trying the formula out on such persons and restraining them when they wanted to get out of the hotel rooms Towns used for his experiments, he perfected the treatment so as to "eliminate all the suffering."

As he gained patients for his treatment, Towns was shunned by the regular medical profession. But in a few years he was somehow able to interest Dr. Alexander Lambert of Cornell in his methods. Although Towns would still not reveal the secret formula, he was able to convince Lambert that he had an effective treatment for addiction. Eventually Lambert . . . introduced Towns to government officials as a "straightforward, honest man—no 'faker,' " who had a most useful treatment for drug addiction. When Towns wanted to find a market for his "cure" in China, Lambert wrote Assistant Secretary of State Robert Bacon, asking him to smooth Towns' way in China so that he could use his treatment there; he reported it had been investigated by the War Department and "really cures morphine and opium addictures."

Towns impressed the American delegation to the Shanghai Opium Commission by his apparent success in China when, in 1908, he claimed to have cured about 4,000 opium addicts there by his method. . . . The delegation wanted Towns to announce to the assembled members of the commission the treatment that he had now decided to give to the world. . . . the unique prominence given the Towns treatment by the delegation was almost an official endorsement.

Source: David F. Musto, *The American Disease: Origins of Narcotic Control*, expanded ed. (New York: Oxford University Press, 1987), 80–81.

* * *

The announcement of this cure was carried by the *New York Times*.

DOCUMENT 171: Announcement of Lambert Cure (*New York Times*, 1908)

The announcement made by Dr. Alexander Lambert . . . visiting physician at Bellevue Hospital and Professor of Clinical Medicine at the Cornell Medical College, that he has at last discovered a speedy cure for the drug habit and alcoholism has aroused much public interest. . . .

The fact that Dr. Lambert is a physician of high repute and a recognized authority in the matter of specifics lends credence to his contention that the most confirmed drug fiends are not beyond cure.

"The obliteration of the craving for narcotics is not a matter of months or weeks . . . but is accomplished in less than five days. The result is often so dramatic that one hesitates to believe it possible."

. . . Here is the specific:

Fifteen per cent tincture of belladonna, the fluid extract of xanthoxylum (prickly ash), and the fluid extract of hyoscyamus, mixed in the certain proportions.

The cure, according to Dr. Lambert, can be effected with a minimum of suffering, and no matter how long the patient has been addicted to the habit, or in what quantities he has been accustomed to take drugs, he will be placed in the same attitude toward them as before he fell into the habit. His health will be in no way impaired by the treatment or the deprivation of the drug; on the contrary, a physiological change comes about whereby, all desire being eliminated, self-confidence is restored to the patient, and his system adjusted to do without it.

. . .

One way in which this treatment differs from all others is that while the specific is being administered, the drug of which the patient is a victim is still taken. For this reason practically all suffering is absent. Regarding this Dr. Lambert says:

"Give with the first dose of the specific from one-half to two-thirds of the usual daily dose of the opium, morphine, or cocaine which the patient is taking at the time of his treatment. Divide the amount of the narcotic in three doses and give them at half-hour intervals by mouth or by hypodermic, as the patient is accustomed to take it."

Source: "Drug Habit Curable, Says Dr. Lambert," *New York Times*, March 28, 1908.

* * *

Describing his cure, Dr. Lambert claimed success with 80 percent of those treated.

DOCUMENT 172: Chapter on Opium and Morphine in Osler and McCrae's *Modern Medicine* (Alexander Lambert, 1914)

The question arises whether they should be treated by the slow withdrawal method, in which they are treated symptomatically for whatever symptom seems most distressing, or whether the drug should be drawn abruptly, and the patients suffer with full intensity, hoping to relieve them in a shorter space of time, or whether some of the more recent methods, using belladonna or hyoscine, should be employed.

The sudden withdrawal method does not seem justifiable. The danger of sudden collapse and death is not a theoretical one. Morphinism or the opium habit is a chronic poisoning and must be treated as such. The only safe method is by the rapid elimination of the drug in the body, the quieting of the withdrawal symptoms with some preparations of the belladonna group, and as rapid a withdrawal of the drug as the condition of the patient will justify. Under these conditions collapse need not be feared, and the elimination of the poison and the restitution to health is soonest accomplished. . . .

The treatment in my hands in some 600 patients has proved so successful that 80% have remained well. This proves the efficacy of this method of treatment and also that most morphinists, if free from their addiction, are anxious to remain clear.

Source: Reprinted in Charles E. Terry and Mildred Pellens, *The Opium Problem* (Bureau of Social Hygiene, 1928; reprint, Montclair, NJ: Patterson Smith Publishing, 1970), 554–555.

* * *

Drs. Herbert Kleber and Charles Riordan, in their review of early drug treatment methods, described some of the dangers of the Towns-Lambert treatment.

DOCUMENT 173: Dangers of Lambert Cure (Herbert D. Kleber and Charles E. Riordan, 1982)

The most famous variant of the hyoscine treatment was called the Towns-Lambert treatment. It was a rapid withdrawal method in which potent purgatives and a variety of belladonna derivatives were given orally. The end point of the successful treatment was a mild belladonna intoxication accompanied by liquid green stools, roughly 2 to 3 days after treatment had started. . . . These treatments were considered successful for so long in spite of the extreme distress they caused patients. . . . In one year in a hospital where 130 patients were given the hyoscine treatment, there were six deaths. To put this into perspective, it should be noted that no deaths have been reported in the English-language literature from uncomplicated heroin withdrawal.

Source: Herbert D. Kleber and Charles E. Riordan, "The Treatment of Narcotic Withdrawal: A Historical Review," *Clinical Psychiatry* 43, no. 6 (Sec. 2) (June 1982): 31.

* * *

In his 1920 book on drug addiction, Ernest Bishop also criticized the Towns-Lambert and other treatments for not reflecting an understanding of the addict and the disease of addiction. Bishop, a physician with extensive experience treating addicts at New York City's Bellevue Hospital, was a strong and vocal proponent of the medical rather than punitive approach to addiction. He also argued in favor of providing maintenance doses of drugs to long-term addicts.

DOCUMENT 174: The Narcotic Drug Problem (Ernest Bishop, 1920)

[The] multitude [of treatments] is conclusive proof of the lack of conception and of understanding of addiction-disease in the past. They have been directed towards incidental and complicating manifestations. They have no more place in the treatment of the addict than they have in the treatment of any other disease condition. I know of no medication that can be called "specific" in the arrest of the mechanism of narcotic drug addiction-disease. There is no more of a specific remedy for narcotic drug addiction than there is for typhoid or pneumonia. The wide advertisement of treatment based on supposed "specific" action of the products of the belladonna and hyoscyamus and similar groups is unfortunate [referring to the Towns-Lambert and similar methods]. They have, in my opinion, no action as curative agents in narcotic drug addiction-disease which can entitle them to consideration as specific or special curative remedies. The drugs of this group are useful in many cases, intelligently applied to meet therapeutic indications. They exhibit wide variation of action and reaction in narcotic drug addicts at different clinical stages and under different clinical conditions, and their dosage presents an extremely wide range of individual measure. They are dangerous drugs in the hands of the inexpert or careless, or used in a routine manner or dosage. The status which they have acquired as specific medication in narcotic addiction disease I hold to be a medical fallacy which should be strongly opposed and early remedied. . . .

Our stumbling block in the past has been that our minds have been too much focused upon the mere use of narcotic drug and upon the stopping of drug use and too little upon the individual we were treating and the mechanism of his disease. We have tended to apply our remedial efforts to narcotic use instead of to narcotic addiction-disease. . . .

The method of gradual reduction of dose to the point of ultimate discontinuance is practical and feasible under conditions and at an expense of time and money which are possible to but very few addicts. The forcible reduction of dose without regard to the environmental, mental, economic, physical or other conditions of the average and individual addict, and absolutely ignoring the considerations of the mechanism and symptomatology of his addiction-disease is barbarous, harmful and futile.

Source: Reprinted in Charles E. Terry and Mildred Pellens, *The Opium Problem* (Bureau of Social Hygiene, 1928; reprint, Montclair, NJ: Patterson Smith Publishing, 1970), 559–561.

* * *

By the late 1800s, some physicians were beginning to recognize addiction as a physical disease, not simply a result of weak moral character or an incorrigible or criminal personality.

DOCUMENT 175: Early Description of Addiction as Disease (Paul Sollier, 1894)

The fundamental mistake in the treatment of morphinism, the one which has given rise to the most fantastic articles and to the most incredible ones, consists of considering morphinism as primarily a psychical malady and secondarily as an organic state. As a matter of fact it is exactly the opposite. Even in emotional addicts the organic condition is the prime consideration as far as treatment is concerned.

The reactions of demorphinism are there for the finding. Elsewhere I have compared what takes place with what occurs in an infectious disease. . . .

[Organic changes] well demonstrate that it is not simply a psychical breaking-up of a habit but that it implies a true crisis, consisting in a violent disturbance of the body, analogous to an acute infectious disease.

Source: Reprinted in Charles E. Terry and Mildred Pellens, *The Opium Problem* (Bureau of Social Hygiene, 1928; reprint, Montclair, NJ: Patterson Smith Publishing, 1970), 540–541.

* * *

In 1924 the crusading journalist Samuel Hopkins Adams wrote a three-part series on drug addiction in the popular and widely circulated magazine *Colliers*. In this series, Adams strongly criticized the Harrison Act and fostered the idea that addiction was a disease that required medical treatment.

DOCUMENT 176: Addiction as a Disease (Samuel Hopkins Adams, 1924)

There could be no more terribly mistaken assumption than the long-implanted idea that narcotic drug addiction is in itself criminal or degenerate, or in any case a mark of moral or mental obliquity.

It is purely and simply a disease, as definitely a disease as cancer or smallpox or pneumonia, and one for which the patient is in 95 per cent of the cases no more responsible or blamable. . . . In recent years, because of the restrictions and uncertainties of a well-intentioned but brutally stupid law, they have lived under the shadow of blackmail from the criminal drug vendors who have a practical monopoly of the supply, and in continual terror of arrest and imprisonment. They are the helpless victims of a popular and legalized error as inhumane as that which, a few centuries ago, cast the insane into chains as possessed of the devil; the error of making a disease a crime.

. . .

The parallel cannot be carried to this limit, however, which would imply that narcotic addiction, once established, is ineradicable. This is not true. It is arrestable—the experts prefer not to use the much-abused word "cure"—and a great majority of the cases which come into the hands of expert practitioners are successfully handled, but not by old-time "dope cure" methods.

. . .

[Dr. Ernest Bishop's treatment] is achieved not by any hard-and-fast system, substitution of other drugs, or patent or secret "cure." Every case must be handled according to its individualized idiosyncracies, for no two are exactly alike. But the method, as practiced by Dr. Bishop and those who follow his teachings, is fundamentally the same in all cases, being based upon the recognition of narcotic drug addiction as a disease which must be combated as such, not a habit which can be thrown off at will.

The problem of the patient thus becomes one of building up the strength of the body until it can, by its own processes, overcome the poison and win back to normal or approximately normal condition. This cannot be done while the sufferer is subjected to the racking agonies of abrupt withdrawal, for then all his vitality is exhausted in the mere effort to endure his torments, leaving none to fight the disease poison, and frequently not enough to keep him alive. By carefully maintaining the balance, however, and by manipulating the intervals at which the drug is taken, it is feasible to reduce the dosage and at a determinable time to stop it entirely without any severe suffering.

Source: Samuel Hopkins Adams, "The Cruel Tragedy of Dope," *Colliers Magazine*, February 23, 1924, 7–8.

* * *

Other support for the view that addiction was a disease that needed to be treated came from Willis Butler, the well-known Shreveport, Louisiana, physician who was one of the pioneers of the short-lived narcotic clinic movement of the early 1920s.

DOCUMENT 177: Addiction as a Disease (Willis P. Butler, 1922)

Morphinism is the same everywhere, yet opinion differs as to what it really is. It is variously considered a vice, a crime, a disease, a purely mental condition, a pathological condition, something that can voluntarily and easily be quit by the user if he wants to quit it, and some say it is a sociologic and legal problem, while still others contend it is a medical problem primarily. No matter what different persons may call the condition, the patient is a sick person, and as such is entitled to and should have proper consideration, care, and treatment, either for the causes that are responsible for him being an addict, or for the addiction itself. There are thousands of addicts, many of them very poor and something has to be done for them, or with them, as the need is urgent. The fact that an addict cannot get his medicine in some legal way does not mean that he will not, or in many cases that he should not get it in some other way. If we fail to provide a legal way for the needy suffering to obtain relief, are we to blame them for seeking relief from some other sources? They suffer with mental and physical troubles and should be given proper and humane consideration.

Source: Willis P. Butler, "How One American City Is Meeting the Public Health Problems of Narcotic Drug Addiction," *American Medicine* 28 (March 1922): 159.

* * *

In 1926 a special committee on heroin and morphine addiction of the British Ministry of Health reviewed the various treatment methods then in use and concluded that the gradual withdrawal method was strongly preferred to either abrupt or rapid withdrawal, due to its lower likelihood of causing physical or mental distress in the patient. The committee also emphasized the importance of taking into account the individual characteristics of the addict. In their report to the Ministry of Health, the committee also presented the rather progressive notion (for that era) that withdrawal from the drug was only the first step in a longer process of recovery from addiction, and that psychological treatment and social factors were important considerations for a positive long-term prognosis.

DOCUMENT 178: British Ministry of Health, Departmental Committee on Morphin and Heroin Addiction (1926)

It was especially insisted upon by several witnesses that the actual withdrawal of the drug of addiction must be looked upon merely as the first stage of treatment, if a complete and permanent cure is to be looked for. . . . A permanent cure will depend in no small measure upon the after-education of the patient's will power, and a gradual consequent change in his mental outlook. To this end it was regarded as essential by one witness that full use be made of psychotherapeutic methods, both during the period of treatment and in the re-education of the patient. It was not considered that a lasting cure could be claimed unless the addict had remained free from his craving for a considerable period—1½ to 3 years—after the final withdrawal of the drug. Scarcely less important than psychotherapy and education of the will is the improvement of the social conditions of the patient, and one physician informed us that he made it a practice, whenever possible, to supplement his treatment by referring the case to some Social Service Agency. . . .

Evidence we have received from most of the witnesses forbids any sanguine estimate as to the proportion of permanent cures which may be looked for from any method of treatment, however thorough. Relapse, sooner or later, appears to be the rule, and permanent cure the exception. With two exceptions, the most optimistic observers did not claim a higher percentage of lasting cures than from 15 to 20 percent.

Source: Reprinted in Charles E. Terry and Mildred Pellens, *The Opium Problem* (Bureau of Social Hygiene, 1928; reprint, Montclair, NJ: Patterson Smith Publishing, 1970), 610.

* * *

Shortly after this British report, Dr. Lawrence Kolb of the U.S. Public Health Service published an article on addiction cures, described below by Terry and Pellens, that also emphasized the importance of psychosocial factors.

DOCUMENT 179: Importance of Psychosocial Factors (Lawrence Kolb, 1927)

In the 210 cases studied, [Kolb] finds that psychic causes produced the susceptibility to opiates and cocaine, and that the cause for relapse was primarily the same as that responsible for the original addiction, reinforced later by memory associations and habit and by the induced physical dependence that gradually developed, the memory associations and habit being part [*sic*] created by physical dependence. The primary psychic factor remained fairly stable during the entire period of addiction, while the other three factors increased in intensity with the passage of time, bringing about a change in the relative importance of the various factors.

Source: Reprinted in Charles E. Terry and Mildred Pellens, *The Opium Problem* (Bureau of Social Hygiene, 1928; reprint, Montclair, NJ: Patterson Smith Publishing 1970), 617–618.

* * *

In the late 1910s and into the 1920s, the New York City Health Department became one of the first municipal agencies to systematically try to treat addicts in a centralized treatment facility. Beginning in 1919, addicts from the city's narcotic clinic who required in-patient care were referred to Riverside Hospital, located on North Brother Island. There the addicts remained until "cured." Riverside Hospital continued to provide most of the city's hospital-based treatment until well into the 1950s. In the following document, Terry and Pellens summarize the Riverside Hospital treatment process as described by Dr. T. F. Joyce of the New York City Health Department.

DOCUMENT 180: Riverside Hospital Treatment Process (Charles E. Terry and Mildred Pellens, 1928)

The patient first is placed in "preparatory" ward where in six days he is brought down to the smallest amount of narcotic that will hold him without the usual signs of drug deprivation—usually two to three grains in 24 hours. During this period of six days' reduction full catharsis is secured but no drastic purgation. Joyce states:

At six o'clock on the morning of the seventh day the patients are given a large dose of castor oil followed shortly afterwards by a small dose of morphine, the last they receive in the institution unless otherwise indicated. About four hours later the first signs of drug deprivation are usually experienced. This is a signal to start using a therapeutic anesthetic. At Riverside Hospital we use the hyoscine hydrobromate. . . .

During this period, which we have termed the period of therapeutic anesthesia, we are combating all the phenomena attending narcotic deprivation, such as vomiting, general restlessness, intestinal colic, cramps in the legs, and a rapid, feeble pulse. These characteristics are held in check by the frequent administration of small doses of hyoscine, usually hypodermically. At the end of thirty-six hours, under favorable conditions the hyoscine is discontinued and we arrive at the period of convalescence.

At this stage of the treatment we produce what might be properly termed a modified twilight sleep. After thirty-six to forty-eight hours of withdrawal treatment the patients are found to be moderately intoxicated by the accumulative action of hyoscine; even after a period of twelve hours they experience all the customary signs of their intoxication and we describe this period as the post-hyoscine hysteria. This is followed in twelve hours by a general feeling of depression and weakness which lasts from two to seven days, depending upon the recuperative powers of the individual and the duration of the addiction. During this early convalescent period they are given hot baths and mild hypnotics, and a restricted diet.

. . . Cocain users often become maniacal and go into convulsions. At this stage a single dose of morphin will counteract these symptoms. Forty-eight hours after the last dose of hyoscine the majority of patients go into the "first convalescent" ward or if not quite ready to the infirmary. The latter are termed "laggards."

After a week or ten days in the first convalescent ward they are transferred to the "second convalescent" ward. Here their physical reconstruction begins. They have light gymnastic exercises and "occupational therapy." Joyce says the chronic user is lazy and it is necessary to teach him to work.

Joyce states that as yet he has found nothing that will remove the psychic trauma that the prolonged use of drugs inflicts.

Source: Charles E. Terry and Mildred Pellens, *The Opium Problem* (Bureau of Social Hygiene, 1928; reprint, Montclair, NJ: Patterson Smith Publishing, 1970), 570–571.

* * *

Given the difficulties of opiate withdrawal and the absence of any effective alternative to opiates in easing withdrawal, most treatment in this era was conducted in hospitals. Moreover, the assumption that most addicts would try to get drugs if given the opportunity made the medical community as well as politicians and policy makers generally opposed to out-patient, or ambulatory, treatment. Although there was considerable debate in the 1920s about the value of ambulatory treatment, it largely remained in disfavor and without policy or financial support until well into the 1950s.

DOCUMENT 181: Ambulatory Treatment a Bad Idea (AMA Committee on Narcotic Drugs, 1921)

Your committee desires to place on record its firm conviction that any method of treatment for narcotic drug addiction, whether private, institutional, official or governmental, which permits the addicted person to dose himself with the habit-forming narcotic drugs placed in his hands for self administration, is an unsatisfactory treatment of addiction, begets deception, extends the abuse of habit-forming narcotic drugs, and causes an increase in crime. Therefore, your committee recommends that the American Medical Association urge both federal and state governments to exert their full powers and authority to put an end to all manner of such so-called addiction, whether practiced by the private physician or the so-called "narcotic clinic" or dispensary.

In the opinion of your committee, the only proper and scientific method of treating narcotic drug addiction is under such conditions of control of both the addict and the drug, that any administration of a habit-forming narcotic drug must be by, or under the direct personal authority of the physician, with no chance of any distribution of the drug from any source other than from the physician directly responsible for the addict's treatment.

Source: Report of the AMA Committee on Narcotic Drugs, *Journal of the American, Medical Association*, 76, no. 24 (1921): 1669–1671.

* * *

Samuel Hopkins Adams also described the difficulties that physicians had treating addicts following the passage of the Harrison Act.

DOCUMENT 182: Doctors Reluctant to Treat Addicts (Samuel Hopkins Adams, 1924)

. . . [T]he drug-sick man may try to get himself admitted to a hospital purporting to treat his addiction, although no State has anything like adequate public facilities, and one such institution in New York City had more than 90 per cent of its "cured" cases revert to their drug promptly upon discharge. Or he may fall back into the toils of one of the numerous quack sanitariums or "treatments" which hold out the lure of "sure cure" at somewhat more expensive rates than those of the illicit peddlers. The remaining, and, as it would seem, sensible resort to a regular licensed medical practitioner. . . .

Any other disease the registered physician may treat according to the best dictates of his knowledge and his conscience, but not this disease. Under the unintelligible, inequitable, and constantly shifting "interpretations" of the [Harrison] law, the treatment of narcotic addiction is rigidly if uncertainly limited, so that no intelligent and honest practitioner can feel himself safe from prosecution in treating one of these cases. . . .

Although no physician who understands this disease will claim to cure it (since some mechanism of the disease is probably always present in the system), nevertheless permanent relief is practical in most cases. But the doctor must appreciate the fact that he is dealing with a disease and not a vice or a habit.

Source: Samuel Hopkins Adams, "How People Become Drug Addicts," *Colliers Magazine*, March 1, 1924, 9.

* * *

By the early 1920s, a number of clinics had been opened to provide morphine and other opiates to addicts. Facing considerable federal pressure to close, public skepticism, and a series of negative Supreme Court decisions, most of these clinics were short-lived. Dr. Willis Butler's Shreveport clinic was perhaps the most highly regarded of these efforts, and seemed to have generated the most solid and consistent local support. It has been the narcotic clinic most commonly cited by drug policy historians as undeservedly criticized by federal authorities.

DOCUMENT 183: Comments on Shreveport Narcotic Clinic (David F. Musto, 1987)

As late as 1955, thirty-two years after its closure, the federal narcotics agency was still condemning Dr. Butler's clinic for permitting "75 percent of the drug addicts in Texas [to make] their headquarters there," and detailing many serious allegations against the Louisiana operation. Dr. Charles E. Terry, however, who had spent seven years as the executive on the Committee on Drug Addiction of the Bureau of Hygiene collecting information on the problem of addiction, wrote Dr. Butler in 1928:

> In looking back over the work that has been done here and there throughout the country, I know of no single piece that can compare with yours as a constructive experiment in the practical handling of cases. The only criticism that I would make is that you did this work probably about twenty years ahead of the time when it could be appreciated, and I have little doubt but that in the next ten or fifteen years your plan will be in widespread operation in this country. If it is not, it will simply mean that rational education of both official and lay groups has been slower than I hope it will be.

Alfred Lindesmith, in comparing the Federal Bureau of Narcotics' account with that in Terry and Pellens' *The Opium Problem* (1928) concludes in 1965, "There is hardly a single general statement about the clinic in the Bureau's account which can be accepted as accurate and which does not require serious qualification." The Shreveport clinic remains the rallying point for those who believe a clinic system should have been established across the nation after 1919.

Source: David F. Musto, *The American Disease: Origins of Narcotic Control*, expanded ed. (New York: Oxford University Press, 1987), 174–175.

* * *

In the next document, Dr. Willis Butler describes the origin, philosophy, and operations of the Shreveport clinic that he founded in 1919.

DOCUMENT 184: Methods Used in Shreveport Clinic (Willis P. Butler, 1922)

In the spring of 1919 a situation arose that had to be met. There were a large number of people living here who were using morphine—some because of suffering from incurable diseases, some from untreated or successfully treated physical conditions . . . and some because they had a morphine habit and either could not get the proper assistance to quit it, or did not try or want to quit. All of these people were in some manner obtaining the drug previously, but now the supply was almost suddenly stopped, and there was great suffering. . . .

There was a general inclination to be rather harsh, stern and unsympathizing with them at first; as a result of this attitude many addicts suffered terribly. Due to a fear or natural disinclination on the part of doctors and druggists to have anything to do with an addict no matter what else might be his trouble (and when it was found out that he was an addict, usually that was enough to cause the doctor to go no deeper into his case), many sick people were caused to suffer terribly, or to seek the peddler. These people began coming to the officers of the law and to the board of health officials begging for relief. . . .

To meet the situation our dispensary was started. Later, our institutional treatment department was opened. At first, our methods were rather crude and we had much difficulty trying to devise the best ways to handle these cases. Gradually improving, within a few months we established our system. Its success is due largely to the fact that we have cooperation, assistance, hearty approval and commendation of every branch of our government locally. . . . We believe it is doing a good work and that in a practical way it is solving our local narcotic situation. That is all that we intend for it to do as we believe that each community or part of the state should be able and be required to care for its problems of this character.

. . .

Morphine is the drug of addiction almost exclusively, and we seldom see a heroin addict. Cocaine being not a habit former, but we believe merely a vice, is not allowed; and no one using it is put on the dispensary; its use, as a rule, is easily detected.

. . .

We insist that all who are able must work, and spend their first money for good food and decent clothes. No vagabonds or loafers are tolerated.

. . .

The amount of morphine dispensed to each patient is the smallest amount that we believe the patient can get along on and keep in drug balance. The dispensary is not intended as a treatment department for a cure, but only as a means of caring for the incurables, and those not at present curable or treatable, but who must have the medicine. There is no longer a systematic and a regular effort at reduction, but each case is judged separately, a certain amount decided on, and this may at times have to be increased or decreased according to the condition of the patient. . . . If too much medicine is allowed there is a temptation to dispose of some; if too little, the tendency would be to buy more, so we try to be as accurate as possible at the same time being reasonable and fair with the patient. . . . The officers say there is little or almost no peddling here, and we have had a number of patients voluntarily request that they be reduced a grain or so, and to actually assist us to cut them down to very small doses. . . .

. . . .

While in the institution being cured everything possible is done to treat the patient properly, humanely and scientifically. . . . He is under absolute restraint, with nurses, attendants, and proper medical supervision.

He is kept there as long as the director thinks necessary. His commitment is legal. Additional to this commitment he signs a request to be placed in the Parish jail to complete the treatment if, for any reason, this may be deemed necessary or advisable by the director. The director[,] who is also the Parish physician, treats him when placed in jail, employing as nearly as possible the same methods as used at the hospital. Several methods of treatment are employed at the hospital, but all are humane and very effective.

Source: Willis P. Butler, "How One American City Is Meeting the Public Health Problems of Narcotic Drug Addiction," *American Medicine* 28 (March 1922): 154–159.

* * *

The Shreveport clinic operated from 1919 until it was closed down in 1923. During these four years of operation, it was the frequent target of investigations by federal narcotics agents as the federal government put strong pressure to close down all the narcotics clinics that emerged in the wake of the Harrison Act. But Dr. Butler's clinic appeared to be a well-run effort that enjoyed substantial support from local residents as well as political leaders of Shreveport and the surrounding parish.

In a 1973 interview, the 85-year-old Butler described the numerous visits by agents of the Narcotics Division of the Treasury Department.

DOCUMENT 185: Statement by Willis Butler (1974)

The government seemed to send agents into Shreveport continually, usually on the sly. Some I saw, some I only heard about. Mostly, they would come attempting to buy drugs from peddlers or get prescriptions from doctors. They were usually discouraged in this because there were no peddlers, and if you went to a doctor to get morphine, they would just tell you to go to my clinic. Both the patients and the doctors told me of these visits, once a newspaper reporter let me know what was going on.

Some agents were gentlemen and completely aboveboard. They came to see me, and I would show them the clinic records and tell them to go see all the officials in the town and ask about the clinic.

Source: Quoted in Dan Waldorf, Martin Orlick, and Craig Reinarman, *Morphine Maintenance: The Shreveport Clinic, 1919–1923* (Washington, D.C.: Drug Abuse Council, 1974), 12–13.

* * *

After several years of unsuccessful pressure to close down the Shreveport clinic, federal narcotics officials increased the pressure on Butler.

DOCUMENT 186: Closing of the Shreveport Clinic (Dan Waldorf, Martin Orlick, and Craig Reinarman, 1974)

Perhaps out of desperation the Narcotic Division sent a "hatchet man" to Shreveport. This was H. H. Wouters who, with a group of Federal agents, proceeded to build a case against Dr. Butler and the clinic. They made two visits to Shreveport. During the first visit, Wouters reported that a group of citizens approached him about an illegal peddler who was said to be paying off one of the clinic's inspectors to stay in business. . . .

On the second visit, they proceeded to interview 50 of the clinic's 129 patients. The object of these interviews was to reveal that the patients were simply drug addicts and not worthy of being maintained, did not work, and were possibly criminal. A personal case was built against Dr. Butler. In the report, he is accused of making money out of the clinic and keeping a large staff from the proceeds.

. . .

[Quoting Dr. Butler:] "During his [Wouters'] last visit here, the patients asked me about him because he was going around questioning them. Wouters was trying to get evidence on the clinic and patients on the sly. I confronted him with it, but he denied it. Eventually, he told one of the patients his intentions (trying to close down the clinic) and the patient told me. I went around to see Sheriff Hughes about it, and Hughes decided to get a local warrant to pick him up. We did not get to him in time. By the time we got to his hotel, he had left. He left a forwarding address in the Virgin Islands."

By this time, Dr. Butler was getting tired of all the battles to keep the clinic open. The numbers of patients had declined to approximately 100, and he was beginning to feel that it was taking too much of his time and effort and possibly was not worth it. Toward the end of January 1923, G. W. Cunningham, a Federal narcotics agent from Richmond, Virginia, was sent to Shreveport on a "diplomatic mission" to close the clinic. He, with two other agents, talked with Judge Jack and Phillip Mecom. Judge Jack stopped by Dr. Butler's house that night and told him of the meeting. Phillip Mecom telephoned the next day and asked Dr. Butler to meet him in his office:

[Quoting Dr. Butler:] "Mecom said that Cunningham was giving him a lot of trouble about the dispensary. Shreveport was the last of the clinics and they wanted it closed. Mecom was taking my part, but Cunningham wanted him to prosecute me. Mecom said there was nothing to prosecute. A meeting was arranged for January 30th."

The meeting took place in the Federal Court House with District Attorney Mecom presiding. Dr. Butler was present with Cunningham and two other agents. After some discussion it was agreed that the clinic would close on February 10, 1923.

Source: Dan Waldorf, Martin Orlick, and Craig Reinarman, *Morphine Maintenance: The Shreveport Clinic, 1919–1923* (Washington, D.C.: Drug Abuse Council, 1974), 14–15.

* * *

The difficulty of curing opiate addicts was recognized early in the 20th century. The passage of the Harrison Act, and subsequent Supreme Court rulings that restricted the prescribing by physicians of maintenance doses of drugs to addicts, made treatment even more difficult.

DOCUMENT 187: Enforcement of Harrison Act and Physicians (*New York Times*, April 13, 1919)

In this country an aggressive campaign will be carried on to check the evil. The Harrison Federal narcotic law, strengthened by amendments and sustained by the Supreme Court, is to be the foundation for the attack. . . .

General hospitals avoid drug patients, and special hospitals are inadequate. In every large community where the Federal law is enforced, deaths of some of the victims would likely result unless there were an organized system of treatment. The cocaine habit can be stopped short and broken with comparative ease, experts say, but not so with morphine and heroin: when these are abruptly taken away from a user, physical collapse, with foaming at the mouth and dangerous internal disorders, usually follows. A rational arrangement for care and treatment is thus considered necessary before strict enforcement of the law can be safely carried out on a wide scale. This is deemed all the more important on account of the fraud connected with the many so-called "cures." . . .

There is no standardized cure for the opium habit; in fact, medical men are in doubt as to the best way to proceed. . . . Some contend that individual treatment by a physician is unsafe, because the patient may be secretly obtaining the drug from some other source, and that therefore he should be in an institution where absolute control can be had over him. There enters into this the fact that the drug habit is much more difficult to treat than the liquor habit. . . .

In seeking to keep the drug evil from extending its grip when the prohibition amendment goes into effect, the authorities in Washington will seek the closer cooperation of physicians. There is no doubt that reputable medical men have unintentionally caused many to fall into the clutches of the drug habit. Morphine given with good intentions to relieve pain often leads to the patient's later slavery to opium. Only a comparative few physicians, it is asserted, are now awake to the dangers of this practice, and fewer still of their liabilities under the Federal narcotics law.

Source: "Spread of Drugs Shown in Government Inquiry," *New York Times*, April 13, 1919.

* * *

With the aggressive enforcement of the Harrison Act, as well as state and local laws against drug use and sale, many addicts during the 1920s came into contact with the criminal justice system. Then, as now, judges wrestled with the dilemma of enforcing the law and punishing those who break the law, while recognizing that treatment was also needed to break the cycle of addiction. The next document is an interesting contemporary view of addiction and the effects of treatment by a New York City criminal court judge who handled many addict cases. Many of the same themes and issues are still relevant today: the high rates of relapse, the factors that trigger relapse, the need for intensive treatment for those involved in the criminal justice system, and the important role of the clinician in promoting recovery. This judge's somewhat negative view of the efficacy of treatment in the 1920s should be tempered by the recognition that as a criminal court judge, he saw mainly the treatment failures. Successfully treated addicts were unlikely to have ended up in his courtroom.

DOCUMENT 188: Perspective of Judge William McAdoo (1923)

. . . I meet a great many addicts, self-complaining in the legal sense, who are seeking admission to the hospitals provided by the state and city for the cure of addiction. . . . During the last four years I have personally examined and committed thousands of addicts. . . .

When the public first became alarmed about drug addiction in New York the city authorities owned a beautiful site in the hills of Orange County, which had been purchased with the intention of making a home for alcoholics, but they turned it over for use as a place to which drug addicts could be committed. . . . I committed many addicts to this place. . . . They used to come back after a sojourn of two or three months and call on me, looking immensely improved in physique.

They all gained weight on the good fare and life spent mostly out of doors. Unfortunately there were not sufficient people to guard the place, and the addicts had no trouble in getting a supply of drugs or alcoholic stimulants smuggled in. Under such conditions effecting lasting cures was not possible.

Then for a considerable time commitments were made to Bellevue Hospital, where the treatment did not extend beyond a couple of weeks. It is no criticism of the physicians at that well-known institution to say that addicts repeatedly told me that they went straight from the hospital to the use of the drug. The period of treatment was not long enough, and the number of addicts was so great as to tax the authorities of the institution to give to each case that painstaking care, that patient treatment, which is necessary. . . .

At both Riker's Island and Bedford Reformatory the doctors have practically adopted the rule that the treatment must be for not less than three months. . . .

. . .

Practically all addicts admit that the usual course is to return to the drug after treatment and that they know it is lack of self-control and the condition of mind that drive them to it. I make it a rule to impress on the addict when he leaves the hospital that he must never on any occasion go with another addict. "Do not keep company with any other person who is an addict even if he is your own brother or a member of your family." When two addicts get together their relapse is inevitable. Mental depression, physical suffering, financial distress, comparison of symptoms—and they both go back to the old remedy. . . .

. . .

In common with others of much more experience it is my judgment that they should be segregated into colonies, carefully guarded, well treated and given light work of a kind suited to them. . . . Above and beyond all medical treatment, which largely consists of purging the system of the poison and then bettering the physical condition, there must positively be sympathetic effort to get the drug out of the addict's mind as well as out of his body.

Source: William McAdoo, "Narcotic Addiction as It Really Is," *Saturday Evening Post*, March 31, 1923, 9ff.

* * *

The 1920s and 1930s saw a number of new treatments and "cures" being developed and tested. Some of these cures do not seem far removed from those unsuccessfully tried in the late 1800s. The next two documents report the use of biological techniques to cure drug addiction.

DOCUMENT 189: "Brain-Washing" Cure (*New York Times*, 1932)

Complete breaking of the morphine habit in six days by a treatment new to medicine was reported today at Cornell University. The narcotic patient was apparently cured with little discomfort.

The treatment is the administration of a compound designed to wash the brain and nervous system clean of the "habit."

This habit, under the Cornell interpretation, is a thickening of proteins in brain cells, a condition which persists after the narcotic is stopped and which accounts for the continuance of the craving. The new antidote, sodium rhodanate, thins the thickened proteins. . . .

The morphine patient was a male nurse, an addict for sixteen years. Cures had been attempted six times previously and he had been recorded as a "mean case." The treatment consisting in reducing him in six days from twelve grains of morphine to none, and substituting sodium rhodanate for the morphine cuts.

Narcotic reduction began on his third day in Ithaca Memorial Hospital. The record as given to the National Academy of Sciences reads:

"Fourth Day—Appetite improved. Neither nervous or apprehensive.

"Fifth Day—More composed, somewhat less talkative and apparently normal, mentally and physically.

"Sixth Day—He boasted that previously he had been able always to tell within one-eighth grain how much his morphine was reduced. This time he invariably guessed 100 per cent or more too high."

On the ninth day the patient was "depressed for the last time," and on the tenth day "completely relaxed and comfortable." He has had no desire for morphine since December 9. The treatment was first tried on dogs.

Source: "Cornell Reports Cure of Morphine Addict," *New York Times*, January 16, 1932. Reprinted by permission of the Associated Press.

DOCUMENT 190: "Frozen Sleep" Cure (*New York Times*, 1939)

The use of "frozen sleep" in the treatment of drug addiction and psychiatric derangement, with "beneficial effects," was reported yesterday before the symposium on temperature of the American Institute of Physics . . . by Dr. L. W. Smith and Dr. Temple Fay of Temple University, Philadelphia, originators of the "frozen sleep" treatment that has been used with considerable success in the alleviation of pain and prolongation of life in thirty cases of hopeless cancer patients.

Two physicians who had become morphine addicts, Dr. Smith reported, apparently have been cured of their addiction after being placed in the refrigeration room, where the temperature of the body is brought down to as low as 75 degrees Fahrenheit, for five days. During that period the patient lives in a state of artificial hibernation, in which bodily activities are at a much lower ebb than normal.

One of the patients, Dr. Smith added, showed a recurrence of the craving for narcotics after six months. He was placed in the refrigerator a second time, and once more lost his addiction. It is too early to tell whether the "cure" will be permanent, it was said, but these treatments give promise that a new avenue of approach to the treatment of narcotic addiction has been opened.

Source: " 'Frozen Sleep' Aids Narcotic Addicts," *New York Times*, November 4, 1939.

* * *

David Musto has also noted the general lack of success in treating drug addiction up to 1930.

DOCUMENT 191: Lack of Treatment Success to 1930 (David F. Musto, 1987)

The year 1930 may be taken as the close of the era of therapeutic optimism with regard to opiate addiction. It had been increasingly difficult since World War I to rouse enthusiasm for an addiction cure and within a decade the full weight of clinical medicine was against any such claims. Everything had been tried and everything failed; the relapse rate was appalling. When Congress established narcotic institutions in 1929 [see Part VIII], the primary reason for federal aid to addiction was not to provide treatment; the . . . narcotic "farms" were unmistakably built for the large number of jailed addicts who had crowded federal penitentiaries. Yet in the debate over authorization, the warm hope was expressed that through these hospitals effective treatment or a new discovery would begin to wipe out the addiction menace.

Source: David F. Musto, *The American Disease: Origins of Narcotic Control*, expanded ed. (New York: Oxford University Press, 1987), 85.

* * *

Perhaps one reason for the relative lack of success of treatment up to this time was the limited recognition that addiction is a chronic disease that requires ongoing follow-up after discharge from treatment. In 1922 Dr. Willis Butler offered one of the first descriptions of the notion of "aftercare."

DOCUMENT 192: Need for Aftercare Treatment (Willis P. Butler, 1922)

If the addict's supply is to be cut off, certainly it is right that arrangements should first be made to care for and treat the curable cases and to dispense to the incurable ones. Places should be provided for the proper after-care of those who are treated and cured, and who are not prepared to properly care for themselves for some weeks or months afterwards. This after-care is very important as it is not so difficult to cure a case of the habit, but it may be very difficult for that case to remain cured unless properly cared for sometime afterwards. The fact that a patient discharged cured will return to the drug at a later day does not prove that he was not cured any more than a patient cured of pneumonia this winter who contracts it again next winter and has to be treated again proves that he was not cured of pneumonia. An addict after being cured might go back to the drug for the same physical or mental reason that he first started on it. Therefore, he should be in proper condition when he takes the treatment, and he should have proper after-care to allow him time to gain back his strength, and get back as nearly to his normal condition as possible. It is to be regretted that this state has no place to care for these cases who need this after-treatment.

Source: Willis P. Butler, "How One American City Is Meeting the Public Health Problems of Narcotic Drug Addiction," *American Medicine* 28 (March 1922): 160.

THE DISCOVERY OF METHADONE

Beginning with World War II, advances in medical and psychological treatment began to lead to more clinically sound and empirically based interventions for addicts. The development of pharmaceutical treatments that blocked the euphoric effects of opiates as well as easing the difficulties of withdrawal was a particularly important advance. The synthetic narcotic that was to have the greatest impact on treatment was methadone. The following is an early description of methadone from a 1948 *Life* magazine article.

DOCUMENT 193: Early Description of Methadone Treatment (*Life*, 1948)

. . . Of the many new substances examined [during World War II], methadon was by far the most important[;] for the Germans, lacking the opium from which to make morphine, had worked hard to produce a synthetic pain killer. Later in the U.S. the pharmaceutical houses of Eli Lilly and Winthrop-Stearns tested the drug chemically and clinically for the first time, while the U.S. Public Health Service coordinated studies all over the country and observed the effects of methadon on federal prisoners at the Lexington, Ky. "Narcotics Farm." . . .

. . .

At [Lexington] addicts are being relieved of their addiction through the substitution of methadon for morphine. Methadon itself is habit-forming, but the methadon habit is not as difficult to break as is morphine addiction. . . . An injection of methadon ends the addict's suffering [from withdrawal symptoms]. . . . Except for drowsiness . . . his condition is normal. In time the patient will transfer his addiction from morphine to methadon. He will then be able to give up drugs without intense suffering, for abstinence from methadon causes no violent reactions. Whether he does so, and for how long, may depend on social and psychological factors. But methadon will help him make the break.

Source: "Methadon," *Life*, August 9, 1948, 87, 90.

* * *

Beginning in the late 1950s into the 1960s, a research team at Rockefeller University, led by Dr. Vincent Dole (a metabolic disease expert) and the psychiatrist Dr. Marie Nyswander (who had worked with addicts at the Lexington narcotics hospital), pioneered the use of methadone as a treatment for heroin addiction. Their work began with investigations regarding methadone's use to ease the difficulties of opiate withdrawal. However, Dole and Nyswander experimented with maintaining some patients on high doses of methadone, rather than reducing the dosage during detoxification. Today, methadone maintenance is one of the most common forms of treatment for heroin addicts, although it remains somewhat controversial.

Edward Brecher described some of the early promising results of the Dole-Nyswander experiments, and the possible reasons for this success.

DOCUMENT 194: Benefits of Methadone (Edward M. Brecher, 1972)

. . . [T]he great majority of addicts placed on methadone, despite such preexisting handicaps as poverty, poor health, little education, prison records, and years of addiction, become self-supporting as well as law-abiding while on methadone—and the longer a group of addicts remains on methadone, the greater the number of members who become self-supporting.

. . .

The two major reasons for the success of methadone maintenance are surely no secret. Methadone is legal; hence the addict who enters a methadone maintenance program casts off his role of hated and hunted criminal. . . . And methadone is cheap. The cost of the usual dose—100 milligrams per day—is ten cents. It is supplied the addict either free or . . . for $10 to $14 per week. . . .

Like morphine and heroin, methadone is a narcotic and therefore, by definition, an addicting drug. This fact is often cited as a disadvantage. Indeed newspapers, politicians, and even some physicians have expressed the hope that a nonaddicting drug for the treatment of heroin addiction can be found.

This hope, however, is based on a misunderstanding. One main advantage of methadone is that it *is* addicting. For an addicting drug . . . is one that an addict continues to take day after day and year after year.

. . .

. . . in four other significant respects, methadone is distinctly superior [to heroin or morphine maintenance]. . . . The first of these advantages is that methadone is fully effective when taken by mouth. Thus the whole long, tragic list of infections spread by injection needles is eliminated. . . .

Second, methadone is a *long-acting* drug. An adequate oral dose in the morning keeps the user on a relatively even keel until the next morning. . . . Addicts on morphine or heroin, in contrast, must "shoot up" several times a day. . . .

Third, some addicts . . . have a tendency to escalate their doses of morphine or heroin. Once stabilized on an adequate dose of methadone, in contrast, patients are content to remain on that dose year after year; some even ask to have the dose reduced. . . .

Methadone's fourth advantage is that it *blocks* the heroin effect. A patient stabilized on an adequate daily dose of methadone who shoots heroin discovers to his own amazement that it has no effect. . . . The higher the methadone maintenance dose, the larger a dose of heroin is thus blocked.

. . .

Finally, methadone staves off not only the acute effects of withdrawal from heroin . . . but the postaddiction syndrome of anxiety, depression, and craving as well.

Source: Edward M. Brecher and the Editors of Consumer Reports, *Licit and Illicit Drugs* (Boston: Little, Brown, 1972), 148, 159, 161–162.

* * *

A somewhat more critical perspective is offered by David Musto.

DOCUMENT 195: Critique of Methadone (David F. Musto, 1987)

The example of institutions and outpatient clinics established in the mid-1960s for methadone maintenance helped create favor for "medical treatment" of heroin addiction. From the care with which it is dispensed, the public appears to believe that methadone is a medicine like an antibiotic rather than what it is—a synthetic and addictive morphine substitute. . . . In the methadone maintenance program, various mental health services are also supplied. The knowledge that methadone substitutes one addiction for another and that only a minority of heroin addicts, very few under twenty-one, want to make the switch is rarely publicized. Dr. Vincent Dole and Dr. Marie Nyswander . . . expressed the belief that opiate addiction creates a permanent biochemical change in physiology so that methadone maintenance might well be necessary for the life of the addict. In their view, therefore, it is not an abstinence cure, but it can be used to stabilize the life styles of those who will cooperate in a treatment program. For a few enthusiasts methadone has become a panacea that will solve the American addiction problem. It is, of course, diametrically opposed to the earlier federal policy of keeping supplies of all addicting drugs as scarce as possible. Every step toward respectability and public financing for methadone maintenance has frayed the traditional view of opiate addiction as inherently perilous.

Source: David F. Musto, *The American Disease: Origins of Narcotic Control*, expanded ed. (New York: Oxford University Press, 1987), 237–238.

EXPANSION OF DRUG TREATMENT SINCE THE 1950s

Another important clinical breakthrough was the developing recognition that abstinence by itself was not sufficient for many addicts to achieve stable and productive lives. Treatment experts increasingly recognized that many addicts had other medical, psychological, and social problems that had to be addressed even after drug use stopped.

The next document, from the New York Academy of Medicine, touches some of these themes from a mid-1950s perspective.

DOCUMENT 196: Difficulties of Successful Treatment (New York Academy of Medicine, 1955)

. . . [M]ere abstinence from narcotics for long periods of time does not cure addiction. A constructive approach to treatment must be based on something more than a mere separation from the drug supply. There is a large psychological element in drug addiction; hence measures to rectify it are a major part of the therapy.

When attempts are made to appraise the success of the therapeutic efforts, two difficulties are encountered: 1) obtaining reliable data; 2) setting standards. . . .

Even if the data were more reliable, it is disappointing, if not misleading, to apply the older and more conventional criterion; namely, the percentage of cures. One source reports that on the basis of five-year follow-ups the results at the U.S. Public Health Service Hospital in Lexington, Kentucky, were 20 per cent known abstinence; 35 per cent known relapse; 40 per cent not heard from or never contacted. It is pointed out that of the 40 per cent on whom data were not obtained, a considerable number may have continued to abstain since no hospital or police record of them could be found. Considering the success of treatment for drug addiction as a whole, another source states that: "Probably less than 50% of treated drug addicts remain free of their habit."

Examination of the record of success of rehabilitation is important for the light that it may shed on the biology of addiction and on the quality and quantity of rehabilitative efforts. Valid conclusions drawn from reliable data assist in answering significant questions about the biology of addiction and particularly its responsiveness to treatment. . . . From all available evidence it may be said with some confidence that addiction is a complex disease and may therefore require a complex therapeutic approach. Certainly with the presently available methods rehabilitation is a relatively long process. With a successive series of therapeutic courses the results show increasing improvement.

. . .

There is valid reason to believe that these [federal] institutions could produce even more effective results in rehabilitation with additional resources. Under the present system, rehabilitation ceases before it is finished. The addict, following his stay at the institution, is given carfare to his home and a warm farewell; then he is dumped as a solitary figure, penniless, very often friendless and without work, in a hostile society. It would test the mettle of a healthy man to undergo this experience; it must be a real trial to the discharged addict. Here is a gap that needs to be filled.

Source: New York Academy of Medicine, "Report on Drug Addiction," *Bulletin of the New York Academy of Medicine* 31, no. 8 (1955): 599–601.

* * *

Here is another 1950s view of addiction as disease and the need for treatment, taken from a popular magazine article that was quite critical of the punitive federal anti-drug policies of that time.

DOCUMENT 197: Importance of Treatment (Roland H. Berg, 1957)

For more than 40 years, state and Federal laws have failed to solve the dope problem. One factor keeps it flourishing: huge profits from the sale of illicit narcotics to addicts. And as long as our laws label the addict a criminal and force him to buy dope illegally at exorbitant prices, the narcotic problem will remain unsolved.

. . .

Many addicts may use twenty or more "caps" a day as their "fix," or dose. At that rate, an addict's habit can cost him up to $100 a day. Unless he has great personal wealth, he must turn criminal to get the money.

Female addicts usually resort to shoplifting or prostitution; men are more likely to become burglars, pickpockets, bunko artists or auto thieves. Even worse, the addict usually will try to get others "hooked" on dope so that he can sell to them and help support his own habit. . . .

Misconceptions about narcotics abound. Contrary to popular belief, the dope-crazed fiend who commits crimes of sex and violence does not exist. Most narcotics, especially heroin—the addict's drug of choice—are pacifiers. Dope soothes and relaxes an addict. Frequently, he falls asleep after a "fix." Once addicted, he must have his shot in order to keep feeling up to par. . . .

Another wrong idea about dope is that it wrecks the body and destroys the brain. However, after exhaustive tests, medical experts found that narcotics produce remarkably little harm to the body. Experts reported no damage to the heart, liver, kidney or brain even in addicts who had been on narcotics for as long as 20 years. Usually an addict loses weight because of the drug's dulling effect on the appetite. But the lack of harmful organic effects should not encourage the use of narcotics. It is a vicious, enslaving habit.

. . .

Less than two years ago, New York's Academy of Medicine proposed a plan [to maintain opiate addicts on drugs]. . . .

The Senate [Judiciary] committee rejected the plan. Instead, it advocated even more stringent punitive laws, which were subsequently adopted [the 1956 Narcotic Act].

Our 40-year record of failure to curb addiction by punitive legislation demands that we take a fresh view of the addict as a patient, not as a criminal.

Source: Roland H. Berg, "We're Bungling the Narcotic Problem," *Look*, October 15, 1957, 46–47.

* * *

The rise in substance and stature of the mental health profession in the 1950s was an important factor that helped improve the climate for expanding psychotherapeutically based drug treatment. With new treatment techniques that had a clinical and scientific basis, the treatment profession began to move far away from the unsound and ineffective "cures" popular prior to World War II. One result was a great expansion of federal funding and support for drug treatment beginning in the late 1960s.

DOCUMENT 198: Increased Importance of Mental Health Approach (David F. Musto, 1987)

After the war the government began to pour money into mental health training and research. By 1969, when the FBN [Federal Bureau of Narcotics] annual budget was about $6 million—only twice the appropriation for 1932—the NIMH [National Institute of Mental Health] budget exceeded $250 million.

. . .

The leaders of the mental health establishment had an attitude toward addiction vastly different from that of the FBN, arguing anew that addiction was a psychological or physical disease and that the medical profession should therefore treat addicts. Their power and persuasiveness, now extensively funded and supported by Congress, suggested that mandatory sentences and rigid control would be modified.

The directors of the Mental Hygiene Division (after 1946, the National Institute of Mental Health) had been either directors or trainees at the federal narcotic "farms." These psychiatrist-administrators had lost faith in policies that in effect turned the treatment centers into prisons; they had reluctantly done the bureau's dirty work since 1935. One of the NIMH's most symbolic actions in the late 1960s was to remove the steel bars from the cells at Lexington and to turn the facility into a recognizable hospital. . . . The NIMH attitude toward social dysfunction and individual behavior gradually replaced the bureau's approach.

Source: David F. Musto, *The American Disease: Origins of Narcotic Control*, expanded ed. (New York: Oxford University Press, 1987), 234–235.

* * *

As a key example of the increased federal attention to and support for the treatment of addiction in this era, the comprehensive reworking of anti-drug laws in 1970 contained a major provision for federal support for research and treatment of addiction. The 1970 act differed substantially from earlier legislation in its more balanced approach to drug control and the separation of marijuana from other drugs.

DOCUMENT 199: Sections on Treatment and Prevention, Comprehensive Drug Abuse Prevention and Control Act (1970)

TITLE I, PART D—NARCOTIC ADDICTION, DRUG ABUSE, AND DRUG DEPENDENCE PREVENTION AND REHABILITATION

. . .

Sec. 253. (a) The Secretary is authorized to make grants to States and political subdivisions thereof and to public or nonprofit private agencies and organizations, and to enter into contracts with other private agencies and organizations, for—

(1) the collection, preparation, and dissemination of educational materials dealing with the use and abuse of drugs and the prevention of drug abuse, and

(2) the development and evaluation of programs of drug abuse education directed at the general public, school-age children, and special high-risk groups.

(b) The Secretary, acting through the National Institute of Mental Health, shall

(1) serve as a focal point for the collection and dissemination of information related to drug abuse;

(2) collect, prepare, and disseminate materials (including films and other educational devices) dealing with the abuse of drugs and the prevention of drug abuse;

(3) provide for the preparation, production, and conduct of programs of public education (including those using films and other educational devices);

(4) train professional and other persons to organize and participate in programs of public education in relation to drug abuse;

(5) coordinate activities carried out by such departments, agencies, and instrumentalities of the federal government as he shall designate with respect to health education aspects of drug abuse;

(6) provide technical assistance to State and local health and educational agencies with respect to the establishment and implementation of programs and procedures for public education on drug abuse; and

(7) undertake other activities essential to a national program for drug abuse education.

. . .

Sec. 256. (a) The Secretary is authorized to make grants to public or nonprofit private agencies and organizations to cover a portion of the costs of programs for treatment and rehabilitation of narcotic addict or drug dependent persons which include one or more of the following: (1) Detoxification services or (2) institutional services (including medical, psychological, educational, or counseling services) or (3) community-based aftercare services.

Source: Public Law 91–513 (Comprehensive Drug Abuse Prevention and Control Act); October 27, 1970.

* * *

The 1972 Drug Abuse Office and Treatment Act established the Special Action Office for Drug Abuse Prevention (SAODAP) within the White House to provide overall planning and policy and to determine priorities for all federal drug abuse prevention activities. For the first time, a president gave priority to prevention and treatment efforts. In addition, this act authorized substantial funding for state programs in prevention and treatment under a formula grant program. The first section of the 1972 act summarizes the prevailing mood of Congress regarding drugs and drug policy, one that tries to strike a balance between a punitive enforcement approach and the recognition of the health and social consequences of drug abuse. Title IV provided for guidelines for giving grants to states to develop and evaluate prevention services. Title V established the National Institute on Drug Abuse within the National Institute of Mental Health, to develop and conduct comprehensive health, education, training, research, and planning programs for the prevention and treatment of drug abuse and for the rehabilitation of drug abusers.

DOCUMENT 200: Drug Abuse Office and Treatment Act (1972)

TITLE I

Sec. 101. The Congress makes the following findings:

(1) Drug abuse is rapidly increasing in the United States and now affects urban, suburban, and rural areas. . . .

(2) Drug abuse seriously impairs individual, as well as societal, health and well-being.

(3) Drug abuse, especially heroin addiction, substantially contributes to crime.

(4) The adverse impact of drug abuse inflicts increasing pain and hard-

ship on individuals, families, and communities and undermines our institutions.

(5) Too little is known about drug abuse, especially the causes, and ways to treat and prevent drug abuse.

(6) The success of Federal drug abuse programs and activities requires recognition that education, treatment, rehabilitation, research, training, and law enforcement efforts are interrelated.

(7) The effectiveness of efforts by State and local governments and by the Federal government to control and treat drug abuse . . . has been hampered by a lack of coordination among the States, between the States and localities, among the Federal Government, States, and localities, and throughout the Federal establishment.

(8) Control of drug abuse requires the development of a comprehensive, coordinated long-term Federal strategy that encompasses both effective law enforcement against illegal drug traffic and effective health programs to rehabilitate victims of drug abuse.

(9) The increasing rate of drug abuse constitutes a serious and continuing threat to national health and welfare, requiring an immediate and effective response on the part of the Federal Government.

. . .

TITLE II—SPECIAL ACTION OFFICE FOR DRUG ABUSE PREVENTION

. . .

Sec. 221. (a) The Director [of SAODAP] shall provide overall planning and policy and establish objectives and priorities for all Federal drug abuse prevention functions. . . .

(b) . . . the Director shall

. . .

(3) review related Federal legislation in the areas of health, education, and welfare providing for medical treatment or assistance, vocational training, or other rehabilitative services and, consistent with the purposes of this Act, assure that the respective administering agencies construe drug abuse as a health problem;

(4) conduct or provide for the conduct of evaluations and studies of the performance and results achieved by Federal drug abuse prevention functions, and of the prospective performance and results that might be achieved by alternative programs and activities supplementary to or in lieu of those currently being administered;

. . .

(6) (A) coordinate the performance of drug abuse prevention functions by Federal departments and agencies;

(7) develop improved methods for determining the extent of drug addiction and abuse in the United States.

Source: Public Law 92–255 (Drug Abuse Office and Treatment Act of 1972), March 1, 1972.

* * *

In contrast to the mostly punitive Anti-Drug Abuse Act of 1986, the Anti-Drug Abuse Act of 1988 placed somewhat more emphasis on treatment and prevention, including the establishment of the Office of Substance Abuse Prevention, the authorization of $100 million for a new Waiting List Reduction Program for treatment services, and increased drug education programs targeting at-risk populations.

Section 2051 of Chapter II authorized funding of $95 million for an Office of Substance Abuse Prevention (OSAP) within the Alcohol, Drug Abuse, and Mental Health Administration (ADAMHA) to provide training to mental health and health professionals in areas of substance abuse, to develop and evaluate substance abuse prevention and education programs, and to conduct other activities under OSAP's mandate. Section 2052 specified a number of areas of annual data on substance abuse and treatment that the ADAMHA should collect.

DOCUMENT 201: Expansion of Treatment and Research (Anti-Drug Abuse Act of 1988)

Sec. 509e. (a) The Secretary, acting through the Administrator, may make grants to public and nonprofit private entities for the purpose of reducing the waiting list of public and nonprofit private programs providing treatment services for drug abuse.

(b) The Secretary may not make a grant under subsection (a) unless the applicant for the grant—

(1) is experienced in the delivery of treatment services for drug abuse;

(2) is, on the date the application is submitted, successfully carrying out a program for the delivery of such services approved by the State;

(3) as a result of the number of requests for admission into the program, is unable to admit any individual into the program any earlier than one month after the date on which the individual makes a request for such admission; and

(4) provides assurances satisfactory to the Secretary that, after funding is no longer available under this section, the applicant will have access to financial resources sufficient to continue the program.

. . .

Sec. 509g. (a)(1) The Secretary, acting through the Administrator, may make grants to public and private entities for demonstration projects—

(A) to determine the feasibility and long-term efficacy of programs providing drug abuse treatment and vocational training in exchange for public service;

(B) to conduct outreach activities to intravenous drug abusers with respect to the prevention of exposure to, and the transmission of, the etiologic agent for acquired immune deficiency syndrome and to encourage intravenous drug abusers to seek treatment for such abuse; and

(C) to provide drug abuse treatment services to pregnant women, post partum women, and their infants.

(2) The Secretary shall, directly or through contracts with public and private entities, provide for evaluations of projects carried out pursuant to subsection (a) and for the dissemination of information developed as [a] result of such models.

(b)(1) The Secretary shall establish demonstration projects that provide grants to States for the purpose of enabling such States to provide effective treatment, and referrals for treatment, to individuals who abuse drugs.

. . .

(3) In awarding grants under subsection (a), the Secretary shall

(A) select projects that focus on at least one of the following areas of treatment:

(i) treatment of adolescents;

(ii) treatment of minorities;

(iii) treatment of pregnant women;

(iv) treatment of female addicts and their children; and

(v) treatment of the residents of public housing projects. . . .

. . .

(7) The Secretary shall require, as a condition of awarding grants under this section, a systematic evaluation of the projects funded under this section on a long term basis to record the impact of such projects on treated individuals, and on the community as a whole. . . .

(c)(1) There are authorized to be appropriated to carry out this section $34,000,000 for fiscal year 1989, and such sums as may be necessary for each of the fiscal years 1990 through 1991.

Source: Public Law 100–690 (Anti-Drug Abuse Act of 1988), November 18, 1988.

* * *

By the end of the 20th century, American drug policy reflected more acceptance of the medical view of addiction as a disease and a more general acceptance of the importance of drug use prevention and drug treatment as part of the nation's efforts to reduce the impact of drug abuse and addiction. Compared with the first half of the century, there is now substantial federal and state support for treatment and prevention. For example, the fiscal year 1998 budgets for the key federal agencies that fund prevention and treatment included more than $1.4 billion for federally funded treatment to the states through the Center for Substance Abuse Treatment of the Department of Health and Human Services, and $157 million for drug prevention through the Center for Substance Abuse Prevention. Research on the effectiveness of treatment and on the medical, behavioral, and social factors affecting drug abuse and addiction also now receive substantial federal support: the budget for fiscal year 1998 was $527 million for the National Institute on Drug Abuse. Yet these funding levels are considered by many to be inadequate relative to the need for drug abuse prevention, treatment, and research. The majority of federal and state anti-drug funding continues to be allocated to the enforcement of anti-drug laws, punishment of arrested drug users and sellers, and drug interdiction.

Treatment is also now more commonly offered to criminal offenders with drug problems than in the past. However, there remains some controversy about the overall effectiveness of drug treatment, and skepticism remains among policy makers about whether treatment really "works" and whether addiction is a biological or a moral disease. Moreover, although the clinical and scientific bases for treatment programs are much stronger than in earlier years, much remains unknown about what services and treatment interventions are most effective for which types of addicts or abusers. Anti-drug policy still places most of its emphasis on enforcement, eradication, and control ("supply" reduction), with about 75 percent of federal anti-drug funds targeted toward these efforts.

As more research becomes available about the effectiveness of treatment and the long-term effects of drugs on brain neurochemistry and other physiological functions, it is likely that treatment will become a growing and more effective part of government policy against drug abuse and addiction.

Part X

Drug Policy in the 1960s and 1970s: A Changing View

With the 1960s came a number of shifts in American drug policy. For the most part, these changes represented a backing away from the escalating harshness of drug policies from the end of World War II through the 1950s. The policy shifts reflected several important issues: an increasing acceptance of drug treatment, a more obvious distinction between drug users and sellers, and an easing of the penalties for marijuana and other drug possession. However, the overall tenor of federal and state anti-drug policy remained primarily punitive. Indeed, one of President Richard Nixon's first major domestic policy initiatives was to declare a war on drugs. Despite this type of rhetoric, however, funding and support for treatment and prevention expanded greatly during the Nixon administration. The spread of drug use beyond poor, urban, disadvantaged populations was a major trend of the 1960s, and probably helped drive some of these policy shifts.

At the beginning of the decade, an important Supreme Court decision had a major effect on the laws and sanctions against drug addicts. Although state and federal laws since the Harrison Act have continued to make possession or sale of illegal drugs a crime, Congress had never made the condition of being addicted to drugs a federal crime. However, this was not true in some states, where until 1962 the mere fact that a person was an addict could subject him or her to arrest, prosecution, and incarceration. In that year the U.S. Supreme Court struck down a California law that made it a crime to be an addict.

DOCUMENT 202: California Law Against Being an Addict (Declared Unconstitutional in 1962)

No person shall use, or be under the influence of, or be addicted to the use of narcotics, excepting when administered by or under the direction of a person licensed by the State to prescribe and administer narcotics. . . . Any person convicted of violating any provision of this section is guilty of a misdemeanor and shall be sentenced to serve a term of not less than 90 days nor more than one year in the county jail. The court may place a person convicted hereunder on probation for a period not to exceed five years and shall in all cases in which probation is granted require as a condition thereof that such person be confined in the county jail for at least 90 days. In no event does the court have the power to absolve a person who violates this section from the obligation of spending at least 90 days in confinement in the county jail.

Source: California Health and Safety Code, Section 11721, before 1962.

* * *

Under this law, a person could be prosecuted even if he or she had never used drugs in California or been guilty of any other crime there. One alleged Los Angeles addict who was arrested, convicted, and sentenced to 90 days in jail appealed his conviction, and in 1962 the Supreme Court, in a 6–2 decision, struck down the California law as unconstitutional. The majority opinion was written by Justice Potter Stewart.

DOCUMENT 203: *Robinson v. California* (1962)

The appellant was convicted after a jury trial in the Municipal Court of Los Angeles. The evidence against him was given by two Los Angeles police officers. Officer Brown testified that . . . he had observed "scar tissue and discoloration on the inside" of the appellant's right arm, and "what appeared to be numerous needle marks." . . . The officer also testified that the appellant under questioning had admitted to the occasional use of narcotics.

Officer Lindquist testified that . . . he had observed discolorations and scabs on the appellant's arms, and he identified photographs which had been taken of the appellant's arms shortly after his arrest the night before. Based upon more than ten years of experience as a member of the Narcotic Division of the Los Angeles Police Department, the witness gave his opinion that "these marks and the discoloration were the result of the injection of hypodermic needles into the tissue into the vein that was not sterile." He stated that the scabs were several days old at the time of his examination, and that the appellant was neither under the influence of narcotics nor suffering withdrawal symptoms at the time he saw him. This witness also testified that the appellant had admitted using narcotics in the past.

The appellant testified in his own behalf, denying the alleged conversations with the police officers and denying that he had ever used narcotics or been addicted to their use. He explained the marks on his arms as resulting from an allergic condition contracted during his military service. His testimony was corroborated by two witnesses.

The trial judge instructed the jury that the statute made it a misdemeanor for a person "either to use narcotics, or to be addicted to the use of narcotics. . . . To be addicted to the use of narcotics is said to be a status or condition and not an act. It is a continuing offense and differs from most other offenses in the fact that [it] is chronic rather than acute; that it continues after it is complete and subjects the offender to arrest at any time before he reforms. The existence of such a chronic condition may be ascertained from a single examination, if the characteristic reactions of that condition be found present."

The judge further instructed the jury that the appellant could be convicted under a general verdict if the jury agreed *either* that he was of the "status" *or* had committed the "act" denounced by the statute. "All that the People must show is either that the defendant did use a narcotic in Los Angeles County, or that while in the City of Los Angeles he was addicted to the use of narcotics. . . ."

Under these instructions the jury returned a verdict finding the appellant "guilty of the offense charged."

An appeal was taken to the Appellate Department of the Los Angeles County Superior Court. . . . Although expressing some doubt as to the constitutionality of "the crime of being a narcotic addict," the reviewing court in an unreported opinion affirmed the judgment of conviction, citing two of its own previous unreported decisions which had upheld the constitutionality of the statute. . . .

The broad power of a State to regulate the narcotic drugs traffic within its borders is not here in issue. . . .

Such regulation, it can be assumed, could take a variety of valid forms. A State might impose criminal sanctions, for example, against the unauthorized manufacture, prescription, sale, purchase, or possession of narcotics, . . . a State might establish a program of compulsory treatment for those addicted to narcotics. . . . And penal sanctions might be imposed for failure to comply with established compulsory treatment procedures. . . . Or a State might choose to attack the evils of narcotics traffic on broader fronts also—through public health education, for example, or by efforts to ameliorate the economic and social conditions under which those evils might be thought to flourish. . . .

It would be possible to construe the statute under which the appellant was convicted as one which is operative only upon proof of the actual use of narcotics within the State's jurisdiction. But the California courts have not so construed this law. Although there was evidence in the present case that the appellant had used narcotics in Los Angeles, the jury were instructed that they could convict him even if they disbelieved that evidence. The appellant could be convicted, they were told, if they found simply that the appellant's "status" or "chronic condition" was that of being "addicted to the use of narcotics." And it is impossible to know from the jury's verdict that the defendant was not convicted upon precisely such a finding.

. . . in their brief in this Court counsel for the State have emphasized that it is "the proof of addiction by circumstantial evidence . . . by the tell-tale track of needle marks and scabs over the veins of his arms, that remains the gist of the section."

This statute, therefore, is not one which punishes a person for the use of narcotics, for their purchase, sale or possession, or for antisocial or disorderly behavior resulting from their administration. It is not a law which even purports to provide or require medical treatment. Rather, we deal with a statute which makes the "status" of narcotic addiction a criminal offense, for which the offender may be prosecuted "at any time before he reforms." California has said that a person can be continuously guilty of this offense, whether or not he has ever used or possessed any narcotics within the State, and whether or not he has been guilty of any antisocial behavior there.

It is unlikely that any State at this moment in history would attempt to make it a criminal offense for a person to be mentally ill, or a leper, or to be afflicted with a venereal disease. A State might determine that the general health and welfare require that the victims of these and other human afflictions be dealt with by compulsory treatment, involving quarantine, confinement, or sequestration. But, in the light of contemporary human knowledge, a law which made a criminal offense of such a disease would doubtless be universally thought to be an infliction of cruel and unusual punishment in violation of the Eighth and Fourteenth Amendments.

We cannot but consider the statute before us as of the same category. In this Court counsel for the State recognized that narcotic addiction is an illness. Indeed, it is apparently an illness which may be contracted innocently or involuntarily. We hold that a state law which imprisons a person thus afflicted as a criminal, even though he has never touched any narcotic drug within the State or been guilty of any irregular behavior there, inflicts a cruel and unusual punishment in violation of the Fourteenth Amendment. To be sure, imprisonment for ninety days is not, in the abstract, a punishment which is either cruel or unusual. But the question cannot be considered in the abstract. Even one day in prison would be a cruel and unusual punishment for the "crime" of having a common cold.

. . .

Reversed.

Source: 370 *U.S. Reports* 660, *Robinson v. California*, decided June 25, 1962.

* * *

In a footnote to the majority opinion, the Supreme Court, for one of the few times since the Linder decision (see Document 65), cited that case in affirming that an addict suffers from a disease.

DOCUMENT 204: Reference to *Linder v. United States* in *Robinson v. California* (1962)

In its brief the appellee stated: "Of course it is generally conceded that a narcotic addict, particularly one addicted to the use of heroin, is in a state of mental and physical illness. So is an alcoholic." Thirty-seven years ago this Court recognized that persons addicted to narcotics "are diseased and proper subjects for medical treatment." *Linder v. United States*, 268 U.S. 5, 18.

Source: 370 *U.S. Reports* 660, *Robinson v. California*, decided June 25, 1962.

* * *

In 1962 President John F. Kennedy called for a White House Conference on Drug Abuse, chaired by his brother, Attorney General Robert Kennedy, to examine all aspects of the drug problem and to search for new solutions. The conference was held September 27–28, 1962. In addition to continuing calls for tough enforcement policies against narcotics importers and dealers, a number of speakers emphasized the need to treat addicts as people with medical and social problems. This recognition of the distinction between drug dealers and the addict victim was a considerable change from previous debates about federal drug policy.

The 1962 White House Conference led to the formation of the Presidential Commission on Narcotic and Drug Abuse, which issued its final report in 1963. The report was somewhat of a departure from the punitive era of the 1950s, recommending more research on addiction and drug abuse, the easing of mandatory minimum sentences, dismantling of the Federal Bureau of Narcotics, and a new role for the Department of Health, Education and Welfare in planning and setting up drug treatment centers. The thrust of the Interim Report of this presidential commission was summarized in the following document.

DOCUMENT 205: Recommendations of 1962 White House Conference (*New York Times*, 1963)

A Presidential advisory group called today for lighter Federal penalties against small peddlers and "victims" of narcotics, coupled with a "massive attack" on importers and large distributors of illegal drugs.

. . .

[President] Kennedy told the White House conference there was "universal agreement" that the two key objectives in this field were eliminating illicit traffic in the drugs and "rehabilitation and restoration to society of the drug addict."

. . .

The report criticized present narcotics laws for establishing mandatory minimum sentences . . . with probation, parole, and suspended sentences permitted only for first offenders. . . .

Most important, "they have made rehabilitation of the convicted narcotics offender virtually impossible, since there is no incentive for rehabilitation where there is no hope for parole," the panel said.

Source: "Narcotics Panel Requests Lighter Penalty for Addicts," *New York Times*, April 5, 1963.

* * *

The commission's final report was issued on November 1, 1963, several weeks before President Kennedy's assassination. Among the specific recommendations were for new federal laws to control the manufacture and sale of depressant and stimulant drugs, and to create a "comprehensive" research program to examine all dimensions of the drug problem. Although many of the proposals were ignored or altered under President Lyndon Johnson's administration, and although the commission's recommendations to some extent continued some of the hard-line rhetoric against drugs, its findings certainly had an impact on subsequent federal policy.

Two years later Congress adopted the Drug Abuse Control Amendments of 1965, which reorganized federal drug control efforts by setting up a Bureau of Drug Abuse Control within the Food and Drug Administration. However, the bureau's enforcement responsibilities were limited to depressants and stimulants—administration of the laws governing narcotics and marijuana remained under the Bureau of Narcotics in the Treasury Department. Another 1965 federal law placed new restrictions on the manufacture, sale, and possession of depressant and stimulant drugs. In the past, little attention had been paid to these drugs in the development of federal or state drug control policy. Earlier efforts to place restrictions on barbiturates in federal legislation had not been successful, in large part because Commissioner Anslinger questioned whether such drugs presented an abuse problem. However, the growing concern in the 1960s over all forms of drug abuse led to the 1965 law amending the federal Food, Drug, and Cosmetic Act.

DOCUMENT 206: First Federal Law Against Depressants and Stimulants (1965)

Sec. 2. The Congress hereby finds and declares that there is a widespread illicit traffic in depressant and stimulant drugs moving in or otherwise affecting interstate commerce [Note: This is to establish federal jurisdiction]; that the use of such drugs, when not under the supervision of a licensed practitioner, often endangers safety on the highways . . . and otherwise has become a threat to the public health and safety, making additional regulation of such drugs necessary regardless of the intrastate or interstate origin of such drugs.

Source: Public Law 89–74, July 15, 1965.

* * *

Section 3 of Public Law 89–74 prohibited (with some exceptions) the manufacture, sale, or possession of depressants or stimulants except for personal use. It also required the maintaining of written records of manufacture or sales, subject to inspection by federal agents. Penalties for a first conviction range up to two years in prison, and up to six years for a second or subsequent conviction.

CIVIL COMMITMENT LAWS

Increasing attention was also paid to education, research, and treatment in the 1960s that in part reflected a growing respect for the mental health and medical professions. In addition to emerging federal interest in community-based treatment centers, the use of civil commitment of addicts to treatment instead of prison began to be examined in some states. It was an important trend in drug policy in the early and mid-1960s. In civil commitment proceedings, a person can be committed to an institution even in the absence of a criminal conviction or even the commission of a criminal act.

By the early 1960s several states had enacted civil commitment laws. For example, New Jersey's law, one of the first in the country, allowed convicted addicts a choice between prison and treatment in a hospital setting for up to the length of the potential prison term. Aftercare treatment was also provided, and addicts could also volunteer to be committed to treatment.

Beginning in 1963, Senators Jacob Javits and Kenneth Keating (and later, Senator Robert Kennedy) from New York introduced a series of bills aimed at providing some type of federal civil commitment program modeled after the programs under way in California and New York. The 1961 California civil commitment law allowed the court to commit an offender convicted of a misdemeanor or nonviolent felony to the Department of Correction for up to three years, with at least the first six months spent at a rehabilitation center. The New York civil commitment program, instituted in 1962 under the Metcalf-Volker Act, was similar, although addicts were placed in the custody of the Department of Mental Hygiene rather than the Corrections Department.

DOCUMENT 207: Metcalf-Volker Act (New York State, 1962)

Section 211.

1. Any person . . . charged with a crime involving the possession of narcotics, or possession with intent to sell, . . . when such crime involves a drug of such nature that dependency upon it would render one a narcotic addict, . . . or charged with possession . . . of hypodermic syringes or needles, shall, upon arraignment before the committing magistrate

. . . be further informed that he may request consideration by the court for civil commitment to a hospital facility, as a narcotic addict. He shall be further informed that if he makes such a request he will have to submit to medical examination and if he is diagnosed to be a narcotic addict, he shall then have to submit to mandatory civil commitment and aftercare supervision, if the court so orders, and that if he successfully completes this medically supervised inpatient and aftercare program, the criminal charges pending against him will abate.

. . .

7. . . . the court shall, before committing the defendant civilly, obtain certification from the commissioner of mental hygiene . . . that he is agreeable to the acceptance of the defendant in a facility certified by the commissioner as having a special unit for the care and treatment of drug addicts. . . .

. . .

Sec. 213.

. . .

3. In no event shall the total time spent . . . under both inpatient care and treatment and aftercare supervision, exceed a total of thirty-six months.

4. . . . criminal charge shall be dismissed, and inpatient and aftercare supervision terminated, upon receipt by the court of a certificate from the commissioner of mental hygiene stating that the defendant's discharge from aftercare in advance of the maximum expiration date is warranted in the judgment of the commissioner by the former addict's condition.

Source: Chapter 204, Article 9, Laws of New York, March 21, 1962.

* * *

In March 1963, in a speech to the New York Academy of Medicine, Senator Javits challenged the Kennedy administration to take strong action against the drug problem.

DOCUMENT 208: Statement by Senator Jacob Javits (1963)

Few social problems in our nation are as grave in their impact on raising the crime rate to dangerous levels as the narcotics and drug addiction problem. Yet, there appears to be almost no prospect of early action on a Federal level to deal adequately with the problem in modern terms. It is time we faced frankly the fact that we are in a state of seemingly endless drift on this issue—characterized by indecision, uncertainty and controversy. It is perhaps a classic example of the governmental technique of inaction by continuous study; new studies and new surveys which are designed to clarify the issue instead add up to new excuses for public officials to avoid making the basic decisions. But the facts are in and the evidence is overwhelming.

I believe the situation calls for a historic decision by the President to set the nation on a new enlightened course to deal with narcotics and drug addiction as an illness rather than a crime. In the current muddle, only the President can make this command decision, and I believe this is the time for him to do it.

Source: Quoted in Rufus King, *The Drug Hang-up* (New York: W. W. Norton, 1972), 241–242.

* * *

The 1966 Narcotic Addict Rehabilitation Act (NARA), adapting the recommendations of the 1963 Presidential Commission, set up a civil commitment system for federal offenders, both prior to and after sentencing. NARA also provided for voluntary civil commitment under court supervision.

The opening section of the act described the philosophy of NARA. Title I of NARA allowed for the civil commitment of certified addicts for up to 36 months instead of prosecution; if the addict successfully completed treatment the original criminal charges would be dismissed. The next document presents excerpts from NARA.

DOCUMENT 209a: Narcotic Addict Rehabilitation Act (1966)

Sec. 2. It is the policy of the Congress that certain persons charged with or convicted of violating Federal criminal laws, who are determined to be addicted to narcotic drugs, and likely to be rehabilitated through treatment, should, in lieu of prosecution or sentencing, be civilly committed for confinement and treatment designed to effect their restoration to health, and return to society as useful members.

It is the further policy of the Congress that certain persons addicted to narcotic drugs who are not charged with the commission of any offense should be afforded the opportunity, through civil commitment, for treatment, in order that they may be rehabilitated and returned to society as useful members and in order that society may be protected more effectively from crime and delinquency which result from narcotic addiction.

TITLE I—Chapter 175. Civil Commitment and Rehabilitation of Narcotic Addicts

. . .

§2902.

(a) If the United States district court believes that an eligible individual is an addict, the court may advise him at his first appearance or thereafter at the sole discretion of the court that the prosecution the criminal charge will be held in abeyance if he elects to submit to an immediate examination to determine whether he is an addict and is likely to be rehabilitated through treatment. . . . the court shall advise him that if he elects to be examined, he will be confined during the examination for a period not to exceed sixty days; that if he is determined to be an addict who is likely to be rehabilitated, he will be civilly committed to the Surgeon General for treatment; that he may not voluntarily withdraw from the examination or any treatment which may follow; that the treatment may last for thirty-six months; that during treatment, he will be confined in an institution and, at the discretion of the Surgeon General, he may be conditionally released for supervised aftercare treatment in the community; and that if he successfully completes treatment the charge will be dismissed, but if he does not, prosecution on the charge will be resumed. . . .

(b) The Surgeon General shall report to the court the results of the examination and recommend whether the individual should be civilly committed. . . . If the court . . . determines that the individual is not an addict or is an addict not likely to be rehabilitated through treatment, the individual shall be held to answer the abeyant charge. If the court determines that the individual is an addict and is likely to be rehabilitated through treatment, the court shall commit him to the custody of the Surgeon General for treatment. . . .

. . .

§2903 . . .

(c) The total period of treatment for any individual committed to the custody of the Surgeon General shall not exceed thirty-six months. If, at the expiration of such maximum period, the Surgeon General is unable to certify that the individual has successfully completed his treatment program the pending criminal proceeding shall be resumed.

(d) Whenever a pending criminal proceeding against an individual is resumed under this chapter, he shall receive full credit toward the service of any sentence which may be imposed for any time spent in the institutional custody of the Surgeon General or the Attorney General or any other time spent in institutional custody in connection with the matter for which sentence is imposed.

Source: Public Law 89–793 (Narcotic Addict Rehabilitation Act), November 8, 1966.

* * *

Title II of NARA included provisions for sentencing *convicted* offenders to treatment instead of prison if the attorney general determined that the offender was an addict and likely to be rehabilitated through treatment. Conditional supervised release was allowed after six months if sufficient progress was made in treatment.

DOCUMENT 209b: Narcotic Addict Rehabilitation Act (1966)

TITLE II—SENTENCING TO COMMITMENT FOR TREATMENT (CHAPTER 314)

. . .

§ 4253. Commitment

(a) Following the examination [to determine whether he is an addict and is likely to be rehabilitated through treatment], if the court determines that an eligible offender is an addict and is likely to be rehabilitated through treatment, it shall commit him to the custody of the Attorney General for treatment. . . . Such commitment shall be for an indeterminate period of time not to exceed ten years, but in no event shall it exceed the maximum sentence that could otherwise have been imposed.

(b) If, following the examination provided for in section 4252, the court determines that an eligible offender is not an addict, or is an addict not likely to be rehabilitated through treatment, it shall impose such other sentence as may be authorized or required by law.

* * *

Title III provided for voluntary commitment of addicts not charged with a crime to a federal hospital for treatment.

DOCUMENT 209c: Narcotic Addict Rehabilitation Act (1966)

TITLE III—CIVIL COMMITMENT OF PERSONS NOT CHARGED WITH ANY CRIMINAL OFFENSE

...

Sec. 302. (a) ... whenever any narcotic addict desires to obtain treatment for his addiction, or whenever a related individual has reason to believe that any person is a narcotic addict, such addict or related individual may file a petition with the United States attorney ... requesting that such addict or person be admitted to a hospital of the Service for treatment of his addiction....

(b) After considering such petition, the United States attorney shall, if he determines that there is reasonable cause to believe that the person named in such petition is a narcotic addict, and the appropriate State or other facilities are not available to such person, file a petition with the United States district court to commit such person to a hospital of the Service for treatment as provided in this title....

Sec. 303. The court shall immediately advise any patient ... of his right to have (1) counsel at every stage of the judicial proceedings under this title ... and (2) present for consultation during any examination conducted under this section, a qualified physician retained by such patient. ... The court shall also advise such patient that if, after an examination and hearing as provided in this title, he is found to be a narcotic addict who is likely to be rehabilitated through treatment, he will be civilly committed to the Surgeon General for treatment; that he may not voluntarily withdraw from such treatment; that the treatment (including posthospitalization treatment and supervision) may last forty-two months; that during treatment he will be confined in an institution; that for a period of three years following his release from confinement he will be under the care and custody of the Surgeon General for treatment and supervision under a posthospitalization program established by the Surgeon General; and that should he fail or refuse to cooperate in such posthospitalization program or be determined by the Surgeon General to have relapsed to the use of narcotic drugs, he may be recommitted for additional confinement in an institution followed by additional posthospitalization treatment and supervision. After so advising the patient, the court shall appoint two qualified physicians, one of whom shall be a psychiatrist, to examine the patient.... Each physician ... shall ... examine the patient and file with the court, a written report with respect to such examination. Each such report shall include a statement of the examining physician's conclusions as to whether the patient examined is a narcotic addict and is likely to be rehabilitated through treatment. . . .

Sec. 304 (a) If both examining physicians (referred to in section 303) conclude in their respective written reports that the patient is not a narcotic addict, or is an addict not likely to be rehabilitated through treatment, the court shall immediately enter an order discharging the patient and dismissing the proceedings under this title. . . .

. . .

Sec. 305. If the court determines after a hearing that such patient is a narcotic addict who is likely to be rehabilitated through treatment, the court shall order him committed to the care and the custody of the Surgeon General for treatment in a hospital of the Service. . . .

Sec. 306. Any patient committed to the care and custody of the Surgeon General pursuant to section 305 of this title shall be committed for a period of six months, and shall be subject to such posthospitalization program as may be established pursuant to section 307 of this title; except that such patient may be released from confinement by the Surgeon General at any time prior to the expiration of such six-month period if the Surgeon General determines that the patient has been cured of his drug addiction and rehabilitated, or that his continued confinement is no longer necessary or desirable.

Sec. 307. . . .

(b) If, at any time during such three-year period, any patient (1) fails or refuses to comply with the directions and orders of the Surgeon General in connection with such patient's posthospitalization treatment and supervision, or (2) is determined by the Surgeon General to be again using narcotic drugs, the Surgeon General may order such patient's immediate return to the committing court which may recommit such patient to a hospital of the Service for additional treatment for a period of not to exceed six months, and may require such patient thereafter to submit to a posthopitalization program in accordance with subsection (a) of this section.

. . .

Sec. 309. Any determination by the court pursuant to this title that a patient is a narcotic addict shall not be deemed a criminal conviction, nor shall such patient be denominated a criminal by reason of that determination. The results of any hearing, examination, test, or procedure to determine narcotic addiction of any patient under this title shall not be used against such patient in any criminal proceeding.

* * *

There were two other main sections of NARA. Title IV authorized the surgeon general to establish outpatient drug treatment programs and to assist state and local governments in developing treatment programs. An annual total of $15 million was authorized for grants to states to develop and test treatment programs, to train treatment program personnel, and to conduct research to assess the effectiveness of state and local treatment programs.

Title V revised the previous federal statutes that disallowed the suspension of sentence or a probation sentence for offenders convicted of a second or subsequent offense. Under the 1966 act, the Board of Parole was directed to review the sentence of any prisoner convicted of a marijuana offense who was denied parole under the previous law. The new act now allowed the release to parole of such a prisoner.

NARA gave civil commitment programs renewed popularity. However, later research on the implementation and impact of these programs found very mixed results. An early cautionary note about civil commitment programs was offered by Alfred Lindesmith in 1965, before the considerable expansion of treatment programs that occurred beginning in the late 1960s.

DOCUMENT 210: Criticism of Civil Commitment Laws (Alfred R. Lindesmith, 1965)

The worst features of the current civil commitment fad may well be connected with its pretense of being something other than punitive. Its current popularity is probably largely due to the fact that it seems to offer advantages to both the police and medical philosophy of addiction. To the former it offers the continuation of the old practices of locking addicts up and of dodging the constitutional guarantees of the Bill of Rights which are built into the procedures of the criminal law. To the liberals and medically oriented it offers a gesture toward a new and more humanitarian approach and a new vocabulary for old practices. For the addict the situation remains substantially unchanged even if he can qualify as one of the select few eligible for civil commitment, except that he may expect to spend more time in institutions. The price of illicit drugs and the illicit traffic are untouched by this program, and the addict must still commit crimes to maintain himself. He still lives in fear of the police and is still exploited by peddlers. If he seeks to quit his habit voluntarily the only establishments to which he has easy access are jails and their equivalents.

Source: Alfred R. Lindesmith, *The Addict and the Law* (Bloomington: Indiana University Press, 1965), 291–292.

LSD IN THE 1960s

The late 1960s saw the emergence of lysergic acid diethylamide (LSD), a psychedelic drug that was popular in the "hippie" culture of that era. LSD caused widespread concern among the public and among policy makers. LSD had been discovered in April 1943 by a Swiss chemist, Dr. Albert Hofmann, working for the pharmaceutical firm Sandoz Laboratories.

Through the 1950s, a number of researchers and psychologists experimented with LSD and similar drugs. It was thought that the hallucinogenic effects of these drugs mimicked mental disorders and thus would be useful in treating psychological problems. During the 1950s, the United States military also experimented with LSD for its possible use as a "brainwashing" tool in wartime. Edward Brecher describes some of these experiments.

DOCUMENT 211: Use of LSD in Psychotherapy (Edward M. Brecher, 1972)

For a time after 1943, LSD was a drug in search of a use. The United States Army tested its usefulness for brainwashing, and for inducing prisoners to talk more freely. Later, LSD was stockpiled in very large amounts by the American armed forces for possible use in disabling an enemy force. Military interest in LSD waned, however, when psychoactive chemicals such as BZ, capable of producing even more bizarre effects, were developed.

Psychiatrists were naturally interested from the beginning in LSD effects. Many of them took the drug themselves, and gave it to staff members of mental hospitals, in the belief that its effects approximate a psychotic state and might thus lead to better understanding of their patients. Some of those who tried LSD reported that it did enable them to achieve greater empathy with their psychotic patients. It was as an adjunct to psychotherapy, however, that LSD came into widespread use.

Drs. Anthony K. Busch and Warren C. Johnson secured a supply of LSD from Sandoz in 1949, and published the first report on its psychotherapeutic use in twenty-one hospitalized psychotic patients in 1950. They concluded that "LSD-25 may offer a means for more readily gaining access to the chronically withdrawn patients. It may also serve as a new tool for shortening psychotherapy. We hope further investigation justifies our present impression." Other reports soon followed. By 1965, it was estimated that between 30,000 and 40,000 psychiatric patients around the world had received LSD therapeutically; and additional thousands of normal volunteers had received it experimentally. Countless experiments had been run on animal species ranging from the spider and the snail to the chimpanzee. It was estimated in 1965 that some 2,000 papers on LSD effects had been published.

Source: Edward M. Brecher and the Editors of Consumer Reports, *Licit and Illicit Drugs* (Boston: Little, Brown, 1972), 349–350.

* * *

By the early 1960s, however, it had become fairly clear that LSD was of limited utility in psychotherapy, and that it had potential psychological hazards for vulnerable individuals. A 1960 study of the use of LSD in psychotherapy found that in many cases patients had negative and sometimes frightening reactions to the drug.

Although LSD lost favor in the world of psychiatry, it became an important recreational drug in the 1960s. Along with marijuana, LSD and related hallucinogenic drugs were widely used by college students and hippies. Psychologist Timothy Leary, a professor at Harvard University, was the best-known and most influential proponent of LSD. His very public promotion of LSD and psilocybin (hallucinogenic mushrooms) at Harvard led to his dismissal from the university. By 1970 there were some estimates that between 1 and 2 million Americans had tried LSD.

DOCUMENT 212: Spread of LSD Use in 1960s (Edward M. Brecher, 1972)

It is impossible to determine which contributed more to the growth of the demand for blackmarket LSD between 1962 and 1969: the warnings or the praise. The combination of warnings and praise triggered a publicity barrage that grew far out of rational proportion. The net effect was to make LSD familiar to everyone in the land, and to arouse nationwide curiosity. From curiosity to experimentation is only one short step.

There were many propagandists for LSD before 1962, but no one paid much attention to them, and they had little effect. This was still true when Timothy Leary, an instructor at Harvard University's Center for Research in Human Personality, first started work with LSD. Leary had been much impressed by the effects of some Mexican psilocybin mushrooms that he had tried in the summer of 1960. "It was the classic visionary voyage and I came back a changed man," he wrote in 1967. "You are never the same after you've had that one flash glimpse down the cellular time tunnel. You are never the same after you've had the veil drawn."

At Harvard that fall, Dr. Leary and an associate, Dr. Richard Alpert, secured a supply of psilocybin from Sandoz for use in an experiment with prisoners at the Massachusetts Correctional Institution in Concord. The first results seemed promising: prisoners released from the institution following a psilocybin trip seemed less likely to be rearrested and returned for parole violation than other parolees. Critics of the experiment noted, however, that it might have been association with the two charismatic young instructors . . . rather than the drug that produced the favorable results. In addition, Leary continued to take trips himself, to confer with other psychedelic enthusiasts such as Aldous Huxley and Allen Ginsberg, and to gather around him a clique of Harvard young people dedicated to the LSD-like drugs. He remained little-known outside his small Cambridge circle.

In 1962, however, Leary's activities attracted the attention of the FDA and Massachusetts law-enforcement officials. . . . Harvard and the Harvard Crimson responded by warning students against taking LSD. The warnings were picked up by the mass media—and were among the first nationally circulated publicity for LSD. As the FDA and state officials continued their investigation, a scandal broke. Leary, the focus of the scandal, became a national figure overnight. He used his new eminence to propagandize for LSD on a national scale.

Source: Edward M. Brecher and the Editors of Consumer Reports, *Licit and Illicit Drugs* (Boston: Little, Brown, 1972), 368–369.

* * *

In Public Law 90–639, enacted on October 24, 1968, Congress added LSD to the drugs covered under the Food, Drug, and Cosmetic Act, reduced some of the penalties for depressant and stimulant violations, and enhanced the penalties for LSD manufacture, sale, or possession. As part of this new law, Congress also called generally for new efforts to educate the public about drug abuse. In addition to this federal legislation, a number of states also passed laws adding or increasing penalties for LSD possession or sale.

DOCUMENT 213: New State Laws Against LSD (Edward M. Brecher, 1972)

The barrage of publicity that popularized LSD was intensified by a wave of prohibitive legislation. New York's 1965 penalties for the "possession, sale, exchange, or giving away" of LSD or LSD-like drugs without a special license provided for a maximum of two years' imprisonment. Sponsors of a bill to increase the penalties cited two newspaper stories as illustrations of the LSD menace: one reported that a five-year-old Brooklyn girl had swallowed an LSD-impregnated sugar cube left in the refrigerator by her young uncle. Her stomach was pumped—a useless measure which, several physicians noted, was probably more traumatic than the drug effect—but she recovered. The other newspaper story reported that a thirty-two-year-old ex-mental patient charged with the brutal murder of his mother-in-law claimed to have been "flying" on LSD, and to remember nothing about the homicide. Law-enforcement officers promptly labeled this case an "LSD murder." (At the man's trial, psychiatrists testified that he suffered from chronic paranoid schizophrenia. He was found not guilty by reason of insanity; the issue of insanity due to LSD was not raised.) These two incidents . . . were interpreted as reasons to increase LSD criminal penalties in 1966 to a maximum of twenty years' imprisonment. . . .

The same year, Donald Grunsky introduced a bill in the California State Senate prohibiting the possession as well as the manufacture, sale, or importation of LSD and DMT [dimethyl tryptamine, a plant-based hallucinogen]. The same New York "LSD murder" case was referred to, and lurid color photographs of a psychotic reaction to LSD were circulated by the state attorney general's office.

Source: Edward M. Brecher and the Editors of Consumer Reports, *Licit and Illicit Drugs* (Boston: Little, Brown, 1972), 370.

* * *

Lurid stories of violence, suicide, and other mayhem committed while under the influence of LSD were common. One widely disseminated story concerned a group of students who were supposedly blinded by staring at the sun while on LSD. The story later was revealed to be a hoax.

DOCUMENT 214: Report on LSD Blindings (*New York Times*, 1968)

Six young college men have suffered total and permanent blindness as a result of staring at the sun while under the influence of LSD.

The six, all juniors at a western Pennsylvania college that officials declined to name, lost their sight after they took the hallucinatory drug together last spring.

Norman Yoder, commissioner of the Office of the Blind in the Pennsylvania State Welfare Department, said the retinal areas of the youths' eyes had been destroyed. . . .

Federal officials questioned about the case said it was the first they had heard of in which total blindness had resulted. . . .

Mr. Yoder said . . . that the six Pennsylvania youths had all taken LSD at least once before. He said they had gone in the morning to a grassy area in a woodland about half a mile from the college and had taken the drug there. Then, he said, they had lain on their backs in the grass "and were not consciously looking at the sun."

Mr. Yoder said doctors guessed that the LSD had put the youths into a trance-like state in which the eyelids remained open while the sun burned the retinas.

The youths were found at the scene, blind and helpless. . . .

"It's a real tragedy," Mr. Yoder said, "when kids can ruin their lives this way. And the parents are asking: 'How can something like this happen?' "

Dr. Leon Jacobs, deputy assistant secretary of welfare for scientific affairs, commented that the case was "another evidence of how disastrous the effects of LSD may be." He said he hoped the "demonstration of what a terrible thing happened to them may keep other kids away from it."

Source: "Six Youths on LSD 'Trip' Blinded by Sun," *New York Times*, January 13, 1968. Reprinted by permission of the Associated Press.

* * *

Six days later the following news story appeared.

DOCUMENT 215: Acknowledgment of LSD Hoax (*New York Times*, 1968)

Gov. Raymond P. Shafer of Pennsylvania labeled as a hoax today the report that six college students were blinded by the sun while they were under the influence of LSD.

The Governor, who yesterday told a news conference that he was convinced the report was true, said his investigators discovered that the story was "a fabrication" by Dr. Norman M. Yoder, commissioner of the Office of the Blind in the Pennsylvania State Welfare Department. He said Dr. Yoder, who was unavailable for comment, had admitted the hoax. . . .

The Governor's investigators . . . described Dr. Yoder as "distraught and sick" and apparently motivated "by his concern over illegal LSD use by children." . . .

Ophthalmologists had doubted that an LSD trance could overcome instincts and keep a person's eyes open long enough for retinal tissue to be burnt out completely by the sun. There was also prevailing skepticism that the simultaneous blinding of six students could have been kept secret for 18 months.

However, the story gained credibility on Tuesday when State Senator Benjamin R. Donolow of Philadelphia said the story was true. . . .

In the Governor's absence—he returned from a vacation in the Virgin Islands Tuesday night—his press secretary, Jack Conmy also said that the blindings had occurred.

Source: "Governor Shafer Calls LSD Blindings a Hoax," *New York Times*, January 19, 1968. Copyright © 1968 by The New York Times. Reprinted by permission.

* * *

Another hoax was perpetrated in the late 1960s about the supposed hallucinogenic effects of banana peels.

DOCUMENT 216: Report on Use of Banana Peels as a Drug (*New York Times*, 1967)

A Federal investigation is under way into the possible hallucinogenic effects of banana peels, Dr. James L. Goddard, Commissioner of the Food and Drug Administration, said today.

The smoking of banana skin pulp is the latest craze among college students and beatniks, some of whom had said that the fad gives the user an effect similar to that produced by marijuana smoking.

Smoking the pulp substance is said to produce a "mild trip," Dr. Goddard said. But he added that the effects might be more psychological than psychedelic.

"We really don't know what agent, if there is any, in the smoke produces the reported effect but we are investigating to see if it might be the methylated form of serotonin," Dr. Goddard said. Some scientists have been studying a possible link between serotonin and schizophrenia. . . .

Banana peel enthusiasts at the University of California at Berkeley have held mass "smokeouts."

The fad spread to New York City where beatniks and students chanted "banana-banana" at a "be-in" in Central Park Easter Sunday. They paraded around the Sheep Meadow carrying a two-foot long wooden banana.

Source: Richard D. Lyons, "Banana Smoking under U.S. Study," *New York Times*, April 5, 1967. Copyright © 1967 by The New York Times. Reprinted by permission.

THE NIXON ADMINISTRATION, THE VIETNAM WAR, AND THE 1970 DRUG CONTROL ACT

Notwithstanding the strong anti-drug rhetoric of the Nixon administration, several important policy changes occurred during his presidency. These were influenced by the spread of drug use to middle-class white people and by the high rate of drug abuse among returning Vietnam War veterans. Both of these trends helped promote a greater acceptance of the need for medical and treatment interventions for addicts.

DOCUMENT 217: Spread of Heroin Addiction to Middle Class (Edward M. Brecher, 1972)

During 1970 and 1971, the mass media carried news of two new and distressing opiate trends. A growing number of white, middle-class young people, in suburbs as well as inner cities, were said to be mainlining heroin. And United States military personnel—primarily in Vietnam, but also at duty stations in the United States and throughout the world—were similarly said to be sniffing, smoking, or mainlining heroin in substantial numbers.

. . .

One very distressing aspect of heroin's spread to the suburbs was that it seemed to signal a crumbling of the long-standing dividing line between heroin and other drugs, licit and illicit. That line had been recognized and accepted by almost all middle-class white young people through all the years from 1914 till late in the 1960s. Young people might risk alcohol, nicotine, marijuana, hashish, LSD, and a variety of other drugs—but heroin? Certainly not—except, of course, for some poverty-stricken denizens of inner cities and a few others.

. . .

After the public was informed, during the summer of 1971, of widespread heroin addiction among the United States armed forces in Vietnam and elsewhere . . . [p]ublic officials from the President . . . down announced that everything possible would be done to "rehabilitate" (which to most people meant "cure") addicts in uniform. . . .

President Nixon's Message to Congress on June 17, 1971, for example, contained such statements as these:

> *Rehabilitation.* A new priority . . . I am asking the Congress for a total of $105 million in addition to funds already contained in my 1972 budget to be used solely for the treatment and rehabilitation of drug-addicted individuals. . . . The nature of drug addiction, and the peculiar aspects of the present problem as it involves veterans, make it imperative that rehabilitation procedures be undertaken immediately. . . . In order to expedite the rehabilitation program of Vietnam veterans, I have ordered the immediate establishment of . . . immediate rehabilitation efforts to be taken in Vietnam. . . . The Department of Defense will provide rehabilitation programs to all servicemen being returned from discharge who want this help, and we will be requesting legislation to permit the military services to retain for treatment any individual who is a narcotic addict. All of our servicemen must be accorded the right to rehabilitation.

Source: Edward M. Brecher and the Editors of Consumer Reports, *Licit and Illicit Drugs* (Boston: Little, Brown, 1972), 183–194.

* * *

The psychiatrist Jerome Jaffe played an important role in the Nixon administration in promoting methadone maintenance and other treatment. Dr. Jaffe was one of the pioneers in methadone treatment in Chicago, and was named by Nixon as the first director of the new Special Action Office for Drug Abuse Prevention (SAODAP), established in 1972.

DOCUMENT 218: Nixon Support for Prevention and Treatment (David F. Musto, 1987)

The other prong of the Nixon strategy was drug abuse prevention, which included research, education, training, rehabilitation, and treatment—efforts to reduce demand for drugs among the American public. Here the monies authorized by the federal government rose from $59 million in FY 1970 to $462 million in FY 1974. Nixon established the Special Action Office for Drug Abuse Prevention (SAODAP) to coordinate the many government programs linked to the drug problem but especially to give leadership to a crash program of treatment services. To head this unparalleled elevation of drug abuse issues to national prominence, Nixon chose Dr. Jerome H. Jaffe, an academic researcher who was familiar with treatment programs, especially methadone maintenance. Dr. Jaffe, who came to be known as the "drug czar," was urged by the President to knock heads together to achieve the high priority of curbing the drug menace.

Source: David F. Musto, *The American Disease: Origins of Narcotic Control*, expanded ed. (New York: Oxford University Press, 1987), 258.

* * *

In 1970 Congress passed the Comprehensive Drug Abuse Prevention and Control Act. For the first time since the Harrison Act, Congress consolidated the numerous existing federal laws. In addition, the 1970 act created a new schedule of controlled substances that remains the template for the classification of illegal drugs under federal and state laws to the present day. This act largely determined federal anti-drug policy and influenced state laws until 1986.

DOCUMENT 219: Enactment of the 1970 Act (Alexander T. Shulgin, 1992)

On October 27, 1970, the Harrison Act was effectively removed from the books with the passage of the Controlled Substances Act of 1970. Title II of this Act was entitled Comprehensive Drug Abuse Prevention and Control Act. The synthetic psychoactive drugs, old and new, are now subjected to the same regulations as the older natural drugs. . . .

With this Act, Congress effectively destroyed the Federal-State relationship that existed between the Harrison Act and the Uniform Narcotic Drug Act. To restore this, the Commission on Uniform State Laws drafted the Uniform Controlled Substances Act [see Document 86]. This Act is structured on the Federal act and requires persons involved in the manufacture, distribution, and dispensing of scheduled drugs to obtain a registration form from the State. Each state can, however, impose its own penalties for violation of these laws.

Source: Alexander T. Shulgin, *Controlled Substances: Chemical and Legal Guide to Federal Drug Laws* (Berkeley, CA: Ronin Publishing, 1992), 247.

* * *

A key aspect of the 1970 act was its attempt to classify drugs according to their potential for abuse and their recognized medical usefulness. Although some of these classifications have been controversial (such as including both marijuana and LSD in the most severe Schedule I category), they were an important effort to make distinctions among the severity of various illegal drugs. In addition, the 1970 act was important in reducing some of the federal penalties for drug possession, notably for marijuana, and eliminating some mandatory minimum sentences. For example, a first offense for possessing a small amount of marijuana was punishable by up to a year of probation. On the other hand, the 1970 act allowed "no-knock" searches by police under certain conditions.

Following are key sections of the 1970 act.

DOCUMENT 220: Comprehensive Drug Abuse Prevention and Control Act (1970)

SCHEDULES OF CONTROLLED SUBSTANCES

Sec. 202.

(a) There are established five schedules of controlled substances. . . . The schedules . . . shall be updated and republished on . . . an annual basis. . . .

(b) . . . a drug or other substance may not be placed in any schedule unless the findings required for such schedule are made with respect to such drug or other substance. The findings required for each of the schedules are as follows:

(I) SCHEDULE I.—[e.g., heroin, LSD]

(A) The drug or other substance has a high potential for abuse.

(B) The drug or other substance has no currently accepted medical use in treatment in the United States.

(C) There is a lack of accepted safety for use of the drug or other substance under medical supervision.

(2) SCHEDULE II.—[e.g., morphine, cocaine]

(A) The drug or other substance has a high potential for abuse.

(B) The drug or other substance has a currently accepted medical use in treatment in the United States or a currently accepted medical use with severe restrictions.

(C) Abuse of the drug or other substances may lead to severe psychological or physical dependence.

(3) SCHEDULE III.—[e.g., barbiturates]

(A) The drug or other substance has a potential for abuse less than the drugs or other substances in schedules I and II.

(B) The drug or other substance has a currently accepted medical use in treatment in the United States.

(C) Abuse of the drug or other substance may lead to moderate or low physical dependence or high psychological dependence.

(4) SCHEDULE IV.—[e.g., tranquilizers]

(A) The drug or other substance has a low potential for abuse relative to the drugs or other substances in schedule III.

(B) The drug or other substance has a currently accepted medical use in treatment in the United States.

(C) Abuse of the drug or other substance may lead to limited physical dependence or psychological dependence relative to the drugs or other substances in schedule III.

(5) SCHEDULE V.—[e.g., cough syrups containing codeine]

(A) The drug or other substance has a low potential for abuse relative to the drugs or other substances in schedule IV.

(B) The drug or other substance has a currently accepted medical use in treatment in the United States.

(C) Abuse of the drug or other substance may lead to limited physical dependence or psychological dependence relative to the drugs or other substances in schedule IV.

. . .

Sec. 308.

(a) It shall be unlawful for any person to distribute a controlled substance in schedule I or II to another except in pursuance of a written order of the person to whom such substance is distributed, made on a form to be issued by the Attorney General. . . .

. . .

(c) (1) Every person who in pursuance of an order required under subsection (a) distributes a controlled substance shall preserve such order for a period of two years, and shall make such order available for inspection and copying by officers and employees of the United States duly authorized for that purpose by the Attorney General, and by officers or employees of States or their political subdivisions who are charged with the enforcement of State or local laws regulating the production, or regulating the distribution or dispensing of controlled substances and who are authorized under such laws to inspect such orders.

. . .

(e) It shall be unlawful for any person to obtain order forms issued under this section for any purpose other than their use, distribution, dispensing, or administration in the conduct of a lawful business in such substances or in the course of his professional practice or research.

PART D—OFFENSES AND PENALTIES

Sec. 401.

(a) Except as authorized by the title, it shall be unlawful for any person knowingly or intentionally—

(1) to manufacture, distribute, or dispense, or possess with intent to manufacture, distribute, or dispense, a controlled substance; or

(2) to create, distribute, or dispense, or possess with intent to distribute or dispense, a counterfeit substance.

[Section (b) describes the allowable penalties for each of the different schedules. If the person has at least one prior federal drug conviction of any type, the potential maximum sentences are doubled. For Schedule I or II substances that are narcotic drugs, the penalty is up to 15 years in prison, a $25,000 fine, or both, plus a "special parole term" of at least three years. The penalty for a Schedule III drug (or a non-narcotic Schedule I or II drug) is up to five years in prison, a $15,000 fine, or both, and a special parole term of at least two years. For a Schedule IV drug, the prison sentence can be up to three years, a fine of $10,000, or both, and a special parole term of at least one year. Finally, the maximum penalty for a Schedule V substance is a prison term of one year, a fine of up to $5,000, or both.]

. . .

PENALTY FOR SIMPLE POSSESSION

Sec. 404

(a) It shall be unlawful for any person knowingly or intentionally to possess a controlled substance unless substance was obtained directly, or pursuant to a valid prescription or from a practitioner, while acting in the course of his professional practice, or except as otherwise authorized by this title. Any person who violates this subsection shall be sentenced to a term of imprisonment of not more than one year, a fine of not more than $5,000, or both, except that if he commits such offense after a prior conviction or convictions under this subsection have become final [he shall] be sentenced to a term of imprisonment of not more than 2 years, a fine of not more than $10,000, or both.

(b) (1) If any person who has not previously been convicted of violating subsection (a) of this section, any other provision of this title or title III, or any other law of the United States relating to narcotic drugs, marihuana or depressant or stimulant substances, is found guilty of a violation of subsection (a) of this section after trial or upon a plea of guilty, the court may, without entering a judgment of guilty and with the consent of such person, defer further proceedings and place him on probation upon such reasonable conditions as it may require and for such period, not to exceed one year, as the court may prescribe. Upon violation of a condition of the probation, the court may enter an adjudication of guilty and proceed as otherwise provided. The court may, in its discretion, dismiss the proceedings against such person and discharge him from probation before the expiration of the maximum period prescribed for such person's probation. If during the period of his probation such person does not violate any of the conditions of the probation then upon expiration of such period the court shall discharge such person and dismiss the proceedings against him. . . . Discharge and dismissal under this section may occur only once with respect to any person.

. . .

DISTRIBUTING TO PERSONS UNDER AGE TWENTY-ONE

Sec. 405

(a) Any person at least eighteen years of age who violates section 401(a)(1) by distributing a controlled substance to a person under twenty-one years of age is (except as provided in subsection (b)) punishable by (1) a term of imprisonment, or a fine, or both, up to twice that authorized by section 401(b), and (2) at least twice any special parole term authorized by section 401(b), for a first offense involving the same controlled substance and schedule. [Note: For a second or subsequent conviction, the maximum penalties are tripled.]

. . .

CONTINUING CRIMINAL ENTERPRISE

Sec. 408. (a)

(1) Any person who engages in a continuing criminal enterprise shall be sentenced to a term of imprisonment which may not be less than 10 years and which may be up to life imprisonment to a fine of not more than $100,000, and to the forfeiture prescribed in paragraph (2); except that if any person engages in such activity after one or more prior convictions of him under this section have become final, he shall be sentenced to a term of imprisonment which may not be less than 20 years and which may be up to life imprisonment, to a fine of not more than $200,000, and to the forfeiture prescribed in paragraph (2).

. . .

(b) For purposes of subsection (a), a person is engaged in a continuing criminal enterprise if—

(1) he violates any provision of this title or title III the punishment for which is a felony, and

(2) such violation is a part of a continuing series of violations of this title or title III—

(A) which are undertaken by such person in concert with five or more other persons with respect to whom such person occupies a position of organizer, a supervisory position, or any other position of management, and

(B) from which such person obtains substantial income or resources.

. . .

POWERS OF ENFORCEMENT PERSONNEL

Sec. 508.

Any officer or employee of the Bureau of Narcotics and Dangerous Drug[s] designated by the Attorney General may—

(1) Carry firearms;

(2) execute and serve search warrants, arrest warrants, administrative inspection warrants, subpenas [*sic*] and summonses issued under the authority of the United States;

(3) make arrests without warrant (A) for any offense against the United States committed in his presence, or (B) for any felony, cognizable under the laws of the United States, if he has probable cause to believe that the person to be arrested has committed or is committing a felony;

(4) make seizures of property pursuant to the provisions of this title and

(5) perform such other law enforcement duties as the Attorney General may designate.

SEARCH WARRANTS

Sec. 509.

(a) [An officer executing a] search warrant relating to offenses involving controlled substances the penalty for which is imprisonment for more than one year may, without notice of his authority and purpose, break open an outer or inner door or window of a building, or any part of the building, or anything therein, if the judge or United States magistrate issuing the warrant (1) is satisfied that there is probable cause to believe that (A) the property sought may and, if such notice is given, will be easily and quickly destroyed or disposed of, or (B) the giving of such notice will immediately endanger the life or safety of the executing officer or another person, and (2) has included in the warrant a direction that the officer executing it shall not be required to give such notice. Any officer acting under such warrant, shall, as soon as practicable after entering the premises, identify himself and give the reasons and authority for his entrance upon the premises.

Source: Public Law 91–513 (Comprehensive Drug Abuse Prevention and Control Act), October 27, 1970.

* * *

Title III of the 1970 act specifies the penalties for importing or exporting a controlled substance. For Schedule I or II drugs, a conviction is punished by up to five years in prison, a fine of not more than $15,000, or both. Penalties could be doubled for a second or subsequent offense.

The 1970 act was the last piece of comprehensive federal legislation on drug control for the next 16 years. The 1972 Drug Abuse Office and Treatment Act created and expanded prevention and treatment, and called for a National Drug Abuse Strategy for drug abuse and drug trafficking prevention.

DOCUMENT 221: Drug Abuse Office and Treatment Act, National Drug Abuse Strategy (1972)

TITLE III—NATIONAL DRUG ABUSE STRATEGY

[This title requires the president to develop a long-term federal strategy for all federal drug abuse and drug traffic prevention functions.]

Sec. 303. The Strategy shall contain:

(1) an analysis of the nature, character, and extent of the drug abuse problem in the United States, including examination of the interrelationships between various approaches to solving the drug abuse problem and their potential for interacting both positively and negatively with one another;

(2) a comprehensive Federal plan, with respect to both drug abuse prevention functions and drug traffic prevention functions, which shall specify the objectives of the Federal strategy and how all available resources, funds, programs, services, and facilities authorized under relevant Federal law should be used; and

(3) an analysis and evaluation of the major programs conducted, expenditures made, results achieved, plans developed, and problems encountered in the operation and coordination of the various Federal drug abuse prevention functions and drug traffic prevention functions.

Source: Public Law 92–255 (Drug Abuse Office and Treatment Act), March 1, 1972.

THE FORD AND REAGAN ADMINISTRATIONS

In the years following Nixon's resignation from the White House in 1974, American drug policy experienced several trends. During the brief administration of President Gerald Ford, and the subsequent Jimmy Carter presidency, there was an increasing acceptance of the inevitability of drug use and much greater tolerance for recreational drug use, especially of marijuana (see Part XI).

DOCUMENT 222: Ford Administration Policies (David F. Musto, 1987)

The departure of President Nixon in August 1974 brought to the White House a man much more relaxed about recreational drug use. President Ford simply did not share Nixon's intense anger at drug users. Ford's attitude facilitated creation of a federal policy that openly acknowledged that drug abuse was here to stay and that hopes of elimination were illusory. His formal recognition of the limits of even the enormous federal effort during the Nixon years was contained in the *White Paper on Drug Abuse*, prepared by the Domestic Council Drug Abuse Task Force and published in September 1975, a year after Ford assumed the presidency. In a wide-ranging review of the anti-drug effort starting in 1969 (which managed never to mention the name of President Nixon), the White Paper drew conclusions marking official recognition of a painful truth: "Total elimination of drug abuse is unlikely, but governmental actions can contain the problem and limit its adverse effects." The White Paper also made a clear statement on the ranking of anti-drug priorities: "All drugs are not equally dangerous, and all drug use is not equally destructive." When a choice must be made, "priority in both supply and demand reduction should be directed toward those drugs which inherently pose a greater risk—heroin, amphetamines (particularly when used intravenously), and mixed barbiturates."

Source: David F. Musto, *The American Disease: Origins of Narcotic Control*, expanded ed. (New York: Oxford University Press, 1987), 264.

* * *

The election of Ronald Reagan in 1980, however, signaled the beginning of a new punitive era in American drug policy that culminated in the emergence of crack cocaine and the passage of the Anti-Drug Abuse Acts of 1986 and 1988 (see Part XII). The conservative President Reagan had little tolerance for illegal drug use and a strong preference for a law enforcement approach to drug policy. During the eight years of the Reagan presidency, federal funds for enforcement rose while treatment and prevention dollars decreased. In numerous speeches, Reagan called for a war on drugs; his key drug policy advisors were strong advocates of the supply reduction approach. Finally, Nancy Reagan began a highly visible campaign ("Just Say No") against drug use. In the following document, drug policy expert James Inciardi describes how military equipment began to be used in the fight against drugs under Reagan.

DOCUMENT 223: President Reagan and Harsher Policies (James A. Inciardi, 1986)

. . . [W]hen President Reagan signed the Department of Defense Authorization Act of 1982 into law, it included several amendments to the century-old Posse Comitatus Act. Although military personnel were still prohibited from physically intercepting suspected drug vessels and aircraft, conducting searches and seizures, and making arrests, the entire war chest of U.S. military power did become available to law enforcement—for training, intelligence gathering, and detection. Moreover, members of the U.S. Army, Navy, Air Force, and Marines could operate military equipment for civilian agencies charged with the enforcement of the drug laws.

Source: James A. Inciardi, *The War on Drugs: Heroin, Cocaine, Crime, and Public Policy* (Mountain View, CA: Mayfield Publishing, 1986), 208–209.

* * *

Until the mid-1980s, American drug policy continued to emphasize law enforcement and supply reduction but with some support for treatment and demand reduction as well. At that point, a renewed wave of concern about drug-related crime (including blatant street drug dealing) and the emergence of crack cocaine generated a series of tougher anti-drug policies that once again increased penalties for drug sale or possession. At the same time, the development of drug treatment programs that began in the mid-1950s continued. The greater tolerance for casual drug use that came out of the 1960s had some influence on American drug policy, especially in the relaxation of anti-marijuana laws.

Part XI

Marijuana Policy after the 1960s

REVISITING HARSH MARIJUANA LAWS

The second half of the 1960s and the early 1970s were characterized by dramatic social upheavals centered around the so-called hippie movement, the growth and glorification of casual drug use (especially marijuana and hallucinogenics), and political protests against the war in Vietnam. In particular, the use of marijuana became widespread: by 1979, 20 percent of adults aged 26 or older, 31 percent of youth aged 12–17, and 68 percent of young adults 18–25 had tried marijuana or hashish. The use of marijuana by millions of middle-class Americans, without apparent harm, made many question the wisdom of stringent laws against the drug's use and sale.

During this time there was considerable debate about the relative dangers of marijuana. The widespread use and popularity made even federal officials question the wisdom of existing harsh state and federal laws against marijuana use, as the next document indicates. In many states, long prison sentences could be imposed for possessing small amounts of marijuana, equivalent to penalties for violent crimes.

DOCUMENT 224: Federal Official Calls for Lower Penalties for Marijuana (*New York Times,* 1969)

The legal punishment of the convicted marijuana user is likely to do him more harm than the illicit cigarette he smoked, a nationally known health expert testified today. . . .

Dr. Stanley F. Yolles, director of the National Institute of Mental

Health, said the legal penalties for marijuana use were strict enough to ruin the life of a first offender and totally disregarded the medical and scientific evidence concerning the drug's effects. . . .

"I am convinced that the social and psychological damage caused by incarceration, is in many cases far greater to the individual and to society than was the offense itself," said Dr. Yolles.

Marijuana is not a narcotic and should be re-classified, he told the hearing [Senate subcommittee hearing on juvenile delinquency]. . . . Dr. Yolles emphasized, however, that marijuana was not harmless and that he was not advocating removal of all restrictions on its use. . . .

The medical scientist said he favored far less severe penalties than at present for simple possession of marijuana. He said severe penalties had never been effective deterrents and that Federal drug laws, in general, should be aimed more at rehabilitation than at repression. . . .

At the outset of his testimony, Dr. Yolles made it clear that he was testifying as an individual and that his views should not be taken as the official position of the Department of Health, Education and Welfare. . . .

Source: H. Schmeck, "U.S. Aide Calls Marijuana Laws More Harmful than the Drug," *New York Times*, September 18, 1969.

* * *

Another debate during this era centered on the classification of marijuana in federal and state laws as a narcotic drug. At least one unsuccessful court case tried to test the constitutionality of anti-drug laws that classified marijuana with narcotic drugs. This debate is still being waged today, and many federal and state laws continue to classify marijuana as a narcotic drug.

By the early 1970s, a major policy shift had occurred as a result of the debate over marijuana use. Many states began easing their anti-marijuana laws, especially for possession and for first offenders, with the support of federal officials. By 1970 at least 27 states had reduced first-time marijuana possession offenses from a felony to a misdemeanor, with lower penalties. The 1972 publication of the National Marihuana Commission's report (see below), calling for reduced penalties for marijuana possession, had a major impact on state policies and laws. As will be discussed in Part XIII, 11 states went so far as to decriminalize the possession of small amounts of marijuana.

Many state governors supported reductions in marijuana penalties. New Jersey, the state that had previously been hailed by Commissioner Anslinger for its tough anti-drug laws, eliminated jail terms for first convictions.

DOCUMENT 225: Reduced Marijuana Penalties Set in New Jersey (*New York Times,* 1970)

The New Jersey Supreme Court established new guidelines today that eliminated prison sentences for persons convicted for the first time of possessing or using marijuana.

The ruling by the state's highest court was described by legal observers as one of the most far-reaching court decisions in the country involving drug abuse penalties. The decision was handed down a week after Gov. William T. Cahill signed into law a bill he had sought that drastically lessened the criminal penalties for first offenders caught with small amounts of marijuana.

. . .

Under the new law . . . the penalty for possessing a small amount of marijuana was reduced from a serious crime carrying a 2-to-15 year prison term to a simple disorderly conduct charge that carries a maximum penalty of six months in jail.

Today's ruling by the court effectively eliminates any six-month sentences, regardless of the amount of marijuana involved, so long as the person caught with it intended it for his own use only.

In a 5-to-2 decision, the court said, "We cannot escape the unhappy fact that our youth have been involved with marijuana in disturbing numbers," but the court emphasized that prison sentences obviously were not the solution, adding that such punishment "is a traumatic experience for anyone."

. . .

The court said that a suspended sentence with an appropriate term of probation generally would be a sufficient penalty.

The decision involved the conviction two years ago of . . . a 20-year old night student at Cumberland County College. The youth, who was 18 years old when he was arrested, was sentenced to two to three years in State prison on charges of possessing $2.50 worth of marijuana in his home, even though he had no prior criminal record.

. . .

Under the new law signed by Mr. Cahill, local judges were given the discretionary power to impose suspended sentences for first-time marijuana offenders. But the Supreme Court's recommendations, which lower court judges generally regard as an order, make suspended sentences virtually mandatory.

Source: R. Sullivan, "Top Jersey Court Ends Jail Term for First Offense on Marijuana," *New York Times*, October 27, 1970. Copyright © 1970 by The New York Times. Reprinted by permission.

NEW FEDERAL CRACKDOWNS ON MARIJUANA

On December 23, 1965, Timothy Leary was arrested in Texas with his two children after crossing the border from Mexico. Three months later he was convicted of transporting marijuana and for failing to pay the marijuana transfer tax and sentenced to a total of 30 years in prison. The conviction was appealed and the case ultimately found its way to the Supreme Court as a test of the constitutionality of the federal laws against importing marijuana: the 1922 Narcotic Drugs Import and Export Act and the 1937 Marihuana Tax Act. The Supreme Court, in a key unanimous decision, reversed Leary's conviction. A summary of the opinion follows.

DOCUMENT 226: *Leary v. United States* (1969)

This case presents constitutional questions arising out of the conviction of the petitioner, Dr. Timothy Leary, for violation of the two federal statutes governing traffic in marihuana.

The circumstances surrounding petitioner's conviction were as follows: On December 20, 1965, petitioner left New York by automobile, intending a vacation trip to Yucatan, Mexico. He was accompanied by his daughter and son, both teenagers, and two other persons. On December 22, 1965, the party drove across the International Bridge between the United States and Mexico at Laredo, Texas. They stopped at the Mexican customs station and, after apparently being denied entry, drove back across the bridge. They halted at the American secondary inspection area, explained the situation to a customs inspector, and stated that they had nothing from Mexico to declare. The inspector then asked them to alight, examined the interior of the car, and saw what appeared to be marihuana seeds on the floor. The inspector then received permission to search the car and passengers. Small amounts of marihuana were found on the car floor and in the glove compartment. A personal search of petitioner's daughter revealed a silver snuff box containing semi-refined marihuana and three partially smoked marihuana cigarettes.

Petitioner was indicted and tried before a jury in the Federal District Court for the Southern District of Texas, on three counts. First, it was alleged that he had knowingly smuggled marihuana into the United States. . . . Second, it was charged that he had knowingly transported and facilitated the transportation and concealment of marihuana which had been illegally imported or brought into the United States, with knowledge that it had been illegally imported or brought in.... Third, it was alleged that petitioner was a transferee of marihuana and had knowingly transported, concealed, and facilitated the transportation and concealment of marihuana, without having paid the transfer tax imposed by the Marihuana Tax Act....

After both sides had presented their evidence and the defense had moved for a judgment of acquittal, the District Court dismissed the first or smuggling count [on the grounds that because the marijuana had been obtained in New York, it could not be "smuggled" back into the country]. The jury found petitioner guilty on the other two counts. He was tentatively sentenced to the maximum punishment [20 years in prison and a $20,000 fine for violating the Import-Export Act, and 10 years in prison and a $20,000 fine for violating the Marihuana Tax Act, sentences to run consecutively], pending completion of a study and recommendations to be used by the District Court in fixing his final sentence. On appeal, the Court of Appeals for the Fifth Circuit affirmed. That court subsequently denied a petition for rehearing *en banc*.

We granted certiorari, to consider two questions: (1) whether petitioner's conviction for failing to comply with the transfer tax provisions of the Marihuana Tax Act violated his Fifth Amendment privileges against self-incrimination; (2) whether petitioner was denied due process by the application of the part of 21 U.S.C. 176a which provides that a defendant's possession of marihuana shall be deemed sufficient evidence that the marihuana was illegally imported or brought into the United States, and that the defendant knew of the illegal importation or bringing in, unless the defendant explains his possession to the satisfaction of the jury.... we hold in favor of the petitioner on both issues and reverse the judgment of the Court of Appeals.

Source: 395 *U.S. Reports* 6, *Leary v. United States*, May 19, 1969.

* * *

The Leary decision made the federal laws against importing marijuana unconstitutional and unenforceable, although state antimarijuana laws as well as federal laws against selling marijuana remained in force. *Leary v. United States* indicated that the federal laws violated the Fifth Amendment's right against self-incrimination.

But the federal government was not finished trying to convict Leary. In the retrial ordered by the Supreme Court, the former Harvard professor was found guilty on January 20, 1970, by a federal court jury in

Laredo, Texas, of helping to import three ounces of marijuana from Mexico. On March 2, 1970, he was sentenced to ten years in federal prison, with the judge calling him "a menace to this country."

In the late 1960s, the rapid spread of marijuana use led to a shortage of the drug and concerns that there would be increased shipments across the Mexican border. The result was an ill-fated federal crackdown on marijuana smuggling called Operation Intercept.

DOCUMENT 227: Failure of Operation Intercept (Edward M. Brecher, 1972)

The extent of marijuana use and distribution . . . was brought to nationwide attention in the spectacular failure of "Operation Intercept," an elaborate and determined effort by the government to shut off the flow of smuggled marijuana from Mexico. The program was based on the belief that Mexico was and would remain the primary source of marijuana for Americans.

Operation Intercept was launched at 2:30 P.M. Pacific Daylight Time on Sunday, September 21, 1969, and abandoned on October 11—just 20 days later. . . .

The drive to close the American border was strategically timed for the September 1969 marijuana harvest. The American marijuana supply was already far short of the demand, and the closure was intended to intensify the shortage.

. . .

"The objective of the [Operation Intercept] program," Secretary of the Treasury David M. Kennedy and Attorney General John N. Mitchell declared in a joint statement . . . "is to reduce the volume of narcotics, marijuana, and dangerous drugs which are smuggled into the United States from Mexico." The statement added that "more than 80 percent of the marijuana smoked in the United States" entered the country illegally from Mexico. If this 80 percent could be cut off, all would be well. That, at least, was the official hope.

Source: Edward M. Brecher and the Editors of Consumer Reports, *Licit and Illicit Drugs* (Boston: Little, Brown, 1972), 434–435.

* * *

Operation Intercept failed to achieve its goals. Border seizures of marijuana did not increase much beyond normal. Moreover, Mexican authorities, as well as other Latin American countries, strongly protested the operation as promoting negative publicity about Mexico and disrupting legitimate border trade between the two countries. The increased border surveillance during Operation Intercept caused massive tie-ups and delays.

NATIONAL COMMISSION ON MARIHUANA AND DRUG ABUSE

Faced with the widespread use of marijuana, and the apparent failure of existing punitive laws to reduce its use, government officials and legislators began questioning the relative harmfulness of marijuana, and whether it should be treated differently than other illegal drugs. The clear consensus that emerged during this period was that marijuana was relatively benign, that large numbers of Americans were using it casually with no apparent ill effects, and that casual personal use should not be punished with criminal sanctions. The result was a general reduction in penalties for marijuana possession in most states. By 1972, 42 of the states and the District of Columbia had adapted the recommendations of the Uniform Controlled Substances Act of the Conference of Commissioners on Uniform State Laws and classified marijuana possession as a misdemeanor. In addition, the 1970 comprehensive federal drug act reduced the possession or casual transfer of marijuana to a misdemeanor, and allowed for the expungement of a criminal record upon satisfactory completion of a probationary period.

Questions about the effects and dangers of marijuana and other drugs in the late 1960s and early 1970s also led many states to appoint special task forces and commissions to study and report on marijuana and other drug abuse. The U.S. Congress directed the Department of Health, Education and Welfare to file annual reports on marijuana and health; in addition, the 1970 act established the National Commission on Marihuana and Drug Abuse. This commission conducted a rigorous and comprehensive study of the current state of drug problems in America.

Prior to the Marihuana Commission, the federal government was questioning the wisdom of severe penalties for marijuana possession. In its ongoing evaluation of federal drug policy, the Nixon administration, despite its reputation for being tough on crime and escalating the "War on Drugs," began to consider distinguishing marijuana from other illegal drugs.

DOCUMENT 228: Federal Review of Harsh Marijuana Penalties (*New York Times,* 1969)

Last month, a 21-year-old Texas man was convicted of selling two marijuana cigarettes—the equivalent in "high" potential, Federal researchers say, of perhaps three or four lunch-time martinis. He was sentenced under state law to 50 years in prison.

Federal law is not substantially more liberal. Even a first offense of simple possession of "pot" carries a mandatory minimum sentence of two years. As Attorney General John N. Mitchell has noted, present Federal marijuana penalties can exceed those for manslaughter or sabotage.

For years, such severity attracted virtually no public notice since the use of marijuana was limited to the ghetto and possibly a few beatniks. But the last five years have seen an explosive growth in the use of pot. Federal officials estimate that users may number 12,000,000. . . .

Now, says a Federal narcotics expert, "the middle class kid is smoking pot" and there is an inevitable corollary. "The middle class parent is waking up to the law. 'For God's sake,' he says, 'throw the book at the trafficker, but don't lock up my kid.' "

. . .

As hinted last week by Administration officials, [John] Ingersoll [director of the Bureau of Narcotics and Dangerous Drugs] is expected to lay before the committee the first Administration proposals for relaxing the harsh present marijuana penalties, and for a sophisticated, flexible approach to all drug sentences.

He will, reportedly, propose a penalty structure which makes two kinds of distinctions. One set differentiates among mere users, peddlers, and large-scale traffickers. The other set distinguishes among four classes of drugs, on the basis of their abuse potential and their medical value [Note: See discussion of 1970 drug act in Part X]. . . .

The administration has progressed from concerned neutrality to unofficial support and now to official near-support for relaxed penalties. . . . Whatever the politics of the matter, however, the larger significance of the anticipated Ingersoll proposals will be a demonstration that the punitive ice is breaking. Eased sentences—allowing, for example, probation on the first offenses—may well pass the Senate and, though over stronger opposition, the House in the current session.

A new Federal law would not affect cases like that of the 50-year sentence in Texas, meted out under state statute. The Federal Government prosecutes only about 400 marijuana cases a year, virtually all involving large-scale operations.

The symbolic importance is great, however. "Virtually every state is wrestling with this problem," says a Narcotics Bureau authority, "and 26 already have asked us for help in rewriting their laws."

Source: J. Rosenthal, "A Fresh Look at Those Harsh Marijuana Penalties," *New York Times*, October 19, 1969.

* * *

The final report of the commission was issued in 1972, and contained a number of recommendations to reduce penalties for marijuana possession and personal use. Following is a summary of some of the key conclusions and recommendations contained in this report. This document sums up the prevailing views of the time that accepted marijuana as a relatively benign drug whose casual use should not be severely punished.

DOCUMENT 229: Report of the National Commission on Marihuana and Drug Abuse (March 1972)

. . . [U]se of [marijuana] has been regarded as a problem of major proportions for less than a decade. We will not find the reasons for contemporary social concern in pharmacology texts or previous governmental reports, for we are dealing with two separate realities: a drug with certain pharmacologic properties and determinable, although variable, effects on man; and a pattern of human behavior, individual and group, which has, *as a behavior*, created fear, anger, confusion, and uncertainty among a large segment of the contemporary American public. . . .

The most apparent feature of the behavior is that it is against the law. But inconsistency between behavior and the legal norm is not sufficient, in itself, to create a social problem. Marihuana has been an illegal substance for several decades; and the widespread violation of laws against gambling and adultery have not excited the public to the same extent as has marihuana-smoking in recent years.

At the same time, we suspect that illegality may play an important role in problem definition where drugs are concerned. Alcohol is of proven danger to individual and societal health and the public is well aware of its dangers, yet use of this drug has not been accorded the same problem status. Marihuana's illegality may have been a necessary condition for the marihuana problem, but the increased violation of the legal proscription does not by itself explain the phenomenon.

The Commission believes that three interrelated factors have fostered the definition of marijuana as a major national problem. First, the illegal behavior is highly visible to all segments of our society. Second, use of the drug is perceived to threaten the health and morality not only of the individual but of the society itself. Third, and most important, the drug has evolved in the late sixties and early seventies as a symbol of wider social conflicts and public issues.

More than anything else, the visibility of marihuana use by a segment of our population previously unfamiliar with the drug is what stirred public anxiety and thrust marihuana into the problem area. . . . For decades, its use was mainly confined to the underprivileged socioeconomic groups in our cities and to certain insulated social groups, such as jazz musicians and artists. As long as use remained confined to these groups and had a negligible impact on the dominant social order, the vast majority of Americans remained unconcerned. . . .

However, all this changed markedly in the mid-1960's. For various reasons, marihuana use became a common form of recreation for many middle and upper class college youth. The trend spread across the country, into the colleges and high schools and into the affluent suburbs as well. Use by American servicemen in Vietnam was frequent. In recent years, use of the drug has spanned every social class and geographic region.

The Commission-sponsored National Survey . . . indicated that some 24 million Americans have tried marihuana at least once and that at least 8.3 million are current users.

Other surveys uniformly indicate that more than 40% of the U.S. college population have tried marihuana. . . . The National Survey indicates that 39% of young adults between 18 and 25 years of age have tried marihuana. The stereotype of the marihuana user as a marginal citizen has given way to a composite picture of large segments of American youth, children of the dominant majority and very much a part of the mainstream of American life.

Public confusion, anger, and fear over this development became increasingly apparent during the mid and late 1960's. Such mass deviance was a problem and the scope of the problem was augmented by frequent publicity. The topic of the usage of marihuana by the young received considerable attention from newspapermen and television reporters. The drug's youthful users abetted the media in this regard by flaunting their disregard of the law. Few of us have not seen or heard of marihuana being used *en masse* at rock concerts, political demonstrations and gatherings of campus activists.

... the sudden increase in marihuana use precipitated extensive research by the medical and scientific communities. By 1969, a consensus emerged holding that many of the earlier beliefs about the effects of marihuana were erroneous. Available U.S. data seemed to indicate that dependence on the drug was rare as was the incidence of psychosis among marihuana users. Particularly important was the recognition that there was little, if any, convincing proof that marihuana caused aggressive behavior or crime. As such findings accumulated, public attention was drawn increasingly to the consequences of existing policy: soaring arrests, convictions and in some states, lengthy sentences.

Policy-makers, in social institutions and government, as well as the public began to believe that the harshness of the criminal penalties was far out of proportion to the dangers posed by the drug. As users were incarcerated, newspapers and television stations often brought the matter to public attention, particularly when the arrested youngster came from a prominent family.

...

RECOMMENDATIONS FOR FEDERAL LAW:

The Commission recommends *only* the following changes in federal law

- POSSESSION OF MARIHUANA FOR PERSONAL USE WOULD NO LONGER BE AN OFFENSE, BUT MARIHUANA POSSESSED IN PUBLIC WOULD REMAIN CONTRABAND SUBJECT TO SUMMARY SEIZURE AND FORFEITURE.
- CASUAL DISTRIBUTION OF SMALL AMOUNTS OF MARIHUANA FOR NO REMUNERATION, OR INSIGNIFICANT REMUNERATION NOT INVOLVING PROFIT WOULD NO LONGER BE AN OFFENSE.

...

RECOMMENDATIONS FOR STATE LAW:

Under existing state marihuana laws, cultivation, distribution and possession with intent to distribute are generally felonies and in most states possession for personal use is a misdemeanor. The Commission strongly recommends uniformity of state laws and in this regard, endorses the basic premise of the Uniform Controlled Substances Act. ... The following are our recommendations for a uniform statutory scheme for marihuana. ...

Existing Law:

- CULTIVATION, SALE OR DISTRIBUTION FOR PROFIT AND POSSESSION WITH INTENT TO SELL WOULD REMAIN FELONIES (ALTHOUGH WE DO RECOMMEND UNIFORM PENALTIES).

Private Activities:

- POSSESSION IN PRIVATE OF MARIHUANA FOR PERSONAL USE WOULD NO LONGER BE AN OFFENSE.
- DISTRIBUTION IN PRIVATE OF SMALL AMOUNTS OF MARIHUANA FOR NO REMUNERATION OR INSIGNIFICANT REMUNERATION NOT INVOLVING A PROFIT WOULD NO LONGER BE AN OFFENSE.

Public Activities:

- POSSESSION IN PUBLIC OF ONE OUNCE OR UNDER OF MARIHUANA WOULD NOT BE AN OFFENSE, BUT THE MARIHUANA WOULD BE CONTRABAND SUBJECT TO SUMMARY SEIZURE AND FORFEITURE.
- POSSESSION IN PUBLIC OF MORE THAN ONE OUNCE OF MARIHUANA WOULD BE A CRIMINAL OFFENSE PUNISHABLE BY A FINE OF $100.
- DISTRIBUTION IN PUBLIC OF SMALL AMOUNTS OF MARIHUANA FOR NO REMUNERATION OR INSIGNIFICANT REMUNERATION NOT INVOLVING A PROFIT WOULD BE A CRIMINAL OFFENSE PUNISHABLE BY A FINE OF $100.
- PUBLIC USE OF MARIHUANA WOULD BE A CRIMINAL OFFENSE PUNISHABLE BY A FINE OF $100.
- DISORDERLY CONDUCT ASSOCIATED WITH PUBLIC USE OF OR INTOXICATION BY MARIHUANA WOULD BE A MISDEMEANOR PUNISHABLE BY UP TO 60 DAYS IN JAIL, A FINE OF $100, OR BOTH.
- OPERATING A VEHICLE OR DANGEROUS INSTRUMENT WHILE UNDER THE INFLUENCE OF MARIHUANA WOULD BE A MISDEMEANOR PUNISHABLE BY UP TO ONE YEAR IN JAIL, A FINE OF UP TO $1,000, OR BOTH, AND SUSPENSION OF A PERMIT TO OPERATE SUCH A VEHICLE OR INSTRUMENT FOR UP TO 180 DAYS.

[From "A Final Comment":]

. . . On the basis of our findings . . . we have concluded that society should seek to discourage use, while concentrating its attention on the prevention and treatment of heavy and very heavy use. The Commission feels that the criminalization of possession of marihuana for personal use is socially self-defeating as a means of achieving this objective. We have attempted to balance individual freedom on one hand and the obligation of the state to consider the wider social good on the other. We believe our recommended scheme will permit society to exercise its control and influence in ways most useful and efficient, meanwhile reserving to the individual American his sense of privacy, his sense of individuality, and, within the context of an interacting and interdependent society, his options to select his own life style, values, goals and opportunities.

. . .

Considering the range of social concerns in contemporary America, marihuana does not, in our considered judgment, rank very high. . . . The existing social and legal policy is out of proportion to the individual and social harm engendered by the use of the drug. To replace it, we have attempted to design a suitable social policy, which we believe is fair, cautious and attuned to the social realities of our time.

Source: National Commission on Marihuana and Drug Abuse, *Marihuana: A Signal of Misunderstanding*, First Report of the National Commission on Marihuana and Drug Abuse (Washington, D.C.: U.S. Government Printing Office, March 1972), 6–7, 107, 152, 153–155, 210–211.

* * *

The legacy of these changes in the views toward marijuana and the lessening of penalties for possession remains today, more than 25 years later. In most states and under federal law, simple possession or personal use of marijuana is generally a misdemeanor or lesser offense, and is rarely punished with a jail or prison sentence.

MEDICAL MARIJUANA

Marijuana continues to be a controversial drug, and a consensus about appropriate policies has not yet been reached. Although the current prevalence of marijuana use remains much lower than its peak in the late 1970s, use among adolescents appears to be increasing. This trend has led to concerns that anti-marijuana laws need to be more punitive in order to deter use. At the same time many believe that more effective drug education and prevention are needed to reduce teen marijuana use.

A new debate has now emerged about marijuana. Several states have recently enacted laws that legalize the prescribing of marijuana by physicians for the treatment of certain conditions. Some believe that marijuana can be an important medicine in the management of the pain and nausea associated with chemotherapy, in the relief of intraocular pressure caused by glaucoma, and for treating other medical conditions. This has led to a spirited debate about whether existing anti-marijuana laws are preventing patients from getting access to an effective medication. Most scientists, however, believe that more research is needed on the effectiveness of marijuana for various medical conditions. Such research is now under way, and this difficult debate is not likely to be resolved for several years.

The authors of the following document believe that there is strong public support for allowing medical marijuana use.

DOCUMENT 230: Support for Medical Marijuana Laws (Lester Grinspoon and James Bakalar, 1993)

There is overwhelming evidence that the American people think medical marijuana should be available to them. In 1991, the Louisiana legislature voted to recognize the medical value of marijuana in the treatment of paraplegic pain and muscle spasms. In 1991, the Cambridge, Massachusetts, City Council approved a "home-rule petition" that would allow physicians to prescribe marijuana after approval by the state government. A month later, San Francisco voters approved an initiative legalizing prescription use of hemp products for any purpose. City officials have said that if state and federal authorities do not intervene, patients who receive prescriptions would be permitted to grow up to six plants on their own.

Source: Lester Grinspoon and James Bakalar, *Marijuana: The Forbidden Medicine* (New Haven, CT: Yale University Press, 1993), 155.

* * *

Other drug policy experts feel strongly that medical marijuana laws are wrong, either because there is insufficient scientific evidence as to marijuana's benefits, or because such laws would open the doors to broader legalization of psychoactive drugs. California and Arizona, in 1996, were the first states to pass so-called medical marijuana laws.

DOCUMENT 231: California Medical Marijuana Law (1996)

§ 11362.5. Use of marijuana for medical purposes

(a) This section shall be known and may be cited as the Compassionate Use Act of 1996.

(b)(1) The people of the State of California hereby find and declare that the purposes of the Compassionate Use Act of 1996 are as follows:

(A) To ensure that seriously ill Californians have the right to obtain and use marijuana for medical purposes where that medical use is deemed appropriate and has been recommended by a physician who has determined that the person's health would benefit from the use of marijuana in the treatment of cancer, anorexia, AIDS, chronic pain, spasticity, glaucoma, arthritis, migraine, or any other illness for which marijuana provides relief.

(B) To ensure that patients and their primary caregivers who obtain and use marijuana for medical purposes upon the recommendation of a physician are not subject to criminal prosecution or sanction.

(C) To encourage the federal and state governments to implement a plan to provide for the safe and affordable distribution of marijuana to all patients in medical need of marijuana.

(2) Nothing in this section shall be construed to supersede legislation prohibiting persons from engaging in conduct that endangers others, nor to condone the diversion of marijuana for nonmedical purposes.

(c) Notwithstanding any other provision of law, no physician in this state shall be punished, or denied any right or privilege, for having recommended marijuana to a patient for medical purposes.

(d) Section 11357, relating to the possession of marijuana, and Section 11358, relating to the cultivation of marijuana, shall not apply to a patient, or to a patient's primary caregiver, who possesses or cultivates marijuana for the personal medical purposes of the patient upon the written or oral recommendation or approval of a physician.

(e) For the purposes of this section, "primary caregiver" means the individual designated by the person exempted under this section who has consistently assumed responsibility for the housing, health, or safety of that person.

Source: Division 10, Chapter 6, Article 2, Uniform Controlled Substances Act, California Health and Safety Code, § 11362.5, 1996. [Adopted by the voters, Prop. 215 § 1, effective November 6, 1996.]

* * *

In addition to providing for medical marijuana use, the 1996 Arizona ballot measure reframed marijuana and other drug abuse as a public health issue, calling for increased access to treatment for offenders in the criminal justice system because of drug abuse problems.

DOCUMENT 232: Arizona Medical Marijuana Law (1996)

Section 2. FINDINGS AND DECLARATIONS

The People of the State of Arizona Find and Declare the Following:

(A) Arizona's current approach to drug control needs to be strengthened. This is evidenced by the fact that, according to the Arizona Criminal Justice Commission, between 1991 and 1993 marijuana use doubled among elementary school students and between 1990 and 1993 quadrupled among middle-school students. In addition to actively enforcing our criminal laws against drugs, we need to medicalize Arizona's drug control policy: Recognizing that drug abuse is a public health problem and treating abuse as a disease. Thus, drug treatment and prevention must be expanded.

. . .

(C) Thousands of Arizonans suffer from debilitating diseases such as glaucoma, multiple sclerosis, cancer, and AIDS, but cannot have access to the necessary drugs they need; allowing doctors to prescribe Schedule 1 controlled substances could save victims of these diseases from loss of sight, loss of physical capacity, and greatly reduce the pain and suffering of the seriously ill and terminally ill.

. . .

Section 3. PURPOSE AND INTENT

The People of the State of Arizona declare their purposes to be as follows . . .

(B) To permit doctors to prescribe Schedule 1 controlled substances to treat a disease, or to relieve the pain and suffering of seriously ill and terminally ill patients.

. . .

Section 6.

Title 13, Chapter 13, Section 13-3412, Arizona Revised Statutes, is amended as follows:

A. The provisions of Sections 13-3402, 13-3403, 13-3404, 13-3404.01 and 13-3405 through 13-3409 do not apply to:

. . .

9. The receipt, possession or use, of a controlled substance included in Schedule 1 of Section 36-2512, by any seriously ill or terminally ill patient, pursuant to the prescription of a doctor in compliance with the provisions of Section 13-3412.01.

. . .

Section 7.

Title 13, Chapter 13, Arizona Revised Statutes, is amended by adding Section 13-3412.01 to read as follows:

Section 13-3412.01 prescribing controlled substances included in Schedule 1 of Section 36-2512 for seriously ill and terminally ill patients[.]

A. Notwithstanding any law to the contrary, any medical doctor licensed to practice in Arizona may prescribe a controlled substance included in Schedule 1 of Section 36-2512 to treat a disease or to relieve the pain and suffering of a seriously ill patient or terminally ill patient, subject to the provisions of Section 13-3412.01. In prescribing such a controlled substance, the medical doctor shall comply with professional medical standards.

B. Notwithstanding any law to the contrary, a medical doctor must document that scientific research exists which supports the use of a controlled substance listed in Schedule 1 of Section 36-2512 to treat a disease, to relieve the pain and suffering of a seriously ill patient or terminally ill patient before prescribing the controlled substance. A medical doctor prescribing a controlled substance included in Schedule 1 of Section 36-2512 to treat a disease, or to relieve the pain and suffering of a seriously ill or terminally ill patient, must obtain the written opinion of a second medical doctor that the prescribing of the controlled substance is appropriate to treat a disease or to relieve the pain and suffering of a seriously ill patient or terminally ill patient. The written opinion of the second medical doctor shall be kept in the patient's official medical file. Before prescribing the controlled substance included in Schedule 1 of Section 36-2512 the medical doctor shall receive in writing the consent of the patient.

C. Any failure to comply with the provisions of this section may be the subject of investigation and appropriate disciplining action by the Board of Medical Examiners.

Source: Arizona Ballot Measure 4, 1996.

* * *

In the 1998 elections, several other states adopted similar medical marijuana laws, and the debate continues over the wisdom of such legislation. The federal government remains strongly opposed to the idea of legalizing controlled substances such as marijuana for medical use, and has threatened legal action against physicians who prescibe marijuana in California and Arizona. Because doctors must obtain a license from the Drug Enforcement Administration in order to prescribe drugs, many physicians are reluctant to risk federal legal action even where state law would allow the prescription of marijuana to patients. A further reason why the medical marijuana laws may not have a widespread impact is that legislatures may move to weaken or repeal laws that were adopted through a public referendum. Thus, the Arizona legislature passed a bill in April 1997 that effectively eliminated the possibility of medical marijuana by requiring that any drug prescribed as a medication must be approved by the U.S. Food and Drug Administration. However, this was overturned by voters in a 1998 ballot measure.

Part XII

Crack Cocaine and Drug Policy from the 1980s

The spread of illicit drug abuse and its social and medical consequences rose to the forefront of social issues during the latter half of the 1980s, coming to a head in the national elections of 1986 and 1988. Although concerns about violent crime and the appropriate response to such behavior were key issues of the early 1980s, illicit drugs were increasingly blamed for many of society's ills. There was considerable media coverage on drugs, and state and federal lawmakers enacted legislation that broadened definitions of illegal drug activity, placed new restrictions on the rights of those accused or convicted of illegal drug sale or possession, increased the penalties for such crimes, and established new civil penalties for drug use.

Although drug abuse has periodically been an important political and social issue in the United States during the 20th century, the late 1980s and early 1990s had a particularly heightened level of rhetoric. Like some previous waves of drug policy concerns, this period emphasized a single drug—crack cocaine. Cocaine is taken by sniffing or snorting the powder, injecting a mixture of cocaine powder and water, or smoking. Smoking allows extremely high doses of cocaine to reach the brain very quickly and brings an intense, immediate, and relatively brief high. "Crack" is the street name given to cocaine that has been processed from cocaine hydrochloride to a free base for smoking. The term "crack" refers to the crackling sound heard when the mixture is smoked (heated). Compulsive cocaine use may develop even more rapidly if smoked in the form of crack rather than snorted. The emergence of crack in the mid-1980s was a key catalyst that fueled a new "War on Drugs," a war that was characterized by a strong moralistic rhetoric, an emphasis on punishment and social control, and a resurgence of public sentiment against the use of any illicit drugs.

Media and political attention toward crack began in late 1985 with several news articles about a "new" form of cocaine. The first mention of crack cocaine in the national media was a story in the November 25, 1984, *Los Angeles Times* about "rock" cocaine use in the poor neighborhoods of Los Angeles. One year later, a *New York Times* story on November 29, 1985, told about several youths seeking treatment for cocaine problems related to smoking crack. Neither of these articles received much national attention. However, within six months, by the spring and summer of 1986, the focus on crack took hold. Newspapers, magazines, and television stations aired sensationalized stories about the terrible effects that crack had on users.

The major newspapers, national magazines, and television networks provided almost daily, prominently displayed coverage of the spread of crack, so it was not surprising that drugs soon came to dominate the list of social issues that concerned the American public. Between 1985 and 1989, the percentage of Americans who believed that drugs were the most serious problem facing the country rose steadily, from 2 percent to 38 percent.

During 1986 public attention toward crack was fueled in part by the well-publicized cocaine deaths of the college basketball star Len Bias and professional football player Don Rogers. The national newspapers, magazines, and networks devoted large amounts of space to coverage of crack. By the November 1986 elections, at least 1,000 articles on crack had appeared in the national print media. In addition, all three major television networks aired documentary programs that presented crack in the direst terms. On September 2, 1986, CBS aired the program "48 Hours on Crack Street," which drew 15 million viewers, making it the most-watched documentary in television history. Three days later, NBC televised its version of the crack story in a show titled "Cocaine Country," which emphasized the "epidemic" nature of the crack phenomenon.

ANTI-DRUG ABUSE ACT OF 1986

The rise of crack to the top of the social policy agenda and the strong response of national and local politicians is clear in the flurry of anti-drug legislation that began in 1986. By 1986 there was intensive publicity about the emerging crack problem, and many politicians joined in expressing strong concerns about the impacts of crack and other drugs. Drug problems became a key issue in 1986 political campaigns, and the 1986 election year culminated in the Anti-Drug Abuse Act. Enacted on October 27, 1986, its emphasis was on the use of punishment and social control to fight drug abuse. As the first comprehensive federal drug legislation since 1970, the 1986 act established increased prison sentences for drug sale and possession, eliminated probation or parole for certain drug offenders, increased fines, and allowed for forfeiture of assets. The United States Code was amended to include "serious drug offenses" under the definition of armed career criminals who were subject to enhanced federal penalties.

Most federal funding authorized under the 1986 act went to law enforcement, prisons, interdiction, and other supply reduction efforts rather than treatment or prevention. A new Drug Law Enforcement Grant program was established to provide funding to state and local jurisdictions for the arrest, prosecution, and imprisonment of drug offenders. The act declared that drugs were a "national security problem" and a threat to the international community. It called for enhanced interdiction efforts by the Defense Department and provided $278 million to purchase or refurbish eight airplanes, eight helicopters, and seven radar aerostats. In all, the 1986 act authorized $1.7 billion in new money to fight drug abuse. Only $231 million (about 14 percent) was allocated for treatment, education, and prevention efforts.

The 1986 act was 192 pages long. Title I specified increased penalties for violations of federal controlled substances laws. Section 1002 in Subtitle A provided for substantial prison terms for selling or possessing large amounts of drugs (for example, 1 kilogram or more of heroin, 1,000 kilograms of marijuana, 5 kilograms of cocaine).

DOCUMENT 233a: Anti-Drug Abuse Act (1986)

Sec. 1002. CONTROLLED SUBSTANCES ACT PENALTIES.

Section 401 (b)(1) of the Controlled Substances Act (21 U.S.C. 84 (b)(1)) is amended— . . .

(1)(A) In the case of a violation of subsection (a) of this section . . . such person shall be sentenced to a term of imprisonment which may not be less than 10 years or more than life and if death or serious bodily injury results from the use of such substance shall be not less than 20 years or more than life, a fine not to exceed the greater of that authorized in accordance with the provisions of title 18, United States Code, or $4,000,000 if the defendant is an individual or $10,000,000 if the defendant is other than an individual, or both. If any person commits such a violation after one or more prior convictions for an offense punishable under this paragraph, or for a felony under any other provision of this title or title III or other law of a State, the United States, or a foreign country relating to narcotic drugs, marihuana, or depressant or stimulant substances, have become final, such person shall be sentenced to a term of imprisonment which may not be less than 20 years and not more than life imprisonment and if death or serious bodily injury results from the use of such substance shall be sentenced to life imprisonment, a fine not to exceed the greater of twice that authorized in accordance with the provisions of title 18, United States Code, or $8,000,000 if the defendant is an individual or $20,000,000 if the defendant is other than an individual, or both. Any sentenced under this subparagraph shall, in the absence of such a prior conviction, impose a term of supervised release of at least 5 years in addition to such term of imprisonment and shall, if there was such a prior conviction, impose a term of supervised release of at least 10 years in addition to such term of imprisonment. Notwithstanding any other provision of law, the court shall not place on probation or suspend the sentence of any person sentenced under this subparagraph. No person sentenced under this subparagraph shall be eligible for parole during the term of imprisonment imposed therein.

Source: Public Law 99–570 (Anti-Drug Abuse Act of 1986), October 27, 1986.

* * *

In paragraph B of this subsection, the act provided for a lower penalty schedule for lesser amounts of drugs (for example, a 5–40 year prison sentence, or 10 years–life if the person had a prior conviction for sale or possession of 100 grams or more of heroin, 500 grams or more of cocaine, or 100 kilograms of marijuana). A suspended or probation sentence was not allowed for these offenses.

In Subtitle B, the "Drug Possession Penalty Act of 1986," penalties for simple possession of drugs were specified. Compared with the 1951 Boggs Act and the 1956 Narcotic Control Act (see Documents 151 and 159, the allowable penalties were relatively lenient: for example, even with two prior convictions, a person convicted of drug possession could be sentenced to as little as 90 days in prison. This subtitle also allowed the conviction of a first offender to be dismissed after the successful completion of a term of probation.

DOCUMENT 233b: Anti-Drug Abuse Act (1986)

Sec. 1052. PENALTY FOR SIMPLE POSSESSION.

Section 404 of the Controlled Substances Act (21 U.S.C. 844) is amended to read as follows:

Sec. 404. (a) It shall be unlawful for any person knowingly or intentionally to possess a controlled substance unless such substance was obtained directly, or pursuant to a valid prescription or order, from a practitioner, while acting in the course of his professional practice, or except as otherwise authorized by this title or title III. Any person who violates this subsection may be sentenced to a term of imprisonment of not more than 1 year, and shall be fined a minimum of $1,000 but not more than $5,000, or both, except that if he commits such offense after a prior conviction under this title or title III, or a prior conviction for any drug or narcotic offense chargeable under the law of any State, has become final, he shall be sentenced to a term of imprisonment for not less than 15 days but not more than 2 years, and shall be fined a minimum of $2,500 but not more than $10,000, except, further, that if he commits such offense after two or more prior convictions under this title or title III, or two or more prior convictions for any drug or narcotic offense chargeable under the law of any State, or a combination of two or more such offenses have become final, he shall be sentenced to a term of imprisonment for not less than 90 days but not more than 3 years, and shall be fined a minimum of $5,000 but not more than $25,000. The imposition or execution of a minimum sentence required to be imposed under this subsection shall not be suspended or deferred. . . .

(b)(1) If any person who has not previously been convicted of violating subsection (a) of this section, any other provision of this subchapter or subchapter II of this chapter, or any other law of the United States relating to narcotic drugs, marihuana, or depressant or stimulant substances, is found guilty of a violation of subsection (a) of this section after trial or upon a plea of guilty, the court may, without entering a judgment of guilty and with the consent of such person, defer further proceedings and place him on probation upon such reasonable conditions as it may require and for such period, not to exceed one year, as the court may prescribe. Upon violation of a condition of the probation, the court may enter an adjudication of guilt and proceed as otherwise provided. The court may, in its discretion, dismiss the proceedings against such person and discharge him from probation before the expiration of the maximum period prescribed for such person's probation. If during the period of his probation such person does not violate any of the conditions of the probation, then upon expiration of such period the court shall discharge such person and dismiss the proceedings against him.

* * *

In Subtitle C, the 1986 Anti-Drug Abuse Act amended the 1970 act to allow for doubling the penalties (imprisonment length or fine amount) for using persons under age 18 to sell or distribute drugs. If the person had a prior conviction, then the allowable sentences could be tripled in severity. In addition, this subsection also provided for increased penalties for selling drugs to minors or to a pregnant woman. Suspended or probation sentences were not allowed under this subsection.

Part M authorized grants to states for law enforcement programs and initiatives aimed at arresting, prosecuting, and incarcerating drug users and sellers, and for programs to disrupt or limit drug supplies.

DOCUMENT 233c: Anti-Drug Abuse Act (1986)

PART M—Grants for Drug Law Enforcement Programs

Sec. 1302. The Director is authorized to make grants to States, for the use of States and units of local government in the States, for the purpose of enforcing State and local laws that establish offenses similar to offenses established in the Controlled Substances Act . . . and to—

(1) provide additional personnel, equipment, facilities, personnel training, and supplies for more widespread apprehension of persons who violate State and local laws relating to the production, possession, and transfer of controlled substances and to pay operating expenses (including the purchase of evidence and information) incurred as a result of apprehending such persons;

(2) provide additional personnel, equipment, facilities (including upgraded and additional law enforcement crime laboratories), personnel training, and supplies for more widespread prosecution of persons accused of violating such State and local laws and to pay operating expenses in connection with such prosecution;

(3) provide additional personnel (including judges), equipment, personnel training, and supplies for more widespread adjudication of cases involving persons accused of violating such State and local laws, to pay operating expenses in connection with such adjudication, and to

provide quickly temporary facilities in which to conduct adjudications of such cases;

(4) provide additional public correctional resources for the detention of persons convicted of violating State and local laws relating to the production, possession, or transfer of controlled substances, and to establish and improve treatment and rehabilitative counseling provided to drug dependent persons convicted of violating State and local laws;

(5) conduct programs of eradication aimed at destroying wild or illicit growth of plant species from which controlled substances may be extracted;

(6) provide programs which identify and meet the needs of drug-dependent offenders; and

(7) conduct demonstration programs, in conjunction with local law enforcement officials, in areas in which there is a high incidence of drug abuse and drug trafficking to expedite the prosecution of major drug offenders by providing additional resources, such as investigators and prosecutors, to identify major drug offenders and move these offenders expeditiously through the judicial system.

* * *

Another section of the 1986 act placed prohibitions on the sale of transport of drug paraphernalia across state lines.

DOCUMENT 233d: Anti-Drug Abuse Act (1986)

Subtitle O—Prohibition on the Interstate Sale and Transportation of Drug Paraphernalia

. . .

Sec. 1822. OFFENSE.

(a) It is unlawful for any person—

(1) to make use of the services of the Postal Service or other interstate conveyance as part of a scheme to sell drug paraphernalia;

(2) to offer for sale and transportation in interstate or foreign commerce drug paraphernalia; or

(3) to import or export drug paraphernalia.

(b) Anyone convicted of an offense under subsection (a) of this section shall be imprisoned for not more than three years and fined not more than $100,000.

. . .

(d) The term "drug paraphernalia" means any equipment, product, or material of any kind which is primarily intended or designed for use in manufacturing, compounding, converting, concealing, producing, processing, preparing, injecting, ingesting, inhaling, or otherwise introducing into the human body a controlled substance in violation of the Controlled Substances Act. It includes items primarily intended or designed for use in ingesting, inhaling, or otherwise introducing marijuana, cocaine, hashish, hashish oil, PCP, or amphetamines into the human body, such as—

[Here 15 examples of types of paraphernalia are given, such as water pipes, roach clips, miniature spoons, and other pipes.]

(e) In determining whether an item constitutes drug paraphernalia, in addition to all other logically relevant factors, the following may be considered:

(1) instructions, oral or written, provided with the item concerning its use;

(2) descriptive materials accompanying the item which explain or depict its use;

(3) national and local advertising concerning its use;

(4) the manner in which the item is displayed for sale;

(5) whether the owner, or anyone in control of the item, is a legitimate supplier of like or related items to the community, such as a licensed distributor or dealer of tobacco products;

(6) direct or circumstantial evidence of the ratio of sales of the item(s) to the total sales of the business enterprise;

(7) the existence and scope of legitimate uses of the item in the community; and

(8) expert testimony concerning its use.

* * *

Title VIII created a President's Media Commission on Alcohol and Drug Abuse Prevention to identify and distribute information about programs to prevent drug and alcohol abuse, and to prepare public service announcements and other media publicity about drug and alcohol abuse prevention.

DOCUMENT 233e: Anti-Drug Abuse Act (1986)

TITLE VIII—PRESIDENT'S MEDIA COMMISSION ON ALCOHOL AND DRUG ABUSE PREVENTION

. . .

Sec. 8003. DUTIES OF COMMISSION.

The Commission shall—

(1) examine public education programs in effect on the date of the enactment of this title which are—

(A) implemented through various segments of mass media; and

(B) intended to prevent alcohol and drug abuse;

(2) act as an administrative and coordinating body for the voluntary donation of resources from—

(A) television, radio, motion picture, cable communications, and print media;

(B) the recording industry;

(C) the advertising industry;

(D) the business sector of the United States; and

(E) professional sports organizations and associations; to assist the implementation of new programs and national strategies for dissemination of information intended to prevent alcohol and drug abuse;

(3) encourage media outlets throughout the country to provide information aimed at preventing alcohol and drug abuse, including public service announcements, documentary films, and advertisements; and

(4) evaluate the effectiveness and assist in the update of programs and national strategies formulated with the assistance of the Commission.

* * *

The 1986 Anti-Drug Abuse Act also established a conference, to be called the White House Conference for a Drug-Free America, which was held during 1987 and 1988 and resulted in the issuance of a final report in June 1988. This report contained very strong rhetoric about America's illicit drug problem. Following are some quotes from the introduction to the final report issued by the conference.

DOCUMENT 234a: White House Conference for a Drug-Free America (1988)

Drugs threaten to destroy the United States as we know it. . . .

From both within and without, this country is being attacked as never before in its history. . . .

The way in which we face the threat of drugs today may well determine the success or failure of our country in the future. . . .

America is at war. We may lose this one. . . .

It is impossible to overstate the danger drug use poses to our country and its citizens. . . .

Source: White House Conference for a Drug-Free America, *Introduction to Final Report* (Washington, D.C.: U.S. Government Printing Office, June 1988), 1–10.

* * *

The recommendations of this report were summarized as follows.

DOCUMENT 234b: White House Conference for a Drug-Free America (1988)

The balance of this Overview will highlight what we must do to rid ourselves of this debilitating evil. The number one national priority our Nation faces today is the need to eliminate illegal drug use.

- We want the resources of the United States mobilized to restore our freedom, safety, health, defense, economic stability, and moral values. Mobilization must take priority over all other issues.
- The President must establish a national leader, a National Drug Director, with nothing on the agenda but controlling illegal drugs. This Director will lead all Federal antidrug efforts and assist in the coordination of State and local efforts, as well as encourage private sector initiatives.
- A Presidential Drug Advisory Council of private citizens must be established.
- A National Drug Prevention Agency must be established, separate and apart from any existing agency, to emphasize, coordinate, and encourage prevention as the key to demand reduction.
- The U.S. national policy must be zero tolerance for illegal drugs.
- We must focus responsibility and sanctions on illegal drug users.
- Parents (or guardians) must be held responsible for their children's behavior.

- Appropriate drug testing is essential in the public and private sectors.
- All workplaces must have strong antidrug programs.
- Policy must be set to achieve drug-free schools.
- We must remove drugged drivers from our highways.
- The military must take a much more active role in reducing the flow of drugs in the country.
- The National Guard and military reservists must be used in domestic drug eradication programs.
- We should consider restructuring the U.S. international diplomatic and law enforcement functions to work with foreign governments to eradicate and destroy narcotic production and laboratory refinement sites.
- Media, entertainment and sports industries should ensure that they have effective self-regulatory standards to deglamorize drugs with strong industry sanctions.
- It is essential to have drug treatment that is adequate, affordable and accountable.
- We must take away the profit from the criminals through uniform and expeditious Federal and State asset seizure laws.
- State and local governments must increase criminal justice resources, build more prisons, and us[e] existing facilities more creatively.
- Mandatory long-term prison sentences must be imposed for dealers, traffickers, manufacturers and distributors of illegal drugs.
- The religious community must get more actively involved.

* * *

This report thus seemed to frame the War on Drugs as a fight for the survival of the United States. Its strong words gave a sense of urgency to the anti-drug crusade that may have made more punitive policies of social control more palatable.

ANTI-DRUG ABUSE ACT OF 1988

Just two years after the 1986 act went into effect, the presidential election campaign of 1988 once again brought drug abuse issues to the forefront of public concern. The result was the passage by Congress of another omnibus drug bill, the Anti-Drug Abuse Act of 1988. Among other features, this act established a new cabinet-level White House Office of National Drug Control Policy. One of the primary responsibilities of this new office was to submit to Congress an annual National Drug Control Strategy, which was to be the blueprint for the nation's short- and long-term goals and strategies for controlling and reducing illicit drug use.

Despite placing somewhat more emphasis on treatment and prevention, most funding authorized in the 1988 act remained for enforcement and punishment. The act contains a number of provisions for enhanced penalties, including calling for the death penalty for murders committed as part of ongoing criminal enterprises such as drug dealing organizations, and increased civil penalties. Moreover, Section 6371 established increased federal penalties for "serious" crack offenses. A first offender convicted of possessing as little as five grams of a substance containing cocaine base was subject to imprisonment for five to twenty years. Second or third time offenders were subject to similar penalties for possessing as little as three grams or one gram, respectively.

The initial versions of the 1988 Anti-Drug Abuse Act, especially as enacted in the House of Representatives, were even more punitive. The original House and Senate versions of the legislation included a death penalty *requirement* for drug-related murders, an easing of illegal search laws to allow evidence seized without search warrant, and provisions for the federal government to impose civil penalties and fines against those accused of using or possessing drugs, even if no criminal conviction occurred.

The Anti-Drug Abuse Act of 1988 also adopted and placed a fair degree of emphasis on the notion of "user accountability" by introducing civil sanctions for possession and casual use. These civil penalties were considered "disincentives" for users. Such disincentives for casual users were viewed as an important concept in the government's policies toward crack and other drugs in the late 1980s.

The 1988 Anti-Drug Abuse Act was approved by Congress on October 22, 1988. The final version was considerably less harsh than the original Senate and House versions. It contained considerably more emphasis on treatment and education than the earlier drafts and compared to the 1986 act; the law called for fully 50 percent of the first year's authorization to be spent on such demand reduction efforts, and 60 percent in succeeding years. The death penalty provisions remained in the act but were made nonmandatory. Treatment on demand was made a goal of federal drug policy. Although the 1988 act permitted the spending of $2.8 billion in additional anti-drug money, only $500 million was actually authorized because of the balanced budget requirements in effect for fiscal year 1989.

A massive piece of legislation, the 1988 act was 364 pages long and contained ten different titles. The following excerpts from this document show the key new provisions of the act. Subtitle F laid out a national policy for a "Drug-Free America," to be achieved by 1995 (a goal obviously not reached).

DOCUMENT 235a: Anti-Drug Abuse Act (1988)

Title V. Subtitle F—DRUG-FREE AMERICA POLICY

Sec. 5251. UNITED STATES POLICY FOR A DRUG-FREE AMERICA BY 1995

(a) FINDINGS—The Congress finds that—

(1) approximately 37 million Americans used an illegal drug in the past year and more than 23 million Americans use illicit drugs at least monthly, including more than 6 million who use cocaine;

(2) half of all high school seniors have used illegal drugs at least once, and over 25 percent use drugs at least monthly;

(3) illicit drug use adds enormously to the national cost of health care and rehabilitation services;

(4) illegal drug use can result in a wide spectrum of extremely serious health problems . . . ;

(5) approximately 25 percent of all victims of AIDS acquired the disease through intravenous drug use;

(6) over 30,000 people were admitted to emergency rooms in 1986 with drug-related health problems, including nearly 10,000 for cocaine alone;

(7) there is a strong link between teenage suicide and use of illegal drugs;

(8) 10 to 15 percent of all highway fatalities involve drug use;

(9) illegal drug use is prevalent in the workplace and endangers fellow workers, national security, public safety, company morale, and production;

(10) it is estimated that 1 of every 10 American workers have their productivity impaired by substance abuse;

(11) it is estimated that drug users are 3 times as likely to be involved in on-the-job accidents, are absent from work twice as often, and incur 3 times the average level of sickness costs as non-users;

(12) the total cost to the economy of drug use is estimated to be over $100,000,000,000 annually;

(13) the connection between drugs and crime is also well-proven;

(14) the use of illicit drugs affects moods and emotions, chemically alters the brain, and causes loss of control, paranoia, reduction of inhibition, and unprovoked anger;

(15) drug-related homicides are increasing dramatically across the Nation;

(16) 8 of 10 men arrested for serious crimes in New York City test positive for cocaine use;

(17) illicit drug use is responsible for a substantially higher tax rate to pay for local law enforcement protection, interdiction, border control, and the cost of investigation, prosecution, confinement, and treatment;

(18) substantial increases in funding and resources have been made available in recent years to combat the drug problem, with spending for interdiction, law enforcement, and prevention programs up by 100 to 400 percent and these programs are producing results—

(A) seizures of cocaine are up from 1.7 tons in 1981 to 70 tons in 1987;

(B) seizures of heroin are up from 460 pounds in 1981 to 1,400 pounds in 1987;

(C) Drug Enforcement Administration drug convictions doubled between 1982 and 1986; and

(D) the average sentence for Federal cocaine convictions rose by 35 percent during this same period;

(19) despite the impressive rise in law enforcement efforts, the supply of illegal drugs has increased in recent years;

(20) the demand for drugs creates and sustains the illegal drug trade; and

(21) winning the drug war not only requires that we do more to limit supply, but that we focus our efforts to reduce demand.

(b) DECLARATION—It is the declared policy of the United States Government to create a Drug-Free America by 1995.

Source: Public Law 100–960 (Anti-Drug Abuse Act of 1988), November 18, 1988.

* * *

Section 1005 of the 1988 act designated some locales as "high intensity drug trafficking areas." Areas so designated would be centers of illegal drug production or distribution, have an impact on drug use in other parts of the country, and be areas where state and local officials were already committing resources to reduce the drug problem. Section 1005 provided for assignment of federal personnel and other resources to assist local authorities. Subtitle L provided enhanced penalties for crack possession, and Subtitle M had several provisions relating to drug enforcement. The two sections presented below illustrate two extremes: a provision of mandatory life imprisonment for someone convicted of a third felony drug offense, and a provision for a civil penalty for personal drug use.

DOCUMENT 235b: Anti-Drug Abuse Act (1988)

Title VI, Subtitle L—SERIOUS CRACK POSSESSION OFFENSES

Sec. 6371 INCREASED PENALTIES FOR CERTAIN SERIOUS CRACK POSSESSION OFFENSES.

Section 404(a) of the Controlled Substances Act . . . is amended by inserting after the second sentence the following new sentence: Notwithstanding the preceding sentence, a person convicted under this subsection for the possession of a mixture or substance which contains cocaine base shall be fined under title 18, United States Code, or imprisoned not less than 5 years and not more than 20 years, or both, if the conviction is a first conviction under this subsection and the amount of the mixture or substance exceeds 5 grams, if the conviction is after a prior conviction for the possession of such a mixture or substance under this subsection becomes final and the amount of the mixture or substance exceeds 3 grams, or if the conviction is after 2 or more prior convictions for the possession of such a mixture or substance under this subsection become final and the amount of the mixture or substance exceeds 1 gram.

Title VI, SUBTITLE N, Sec. 6452. LIFE IN PRISON FOR THREE-TIME DRUG OFFENDER

(a) PENALTY FOR THIRD OFFENSE—Section 401(b)(1)(A) of the Controlled Substances Act . . . is amended—

. . .

(2) adding after such sentence the following: "If any person commits a violation of this subparagraph or of section 405, 405A, or 405B after two or more prior convictions for a felony drug offense have become final, such person shall be sentenced to a mandatory term of life imprisonment without release and fined in accordance with the preceding sentence. For purposes of this subparagraph, the term "felony drug offense" means an offense that is a felony under any provision of this title or any other Federal law that prohibits or restricts conduct relating to narcotic drugs, marihuana, or depressant or stimulant substances or a felony under any law of a State or a foreign country that prohibits or restricts conduct relating to narcotic drugs, marihuana, or depressant or stimulant substances.

. . .

Sec. 6486. CIVIL PENALTY FOR POSSESSION OF SMALL AMOUNTS OF CERTAIN CONTROLLED SUBSTANCES.

(a) IN GENERAL—Any individual who knowingly possesses a controlled substance that is listed in section 401(b)(1)(A) of the Controlled Substances Act . . . in violation of section 404 of that Act . . . in an amount that, as specified by regulation of the Attorney General, is a personal use amount shall be liable to the United States for a civil penalty in an amount not to exceed $10,000 for each such violation.

. . .

(c) PRIOR CONVICTION—A civil penalty may not be assessed under this section if the individual previously was convicted of a Federal or State offense relating to a controlled substance as defined in section 102 of the Controlled Substances Act.

* * *

Title VII contains the provision for the death penalty for drug-related killings.

DOCUMENT 235c: Anti-Drug Abuse Act (1988)

TITLE VII, SUBTITLE A—DEATH PENALTY

Sec. 7001. DEATH PENALTY FOR DRUG-RELATED KILLINGS.

(a) ELEMENTS OF OFFENSE—Section 408 of the Controlled Substances Act . . . is amended [as follows]—

(e)(i) In addition to the other penalties set forth in this section—

(A) any person engaging in or working in furtherance of a continuing criminal enterprise, or any person engaging in an offense punishable under section 841(b)(1)(A) or section 960(b)(1) who intentionally kills or counsels, commands, induces, procures, or causes the intentional killing of an individual and such killing results, shall be sentenced to any term of imprisonment, which shall not be less than 20 years, and which may be up to life imprisonment, or may be sentenced to death; and

(B) any person, during the commission of, in furtherance of, or while attempting to avoid apprehension, prosecution or service of a prison sentence for, a felony violation of this title or title III who intentionally kills or counsels, commands, induces, procures, or causes the intentional killing of any Federal, State, or local law enforcement officer engaged in, or on account of, the performance of such officer's official duties and such killing results, shall be sentenced to any term of imprisonment, which shall not be less than 20 years, and which may be up to life imprisonment, or may be sentenced to death.

* * *

The remainder of this section of the act describes the various legal and court procedures and rules to be followed in a death penalty case, including mitigating or aggravating factors that might affect the imposition of the death penalty, and a provision that calls for protections against discrimination in the application of the death penalty and future research to assess whether discrimination has occurred.

The news media coverage of the crack problem before and after the enactment of the 1988 act illustrates the substantial and continuing level of concern about the effects of crack that help us to understand why this act contained even stricter penalties for violating federal drug laws than the 1986 act.

In addition, the murder in February 1988 of police officer Edward Byrne while guarding the house of a citizen informer in New York City was a watershed event. Carried out under the orders of one of the major crack gangs in New York, the killing illustrated the cold-blooded violence that could be associated with the crack trade and helped to galvanize public support for tougher measures against crack dealers.

Media coverage during this phase began centering on the involvement of gangs in the crack trade and their tendency toward violence, and the spread of crack into all corners of the nation. These articles almost always quoted local or national law enforcement officials as the sources of information about gang involvement and their role in the spread of crack. For example, a *Washington Post* article on February 22, 1988, headlined "Crack Wars in DC," described how "out-of-towners" (namely, Jamaican posses) had introduced crack to DC, and quoted a Narcotics Task Force officer as stating that "crack is just taking over." Two of the major *Time* magazine stories about crack during 1988 (March 14, 1988, and December 5, 1988), relied almost exclusively on the views of police officials and prosecutors in concluding that the crack "war" was being lost as gangs invaded American cities and set up lucrative crack businesses, and that crack had "caused" a homicide epidemic. The CBS network, in an effort to capitalize on the revived crack hysteria, inaugurated its 1989–1990 season on *48 Hours* with a three-hour special, "Return to Crack Street." Typical quotes from national media coverage on crack during this period include the following: "The booming crack business is just tearing the heart out of US cities"; "after three years, the crack plague in New York grows worse"; "spreading plague"; "crack, a disaster of historic dimensions, still growing"; "cracks's destructive sprint across America"; "the spreading web of crack"; "[the] enormous spread of crack is creating a spiral of violence that places both police officers and civilian bystanders at risk"; "the crack trade, with its staggering profits, is now entrenched in the ghettos of dozens of American cities"; "slaughter in the streets: Crack touches off a homicide epidemic"; "[crack] has turned many American cities into virtual war zones."

These quotes illustrate several themes that typified the reporting about crack during this period. First, the coverage associated crack with terrible violence that was portrayed as overwhelming American cities. Second, crack use was described as being out of control and extending its reach into white middle America. Third, crack was presented as the worst drug plague in history, with the United States in danger of quickly succumbing to this "plague."

STATE ANTI-CRACK INITIATIVES

The war against crack was also carried out at the state and local level, with a number of legislatures passing laws to increase penalties for crack possession and sale. For example, the New York State Penal Law was amended on November 1, 1988, making it a felony to possess 500 milligrams or more (gross weight) of a substance containing crack (about five or six vials, or 1/50 ounce). Previously, possession of one-eighth of an ounce, about 30 vials, was required for a felony charge. In signing the law, Governor Mario Cuomo made the following statement.

DOCUMENT 236: Statement on New Crack Possession Law (Governor Mario M. Cuomo, 1988)

The bill, which is part of my 1988 Legislative program, amends section 220.06 of the Penal Law to make possession of 500 milligrams or more of cocaine a class D felony.

Crack—the extraordinarily potent, highly addictive and relatively inexpensive cocaine derivative—has reached into virtually every corner of the State; crack's devastating effect on young lives cannot be overstated. The lightning speed with which this lethal drug has spread through society is evident in substantial increases in drug-related deaths and babies born addicted to drugs. Crack use has also been accompanied by rising incidences of violent crime, including robberies and murders.

—Even small amounts of crack are extremely dangerous.

The current law measures cocaine possession on an aggregate weight basis; this standard is clearly inappropriate in the case of crack, which is extremely low in weight but high in concentration and purity. . . . Given the minute quantities required for a devastating effect, the current law's weight requirements for felony possession are clearly inadequate and must be changed to accurately reflect the potency of this new form of cocaine.

The bill adopts a pure weight standard and classifies the possession of 500 milligrams or more of cocaine, which is approximately four to six one-grain vials, as a Class D felony, punishable by a maximum sentence of seven years in prison.

Crack is a relatively new phenomenon. The bill sends a clear message that the possession of crack will be treated with the severity that it deserves. By taking a tough stand now, we can prevent crack from becoming a permanent part of the drug subculture.

Source: Statement by Governor Mario M. Cuomo, approving Chapter 178, Laws of 1988, New York State, June 27, 1988.

* * *

In 1989 the Minnesota state legislature passed a law that imposed harsher penalties for sale or possession of crack than for sale or possession of cocaine. This new law amended the previous anti-drug statutes by allowing the same penalties for a lower weight of cocaine base (which includes crack) than for cocaine powder. For example, section 10 of the new law (Controlled Substance Crime in the Third Degree) provided for a four-year prison term for first-time offenders convicted of possession of three grams (about 30 vials) of crack, while possession of three grams of powdered cocaine was subject to probation sentences. More severe penalties were allowed for first and second degree drug crimes.

DOCUMENT 237: Minnesota Anti-Crack Law (1989)

Sec. 8. *Controlled Substance Crime in the First Degree*

Subd. 1. A person is guilty of controlled substance crime in the first degree if:

(1) on one or more occasions within a 90-day period the person unlawfully sells one or more mixtures containing ten grams or more of cocaine base;

(2) on one or more occasions within a 90-day period the person unlawfully sells one or more mixtures of a total weight of 50 grams or more containing a narcotic drug. . . .

Subd. 2. A person is guilty of a controlled substance crime in the first degree if:

(1) the person unlawfully possesses one or more mixtures containing 25 grams or more of cocaine base;

(2) the person unlawfully possesses one or more mixtures of a total weight of 500 grams or more containing a narcotic drug. . . .

Subd. 3. (a) A person convicted under subdivision 1 or 2 may be sentenced to imprisonment for not more than 30 years or to payment of a fine of not more than $1,000,000, or both.

(b) If the conviction is a subsequent controlled substance conviction, a person convicted under subdivision 1 or 2 shall be sentenced to not less than four years nor more than 40 years or to a payment of a fine of not more than $1,000,000, or both.

Source: Chapter 290, Article 3, Laws of Minnesota, 1989.

* * *

By early 1991, half the states had passed similar laws or were drafting similar anti-crack statutes. Citing a lack of scientific evidence that crack was more harmful and dangerous than powdered cocaine, a Minnesota district judge challenged this law by dismissing crack possession charges against five black defendants in December 1990. She declared the law unconstitutional because it discriminated against blacks—most crack defendants in Minnesota were black, and most powdered cocaine defendants were white. Challenged by prosecutors, this ruling was subsequently upheld by the Minnesota Supreme Court, which overturned the crack possession law because it denied equal protection. The Minnesota legislature responded to this ruling by passing a new law in early 1992 that increased allowable sentences for cocaine offenses generally.

DOCUMENT 238: Minnesota Supreme Court Decision Overturning Crack Law (1991)

Evidence did not establish existence of rational basis for statutory distinction drawn between quantity of crack cocaine possessed and quantity of cocaine powder—person was guilty of third-degree offense if he or she possessed three or more grams of crack cocaine, while person had to possess ten or more grams of cocaine powder to be guilty of the same offense and punished accordingly—and statute violated equal protection provision of State Constitution due to its discriminatory impact on blacks; testimony before state legislature by single expert regarding respective amounts of drugs that indicated street-level dealing did not establish substantial and genuine distinction between crack users and powder users, evidence regarding effects of two substances on users was based on manner of ingestion rather than different properties of two substances, and statutory distinction did not further allege purpose of penalizing street-level dealers; moreover, statutory distinction created irrebuttable presumption of intent to sell based solely on amount possessed.

Source: State v. Russell, 477 N.W. 2nd 886, 1991.

* * *

THE NATIONAL DRUG CONTROL STRATEGIES

The administration of President George Bush issued the first series of annual National Drug Control Strategies mandated by the Anti-Drug Abuse Act of 1988 and prepared by the newly created White House Office of National Drug Control Policy. An examination of the 1989 and 1991 strategies illustrates the strong reaction to the emergence of crack and the gradual lessening of concern about this drug over time. These documents express two underlying themes. First, the strategies tended to emphasize a law enforcement and punishment response to illicit drug use, and individual accountability for drug use. Second, the strategies were a distillation of three years of media and political concern about drugs, especially in response to the emergence of crack.

The first National Drug Control Strategy, released in 1989, made user accountability a key touchstone, holding occasional, functional users of illicit drugs as responsible for the social problems of drug abuse as major drug traffickers. The 1989 strategy also contains numerous references to crack and its dangers. As did the White House Conference for a Drug-Free America, it portrays this drug as a potential scourge of America. Not only were crack and cocaine the primary drugs specifically discussed in the strategy, their effects on American society were painted in dire terms. The following is an excerpt from the Introduction to the 1989 National Drug Control Strategy.

DOCUMENT 239: Introduction to National Drug Control Strategy (1989)

In late July of this year, the Federal government's National Institute on Drug Abuse (NIDA) released the results of its ninth periodic National Household Survey on Drug Abuse. . . . Much of the news in NIDA's report was dramatic and startling. The estimated number of Americans using any illegal drug . . . (at least once in the 30-day period preceding the survey) has dropped 37 percent: from 23 million in 1985 to 14.5 million last year. Current use of the two most common illegal substances—marijuana and cocaine—is down 36 and 48 percent respectively.

This is all good news—very good news. But it is also, at first glance, difficult to square with commonsense perceptions. Most Americans remain firmly convinced that drugs represent the gravest present threat to our national well-being—and with good reason. Because a wealth of other, up-to-date evidence suggests that our drug problem is getting worse, not better.

. . .

Not so long ago, drug use was an activity widely thought of as harmless fun or isolated self-indulgence. Today it is seen—just as widely, and far more accurately—to be a personal, social, medical, and economic catastrophe. In less than a decade, parents, educators, students, clergy, and local leaders across the country have changed and hardened American opinion about drugs. The effectiveness of their activism is now largely vindicated. Despite the persistent widespread availability of illegal drugs, many millions of Americans who once used them regularly appear to have recently given them up altogether. Many others—young people for the most part—have been successfully induced not to try drugs in the first place.

What, then, accounts for the intensifying drug-related chaos that we see every day in our newspapers and on television? One word explains much of it. That word is crack.

. . .

Estimated "frequent" use of cocaine in any form . . . has doubled since 1985. Not coincidentally, 1985 was the first year in which crack became an almost ubiquitous feature of American inner-city life. It is an inexpensive, extremely potent, fast-acting derivative of cocaine with a limited-duration "high" that encourages compulsive use. It is, in fact, the most dangerous and quickly addictive drug known to man.

Crack is responsible for the fact that vast patches of the American urban landscape are rapidly deteriorating beyond effective control by civil authorities. Crack is responsible for the explosion in recent drug-related medical emergencies—a 28-fold increase in hospital admissions involving smoked cocaine since 1984. Crack use is increasingly responsible for the continued marketing success enjoyed by a huge international cocaine trafficking industry, with all its consequential evils. And crack use is spreading—like a plague.

. . .

Few American communities can afford to assume they are immune to cocaine. The drug black market has proved itself remarkably flexible and creative. Crack is an innovation in cocaine retailing that takes uncanny advantage of the nation's changing drug use patterns. And because it is so horribly seductive and "new," it threatens to reverse the current trend and send a fresh wave of cocaine use back out of our cities and into the country at large. Indeed, to some extent at least, it is happening already: almost every week, our newspapers report a new first sighting of crack—in the rural South or in some midwestern suburb, for example.

. . .

. . . our most intense and immediate problem is inner-city crack use. It is an acid that is fast corroding the hopes and possibilities of an entire generation of disadvantaged young people. They need help. Their neighborhoods need help. A decent and responsible America must fully mobilize to provide it.

. . .

We should be tough on drugs—much tougher than we are now. Our badly imbalanced criminal justice system, already groaning under the weight of current drug cases, should be rationalized and significantly expanded. But we cannot afford to delude ourselves that drug use is an exclusively criminal issue. Whatever else it does, drug use degrades human character, and a purposeful, self-governing society ignores its people's character at great peril. Drug users make inattentive parents, bad neighbors, poor students, and unreliable employees—quite apart from their common involvement in criminal activity. Legal sanctions may help to deter drug use, and they can be used to direct some drug users to needed treatment. But locking up millions of drug users will not by itself make them healthy and responsible citizens.

. . .

First, we must come to terms with the drug problem in its essence: use itself. Worthy efforts to alleviate the symptoms of epidemic drug abuse—crime and disease, for example—must continue unabated. But a largely ad-hoc attack on the holes in our dike can have only an indirect and minimal effect on the flood itself. By the same token, we must avoid the easy temptation to blame our troubles first on those chronic problems of social environment—like poverty and racism—which help to breed and spread the contagion of drug use. We have been fighting such social ills for decades: that fight, too, must continue unabated. But we need not—and cannot—sit back and wait for that fight to be won for good. Too many lives will be lost in the interim. The simple problem with drugs is painfully obvious: too many Americans still use them. And so the highest priority of our drug policy must be a stubborn determination further to reduce the overall level of drug use nationwide—experimental first use, "casual" use, regular use, and addiction alike.

. . .

The proposed national strategy outlined in this report takes pains to avoid the artificial and counter-productive distinctions so often drawn among the various fronts necessary to a successful fight against epidemic drug use. Instead it seeks to draw each of them into full participation in a coherent, integrated, and much improved program. The next five chapters . . . describe a coordinated and balanced plan of attack involving all basic anti-drug initiatives and agencies: our criminal justice system; our drug treatment system; our collection of education, workplace, public awareness, and community prevention campaigns; our international policies and activities; and our efforts to interdict smuggled drugs before they cross our borders.

Source: White House Office of National Drug Control Policy, *National Drug Control Strategy 1989* (Washington, DC: U.S. Government Printing Office, 1989), 1–13.

* * *

Within two years of the initial strategy, however, the emphasis on crack had diminished considerably. The 1991 National Drug Control Strategy reflected the diminution in media and political attention toward crack, even as the exact nature of the crack phenomenon and its effects on drug use, health, and crime were still being studied and only beginning to be understood. Thus the 1991 strategy mentioned crack only three times in the entire 122-page document, and crack is mentioned only once in the Introduction. Not once in the 1991 strategy was crack referred to as a particularly dangerous drug or a threat to American society. Indeed, in the section on emerging drug trends, neither crack nor cocaine was even mentioned. By 1991 crack seemed to have ceased to be of special concern to our national leaders.

There are several explanations for this change in emphasis. First, the plague of crack use that was forecast early on in the crack era did not materialize. Data from national drug use surveys and ethnographic research within the crack subculture indicated that crack use actually was declining over this period. This was especially apparent among high school and college students and the middle class. There were indications from the inner city as well that crack use was declining in popularity, and that "crackheads" were increasingly being viewed disparagingly by other drug users.

The decline in crack and cocaine use among students (continuing a pattern that had begun some time prior to the "War on Crack"), also allowed national political leaders to claim credit for gains in the fight against crack. Thus, now that the threat of the spread of crack to white middle America failed to occur, it became much less of specific concern to White House drug strategists.

Second, despite the continuing intractability of many social problems, and ongoing problems of drug abuse, the United States had not been destroyed by crack. Third, more empirical research about crack was becoming available and being disseminated. These research findings provided a more reasoned picture of the actual dimensions of the crack problem, showed how the effects of crack were in many ways similar to those of powdered cocaine, and documented the complexity of the crack phenomenon.

Finally, by the early 1990s many policy makers, including law enforcement and prison officials, were beginning to realize that arrest and imprisonment were relatively expensive and ineffective strategies for controlling illicit drug use. As crack offenders continued to be recycled through the criminal justice system, crowding prisons and jails, support for treatment and education/prevention efforts against crack began growing. Even among relatively conservative law enforcement and prison officials, the limitations of a strictly punitive anti-drug policy, in the absence of drug treatment, economic opportunity, and social stability, were becoming more apparent.

DOCUMENT 240: Introduction to National Drug Control Strategy (1991)

This third National Drug Control Strategy reaffirms the main arguments about the drug problem advanced in the first two Strategies, and, like those documents, argues that to fight drugs successfully we must . . . exert pressure on all parts of this problem simultaneously. We must have meaningful efforts to prevent people from using drugs in the first place, and we must provide effective treatment for those who need it and can benefit from it. On the presumption that law enforcement not only punishes but also instructs, we must hold users accountable for their actions and thereby deter others from using drugs. We must prosecute dealers and traffickers. . . . We must disrupt the flow of drugs, drug money, and related chemicals. We must engage other nations in efforts to reduce the growth, production, and distribution of drugs. We must support basic and applied research in behavior, medicine, and technology. And we must improve our intelligence capabilities in order to attack drug trafficking organizations better. . . .

Under this Administration, Federal funding to fight drugs has grown

64 percent to $10.5 billion in Fiscal Year 1991. The President is requesting a total of $11.7 billion for Fiscal Year 1992, an increase of 11 percent above the Fiscal Year 1991 level, and 82 percent since this Administration took office. . . .

There are some who believe that the Federal effort should be evenly divided among what are loosely called "supply reduction" and "demand reduction" activities. This notion ignores the fact that the mission of the Federal government includes activities that *only* the Federal government can undertake, such as efforts in countries where drugs are grown and produced, as well as broader initiatives to engage the international community to take strong measures against money laundering. It ignores the fact that much of our interdiction effort occurs offshore, on the high seas, or in international airspace, and requires the use of expensive assets, including ships, aircraft, and sophisticated air-, sea-, and land-based radar systems. It also ignores the fact that law enforcement, sometimes conceived of as only a "supply reduction" activity, has a deterrent—i.e., "demand reduction"—effect, an effect widely acknowledged. Indeed, some would even argue that deterrence is law enforcement's main effect, or main justification. In any case, simple distinctions between "supply reduction" and "demand reduction" are artificial and at times even meaningless.

. . .

Neither the original National Drug Control Strategy nor its January 1990 companion proceeds from the assumption that the Federal government's programs and money alone can solve the drug problem. Both documents offer extensive attention and advice to State and local governments, private civic and service organizations, schools, churches, synagogues, businesses, families, and individuals—all of whom must devote concentrated and persistent effort to the drug problem in their particular spheres. It should be noted that a major feature of this Strategy is that it challenges States, localities, and the private sector to join with the Federal government in committing themselves to expanding the capacity of the national treatment system. The Federal government will continue to do its part by increasing funding significantly. Others must do their part, too.

Source: White House Office of National Drug Control Policy, *National Drug Control Strategy 1991* (Washington, DC: U.S. Government Printing Office, 1991), 2–3.

SUPREME COURT DECISIONS ON "NO-KNOCK" LAWS

Finally, two Supreme Court cases in the 1990s addressed the constitutionality of "no-knock" searches such as those allowed in the 1970 drug abuse act, which became more common as the war against crack escalated in the late 1980s. In the first decision, *Wilson v. Arkansas*, the Supreme Court unanimously held that the Fourth Amendment to the Constitution, in banning "unreasonable" searches, generally required the police to knock and announce their presence before entering. However, the Supreme Court also noted that there may be special circumstances (left for the state courts to define) where an unannounced entry might be justified. In the second case, *Richards v. Wisconsin*, the Court held that the Fourth Amendment did not automatically allow no-knock searches whenever they involved a felony drug investigation, but that unannounced entries must be justified on a case-by-case basis. Both of these opinions were unanimous.

DOCUMENT 241: *Wilson v. Arkansas* (1995)

[Summary of Opinion, delivered by Justice Clarence Thomas]

Petitioner was convicted on state-law drug charges after the Arkansas trial court denied her evidence-suppression motion, in which she asserted that the search of her home was invalid because the police had violated the common-law principle requiring them to announce their presence and authority before entering. The State Supreme Court affirmed, rejecting petitioner's argument that the common-law "knock and announce" principle is required by the Fourth Amendment.

Held: The common-law knock-and-announce principle forms a part of the Fourth Amendment reasonableness inquiry.

(a) An officer's unannounced entry into a home might, in some circumstances, be unreasonable under the Amendment. In evaluating the scope of the constitutional right to be secure in one's house, this Court has looked to the traditional protections against unreasonable searches and seizures afforded by the common law at the time of the framing. Given the longstanding common-law endorsement of the practice of announcement, and the wealth of founding-era commentaries, constitutional provisions, statutes, and cases espousing or supporting the knock-and-announce principle, this Court has little doubt that the Amendment's Framers thought that whether officers announced their presence and authority before entering a dwelling was among the factors to be considered in assessing a search's reasonableness. Nevertheless, the common-law principle was never stated as an inflexible rule requiring announcement under all circumstances. Countervailing law enforcement interests—including, e.g. the threat of physical harm to police, the fact that an officer is pursuing a recently escaped arrestee, and the existence of reason to believe that evidence would likely be destroyed if advance notice were given—

may establish the reasonableness of an unannounced entry. For now, this Court leaves to the lower courts the task of determining such relevant countervailing factors.

(b) Respondent's [i.e., the State of Arkansas] asserted reasons for affirming the judgment below—that the police reasonably believed that a prior announcement would have placed them in peril and would have produced an unreasonable risk that petitioner would destroy easily disposable narcotics evidence—may well provide the necessary justification for the unannounced entry in this case. The case is remanded to allow the state courts to make the reasonableness determination in the first instance.

Source: Wilson v. Arkansas (Case 94–5707), May 22, 1995.

DOCUMENT 242: *Richards v. Wisconsin* (1997)

Certorari to the Supreme Court of Wisconsin
Justice Stevens delivered the opinion for a unanimous Court.

In *Wilson v. Arkansas*, 514 U.S. 927 (1995), we held that the Fourth Amendment incorporates the commonlaw requirement that police officers entering a dwelling must knock on the door and announce their identity and purpose before attempting forcible entry. At the same time, we recognized that the "flexible requirement of reasonableness should not be read to mandate a rigid rule of announcement that ignores countervailing law enforcement interests," and left "to the lower courts the task of determining the circumstances under which an unannounced entry is reasonable under the Fourth Amendment."

In this case, the Wisconsin Supreme Court concluded that police officers are never required to knock and announce their presence when executing a search warrant in a felony drug investigation. In so doing, it reaffirmed a pre-Wilson holding and concluded that Wilson did not preclude this per se rule. We disagree with the court's conclusion that the Fourth Amendment permits a blanket exception to the knock-and-announce requirement for this entire category of criminal activity. But because the evidence presented to support the officers' actions in this case establishes that the decision not to knock and announce was a reasonable one under the circumstances, we affirm the judgment of the Wisconsin court.

I. On December 31, 1991, police officers in Madison, Wisconsin obtained a warrant to search Steiney Richards' hotel room for drugs and related paraphernalia. The search warrant was the culmination of an investigation that had uncovered substantial evidence that Richards was one of several individuals dealing drugs out of hotel rooms in Madison.

The police requested a warrant that would have given advance authorization for a "no-knock" entry into the hotel room, but the magistrate explicitly deleted those portions of the warrant.

. . .

Richards sought to have the evidence from his hotel room suppressed on the ground that the officers had failed to knock and announce their presence prior to forcing entry into the room. The trial court denied the motion, concluding that the officers could gather from Richards' strange behavior when they first sought entry that he knew they were police officers and that he might try to destroy evidence or to escape. The judge emphasized that the easily disposable nature of the drugs the police were searching for further justified their decision to identify themselves as they crossed the threshold instead of announcing their presence before seeking entry. Richards appealed the decision to the Wisconsin Supreme Court and that court affirmed.

II. We recognized in Wilson that the knock-and-announce requirement could give way "under circumstances presenting a threat of physical violence," or "where police officers have reason to believe that evidence would likely be destroyed if advance notice were given." It is indisputable that felony drug investigations may frequently involve both of these circumstances. The question we must resolve is whether this fact justifies dispensing with case-by-case evaluation of the manner in which a search was executed.

. . .

In order to justify a "no-knock" entry, the police must have a reasonable suspicion that knocking and announcing their presence, under the particular circumstances, would be dangerous or futile, or that it would inhibit the effective investigation of the crime by, for example, allowing the destruction of evidence. This standard—as opposed to a probable cause requirement—strikes the appropriate balance between the legitimate law enforcement concerns at issue in the execution of search warrants and the individual privacy interests affected by no-knock entries. . . .

III. Although we reject the Wisconsin court's blanket exception to the knock-and-announce requirement, we conclude that the officers' no-knock entry into Richards' hotel room did not violate the Fourth Amendment. We agree with the trial court . . . that the circumstances in this case show that the officers had a reasonable suspicion that Richards might destroy evidence if given further opportunity to do so.

The judge who heard testimony at Richards' suppression hearing concluded that it was reasonable for the officers executing the warrant to believe that Richards knew, after opening the door to his hotel room the first time, that the men seeking entry to his room were the police. Once the officers reasonably believed that Richards knew who they were, the court concluded, it was reasonable for them to force entry immediately given the disposable nature of the drugs.

In arguing that the officers' entry was unreasonable, Richards places great emphasis on the fact that the magistrate who signed the search warrant for his hotel room deleted the portions of the proposed warrant that would have given the officers permission to execute a no-knock entry. But this fact does not alter the reasonableness of the officers' decision, which must be evaluated as of the time they entered the hotel room. At the time the officers obtained the warrant, they did not have evidence sufficient, in the judgment of the magistrate, to justify a no-knock warrant. Of course, the magistrate could not have anticipated in every particular the circumstances that would confront the officers when they arrived at Richards' hotel room.

Accordingly, although we reject the blanket exception to the knock-and-announce requirement for felony drug investigations, the judgment of the Wisconsin Supreme Court . . . is affirmed.

Source: Richards v. Wisconsin (Case 96–5955), April 28, 1997.

* * *

Crack had important effects on anti-drug policy in the United States in the 1980s and the beginning of the 1990s. The strong reaction to crack was probably grounded in the simultaneous development of several social, economic, and political trends: concerns about the intractability of a growing underclass, economic problems, and a continuing trend away from rehabilitation and toward punishment of criminals. In addition, crack appeared at a time when community frustrations over the spread of open-air drug markets had been growing for several years. The proliferation of frightening information about crack and its effects by politicians and the media did much to fuel the punitive anti-drug atmosphere of the latter half of the 1980s.

The policy response to crack provides important lessons for understanding American drug policy. First, policy makers need a better understanding of the complexity of psychoactive drug use and the social psychological processes that affect the degree of drug use. Second, as with previous drug "epidemics," crack use has declined over time. Finally, purely punitive policies to control drugs are limited in their effects among those populations most at risk to use illicit drugs; the harmfulness of a drug's effects has as much to do with surrounding social and economic conditions as with the drug's psychopharmacological actions. One legacy of the "war on crack" has been the huge growth in America's prison population, with a disproportionate effect on minority groups.

Part XIII

The Debate over Drug Legalization

Over the past decade, a sometimes contentious debate has arisen over whether the use of currently illegal drugs should be made legal. Since the Harrison Act, periodic movements have aimed to shift America's anti-drug policies away from an enforcement and punishment model toward a model that recognizes the reality of drug use, and that treats addiction as a medical and social problem requiring a public health response. Driven by concerns about the impact of punitive drug laws, and by a seemingly intractable drug problem, proposals for legalizing drugs have again received wide publicity in recent years. These have taken a number of different forms, ranging from a total free market in drugs without any government controls to allowing limited decriminalization of certain drugs, especially marijuana. Even the most far-reaching proposals for legalization, however, generally retain some government controls such as those that tax and regulate alcohol and tobacco, and include restrictions on use by or sale to minors.

More recently, many critics of American drug policy have begun to step back from seeking wholesale legalization of drugs, preferring to argue for policies that reduce the harms to individuals and society exacerbated by harsh anti-drug laws: long prison sentences, infectious diseases such as AIDS and tuberculosis, and lack of access to drug treatment.

HISTORICAL OVERVIEW

An overview of the most recent wave of legalization proposals is provided by sociologist Erich Goode in his book on the legalization debate.

DOCUMENT 243: Overview of Legalization Proposals (Erich Goode, 1997)

Beginning in the late 1980s, a taboo, almost unthinkable proposal—the decriminalization or legalization of the currently illegal drugs—began to be advanced with remarkable frequency and urgency. Dozens of books, hundreds of magazine and newspaper articles, uncountable editorials and op-ed pieces, and scores of prominent spokespersons have urged the repeal of the drug laws. Drug legalization has become a major focus of debate in recent years, joining such controversial subjects as abortion, pornography, the environment, the economy, gun control, and homosexual rights, women's rights, minority rights, and affirmative action as yet another battlefield of controversy.

It must be emphasized that legalization is not a single proposal. Instead, it is a *cluster* of proposals that stands toward one end of a *spectrum* of degrees of regulation and availability. . . . [V]ery few, if any, legalization advocates argue that there should be absolutely *no* controls on drugs whatsoever—for instance, that minors be allowed to purchase heroin and cocaine from whoever is willing to sell to them. Instead, all agree that *some* sorts of controls will be necessary; the question is, how far along the spectrum of control to decontrol—and whether those controls should be legal or some other type—the currently illlegal drugs should be moved. Consequently, both the similarities and differences among the various legalization programs have to be considered.

Source: Erich Goode, *Between Politics and Reason: The Drug Legalization Debate* (New York: St. Martin's Press, 1997), 73–74.

* * *

The recent wave of legalization proposals has ranged from outright legalization of one or more drugs, to decriminalization of possession of small amounts of drugs for personal use, to allowing doctors to prescribe currently illegal drugs to addicts.

DOCUMENT 244: Common Legalization Terms (Herbert D. Kleber, Joseph A. Califano, Jr., and John C. Demers, 1997)

Four terms are commonly used: legalization, decriminalization, medicalization, and harm reduction—with much variation in each.

Legalization usually implies the most radical departure from current policy. Legalization proposals vary from making marihuana cigarettes as available as tobacco cigarettes to establishing an open and free market for all drugs. Variations on legalization include: making drugs legal for the adult population, but illegal for minors; having only the government produce and sell drugs, and/or allowing a private market in drugs, usually with restrictions on advertising, dosage, and place of consumption.

Decriminalization proposals retain laws that forbid manufacture, importation, and sale of illegal drugs, but remove criminal sanctions for possession of small amounts of drugs for personal use. Most commonly advocated for marihuana, such proposals suggest that possession of drugs for personal use be legal or subject only to civil penalties such as fines.

Medicalization refers to the prescription of currently illegal drugs by physicians to addicts already dependent on such drugs. The most frequently mentioned variation is heroin maintenance. Proponents argue that providing addicts with drugs prevents them from having to commit crimes to finance their habit and ensures that the drugs they ingest are pure.

Harm reduction generally implies that government policies should concentrate on lowering the harm to the individual associated with drug use, especially the risk of AIDS, rather than on reducing use itself or getting an addict off drugs. Beginning with the proposition that drug use is inevitable, harm reduction proposals can include the prescription of heroin and cocaine to addicts; removal of penalties for personal use of marihuana; advocating "responsible" drug use as opposed to no drug use; needle-exchange programs for injection drug users to prevent the spread of HIV infection; and "low threshold" methadone maintenance which does not require counseling or regular attendance.

Variations on these options are numerous. Some do not require any change in the legal status of these drugs. The government could, for instance, allow needle exchanges while maintaining current laws banning heroin, the most commonly injected drug. Others, however, represent a major shift from the current role of government and the goal of its policies with regard to drug use and availability.

Source: Herbert D. Kleber, Joseph A. Califano, Jr., and John C. Demers, "Clinical and Societal Implications of Drug Legalization." In Joyce H. Lowinson, Pedro Ruiz, Robert B. Millman, and John G. Langrod, eds., *Substance Abuse: A Comprehensive Textbook* (Baltimore: Williams and Wilkins, 1997), 855.

* * *

Some historical perspective is useful. Prior to the current debate, there were at least two previous periods where some calls for "legalization" occurred, primarily from a medical establishment concerned about the criminalization of the addict and physician and the inability of physicians to prescribe drugs to maintain addicts. The first period was a few years after passage of the Harrison Act in 1914, when some groups called for providing drugs to addicts. Then, as now, such maintenance models were driven by the belief that addiction is a disease requiring a medical rather than a legal enforcement approach. These proposals were strongly resisted by federal drug control officials, and ultimately were derailed by the Supreme Court decisions that upheld the government's policies and laws against the dispensing of illegal drugs for the purpose of maintaining an addiction.

Most prominent among these efforts were the various drug maintenance clinics that began operating shortly after the Harrison Act. In a number of cities, health departments, hospitals, and physicians set up clinics to dispense opiates to addicts in order to relieve withdrawal suffering and maintain their addiction. Although some of these opiate maintenance clinics seemed to be well run and successful (such as the Shreveport clinic), others were badly managed and regulated. Strong opposition by federal anti-drug authorities and the various anti-maintenance Supreme Court decisions forced all these clinics to close down within a few years. These clinics are discussed in more detail in Part IX.

DOCUMENT 245: Early Opiate Maintenance Clinics (Edward M. Brecher, 1972)

The suggestion that heroin addicts receive their drug legally is hardly new or revolutionary. Indeed, narcotics-dispensing clinics were established in Florida and Tennessee back in 1912 and 1913. Following passage of the Harrison Narcotic Act in 1914, clinics for supplying addicts with legal heroin at low cost or without charge spread throughout the country; at least 44 of them are known to have been opened by 1920 or 1921.

Some of these clinics actually dispensed morphine or heroin or both. Others gave addicts prescriptions. . . . If enough addicts were thus supplied, it was reasoned, the narcotics black market would wither away; it could hardly support itself by selling opiates solely to nonaddicts.

Source: Edward M. Brecher and the Editors of Consumer Reports, *Licit and Illicit Drugs* (Boston: Little, Brown, 1972), 115.

* * *

Brecher also reported, based on interviews with elderly addicts in the 1960s, that in some southern states physicians continued to prescribe opiates to addicts who had been getting their drugs from physicians prior to the post–Harrison Act crackdown. These opiates were dispensed with the knowledge and tacit acceptance of federal narcotics agents.

The second period of interest in legalization occurred in the early 1950s. As federal anti-drug laws became harsher, various medical and legal groups proposed allowing the maintenance of addicts with legally available, cheap drugs under medical supervision. One prime example is a 1955 proposal by the New York Academy of Medicine (NYAM) to provide drugs to addicts in round-the-clock clinics. Developed to counter the increasingly punitive discussion that surrounded the drafting of the federal Narcotic Control Act of 1956, the NYAM proposal received a fair amount of attention but was never adopted by federal or state policy makers. The NYAM clinic proposal is an example of a *medicalization* model, falling far short of legalization. But the idea of freely dispensing drugs to addicts was still much too controversial in the 1950s, as today, so the proposal was never adopted.

DOCUMENT 246: Proposal for Dispensing Drugs to Addicts (New York Academy of Medicine, 1955)

2. The Academy believes that the most effective way to eradicate drug addiction is to take the profit out of the illicit drug traffic. The causes of addiction are cited as: maladjustment; underprivilege; broken home; poverty. Such conditions may well be contributory factors, but they are not of themselves the prime cause. Rather, profit looms large as the principal factor.

. . .

The addict should be able to obtain his drugs at low cost under Federal control, in conjunction with efforts to have him undergo withdrawal. Under this plan, these addicts, as sick persons, would apply for medical care and supervision. Criminal acts would no longer be necessary in order to obtain a supply of drugs and there would be no incentive to create new addicts. Agents and black markets would disappear from lack of patronage. Since about eighty-five per cent of the "pushers" on the streets are said to be addicts, they would be glad to forego this dangerous occupation if they were furnished with their needed drug.

. . .

It is suggested therefore that there be developed a program whereby sufficient amounts of drugs can be legally and inexpensively supplied to addicts, while attempts are being made to have them undergo treatment. This service for narcotic addicts should be instituted in dispensary-clinics, preferably attached to hospitals, whether Federal, municipal or voluntary. No person should be given drugs at such a service clinic unless he is willing to enter a hospital for evaluation of his drug needs. After careful medical evaluation he should receive at cost from the service clinic the amount of drug which it has been medically determined that he requires.

The service clinic should be in operation twenty-four hours a day, seven days a week, to insure that no addict has the excuse that he could not obtain his supply from a legitimate source and was thus forced by his discomfort to seek his supply from illicit dispensers. At no time should he be given a supply of narcotics adequate for more than two days; if he is found to have sold or given away any of the supply to another person, he shall be liable to commitment to a hospital with attempted rehabilitation.

. . .

Needless to say, all addicts receiving drugs from the service clinic or entering a hospital for evaluation and treatment should be photographed and fingerprinted; copies of such photographs and fingerprints should be sent to a central agency, while one copy is retained at the original clinic. By means of a punchcard system, monthly checks should be made by the central agency to insure that an addict is not obtaining supplies from more than one clinic. If such a violation is found to exist, the offending addict shall immediately be subject to commitment as a hospital patient.

It is visualized that such service clinics will be established all over the country. Thus it will be possible for an addict desiring to change his residence to transfer from one service clinic to another without encountering difficulties in maintaining his supply. . . .

Strictly enforced, these safeguards should eliminate any possibility of the use of the illicit market and should insure that only those with intractable addiction are actually receiving narcotics. . . .

. . .

4. . . . It should be emphasized that the law should draw a distinction between the addict and non-addict in its provision. The convicted non-addict trafficker should feel its full force.

Source: New York Academy of Medicine, "Report on Drug Addiction," *Bulletin of the New York Academy of Medicine* 31, no. 8 (1955): 603–607.

* * *

In addition, a Joint Committee of the American Bar Association (ABA) and the American Medical Association (AMA) on Narcotic Drugs was established in 1956 to explore alternatives to current anti-drug policies. Among its key recommendations was the establishment of an experimental clinic to dispense narcotics to addicts. Although the ABA-AMA report recognized the difficulties in setting up such a clinic and acknowledged the arguments against such a clinic, it concluded that it was a worthy plan to test.

DOCUMENT 247: Recommendation to Establish Experimental Narcotics Clinic (Joint ABA-AMA Committee, 1961)

The Committee should sponsor an experimental clinic for the outpatient treatment of drug addicts. . . . The clinic should provide facilities for the thoroughgoing study and diagnosis of each addict. . . . After the diagnosis and study, the attempt should be made to take the addicts off drugs and keep them off drugs through the use of all the techniques available. . . .

. . .

If the clinic does not succeed in taking and keeping the addict patient off drugs after a period of intensive treatment, its personnel then should consider supplying the addict with sufficient drugs for his needs, so that he does not have to patronize the illicit peddler.

. . .

In proposing the experimental clinic, the author is not unaware of the legal problems involved in supplying drugs to addicts. However, it is his belief that the operation of the experimental clinic proposed herein will not violate present federal statutes on narcotics, as interpreted by our courts. . . . The addicts coming to the experimental clinic will be treated as patients in the effort to overcome their addiction, and will only be supplied with drugs when it is determined that such drugs are absolutely necessary to their health and well-being and their ability to function as productive individuals in the community.

Source: Joint Committee of the American Bar Association and the American Medical Association on Narcotic Drugs: Interim and Final Reports, *Drug Addiction: Crime or Disease?* (Bloomington: Indiana University Press, 1961), 103–107.

* * *

Partly in response to the growing punitiveness of anti-drug laws, the 1950s produced a number of proposed legalization or medicalization approaches from various observers and critics of drug policy. In the next document the writer emphasizes the need for a medical approach and criticizes the use of the Harrison Act and other drug laws to punish rather than treat addicts.

DOCUMENT 248: "Make Dope Legal" (Alden Stevens, 1952)

This damaging misinterpretation of the Harrison Act has not gone unobserved. Doctors, welfare workers, and even the Supreme Court of the United States have noted it. The entire matter was succinctly and completely aired in Congress on June 15, 1938, by Congressman John M. Coffee of Washington. Mr. Coffee wanted to transfer the entire narcotics enforcement problem from the Bureau of Narcotics to the U.S. Public Health Service. He spoke of the $2,735,000,000 a year cost of addiction as a "needless burden imposed on the people, not by conditions inherent in the problem of drug addiction, and not by the operation of the law, but by the mistaken interpretation of law made by the Federal Narcotics Bureau." Continuing, he pointed out that "in examining the Harrison Special Tax Act we are confronted with the anomaly that a law designed (as its name implies) to place a tax on certain drugs, and revenue thereby, resulted in . . . developing a smuggling industry not before in existence. Through operation of the law as interpreted there has developed the racket of dope peddling; in a word, the whole gigantic structure of the illicit drug racket, with direct annual turnover of upward of a billion dollars."

. . . Said Coffee: "The Narcotics Bureau ignores these [Supreme Court] decisions and assumes authority to prevent physicians from even the attempt to cure narcotic addicts unless the patients are under forced confinement." Coffee went on to recommend putting addicts in the care of physicians who would prescribe what medicine they might need, presumably including narcotics. Confidently predicting the end of the narcotics traffic if this were done, Coffee asked why the Harrison Act should not function as originally intended and the Supreme Court said it should. In reply to this question he said "the opposition comes from a small coterie of persons in authority who are in a position to benefit from the status quo." He particularly desired "to question the Commissioner of Narcotics and to observe how he may endeavor to justify the activities that cost the American people not far from $3,000,000,000 per year."

Source: Alden Stevens, "Make Dope Legal," *Harper's Magazine*, November 1952, 43–44.

* * *

In criticizing both the 1951 Boggs Act and the 1956 Narcotic Control Act, drug policy reformer Alfred Lindesmith argued that these laws had a disproportionate impact on addicts, small-time dealers, and members of minority groups in comparison to major drug traffickers. A similar view is held by most contemporary proponents of various legalization scenarios.

DOCUMENT 249: Negative Effects of Drug Policies on Addicts (Alfred R. Lindesmith, 1957)

One of the basic injustices of the narcotic laws in general, and of the recent laws in particular, is that the penalties fall mainly upon the victims of the traffic—the addicts—rather than upon the dope racketeers against whom they are designed.

. . .

In the Chicago Narcotics Court and in other similar courts in our large cities, there is a long, shabby, pitiful parade of indigent drug users and petty offenders, mostly Negroes. These persons, except in the rare instances when they happen to be represented by lawyers, are hustled through the courts with such haste that a decent defense is precluded. The notion that punishing these victims will deter the lords of the dope traffic is as naive as supposing that the bootlegging enterprises of the late Al Capone could have been destroyed by arresting drunks on West Madison Street or Times Square.

Apart from the fact that jails and prisons are not currently supposed to be regarded as appropriate places for diseased persons, the incarceration of addicts is bad on other grounds as well. James V. Bennett, Director of the Federal Bureau of Prisons, criticized the 1951 act as follows: "I feel the law is a mistake. It is certainly a mistake so far as addicts are concerned. I feel that it has handicapped our efforts to salvage and rehabilitate them and has complicated our institutional problems." Association within a prison tends to spread addiction among criminals and criminality among addicts. The stigma of criminality and the influence of prison associations make the drug habit more difficult to break.

Even if it were possible to establish institutions in which all known addicts could be locked up for the rest of their lives, such a program would be futile. The big-shot dealers would still be at large, creating new generations of users. There is, in short, no substitute for punishment of the guilty. As long as addicts rather than peddlers bear the brunt of the penalties, the traffic is bound to continue.

Source: Alfred R. Lindesmith, "Dope: Congress Encourages the Traffic." Reprinted with permission from the March 16, 1957 issue of *The Nation*.

* * *

A similar theme was sounded by Dr. Lawrence Kolb.

DOCUMENT 250: Need for a Medical Approach to Addiction (Lawrence Kolb, 1956)

In my opinion, . . . [m]ost drug addiction is neither menace nor mortal sin, but a health problem—indeed, a minor health problem when compared with such killers as alcoholism, heart disease and cancer.

I make that statement with deep conviction. My work has included the psychiatric examination and general treatment of several thousand addicts. I know their habit is a viciously enslaving one, and we should not relax for a moment our efforts to stop its spread and ultimately to stamp it out completely. But our enforcement agencies seem to have forgotten that the addict is a sick person who needs medical help rather than longer jail sentences. . . . He needs help which the present Narcotics Bureau regulations make it very difficult for doctors to give him. Moreover, no distinction has been made, in the punishment of violators, between the non-addicted peddler who perpetuates the illicit traffic solely for his own profit and the addict who sells small amounts to keep himself supplied with a drug on which he has become physically and psychologically dependent.

The Council of the American Psychiatric Association in a public statement issued after the Senate passed its bill, declared that this and a companion measure introduced in the House, "represent backward steps in attacking this national problem." The association . . . concludes by remarking that "additional legislation concerning drug addiction should be directed to making further medical progress possible, rather than discouraging it. The legislative proposals now under consideration would undermine the progress that has been made and impede further progress. Thus, they are not in the public interest."

. . .

Existing measures and those which are advocated defy common sense and violate sound principles of justice and penology. There is nothing about the nature of drug addicts to justify such penalties. They only make it difficult to rehabilitate offenders who could be helped by a sound approach which would take into account both the offense and the psychological disorders of the offender.

Drug addiction is an important problem which demands the attention of health and enforcement officials. However, the most essential need now is to cure the United States of its hysteria, so that the problem can be dealt with rationally. A major move in the right direction would be to stop the false propaganda about the nature of drug addiction and present it for what it is—a health problem which needs some police measures for adequate control. Our approach so far has produced tragedy, disease and crime.

Source: Lawrence Kolb, "Let's Stop This Narcotics Hysteria!," *Saturday Evening Post*, July 28, 1956.

* * *

With the growing popularity of drugs in the 1960s, and the political and social upheaval of that era, attitudes toward the "softer" drugs such as marijuana began to moderate; policy makers began to consider relaxing anti-marijuana drug laws. The 1972 report of the National Commission on Marihuana and Drug Abuse (see Document 229), calling for consideration of a limited decriminalization of the personal use of small amounts of marijuana, spurred the actual enactment of such laws in some states. The 1972 commission report is still cited today by proponents of legalization, who point out that even a commission appointed by a conservative Republican president, Richard Nixon, called for a relaxation of laws against personal drug use. Following the commission's report, the National Commission on Uniform State Laws incorporated the decriminalization recommendations as amendments to the Uniform Controlled Substances Act. This prompted some states to incorporate such provisions into their own laws.

In the following document, Richard Bonnie, who has extensively studied the legal and policy issues opposing marijuana, comments on the 1972 commission recommendations on decriminalization and several state initiatives that followed.

DOCUMENT 251: State Decriminalization Laws (Richard J. Bonnie, 1981)

In 1973, the National Conference of Commissioners on Uniform State Laws promulgated amendments to the Uniform Controlled Substances Act which codified the recommendations of the National Commission. Some form of decriminalization was endorsed during the same year by a variety of national organizations, including the American Bar Association and numerous state and local bar associations, the National Education Association, the Consumer's Union, the National Council of Churches, the American Public Health Association, and the Governing Board of the American Medical Association.

In 1973, Oregon became the first state to decriminalize possession of small amounts of marijuana. As of this writing, 10 additional states have eliminated incarceration as a penalty for simple possession, usually substituting a $100 fine.... Five of these states have made possession a "civil" offense; in others it remains a criminal offense but the law usually contains a provision for expungement of criminal records after specified periods of time. In Alaska, because of a Supreme Court ruling in that state, possession by adults in the home for personal use is not an offense at all.

While these 11 states share the feature of having eliminated incarceration as a penalty for some consumption-related behavior, at least for first offenders, the reform statutes vary in significant respects. The conduct which has been "decriminalized" is not uniformly defined and the reform jurisdictions differ in their prescriptions of the residual sanctions which can still be imposed on persons who are apprehended for, and convicted of, "decriminalized" offenses.

Source: Richard Bonnie, "The Meaning of 'Decriminalization': A Review of the Law," *Contemporary Drug Problems* 8, no. 3 (Fall 1981): 278, 283.

* * *

The next document presents the key provisions of Oregon's statute.

DOCUMENT 252: Oregon Marijuana Law (1973)

(1) A person commits the offense of criminal activity in drugs if he knowingly and unlawfully manufactures, cultivates, transports, possesses, furnishes, prescribes, administers, dispenses or compounds a narcotic or dangerous drug.

(2) Except as provided in subsections (3) and (4) of this section, criminal activity in drugs is a Class B felony, or the court may, under the criteria set forth in ORS 161.705, enter judgment for a Class A misdemeanor and impose sentence accordingly.

. . .

(4) Notwithstanding subsection (2) of this section, if the conviction is for possession of less than one avoirdupois ounce of marijuana it is a violation punishable by a fine of not more than $100.

Sec. 167.217 Criminal use of drugs.

(1) A person commits the offense of criminal use of drugs it he knowingly uses or is under the influence of a narcotic or dangerous drug, except when administered or dispensed by or under the direction of a person authorized by law to prescribe and administer narcotic drugs and dangerous drugs to human beings.

. . .

(2) Criminal use of drugs is a Class A misdemeanor.

(3) Notwithstanding subsection (2) of this section, if the conviction is for criminal use of marijuana, criminal use of drugs is a violation punishable by a fine of not more than $100.

Source: Chapter 167, Section 207, Oregon Revised Statutes, 1973.

* * *

Sociologist Erich Goode prefers to call these marijuana law reforms *partial decriminalization*, noting that possession of larger amounts, sale, or cultivation of marijuana are criminal offenses. Further, he notes that two of the eleven states later recriminalized marijuana possession, at least in part.

DOCUMENT 253: Overview of State Decriminalization of Marijuana (Erich Goode, 1997)

A small exception to the punitive policy toward Schedule I drugs is provided by the *partial decriminalization* of marijuana in nine states . . . : California, Colorado, Maine, Minnesota, Mississippi, Nebraska, New York, North Carolina, and Ohio. (In 1989 and 1990, the electorate of two states, Oregon and Alaska, voted—at least partially—to recriminalize small-quantity marijuana possession.) In these partially decriminalized states, possession of small quantities of marijuana (the amount varies from one state to another) is not a crime. . . . For such an offense, one will receive a citation much like a traffic ticket, and pay a small fine. The *sale* or *transfer* and the *cultivation* of marijuana, and the possession of *more* than the stipulated amount, remain on the books as crimes in those states; only the possession of small quantities is exempt. All the partial decriminalization statutes were enacted in the 1970s; since 1980, no state has decriminalized marijuana possession.

Source: Erich Goode, *Between Politics and Reason: The Drug Legalization Debate* (New York: St. Martin's Press, 1997), 48.

* * *

In the late 1970s, the support of President Jimmy Carter and his drug policy advisors for the decriminalization of marijuana signaled a more tolerant approach to casual drug use.

DOCUMENT 254: President Carter's Policies (David F. Musto, 1987)

Carter's narrow victory in 1976 gave hope to those who wanted a more unequivocally tolerant approach to drugs, much as Nixon's close victory in 1968 buoyed those who wanted an assertion of "law and order." . . .

Carter favored decriminalizing the possession of a small amount of marihuana. One ounce was chosen as that small amount. Civil penalties—for example, a small fine—might still be imposed, but criminal sanctions, such as a jail sentence, would be removed. . . .

In March 1977, less than two months after Carter's inauguration and forty years after the Marihuana Tax Act Hearings, [Dr. Peter] Bourne [Special Assistant to the President for Health Issues] and high officials from DEA, the State Department, NIDA, NIMH, the Customs Service, and the Justice Department appeared before the House Select Committee on Narcotics Abuse and Control to argue for the decriminalization of marihuana. Bourne, acknowledging that marihuana could pose some of the same dangers as alcohol does when, for example, a driver is intoxicated by either drug, explained that marihuana "is not physically addicting and in infrequent or moderate use, probably does not pose an immediate substantial health hazard to the individual." He recommended that federal law be amended in this area so that the states would have the option to determine what penalty to apply to the possession of small amounts. He noted that federal law "is now rarely enforced with regard to simple possession." Legalization, Bourne argued, "would only serve to encourage the use of the drug when we seek to deter it," and furthermore, "legalization would violate the 1961 Single Convention of which the United States is a signatory."

Source: David F. Musto, *The American Disease: Origins of Narcotic Control*, expanded ed. (New York: Oxford University Press, 1987), 266.

THE ARGUMENTS FOR LEGALIZATION

The most visible spokesperson for recent legalization proposals has been Dr. Ethan Nadelmann, whose two 1988 essays spawned the new debate on legalization and decriminalization. Nadelmann, currently director of the Lindesmith Center (a drug policy reform organization), has remained one of the most active advocates of major drug policy reform. Following are excerpts from those two controversial documents.

DOCUMENT 255: Legalization Proposal Overview (Ethan Nadelmann, 1988)

In between [a free market in drugs and strict government controls] lies a strategy that may prove more successful than anything yet tried in stemming the problems of drug abuse and drug-related violence, corruption, sickness, and suffering. It is one in which government makes most of the substances that are now banned legally available to competent adults, exercises strong regulatory powers over all large-scale production and sale of drugs, makes drug-treatment programs available to all who need them, and offers honest drug-education programs to children. This strategy, it is worth noting, would also result in a net benefit to public treasuries of at least ten billion dollars a year, and perhaps much more.

There are three reasons why it is important to think about legalization scenarios, even though most Americans remain hostile to the idea. First, current drug-control policies have failed, are failing, and will continue to fail, in good part because they are fundamentally flawed. Second, many drug-control efforts are not only failing, but also proving highly costly and counter-productive; indeed, many of the drug-related evils that Americans identify as part and parcel of the "drug problem" are in fact caused by our drug-prohibition policies. Third, there is good reason to believe that repealing many of the drug laws would not lead, as many people fear, to a dramatic rise in drug abuse.

. . .

[Legalization] . . . is not a capitulation to the drug dealers—but rather a means to put them out of business. It is not an endorsement of drug use—but rather a recognition of the rights of adult Americans to make their own choices free of the fear of criminal sanctions. It is not a repudiation of the "just say no" approach—but rather an appeal to government to provide assistance and positive inducements, not criminal penalties and more repressive measures, in support of that approach. It is not even a call for the elimination of the criminal-justice system from drug regulation—but rather a proposal for the redirection of its efforts and attention.

There is no question that legalization is a risky policy, since it may lead to an increase in the number of people who abuse drugs. But that is a risk—not a certainty. . . . The past twenty years have demonstrated that a drug policy shaped by exaggerated rhetoric designed to arouse fear has only led to our current disaster. Unless we are willing to honestly evaluate our options, including various legalization strategies, we will run a still greater risk: we may never find the best solution for our drug problems.

Source: Ethan Nadelmann, "The Case for Legalization," *The Public Interest* 92 (Summer 1988): 5–6, 30–31.

DOCUMENT 256: Rationale for Legalization (Ethan Nadelmann, 1988)

The case for legalization is particularly convincing when the risks inherent in alcohol and tobacco use are compared with those associated with illicit drug use. . . . in the United States, the health costs exacted by illicit drug use pale in comparison with those associated with tobacco and alcohol use. In September 1986, the Department of Health and Human Services reported that in the United States, alcohol was a contributing factor in 10 per cent of work-related injuries, 40 per cent of suicide attempts, and also 40 per cent of the approximately 46,000 traffic deaths in 1983. That same year the total cost of alcohol abuse to American society was estimated at more than $100 billion. An estimated 18 million Americans are currently reported to be either alcoholics or alcohol abusers. Alcohol has been identified as the direct cause of 80,000 to 100,000 deaths annually and as a contributing factor in an additional 100,000 deaths. The health costs of tobacco use in the United States and elsewhere are different but of similar magnitude. In the United States alone in 1984, more than 320,000 deaths were attributed to tobacco consumption. All of the health costs of marijuana, cocaine, and heroin combined amount to only a fraction of those of either of the two licit substances.

According to the National Council on Alcoholism, only 3,562 people were known to have died in 1985 from use of all illegal drugs combined. . . . However, most people seem to believe that there is something fundamentally different about alcohol and tobacco that legitimates the legal distinction between those two substances and the illicit ones. The most common distinction is based on the assumption that the illicit drugs are more dangerous than the licit ones. . . . They are also believed to be more addictive and more likely to cause dangerous and violent behavior than are alcohol and tobacco. All use of illicit drugs is typically equated with drug abuse. . . .

Many Americans also make the fallacious assumption that the government would not criminalize certain psychoactive substances if they were not in fact dangerous. They then jump to the conclusion that any use of those substances is a form of abuse. . . . [It is a fact that] the vast majority of Americans who have used illicit drugs have done so in moderation, that relatively few have suffered negative short-term consequences, and given available evidence, that few are likely to suffer long-term harm.

. . .

It is both insightful and important to think about the illicit drugs in the same way as alcohol and tobacco. Like tobacco, many of the illicit substances are highly addictive, but many people can consume them on a regular basis for decades without any demonstrable harm. Like alcohol, most of the substances can be, and are, used by most consumers in moderation with little in the way of harmful effects; but like alcohol they also lend themselves to abuse by a minority of users who become addicted or otherwise harm themselves or others as a consequence. And like both the legal substances, the psychoactive effects of each of the illegal drugs vary greatly from one person to another. . . .

Clearly, then, there is no valid basis for distinguishing between alcohol and tobacco, on the one hand, and most of the illicit substances, on the other, as far as their relative dangers are concerned.

. . .

Of all the drugs that are currently illicit, marijuana perhaps presents the easiest case for repeal of the prohibition laws, in good part because it presents relatively few serious risks to users and is less dangerous in most respects than both alcohol and tobacco.

. . .

Cocaine, heroin, and the various amphetamines, barbiturates, and tranquilizers that people consume illegally present much tougher policy problems. If they were legally available at reasonable prices, would millions more Americans use and abuse them? Drawing comparisons with other countries and historical periods provides clues but no definitive answers for the simple reason that culture and personality often prove to be the most important determinants of how drugs are used in a society. Availability and price play important roles, but not as important as cultural variables. There is good reason to assume that even if all the illegal drugs were made legally available, the same cultural restraints that now keep most Americans from becoming drug abusers would persist and perhaps even strengthen.

Source: Ethan Nadelmann, "U.S. Drug Policy: A Bad Export," *Foreign Policy* 70 (Spring 1988): 92–93, 95–96, 106–107.

* * *

One of the key proponents of the most far-reaching legalization proposals has been Arnold Trebach, a longtime vocal foe of American drug policy. Professor Trebach states the essence of his libertarian position in the next document.

DOCUMENT 257: Legalization Proposal (Arnold S. Trebach, 1993)

My preferred plan of legalization seeks essentially to turn the clock back to the last century, before we made the terrible mistake of starting the war on opium smoking. With some modern adaptations—such sensible rules regarding purity, labeling, places and hours of sale, and age limits for purchasers—we should return to the people the freedom of choice regarding drugs which was unwisely taken away from them at the turn of the century. This plan springs from a judgment that we should trust our adult citizens more than government officials to make choices as to what goes into their bodies.

In concrete terms, then, my major proposal is that we deal with virtually all illegal drugs as we now deal with alcohol. . . .

. . . the process of reform should start now: repeal national drug prohibition. Just do it—in the same way Prohibition was repealed in 1933, in the same way its people dismantled the former Soviet Union—with speed, courage, and the confidence that the future cannot be worse than the present.

Source: Arnold S. Trebach and James A. Inciardi, *Legalize It? Debating American Drug Policy* (Washington, DC: American University Press, 1993), 79–80.

* * *

Kurt Schmoke, a former prosecutor and the mayor of Baltimore, has been another active and popular advocate of drug legalization. Schmoke's arguments center around the impact of current policies on crime and the enormous profits associated with illegal drug trafficking, and his view that money spent for the enforcement of anti-drug laws would be better spent on treatment and prevention to reduce the demand for illegal drugs. He has remained one of the few politicians to openly discuss drug legalization policy options.

DOCUMENT 258: Legalization Proposal (Mayor Kurt L. Schmoke, 1988)

There are three basic arguments in favor of decriminalization: libertarianism, economics and health. I don't subscribe to the libertarian view that people should have a right to injure themselves with drugs if they so choose. Drugs—even if decriminalized—also pose a danger to third parties. But the other two arguments are compelling enough for Congress at least to study the question.

Economics. Just as Prohibition banned something millions of people want, our current drug laws make it illegal to possess a commodity that is in very high demand. As a result, the price of that commodity has soared far beyond its true cost.

This has led to enormous profits from illegal drugs and turned drug trafficking into the criminal enterprise of choice for pushers and manufacturers alike. . . .

First, drug traffickers . . . care very little about the sanctions of the criminal justice system. Going to jail is just part of the cost of doing business. It's a nuisance, not a deterrent.

Second, drug dealers fear one another far more than they fear law-enforcement officials. They know that the police must give them due process, but competing drug dealers will kill them at a moment's notice.

Finally, profit is the engine driving drug trafficking. Neither criminal sanctions nor even the competitive business practices (murder, extortion, kidnapping) of their fellow dealers have much, if any, effect on people who trade in drugs.

But take the profit out of their enterprise—and you'll get their attention. . . . Decriminalization would take the profit out of drugs and greatly reduce, if not eliminate, the drug-related violence that is currently plaguing our streets. Decriminalization will not solve this country's drug abuse problem, but it could solve our most intractable crime problem. . . .

Health. Some will argue that the public-health risks from drugs will only worsen if they are decriminalized . . . but there is every reason to believe that decriminalization would improve public health.

First, violent crime associated with illegal sale of drugs would fall dramatically. For those who doubt that, imagine how violent crime would increase if we once again made the sale and use of alcohol illegal.

Secondly, decriminalization would allow billions of dollars now used for interdiction and enforcement to be redirected toward prevention and treatment. . . .

. . . we have made the policy decision to treat tobacco as a health problem, not a crime problem, and we are making real progress. The number of people smoking continues to fall because of a concerted public education campaign about the health effects of smoking.

There is no reason that we could not do the same with drugs. And then we could find the money we need to educate our young people on the harmful effects of drugs and treat those who are currently addicted.

Source: Kurt L. Schmoke, "Decriminalizing Drugs: It Just Might Work—And Nothing Else Does," *Washington Post*, May 15, 1988.

* * *

Other prominent citizens from both ends of the political spectrum, such as well-known conservative writer William F. Buckley, Nobel Prize economist Milton Friedman, and federal judge Robert Sweet, have echoed the sentiments of Mayor Schmoke. In its February 12, 1996, issue, the conservative magazine *National Review* published a featured article ("The War on Drugs Is Lost") calling for an end to the War on Drugs and a consideration of drug legalization. Editor William F. Buckley, calling for the legalization of the sale of drugs (except to minors), noted "the cost to our society of the astonishing legal weapons available now to policemen and prosecutors; of the penalty of forfeiture of one's home and property for violation of laws . . . designed to advance the war against drugs . . ." and that "it is outrageous to live in a society whose laws tolerate sending young people to life in prison because they grew, or distributed, a dozen ounces of marijuana." In the same article, federal judge Robert W. Sweet questioned the distinction between illegal drugs and the addictive but legal alcohol and tobacco, which cause many more health problems, and recommended an end to laws against drug use and sale. Judge Sweet felt that all drugs should be treated like alcohol, "restricted by the individual states as to time and place of sale, barred from minors, subject to truth in advertising, and made the source of tax revenue. As with alcohol, those who harm or pose a threat to others while under the influence of drugs would face criminal sanctions."

THE HARM REDUCTION APPROACH

One recently popular notion is the so-called harm reduction approach, which aims to alter anti-drug laws in a way that will maintain controls over drug use and sale but that reduces the scope of such laws in a way that can minimize the harms to individuals and communities caused by drug abuse. The following document describes some key elements of the harm reduction approach and the difficulties inherent in implementing such a policy.

DOCUMENT 259: Overview of Harm Reduction Approach (Erich Goode, 1997)

Harm reduction represents an eclectic or mixed bag of policy proposals. . . . Rather than attempting to wipe out drug distribution, addiction, and use—an impossibility, in any case—its goal is for drug policy to attempt to minimize harm. Legal reform, likewise, is secondary; the emphasis is on practicality—what works in concrete practice rather than what seems to look good on paper or in theory. A needle exchange stands high on the list of particulars of any harm reduction advocate: Addicts can turn in used needles at distribution centers and receive clean, fresh ones free of charge. This is designed to keep the rate of new AIDS/HIV infections in check. . . .

In short, harm reduction means: Stress treatment and rehabilitation; underplay the punitive, penal, or police approach, and explore nonpenal alternatives to trivial drug offenses. Expand drug maintenance, especially methadone programs; expand drug education programs; permit heroin and marijuana to be used by prescription for medical treatment. . . .

No one who supports a harm reduction proposal questions the fact that there are theoretical and practical difficulties and dilemmas in implementing such a policy. Some tough and troubling questions demand an answer. For instance, how do we measure or weigh one harm against another? What if our policy results in fewer deaths and more addicts? Less crime and more drug use? If we are truly worried about harm from drug abuse, why concentrate on legalizing or decriminalizing the illegal drugs—why not focus on ways of reducing the use, and therefore the harm, that the *legal* drugs cause? What if our policy improves conditions for one group or category in the population but harms another? And will harm reduction really result in less state control of the drug addict, abuser, and user? Government regulations and programs designed to reduce drug-related harm is likely to result in far *more* state intervention into the lives of persons affected by them. . . . No advocates of a harm reduction program suggest that it is a problem-free panacea or cure-all, but all believe that these and other criticisms are not fatal, and that its problems can be resolved with the application of reliable information and good common sense.

Source: Erich Goode, *Between Politics and Reason: The Drug Legalization Debate* (New York: St. Martin's Press, 1997), 81–83.

* * *

Ethan Nadelmann has been a vocal proponent of the harm reduction approach.

DOCUMENT 260: Argument for Harm Reduction (Ethan Nadelmann, 1996)

Drugs are here to stay. The time has come to abandon the concept of a "drug-free society." We need to focus on learning to live with drugs in such a way that they do the least possible harm. So far as I can ascertain, the societies that have proved most successful in minimizing drug-related harm aren't those that have sought to banish drugs, but those that have figured out how to control and manage drug use through community discipline, including the establishment of powerful social norms. That is precisely the challenge now confronting American society regarding alcohol: How do we live with a very powerful and dangerous drug—more powerful and dangerous than many illicit drugs—that, we have learned, cannot be effectively prohibited?

. . .

There is a wide range of choice in drug-policy options between the free-market approach favored by Milton Friedman and Thomas Szasz, and the zero-tolerance approach of William Bennett. These options fall under the concept of harm reduction. That concept holds that drug policies need to focus on *reducing harm*, whether engendered by drugs or by the prohibition of drugs. And it holds that disease and death can be diminished even among people who can't, or won't, stop taking drugs. This pragmatic approach is followed in the Netherlands, Switzerland, Australia, and parts of Germany, Austria, Britain, and a growing number of other countries.

Source: Ethan Nadelmann, in "The War on Drugs Is Lost," *National Review*, February 12, 1996.

THE ARGUMENTS AGAINST LEGALIZATION

Many drug policy experts have strongly opposed the idea of legalization or even decriminalization. Among their primary concerns are that increased illegal drug use would result from any relaxation of anti-drug laws, that an illegal market in drugs would remain, that it would be difficult to control access to drugs by youth, and that the negative consequences of legalization are impossible to predict and too risky to chance. Joseph A. Califano, Jr. (chairman and president of the National Center on Addiction and Substance Abuse [CASA] at Columbia University and former Secretary of Health, Education, and Welfare), and Dr. Herbert Kleber (professor of psychiatry at Columbia University, CASA's medical director at Columbia University, and former deputy director for demand reduction for the White House Office of National Drug Control Policy) have been vocal opponents of legalization. The next document presents some of their arguments against various forms of legalization.

DOCUMENT 261: Overview of Arguments Against Legalization (Herbert D. Kleber, Joseph A. Califano, Jr., and John C. Demers, 1997)

Advocates of medicalization argue that while illicit drugs should not be freely available to all, doctors should be allowed to prescribe them . . . to addicts. They contend that giving addicts drugs assures purity and eliminates the need for addicts to steal in order to buy them.

Giving addicts drugs like heroin, however, poses many problems. Providing them by prescription raises the danger of diversion for sale on the black market. The alternative—insisting that addicts take drugs on the prescriber's premises—entails at least two visits a day, thus interfering with the stated goal of many maintenance programs to enable addicts to hold jobs. . . .

Heroin addicts require two to four shots each day in increasing doses as they build tolerance to its euphoric effect. On the other hand, methadone can be given at a constant dose since euphoria is not the objective. Addicts maintained on methadone need only a single oral dose each day, eliminating the need for injection. Because cocaine produces an intense but short euphoria and an immediate desire for more, addicts would have to be given the drug even more often than heroin in order to satisfy their craving sufficiently to prevent them from seeking additional cocaine on the street. The binge nature of cocaine use renders it unlikely that cocaine could be given on a "medicalization" basis. Because powder cocaine can be readily converted into crack, any proposal to expand availability of the former will increase the number of crack users and addicts.

. . . Distributing free needles does not ensure that addicts desperate for a high at inconvenient times would not continue to share them. But to the extent that needle exchange programs are effective in reducing the spread of the HIV virus, they can be adopted without legalizing drugs. Studies of whether needle exchange programs increase drug use, however, have generally focused on periods of no longer than 12 months. While use does not seem to increase in this period, data are lacking on the long-term effects of such programs and whether they prompt attitude shifts that in turn lead to increased drug use.

Source: Herbert D. Kleber, Joseph A. Califano, Jr., and John C. Demers, "Clinical and Societal Implications of Drug Legalization." In Joyce H. Lowinson, Pedro Ruiz, Robert B. Millman, and John G. Langrod, eds., *Substance Abuse: A Comprehensive Textbook* (Baltimore: Williams and Wilkins, 1997), 858–861.

* * *

Other drug policy experts have responded strongly against calls for legalizing or decriminalizing drugs, as in the following document.

DOCUMENT 262: Official Reactions to Legalization Proposals (May 15, 1988)

Macdonald [director of the White House Office of Drug Abuse Policy Dr. Donald I. Macdonald] agrees that crime rates might fall under a legalization plan, but said that "all the other consequences of drug use would get worse. Legalization makes drugs more available, more acceptable and more used," contributing to an increase in drug-related accidents and crime, family and child abuse and drug-related diseases such as AIDS.

Rep. Charles B. Rangel (D-NY), chairman of the House Select Committee on Narcotics Abuse and Control, said legalization would, "in effect, be sanctioning the mass poisoning of an entire society . . ." and charged that its proponents do not have the slightest idea of how such a plan would work.

. . .

Dr. Robert L. DuPont, former director of the National Institute on Drug Abuse, said all proponents of legalization run into the same problems: Their plans cannot work. If they propose selling all illegal drugs to "whoever shows up . . . then they're politically dead." If they refuse to legalize a drug, such as crack, then they "undercut their position because the demand for crack will create a black market."

DuPont said legalization proponents often point to the British system as their model, but it is "a fabrication. . . . The British never legalized."

Source: Saundra Torry, "Call to Debate Legalization of Drugs Becomes Louder," *Washington Post*, May 15, 1988.

* * *

In a 1990 article, law professor James B. Jacobs argued that legalization proponents had not provided sufficient details about various legalization options to allow for an assessment of their impact. In considering how legalization might actually work in practice, Jacobs concluded that most contemporary legalization scenarios carried a substantial risk of worsening America's drug problems.

DOCUMENT 263: Risks of Legalization (James B. Jacobs, 1990)

It is mere speculation that making psychoactive drugs legal and inexpensive will reduce drug-related crime. It is also possible that, in a world of legal drugs, drug experimenters and regular users will wish to increase their consumption; if so, they might still need as much money as they did under prohibition when drugs were more expensive. Moreover, legalization would cause economic hardship for many drug users because it would deprive them of the income that they currently derive from participation in the black market distribution system. Black-market wholesalers and distributors, unless they are given a profitable role in the legalized distribution system, cannot be expected simply to wither away. More likely, they will continue to compete fiercely with one another and with the legalized market for as much of the drug market as possible. That might mean underpricing the legal market and providing more powerful drugs than are available on the legal market.

Furthermore, as consumption of mood- and mind-altering drugs increases, so too will the number of crimes committed under the influence of drugs. Consider just the crime of driving while intoxicated. Experts have come increasingly to see that drunk driving is a drug problem. This is a massive understatement. Drug legalization would be more like a cultural revolution than a change in policy.

. . .

Given the extraordinary risks of such an experiment, and the fact that no other country in the world has sought to try it, one might have expected many people who today proclaim themselves to be "for legalization" to have demanded to know just what is meant by legalization, how it would work, and how it would affect key institutions of American society. These questions are being asked all too infrequently. The legalization debate continues to be waged at an abstract and simplistic level. Perhaps the most important negative effect of this current debate is that it is diverting time, resources, and attention from the more pressing question of how to reform the war on drugs so as to reduce drug use more effectively, and to minimize social and economic costs while preserving civil liberties.

Source: James B. Jacobs, "Imagining Drug Legalization." Reprinted with permission of the author from: *The Public Interest*, No. 101 (Fall 1990), pp. 28–42. © 1990 by National Affairs, Inc.

WOULD LEGALIZATION INCREASE DRUG USE?

One of the key areas in which drug policy experts have disagreed is whether legalization would result in increased drug use, among other possible adverse consequences. Opponents of legalization argue that use could substantially increase, while proponents argue just as emphatically that drug use would not increase. Dr. Michael Gazzaniga, Andrew W. Thomson Jr. Professor of Psychiatry (Neuroscience) at Dartmouth Medical School, has argued that drug consumption and drug abuse rates would not change significantly under the type of plan in which the federal government would sell drugs. In an interview in the February 5, 1990 edition of the *National Review* ("The Federal Drugstore"), Gazzaniga noted that drugs are already ubiquitous and that people often like to alter their consciousness with drugs, but that most are able to moderate their use: "I think illegality has little if anything to do with drug consumption. . . . Drugs are everywhere. . . . In terms of availability, drugs might just as well be legal as illegal. . . . [H]uman beings in all cultures tend to seek out means of altering their mental state, and . . . although some will shop around and lose the powers of self-discipline, most will settle down to a base rate of use, and a much smaller rate of abuse, and those rates are pretty much what we have in the United States right now." However, Gazzaniga went on to acknowledge that although it would be greatly reduced, black market activity would not be eliminated if there were so-called federal drugstores: "The criminal is ever inventive. Special services will be supplied, like home-delivery services, and the inevitable (and positively illegal) pushing to children. There will be new drugs dreamed up, and they will have their own market until they are isolated, and then will be sold legally. But, the vast majority of the crime network ought to crumble. The importance of that cannot be underestimated."

Law professor Steven Duke has also argued that having cheaper or more easily available drugs would not lead to increases in drug consumption. Pointing out that national surveys find about 3 million Americans use cocaine (fewer than 500,000 using it weekly), Duke discounts predictions that many millions would abuse cocaine if it were legal. As evidence he points to other countries with more tolerant drug laws: "In many countries, heroin and cocaine are cheap and at least de facto legal. Mexico is awash in cheap drugs, yet our own State Department says that Mexico does 'not have a serious drug problem.' Neither cocaine nor heroin is habitually consumed by more than a small fraction of the residents of any country in the world. There is no reason to suppose that Americans would be the single exception" (*National Review*, February 12, 1996).

Not surprisingly, Ethan Nadelmann concurs, believing that legalization of certain drugs would not lead to substantial increases in use.

DOCUMENT 264: Drug Use Would Not Increase (Ethan Nadelmann, 1988)

. . . The lessons that can be drawn from other societies are mixed. China's experience with the British opium pushers of the nineteenth century, when millions became addicted to the drug, offers one worst-case scenario. The devastation of many native American tribes by alcohol presents another. On the other hand, the legal availability of opium and cannabis in many Asian societies did not result in large addict populations until recently. Indeed, in many countries U.S.-inspired opium bans imposed during the past few decades have paradoxically contributed to dramatic increases in heroin consumption among Asian youth. Within the United States, the decriminalization of marijuana by about a dozen states during the 1970s did not lead to increases in marijuana consumption. . . . Finally, late nineteenth-century America was a society in which there were almost no drug laws or even drug regulations—but levels of drug use then were about what they are today. Drug abuse was considered a serious problem, but the criminal-justice system was not regarded as part of the solution.

. . .

Perhaps the most reassuring reason for believing that repeal of the drug-prohibition laws will not lead to tremendous increases in drug-abuse levels is the fact that we have learned something from our past experiences with alcohol and tobacco abuse. We now know, for instance, that consumption taxes are an effective method of limiting consumption rates. We also know that restrictions and bans on advertising, as well as a campaign of negative advertising, can make a difference. The same is true of other government measures, including restrictions on time and place of sale, prohibition of consumption in public places, packaging requirements, mandated adjustments in insurance policies, crackdowns on driving while under the influence, and laws holding bartenders and hosts responsible for the drinking of customers and guests. There is even some evidence that government-sponsored education programs about the dangers of cigarette smoking have deterred many children from beginning to smoke.

Source: Ethan Nadelmann, "The Case for Legalization," *The Public Interest*, no. 92 (Summer 1988): 28–31.

* * *

The next three documents argue that there is a danger of increased drug use if drug prohibitions were to be relaxed.

DOCUMENT 265: Drug Use Would Increase (Herbert D. Kleber, Joseph A. Califano, Jr., and John C. Demers, 1997)

Legalization proponents point out that alcohol and tobacco cost society much more in lost productivity, increased health care, and criminal justice expenditures and lead to more deaths than all illegal drugs combined. From that, they conclude that we spend too much time and energy fighting illegal drugs, as compared to legal drugs. Alcohol and tobacco are indeed responsible for far more deaths and costs to society than illegal drugs, but this is precisely because alcohol and tobacco are legal and therefore widely available, used, and abused.

. . .

For [many] reasons, particularly the increased number of users and addicts and the threat to our children, legalization would open a dangerous Pandora's box. The claimed panacea—change the legal status of drugs and the problems associated with them will disappear—is illusory. More questions and problems arise than are answered by proponents.

Legalization is a policy of despair, one that would write off millions of our citizens and lead to a terrible game of Russian roulette, particularly for children. It is not born of any new evidence regarding the nature of addiction or the pharmacological, public health, or criminal effects of drug use. At the beginning of the century, the visible results of widespread recreational opiate and cocaine use prompted the first antidrug laws. With so much more new knowledge about the devastating consequences of drug use, it would be foolhardy to turn back the clock.

Source: Herbert D. Kleber, Joseph A. Califano, Jr., and John C. Demers, "Clinical and Societal Implications of Drug Legalization." In Joyce H. Lowinson, Pedro Ruiz, Robert B. Millman, and John G. Langrod, eds., *Substance Abuse: A Comprehensive Textbook* (Baltimore: Williams and Wilkins, 1997), 862.

DOCUMENT 266: Drug Use Would Increase (James B. Jacobs, 1990)

The drug-legalization movement is urging us to consider the transformation of American society from an alcohol culture to a poly-drug culture in which a wide range of psychoactive drugs . . . would instantly be made the legal equivalents of alcohol. . . .

Advocates of drug legalization in effect are urging the country to engage in a massive experiment. Incredibly, their hypothesis is that by legalizing drugs and reducing their cost, the drug problem will decline if not wither away. This defies everything we know about markets, deterrence, and the propensity of people . . . to seek chemical solutions to life's real or imagined problems and challenges. Moreover, if the legalization movement's hypothesis proves wrong it will be too late to go back to the *status quo ante*. Returning to prohibition after a period in which millions of consumers developed a taste for new drugs would be a daunting challenge, to say the least.

Source: James B. Jacobs, "Imagining Drug Legalization." Reprinted with permission of the author from: *The Public Interest*, No. 101 (Fall 1990), pp. 28–42. © 1990 by National Affairs, Inc.

DOCUMENT 267: Drug Use Would Increase (David T. Courtwright, 1991)

. . . [S]hould [society] risk an unknown increase in drug abuse and addiction in order to bring about an unknown reduction in illicit trafficking and other costs of drug prohibition? Controlled legalization would take some, but by no means all, of the crime out of it. Just how much and what sort of crime would be eliminated would depend upon which groups were to be denied which drugs; the overall level of taxation; and differences in state tax and legalization policies. If the excluded groups were few and all states legalized all drugs and all governments taxed at uniformly low levels, then the black market would be largely eliminated. But these are precisely the conditions that would be most likely to bring about an unacceptably high level of drug abuse. The same variables that would determine how successful the controlled legalization policy would be in eliminating the black market would also largely determine how unsuccessful it was in containing drug addiction.

Source: David T. Courtwright, "Drug Legalization, the Drug War, and Drug Treatment in Historical Perspective," *Journal of Policy History* 3, no. 4, p. 406. Copyright 1991 by The Pennsylvania State University. Reproduced by permission of The Pennsylvania State University Press.

A MIDDLE GROUND?

A middle ground has also been proposed by some drug policy experts. This approach recognizes the problems cited by legalization proponents that have accompanied the punitive anti-drug policies of this century, but identifies a number of risks and difficulties in legalizing or decriminalizing drugs. This middle ground generally includes an acceptance of current anti-drug policies, but with increased support and funding for drug treatment and prevention. In addition, this viewpoint argues that drug policies should recognize that illegal drug use is likely to continue, and that it is important to acknowledge the health consequences of illegal drug use and attempt to reduce the harm caused by these effects.

Drug policy historian David Courtwright argues for a modified harm reduction approach that would retain some elements of drug control short of legalization, but shift more resources into treatment and prevention under a balanced medical-enforcement approach.

DOCUMENT 268: Argument for a Balanced Policy (David T. Courtwright, 1991)

. . . My principal conclusion is that neither the drug war as presently configured nor controlled legalization is likely to effect the greatest reduction of misery or death. Public health efforts backed by coercion are a better and more rational way of minimizing the long-term consequences of drug abuse.

. . .

The assumption upon which the controlled legalization argument rests is that legal sales would largely eliminate the illicit traffic and its attendant evils. The history of drug use, regulation, and taxation in the United States suggests otherwise. The concept of controlled legalization implies not making drugs available to certain groups. Minors are the most obvious exception. [Ethan] Nadelmann has stressed that the sale of drugs to children should remain illegal. Presumably selling drugs to anyone under twenty-one would remain a criminal offense. . . .

Forbidding the sale of powerful psychoactive drugs to young people makes social, moral, and political sense. Unfortunately, illicit drug abuse in this century has become concentrated among the young, that is, among those who are most likely to be made exceptions to the rule of legal sales.

[The growing number of young drug users entering the criminal justice system] has important implications for a controlled-legalization system predicated on the denial of sales to those under twenty-one. . . . a quarter, a third, or more of all customers would be underage, and there would be a great deal of money to be made by selling drugs to them. The primary source of supply would likely be diversion. Adults who had legally purchased drugs would sell all or part of their supply to those who were below the legal age. . . . There might well be turf disputes and hence violence among those who resold drugs. Some of the dealers and their underage purchasers would be caught, prosecuted, and imprisoned, with the result that the criminal justice system would still be involved with and burdened by drug arrests. The black market would be altered and diminished, but would not disappear.

The potential for illegal sales and use goes beyond minors . . . Pilots, policemen, firemen, bus, train, taxi, and ambulance drivers, surgeons, active-duty military personnel, and others whose drug use would jeopardize public safety and security would be denied access to at least some drugs. Yet those among them who began or persisted in drug use would be liable to criminal and in some instances civil actions, as would their suppliers. Pregnant and possibly nursing women would also pose a problem. . . . The point to be made here is simply that every time an exception is made for good and compelling reasons—every time the accent is placed on "controlled" as opposed to "legalization"—the likelihood of continued illicit sales and use increases.

. . .

Drugs like cocaine and heroin are more compact, more profitable, and very easy to conceal. Smuggling these drugs to take advantage of state tax differentials would consequently be much more difficult to detect and deter. If, for example, taxed cocaine retailed in Vermont for ten dollars a gram and in New York for twelve dollars a gram, anyone who bought just five kilograms at Vermont prices, transported them, and sold them (illegally) at New York prices would realize a profit of $10,000. Five kilograms is an amount that could be concealed in an attache case.

Should all states legalize drugs and tax them at the same rate, this sort of illegal activity would not exist. The difficulty is that it is constitutionally and politically infeasible to ensure uniform rates of state taxation. . . . States with older, more rural populations typically have fewer drug problems and hence would have less incentive to impose heavy taxes to finance treatment programs or discourage consumption. The opposite would be true of states with younger, more urban populations.

. . .

Federalism poses other challenges. Laws against drug use and trafficking have been enacted at the local, state, and federal levels. It is probable that if Congress repeals or modifies the national drug laws some states will go along with controlled legalization, but others will not. Nevada, long in the legalizing habit, might jettison its drug laws, but conservative, Mormon-populated Utah might not. . . . Virginia and Maryland might experiment with the decriminalization of marijuana, the least risky legalization option, but retain prohibition of the nonmedical use of other drugs. The result would again be smuggling. . . . it is hard to see how any state that chose to retain laws against some or all drugs could possibly stanch the influx of prohibited drugs from adjacent states that opted for their legalization.

. . .

The dilemmas and dangers of controlled legalization do not mean that the drug war is the only alternative. A case also can be made for the reallocation of resources and for selective legal changes that stop short of making drugs legally available. . . .

Prosecutorial efforts should not be abandoned. The mere fact that some potentially harmful drugs are illegal, and that their possession and sale are occasionally detected and punished, is sufficient to deter the majority of the population from using them. The essential point about law enforcement and interdiction efforts is not that they fail, but that large investments in them produce diminishing returns. Additional appropriations for the drug war would be better spent on educational and therapeutic efforts. In both budgetary and strategic terms it is possible to move closer to the center-right of the spectrum—that is, toward a more balanced medical-police approach—without embracing legalization, controlled or otherwise.

Source: David T. Courtwright, "Drug Legalization, the Drug War, and Drug Treatment in Historical Perspective," *Journal of Policy History* 3, no. 4, pp. 393, 398–399, 404–405, 406–407. Copyright 1991 by the Pennsylvania State University. Reproduced by permission of the Pennsylvania State University Press.

* * *

Criminologist James Inciardi, a strong proponent of using the coercive power of the criminal justice system to engage and keep drug abusers and addicts in treatment, takes a negative view of legalization efforts while arguing for reforms in current drug policy.

DOCUMENT 269: Reform without Legalization (James A. Inciardi, 1993)

The arguments *for* legalization are seemingly based on the fervent belief that America's prohibitions against . . . drugs impose far too large a cost in terms of tax dollars, crime, and infringements on civil rights and individual liberties. And while the overall argument may be well-intentioned and appear quite logical, I find it to be highly questionable in its historical, sociocultural, and empirical underpinnings, and demonstrably naïve in its understanding of the negative consequences of a legalized drug market. . . .

1. Although drug prohibition policies have been problematic, it would appear that they have managed to keep drugs away from most people. High school and general population surveys indicate that most Americans don't use drugs, have never even tried them, and don't know where to get them. Thus, the numbers "at risk" are dramatically fewer than is the case with the legal drugs. Or stated differently, there is a rather large population who might be at risk if illicit drugs were suddenly available.
2. Marijuana, heroin, cocaine, crack, and the rest are not "benign" substances. Their health consequences, addiction liability, and/or abuse potential are considerable.
3. There is extensive physiological, neurological, and anthropological evidence to suggest that people are of a species that has been honed for pleasure. Nearly all people want and enjoy pleasure, and the pursuit of drugs . . . seems to be universal and inescapable. . . . Moreover, history and research ha[ve] demonstrated that "availability created demand."

. . .

7. The focus on the war on drugs can be shifted. I believe that we do indeed need drug enforcement, but it is stressed far too much in current policy. Cut it in half, and shift those funds to criminal justice-based treatment programs. . . .
8. Since the "war on drugs" will continue, then a more humane use of the criminal justice system should be structured. This is best done through treatment in lieu of incarceration, and corrections-based treatment for those who do end up in jails and prisons.

Source: Arnold S. Trebach and James A. Inciardi, *Legalize It? Debating American Drug Policy* (Washington, DC: American University Press, 1993), 203–205.

* * *

Sociologist Erich Goode, however, believes that the debate over legalization has been useful, and that in the future at least some of the less extreme proposals made by its proponents and other drug policy reformers will be adopted.

DOCUMENT 270: Benefits of the Legalization Debate (Erich Goode, 1997)

Given the dense entanglement of the issue of legalization in ideological and political considerations, it is unlikely that it will be decided on empirical or consequentialist grounds alone. It is unlikely that any of the more radical proposals laid out by the legalizers will be adopted any time in the foreseeable future. However, what the debate has done is introduce some critical issues to the public arena. The debate has been healthy. It will force a reconsideration of our current and very harmful strategy of criminalizing the addict and user. However, legitimate criticism of the present system is not the same thing as devising a viable alternative strategy. Still, perhaps when the current wave of conservatism has subsided, some of the legalizers' more moderate proposals will be given a fair hearing. It is entirely likely that a number of them will be adopted within a generation. While some of them are, in my view, seductively appealing but do not hold up under scrutiny, some others make a great deal of sense. Perhaps a detailed and systematic study will manage to sort out the productive from the harmful.

Source: Erich Goode, *Between Politics and Reason: The Drug Legalization Debate* (New York: St. Martin's Press, 1997), 156.

* * *

Despite the considerable attention accorded to the debate over legalization and decriminalization over the past ten years, it remains quite unlikely that either the United States government or any states will relax anti-drug laws in any meaningful way, at least in the foreseeable future. The likelihood that even modest pilot proposals will be implemented and tested is also unlikely. The strong and rapid government response to the California and Arizona medical marijuana referenda of 1996 is a case in point (see Part XII). The following statement from the 1988 White House Conference still reflects the current views of nearly all political leaders.

DOCUMENT 271: Statement Against Legalization (White House Conference for a Drug-Free America, 1988)

The legalization of illicit drugs is not a solution, but rather a profound mistake. Legalization appears seductively simple and yet, like most simplistic solutions to complex problems it would create problems even more difficult than it purports to solve. To legalize drugs is to make them more readily available, and as an inevitable consequence, more widely used, and this is simply unacceptable. Illicit drugs are far too destructive to the health of our citizens and the strength of our national character. If our methods for eliminating such a deadly force from within our midst are not working well, the answer lies in improving them—not in giving up and unleashing destruction in our land.

Source: White House Conference for a Drug-Free America, *Final Report* (Washington, DC: U.S. Government Printing Office, June 1988), 2.

* * *

Proponents of various forms of legalization have sparked some contentious debate in recent years. As should be clear from the documents cited in this part, the range of opinions of drug policy experts is considerable. Some believe that illegal drug use will increase following legalization or decriminalization; others argue that it would not. Some point to a low prevalence of heavy drug use as evidence that many more users are potentially at risk and that current policies are responsible for deterring users. Others argue that the small percentage of abusers demonstrates that despite the widespread availability of illegal drugs, most people do not use drugs or are able to use drugs in moderation. Many experts are concerned that legalization would lead to unknown and possibly harmful effects on youth, health, and crime. Legalization proponents counter by pointing out that the negative effects and huge costs of current punitive drug policies make it worth testing out various legalization scenarios.

Whatever the outcome of the current debate, it is probable that currently illegal drugs will remain that way for some time. The debate over the limitations of current policies, however, has helped to spur a reexamination of punitive policies that may lead to some reforms that nevertheless fall far short of legalization.

Suggested Readings

Anslinger, Harry J., and Will Oursler. *The Murderers*. New York: Farrar, Straus and Cudahy, 1961.

Anslinger, Harry J., and William F. Tompkins. *The Traffic in Narcotics*. New York: Funk and Wagnalls, 1953.

Bonnie, Richard J., and Charles H. Whitebread. *The Marihuana Conviction: A History of Marihuana Prohibition in the United States*. Charlottesville: University Press of Virginia, 1974.

Brecher, Edward M., and the Editors of Consumer Reports. *Licit and Illicit Drugs*. Boston: Little, Brown, 1972.

Courtwright, David T. *Dark Paradise: Opiate Addiction in America Before 1940*. Cambridge, MA: Harvard University Press, 1982.

———. "Drug Legalization, the Drug War, and Drug Treatment in Historical Perspective." *Journal of Policy History* 3, no. 4 (1991).

Domestic Council Drug Abuse Task Force. *White Paper on Drug Abuse: A Report to the President*. Washington, DC: U.S. Government Printing Office, September 1975.

Goode, Erich. *Between Politics and Reason: The Drug Legalization Debate*. New York: St. Martin's Press, 1997.

Himmelstein, Jerome. *The Strange Career of Marihuana*. Westport, CT: Greenwood Press, 1983.

Jacobs, James B. "Imagining Drug Legalization." *The Public Interest*, no. 101 (Fall 1990): 28–42.

Joint Committee of the American Bar Association and the American Medical Association on Narcotic Drugs: Interim and Final Reports. *Drug Addiction: Crime or Disease?* Bloomington: Indiana University Press, 1961.

King, Rufus. *The Drug Hang-up*. New York: W. W. Norton, 1972.

Kleber, Herbert D., Joseph A. Califano, Jr., and John C. Demers. "Clinical and Societal Implications of Drug Legalization." In Joyce H. Lowinson, Pedro Ruiz, Robert B. Millman, and John G. Langrod, eds., *Substance Abuse: A Comprehensive Textbook*. Baltimore: Williams and Wilkins, 1997.

Lindesmith, Alfred R. *The Addict and the Law*. Bloomington: Indiana University Press, 1965.

Mayor's Committee on Marihuana. *The Marihuana Problem in the City of New York*. Lancaster, PA: Cattell Press, 1944.

Morgan, H. Wayne. *Yesterday's Addicts: American Society and Drug Abuse, 1865–1920*. Norman: University of Oklahoma Press, 1974.

Musto, David F. *The American Disease: Origins of Narcotic Control*, expanded ed. New York: Oxford University Press, 1987.

Nadelmann, Ethan. "The Case for Legalization." *The Public Interest*, no. 92 (Summer 1988).

National Commission on Marihuana and Drug Abuse. *Marihuana: A Signal of Misunderstanding*. First Report of the National Commission on Marihuana and Drug Abuse. Washington, D.C.: U.S. Government Printing Office, March 1972.

New York Academy of Medicine. "Report on Drug Addiction." *Bulletin of the New York Academy of Medicine* 31, no. 8 (1955): 592–607.

Office of National Drug Control Policy. *National Drug Control Strategy*. Washington, DC: U.S. Government Printing Office, 1989–1999 (annual).

President's Commission on Model State Drug Laws. *Final Report*, 6 vols. Washington, DC: The White House, 1993.

Spillane, Joseph. *Modern Drug, Modern Menace*. Santa Monica, CA: RAND Corporation, 1994.

Taylor, Arnold. *American Diplomacy and the Narcotics Traffic, 1900–1939*. Durham, NC: Duke University Press, 1969.

Terry, Charles E., and Mildred Pellens. *The Opium Problem*. Bureau of Social Hygiene, 1928. Reprint, Montclair, NJ: Patterson Smith Publishing, 1970.

Trebach, Arnold S., and James A. Inciardi. *Legalize It? Debating American Drug Policy*. Washington, DC: American University Press, 1993.

Walton, Robert. *Marijuana, America's New Drug Problem*. Philadelphia: J. B. Lippincott, 1938.

White House Conference for a Drug-Free America. *Final Report*. Washington, DC: U.S. Government Printing Office, June 1988.

Index

About the Editor

STEVEN R. BELENKO is Senior Research Associate at the National Center on Addiction and Substance Abuse, Columbia University. He is the author of *Crack and the Evolution of Drug Policy* (Greenwood, 1993).

Primary Documents in American History and Contemporary Issues

The Abortion Controversy
Eva R. Rubin, editor

The AIDS Crisis
Douglas A. Feldman and Julia Wang Miller, editors

Capital Punishment in the United States
Bryan Vila and Cynthia Morris, editors

Constitutional Debates on Freedom of Religion
John J. Patrick and Gerald P. Long, editors

The Environmental Debate
Peninah Neimark and Peter Rhoades Mott, editors

Founding the Republic
John J. Patrick, editor

Free Expression in America
Sheila Suess Kennedy, editor

Genetic Engineering
Thomas A. Shannon, editor

The Gun Control Debate
Marjolijn Bijlefeld, editor

Major Crises in Contemporary American Foreign Policy
Russell D. Buhite, editor

The Right to Die Debate
Marjorie B. Zucker, editor

The Role of Police in American Society
Bryan Vila and Cynthia Morris, editors

Sexual Harassment in America
Laura W. Stein

States' Rights and American Federalism
Frederick D. Drake and Lynn R. Nelson, editors

U.S. Immigration and Naturalization Laws and Issues
Michael LeMay and Elliott Robert Barkan, editors

Women's Rights in the United States
Winston E. Langley and Vivian C. Fox, editors